Olympic
Games

The Records

Olympic Games
The Records

Stan Greenberg

EDITOR: Beatrice Frei
DESIGN AND LAYOUT: Michael Morey

© Stan Greenberg and Guinness Superlatives Ltd, 1987
Published by Guinness Superlatives Ltd.
33 London Road, Enfield, Middlesex

Typeset in 9/10 Century (Schoolbook)
by Input Typesetting Ltd, London SW19 8DR
Printed and bound in Great Britain by
R.J. Acford Ltd, Chichester, Sussex

'Guinness' is a registered trade mark of Guinness Superlatives Ltd

British Library Cataloguing in Publication Data

Greenberg, Stan
    Guinness Olympic Games: the records.
    1. Olympic Games — Records
    I. Title
    796.4'8'09   GV721.8

ISBN 0-85112-896-3 Pbk

R
796.48
G 798 O
234717

CONTENTS

ACKNOWLEDGEMENTS

Any book about the Olympic Games must rely very heavily on the original research previously done by a dedicated few, principally Erich Kamper (AUT), whose *Enzyklopädie der Olympischen Spiele* (1972), *Lexicon der Olympischen Winter Spiele* (1964) and *Lexicon der 14,000 Olympioniken* (1983) are recognized as the basic texts on the Games. Also particular mention must be made of *Die Olympischen Spiele von 1896 bis 1980* by Volker Kluge (GDR) who has taken up where Kamper left off, as well as adding some new material to the earlier research. Other main sources are, in alphabetical order:

The Associated Press and Grolier – *Pursuit of Excellence, The Olympic Story* (1979)
Pat Besford (GBR) – *Encyclopaedia of Swimming* (1976)
Sándor Barcs (HUN) – *The Modern Olympics Story* (1964)

John Durant (USA) – *Highlights of the Olympics* (1961)
Lord Killanin (IRE) and John Rodda (GBR) – *The Olympic Games* (1976)
Peter Matthews (GBR) – *Track and Field Athletics – The Records* (1986)
Norris and Ross McWhirter (GBR) – *The Guinness Book of Olympic Records* (1980)
Melvyn Watman (GBR) – *The Encyclopaedia of Track and Field Athletics* (1981)

Other experts and organizations whose publications and personal help have been invaluable include:

Richard Ayling, Howard Bass, Ian Buchanan, Harry Carpenter, Jim Coote, Peter Diamond (USA), Maurice Golesworthy, John Goodbody, Marc Heller, Richard Hymans, Peter Johnson, Bill Mallon (USA), Ferenc Mézo (HUN), Ron Pickering, Jack Rollin, Bob Sparks, Stuart Storey, Dave Terry, Lance Tingay, Martin Tyler, David Vine, David Wallechinsky, Alan Weeks, Dorian Williams, Don Wood. The Association of Track and Field Statisticians (ATFS) and its members, British Olympic Association, International Amateur Athletic Federation (IAAF), International Olympic Committee publications, International Weightlifting Federation, National Ski Federation of Great Britain, National Union of Track Statisticians (NUTS) and its members, *New York Times* publications, *Sports Illustrated*, *The Times*, *Track and Field News* publications, and many national and international governing bodies and individuals.

Where contradictions have been found in different sources I have invariably used Kamper and Kluge as the final arbiters.

OFFICIAL ABBREVIATIONS AND PARTICIPATION

	Country	Summer Games		Winter Games	
		Debut	Number attended	Debut	Number attended
AFG	Afghanistan	1936	8	–	
AHO	Netherlands Antilles	1952	7	–	
ALB	Albania	1972	1	–	
ALG	Algeria	1964	5	–	
AND	Andorra	1976	3	1976	3
ANG	Angola	1980	1	–	
ANT	Antigua	1976	2	–	
ARG	Argentina	1920	14	1908	10
AUS	Australia[1]	1896	21	1936	10
AUT	Austria[2]	1896	20	1924	14
BAH	Bahamas	1952	8	–	
BAN	Bangladesh	1984	1	–	
BAR	Barbados	1968	4	–	
BEL	Belgium	1900	19	1920	13
BEN	Benin	1980	2	–	
BER	Bermuda	1936	10	–	
BHU	Bhutan	1984	1	–	
BIR	Burma	1948	9	–	
BIZ	Belize (ex British Honduras)	1968	4	–	
BOH	Bohemia (prior to 1920)[13]	–		–	
BOL	Bolivia	1936	6	1956	3
BOT	Botswana	1980	2	–	
BRA	Brazil	1920	14	–	
BRN	Bahrain	1976	2	–	
BRU	Brunei	nya	–	–	
BUL	Bulgaria	1896	12	1936	11
CAF	Central African Republic	1968	2	–	
CAN	Canada	1900	19	1920	15
CAY	Cayman Islands	1976	2	–	
CGO	Congo	1964	4	–	
CHA	Chad	1964	4	–	
CHI	Chile	1896	15	1948	8
CHN	China	1932	5	1980	2
CIV	Ivory Coast	1964	5	–	
CMR	Cameroun	1964	6	–	
COL	Colombia	1932	11	–	
CRC	Costa Rica	1936	7	1984	1
CUB	Cuba	1900	13	–	
CYP	Cyprus	1980	2	1980	2
DEN	Denmark	1896	20	1948	5
DJI	Djibouti	1984	1	–	
DOM	Dominican Republic	1964	6	–	
ECU	Ecuador	1924	6	–	
EGY	Egypt[3]	1906	15	1984	1
ESA	El Salvador	1968	3	–	
ESP	Spain	1900	15	1936	11
EST	Estonia (prior to 1948)[4]	1920	5	1928	2
ETH	Ethiopia	1956	6	–	
FIJ	Fiji	1956	6	–	
FIN	Finland	1906	18	1920	15
FRA	France	1896	21	1920	15
FRG	Federal Republic of Germany[5]	1896	17	1908	13
GAB	Gabon	1972	2	–	
GAM	Gambia	1984	1	–	
GBR	Great Britain	1896	21	1908	16
GDR	German Democratic Republic[6]	1968	4	1968	5
GEQ	Equatorial Guinea	1984	1	–	
GER	Germany (prior to 1968)	–		–	
GHA	Ghana (ex Gold Coast)	1952	6	–	
GRE	Greece	1896	21	1936	10
GRN	Grenada	1984	1	–	
GUA	Guatemala	1952	6	–	
GUI	Guinea	1968	3	–	
GUY	Guyana (ex British Guiana)	1948	9	–	
HAI	Haiti	1900	8	–	
HKG	Hong Kong	1952	8	–	
HOL	Netherlands	1900	19	1928	12
HON	Honduras	1968	3	–	
HUN	Hungary[2]	1896	19	1924	14
INA	Indonesia	1952	7	–	
IND	India	1900	16	1964	2
IRL	Ireland[7]	1924	13	–	
IRN	Iran	1948	8	1956	5
IRQ	Iraq	1948	6	–	
ISL	Iceland	1908	13	1948	9
ISR	Israel	1952	8	–	
ISV	Virgin Islands	1968	4	1984	1
ITA	Italy	1900	19	1924	14
IVB	British Virgin Islands	1984	1	–	
JAM	Jamaica[8]	1948	10	–	
JOR	Jordan	1980	2	–	
JPN	Japan	1912	14	1928	12

	Country	Summer Games		Winter Games	
		Debut	Number attended	Debut	Number attended
KEN	Kenya	1956	6	–	
KOR	Korea[9]	1948	9	1928	9
KUW	Kuwait	1968	5	–	
LAO	Laos	1980	1	–	
LAT	Latvia (prior to 1948)[4]	1924	4	1924	3
LBA	Libya	1968	3	–	
LBR	Liberia	1956	6	–	
LES	Lesotho	1972	3	–	
LIB	Lebanon	1948	9	1948	10
LIE	Liechtenstein	1936	9	1936	10
LIT	Lithuania (prior to 1948)[4]	1924	2	1928	1
LUX	Luxembourg	1912	15	1928	2
MAD	Madagascar	1964	5	–	
MAL	Malaysia[10]	1956	7	–	
MAR	Morocco	1960	6	1968	2
MAW	Malawi	1972	2	–	
MDV	Maldives	nya	–	–	
MEX	Mexico	1924	14	1928	2
MGL	Mongolia	1964	5	1964	5
MLI	Mali	1964	5	–	
MLT	Malta	1928	8	–	
MON	Monaco	1920	12	1984	1
MOZ	Mozambique	1980	2	–	
MRI	Mauritius	1984	1	–	
MTN	Mauretania	1984	1	–	
NCA	Nicaragua	1968	5	–	
NEP	Nepal	1964	5	–	
NGR	Nigeria	1952	8	–	
NGU	Papua-New Guinea	1976	2	–	
NIG	Niger	1964	4	–	
NOR	Norway	1900	19	1920	15
NZL	New Zealand	1908[1]	17	1952	7
OMA	Oman	1984	1	–	
PAK	Pakistan	1948	9	–	
PAN	Panama	1928	9	–	
PAR	Paraguay	1968	4	–	
PER	Peru	1936	10	–	
PHI	Philippines	1924	13	1972	1
POL	Poland	1924	13	1924	14
POR	Portugal	1912	16	1952	1
PRK	Democratic People's Republic of Korea[9]	1972	3	1964	4
PUR	Puerto Rico	1948	10	1984	1
QAT	Qatar	1984	1	–	
ROM	Romania	1924	12	1928	12
RWA	Rwanda	1984	1	–	
SAF	South Africa[11]	1904	13	1960	1
SAM	Western Samoa	1984	1	–	
SAR	Saar[12]	1952	1	–	
SAU	Saudi Arabia	1976	2	–	
SEN	Senegal	1964	6	1984	1
SEY	Seychelles	1980	2	–	
SIN	Singapore[10]	1948	9	–	
SLE	Sierra Leone	1968	3	–	
SMR	San Marino	1960	5	1976	2
SOL	Solomon Islands	1984	1	–	
SOM	Somalia	1972	2	–	
SRI	Sri Lanka (ex Ceylon)	1948	9	–	
SUD	Sudan	1960	4	–	
SUI	Switzerland	1896	21	1920	15
SUR	Surinam	1968	4	–	
SWE	Sweden	1896	20	1908	16
SWZ	Swaziland	1972	2	–	
SYR	Syria	1948	5	–	
TAN	Tanzania	1964	5	–	
TCH	Czechoslovakia[13]	1900	18	1920	15
THA	Thailand	1952	8	–	
TOG	Togo	1972	2	–	
TON	Tonga	1984	1	–	
TPE	Taipei (ex Formosa/Taiwan)	1956	6	1972	3
TRI	Trinidad & Tobago[8]	1948	10	–	
TUN	Tunisia	1960	6	–	
TUR	Turkey	1908	14	1936	8
UAE	United Arab Emirates	1984	1	–	
UGA	Uganda	1956	7	–	
URS	Soviet Union[14]	1952	8	1956	8
URU	Uruguay	1924	13	–	
USA	United States	1896	20	1908	16
VEN	Venezuela	1948	10	–	
VIE	Vietnam[15]	1952	7	–	
VOL	Upper Volta (Burkina Faso)	1972	1	–	
YAR	Yemen Arab Republic	1984	1	–	
YMD	Yemen Democratic Republic	nya		–	
YUG	Yugoslavia	1912	16	1924	12
ZAI	Zaire	1968	2	–	
ZAM	Zambia (ex Northern Rhodesia)	1964	5	–	
ZIM	Zimbabwe (ex Rhodesia)	1928	5	–	

1 Australia and New Zealand combined as Australasia 1908–1912.
2 Not invited in 1920.
3 As United Arab Republic 1960–1972.
4 Annexed by the Soviet Union in 1940.
5 Not invited 1920, 1924 and 1948.
6 Separate team from 1968; part of combined German team 1956–1964.
7 Part of Great Britain team until 1924.
8 Jamaica & Trinidad combined as Antilles in 1960.
9 Country divided in 1945, separate regimes established in 1948.
10 Prior to 1964 consisted of Malaya and North Borneo; in 1964 also included Singapore.
11 Not invited since 1960.
12 Independent 1947–1957, then incorporated in Germany
13 Czechoslovakia was represented by Bohemia up to 1912.
14 As Czarist Russia 1900–1912.
15 From 1952 to 1972 only a South Vietnamese team competed.

PARTICIPATING COUNTRIES

Only five countries have never failed to be represented at all celebrations of the Summer Games since 1896 (including those of 1906):

Australia, France, Greece, Great

Britain and Switzerland. Of these only France and Great Britain have been present at all Winter Games as well. However, only Great Britain also competed in the skating and ice hockey events of 1908 and 1920.

CELEBRATIONS OF THE MODERN OLYMPIC GAMES

Summer

	Year	Venue	Date	Nations	Women	Men	Total
I	1896	Athens, Greece	6–15 April[1]	13	–	311	311
II	1900	Paris, France	20 May–28 October	22	12	1318	1330
III	1904	St Louis, USA	1 July–23 November	13[2]	8	617	625
*	1906	Athens, Greece	22 April–2 May	20	7	877	884
IV	1908	London, England	27 April–31 October	22	36	2020	2056
V	1912	Stockholm, Sweden	5 May–22 July	28	55	2491	2546
VI	1916	Berlin, Germany	Not held due to war	–	–	–	–
VII	1920	Antwerp, Belgium	20 April–12 September	29	64	2628	2692
VIII	1924	Paris, France	4 May–27 July	44	136	2956	3092
IX	1928	Amsterdam, Netherlands	17 May–12 August	46	290	2724	3014
X	1932	Los Angeles, USA	30 July–14 August	37	127	1281	1408
XI	1936	Berlin, Germany	1–16 August	49	328	3738	4066
XII	1940	Tokyo, then Helsinki	Not held due to war	–	–	–	–
XIII	1944	London, England	Not held due to war	–	–	–	–
XIV	1948	London, England	29 July–14 August	59	385	3714	4099
XV	1952	Helsinki, Finland	19 July–3 August	69	518	4407	4925
XVI	1956	Melbourne, Australia[3]	22 November–8 December	67	371	2813	3184
XVII	1960	Rome, Italy	25 August–11 September	83	610	4736	5346
XVIII	1964	Tokyo, Japan	10–24 October	93	683	4457	5140
XIX	1968	Mexico City, Mexico	12–27 October	112	781	4749	5530
XX	1972	Munich, FRG	26 August–10 September	122	1070	6086	7156
XXI	1976	Montreal, Canada	17 July–1 August	92	1251	4834	6085
XXII	1980	Moscow, Soviet Union	19 July–3 August	81	1088	4238	5326
XXIII	1984	Los Angeles, USA	28 July–12 August	140	1620	5458	7078
XXIV	1988	Seoul, South Korea	17 September–2 October	–	–	–	–
XXV	1992	Barcelona, Spain	–	–	–	–	–

*This celebration (to mark the tenth anniversary of the Modern Games) was officially intercalated but is not numbered.
[1] Actually 25 March–3 April by the Julian Calendar then in force in Greece.
[2] Including recently discovered French national.
[3] The equestrian events were held in Stockholm, Sweden, 10–17 June with 158 competitors (13 women and 145 men) from 29 countries.

Winter

	Year	Venue	Date	Nations	Women	Men	Total
I	1924	Chamonix, France	25 January–4 February	16	13	281	294
II	1928	St Moritz, Switzerland	11–19 February	25	27	468	495
III	1932	Lake Placid, USA	4–15 February	17	32	274	306
IV	1936	Garmisch-Partenkirchen, Germany	6–16 February	28	80	675	755
–	1940	Sapporo, then St Moritz, then Garmisch-Partenkirchen	Not held due to war	–	–	–	–
–	1944	Cortina d'Ampezzo, Italy	Not held due to war	–	–	–	–
V	1948	St Moritz, Switzerland	30 January–8 February	28	77	636	713
VI	1952	Oslo, Norway	14–25 February	30	109	623	732
VII	1956	Cortina d'Ampezzo, Italy	26 January–5 February	32	132	687	819
VIII	1960	Squaw Valley, USA	18–28 February	30	144	521	665
IX	1964	Innsbruck, Austria	29 January–9 February	36	200	986	1186
X	1968	Grenoble, France	6–18 February	37	212	1081	1293
XI	1972	Sapporo, Japan	3–13 February	35	217	1015	1232
XII	1976	Innsbruck, Austria	4–15 February	37	228	900	1128
XIII	1980	Lake Placid, USA	13–24 February	37	234	833	1067
XIV	1984	Sarajevo, Yugoslavia	8–19 February	49	276	1002	1278
XV	1988	Calgary, Canada	13–28 February	–	–	–	–
XVI	1992	Albertville, France	–	–	–	–	–

TABLE OF OLYMPIC MEDAL WINNERS BY NATION 1896–1984

These totals include all first, second and third places, including those events no longer on the current (1988) schedule. The 1906 Games which were officially staged by the International Olympic Committee (IOC) have also been included. However, the medals won in the Art Competitions 1912–48 have *not* been included.

Note: Medals won in 1896, 1900 and 1904 by mixed teams from two countries have been counted for both countries.

Figures in brackets denote positions in medal tables for both Summer and Winter Games.

		Summer				Winter					Combined
		Gold	Silver	Bronze	Total	Gold	Silver	Bronze	Total		Total
1	United States	710	529	448	1687	(1) 40	46	31	117	(3)	1804
2	Soviet Union	340	292	253	885	(2) 68	48	50	166	(1)	1051
=3	Great Britain	168	212	197	577	(4) 7	4	10	21	(14)	598
=3	Germany (FRG)[1]	146	193	192	631	(3) 24	22	21	67	(8)	598
5	France	147	163	171	481	(5) 12	10	15	37	(11)	518
6	Sweden	131	135	162	428	(6) 32	25	29	86	(6)	514
7	Italy	141	117	120	378	(7) 12	9	7	28	(13)	406
8	GDR[2]	116	94	97	307	(9) 30	26	29	85	(7)	392
9	Finland	96	74	108	278	(10) 29	42	32	103	(4)	381
10	Hungary	113	106	130	349	(8) –	2	4	6	(=17)	355
11	Norway	40	30	33	103	(22) 54	57	52	163	(2)	266
12	Japan	83	72	75	230	(11) 1	4	1	6	(=17)	236
13	Switzerland	40	63	56	159	(16) 18	20	20	58	(9)	217
14	Australia	68	61	82	211	(12) –	–	–	–		211
15	Canada	36	60	68	164	(15) 14	10	15	39	(10)	203
=16	Netherlands	41	45	58	144	(17) 10	15	10	35	(12)	179
=16	Poland	38	51	86	175	(14) 1	1	2	4	(=19)	179
18	Romania	48	53	76	177	(13) –	–	1	1	(=21)	178
19	Austria	18	27	33	78	(24) 25	33	30	88	(5)	166
20	Czechoslovakia	42	45	47	134	(19) 2	7	11	20	(15)	154
21	Denmark	31	57	52	140	(18) –	–	–	–		140
22	Belgium	35	48	40	123	(20) 1	1	2	4	(=19)	127
23	Bulgaria	27	50	39	116	(21) –	–	1	1	(=21)	117
24	Greece	22	39	38	99	(23) –	–	–	–		99
25	Yugoslavia	23	25	23	71	(25) –	1	–	1	(=21)	72
26	Cuba	23	21	15	59	(26) –	–	–	–		59
27	South Africa[3]	16	15	21	52	(27) –	–	–	–		52
28	Turkey	23	12	10	45	(28) –	–	–	–		45
29	Argentina	13	18	13	44	(29) –	–	–	–		44
30	New Zealand	23	4	25	42	(30) –	–	–	–		42
=31	Mexico	9	12	16	37	(=31) –	–	–	–		37
=31	Korea (South)	7	12	18	37	(=31) –	–	–	–		37
33	China	15	8	9	32	(33) –	–	–	–		32
34	Brazil	6	7	17	30	(34) –	–	–	–		30
35	Iran	4	10	15	29	(35) –	–	–	–		29
=36	Kenya	6	7	9	22	(36) –	–	–	–		22
=36	Spain	3	11	7	21	(=37) 1	–	–	1	(=21)	22
38	Estonia[4]	6	6	9	21	(=37) –	–	–	–		21
39	Jamaica	4	8	8	20	(39) –	–	–	–		20
40	Egypt	6	6	6	18	(40) –	–	–	–		18
41	India	8	3	3	14	(41) –	–	–	–		14
=42	Ireland	4	4	5	13	(42) –	–	–	–		13
=42	North Korea (PRK)[5]	2	5	5	12	(=43) –	1	–	1	(=21)	13
44	Portugal	1	4	7	12	(=43) –	–	–	–		12
=45	Ethiopia	5	1	4	10	(=45) –	–	–	–		10
=45	Mongolia	–	5	5	10	(=45) –	–	–	–		10
47	Uruguay	2	1	6	9	(47) –	–	–	–		9
=48	Pakistan	3	3	2	8	(=48) –	–	–	–		8
=48	Liechtenstein	–	–	–	–	2	2	4	8	(16)	8
=48	Venezuela	1	2	5	8	(=48) –	–	–	–		8
=51	Trinidad	1	2	4	7	(=50) –	–	–	–		7
=51	Chile	–	5	2	7	(=50) –	–	–	–		7
53	Philippines	–	1	5	6	(52) –	–	–	–		6
=54	Uganda	1	3	1	5	(=53) –	–	–	5		5
=54	Tunisia	1	2	2	5	(=53) –	–	–	–		5
=56	Colombia	–	2	2	4	(=55) –	–	–	–		4
=56	Lebanon	–	2	2	4	(=55) –	–	–	–		4
=56	Nigeria	–	1	3	4	(=55) –	–	–	–		4
=56	Puerto Rico	–	1	3	4	(=55) –	–	–	–		4
=60	Morocco	2	1	–	3	(=59) –	–	–	–		3
=60	Latvia[4]	–	2	1	3	(=59) –	–	–	–		3
=60	Ghana	–	1	2	3	(=59) –	–	–	–		3
=60	Taiwan (Taipei)	–	1	2	3	(=59) –	–	–	–		3
=64	Luxembourg	1	1	–	2	(=63) –	–	–	–		2
=64	Peru	1	1	–	2	(=63) –	–	–	–		2
=64	Bahamas	1	–	1	2	(=63) –	–	–	–		2
=64	Tanzania	–	2	–	2	(=63) –	–	–	–		2
=64	Cameroun	–	1	1	2	(=63) –	–	–	–		2
=64	Haiti	–	1	1	2	(=63) –	–	–	–		2
=64	Iceland	–	1	1	2	(=63) –	–	–	–		2
=64	Thailand	–	1	1	2	(=63) –	–	–	–		2

		Summer				Winter				Combined
		Gold	Silver	Bronze	Total	Gold	Silver	Bronze	Total	Total
=64	Algeria	–	–	2	2	(=63) –	–	–	–	2
=64	Panama	–	–	2	2	(=63) –	–	–	–	2
=74	Zimbabwe	1	–	–	1	(=73) –	–	–	–	1
=74	Ivory Coast	–	1	–	1	(=73) –	–	–	–	1
=74	Singapore	–	1	–	1	(=73) –	–	–	–	1
=74	Sri Lanka	–	1	–	1	(=73) –	–	–	–	1
=74	Syria	–	1	–	1	(=73) –	–	–	–	1
=74	Bermuda	–	–	1	1	(=73) –	–	–	–	1
=74	Dominican Rep.	–	–	1	1	(=73) –	–	–	–	1
=74	Guyana	–	–	1	1	(=73) –	–	–	–	1
=74	Iraq	–	–	1	1	(=73) –	–	–	–	1
=74	Niger	–	–	1	1	(=73) –	–	–	–	1
=74	Zambia	–	–	1	1	(=73) –	–	–	–	1

[1]Germany 1896–1964, West Germany from 1968. [2]GDR, East Germany, from 1968.
[3]South Africa, up to 1960. [4]Estonia and Latvia, up to 1936. [5]From 1964.

OFFICIAL OPENINGS

The Olympic Games traditionally are opened by a member of the Royal Family or a representative of the national government of the host country. They have included:

Summer
1896	King George I
1900	–
1904	–
1906	–
1908	King Edward VII
1912	King Gustav V
1920	King Albert
1924	President Gaston Doumergue
1928	HRH Prince Hendrik
1932	Vice President Charles Curtis
1936	Chancellor Adolf Hitler
1948	King George VI
1952	President Juho Paasikivi
1956	HRH The Duke of Edinburgh
1960	President Giovanni Gronchi
1964	Emperor Hirohito
1968	President Gustavo Diaz Ordaz
1972	President Gustave Heinemann
1976	Queen Elizabeth II
1980	President Leonid Brezhnev
1984	President Ronald Reagan

Winter
1896	
1900	–
1904	–
1906	–
1908	–
1912	–
1920	–
1924	Under Secretary Gaston Vidal
1928	President Edmund Schulthess
1932	Governor Franklin D Roosevelt
1936	Chancellor Adolf Hitler
1948	President Enrico Celio
1952	HRH Princess Ragnhild
1956	President Giovanni Gronchi
1960	Vice President Richard Nixon
1964	President Adolf Schärf
1968	President Charles de Gaulle
1972	Emperor Hirohito
1976	President Rudolf Kirchschläger
1980	Vice President Walter Mondale
1984	President Mika Spiljak

THE OLYMPIC OATH

At the opening ceremony a representative of the host country, usually a veteran of previous Games, mounts the rostrum, holds a corner of his national flag and, with the flag bearers of all the other countries drawn up around him in a semicircle, pronounces the oath: 'In the name of all competitors, I promise that we will take part in these Olympic Games, respecting and abiding by the rules which govern them, in the true spirit of sportsmanship, for the glory of sport and the honour of our teams.'

The following have taken the Olympic oath:

1920	Victor Boin	Water Polo/Fencer
1924	Georges André	Athlete
1928	Harry Denis	Footballer
1932	George Calnan	Fencer
1936	Rudolf Ismayr	Weightlifter
1948	Donald Finlay	Athlete
1952	Heikki Savolainen	Gymnast
1956	John Landy	Athlete
1960	Adolfo Consolini	Athlete
1964	Takashi Ono	Gymnast
1968	Pablo Garrido	Athlete
1972	Heidi Schüller	Athlete
1976	Pierre St Jean	Weightlifter
1980	Nikolai Andrianov	Gymnast
1984	Edwin Moses	Athlete

Winter
1924	All flag bearers	
1928	Hans Eidenbenz	Skier
1932	Jack Shea	Speed skater
1936	Wilhelm Bogner	Skier
1948	Richard Torriani	Ice hockey player
1952	Torbjörn Falkanger	Ski jumper
1956	Guiliana Chenal-Minuzzo*	Skier
1960	Carol Heiss	Figure skater
1964	Paul Aste	Bobsledder
1968	Leo Lacroix	Skier
1972	Keichi Suzuki	Speed skater
1976	Werner Delle-Barth	Bobsledder
1980	Eric Heiden	Speed skater
1984	Bojan Krizaj	Skier

*First woman in Olympic history to take the oath.

THE OLYMPIC FLAME

The Olympic flame was introduced to the modern Games at Amsterdam in 1928, and since then has always burned throughout the duration of a Games. It symbolizes the endeavour for perfection and struggle for victory. The torch relay from Olympia to the Games venue was first staged in 1936 (and for the Winter Games in 1964). The torch first travelled by air when the Games were held in Melbourne in 1956.

The following have lit the Olympic flame in the stadium:

1936	Fritz Schilgen
1948	John Mark
1952	Paavo Nurmi (Hannes Kolehmainen on tower)
1956	Ron Clarke
1960	Giancarlo Peris
1964	Yoshinori Sakai
1968	Enriqueta Basilio
1972	Günter Zahn
1976	Stéphane Préfontaine and Sandra Henderson
1980	Sergei Belov
1984	Rafer Johnson

The Games

THE ANCIENT GAMES

The Olympic Games originally evolved from legendary conflicts among the Greek Gods and the religious ceremonies held in their honour. Historical evidence dates the Games from about 900 BC, but there is good reason to believe that a similar festival existed four centuries previously. The word 'athlete' derives from Aethlius, King of Elis, the area in which Olympia lies, and it was a successor, Iphitus, who revived the faltering concept in the late 9th century BC. The first firm record dates from 776 BC, and the Games were numbered at four-yearly intervals from then. At that time there was only one event, the *stade* race of approximately 192 metres, and the first recorded Olympic champion was Coroibis of Elis. Later the *diaulus* (two stade) and the *dolichus* (24 stade) followed. In 708 BC came the *pentathlon*, consisting of running, jumping, throwing the discus and javelin, and wrestling, and in 648 BC the *pankration*, a brutal mix of boxing and wrestling.

Initially contestants wore simple shorts-like garments, but from about 720 BC they competed in the nude, and until 692 BC the Games only lasted for a single day. For six centuries the fame of Olympia spread, and the winners, who only won a crown of wild olive leaves at the Games, were often richly rewarded by their home states. It has been estimated that the Stadium at Olympia could hold over 20 000 spectators. Possibly the most famous champion of early times was Leonidas of Rhodes who won 12 events from 164–152 BC. Other famous champions included the Spartan runner Chionis, and six-time wrestling champion Milon of Croton. Eventually the very success of the Games led to professionalism and corruption, and with the dawn of the Christian Era the religious and physical backgrounds of the Games were attacked. The Games declined under Roman influence, so much so that in AD 67 a drunken Emperor Nero was crowned victor of the chariot race despite the fact that there were no other entrants and he failed to finish the course. In AD 393 Emperor Theodosius I issued a decree in Milan which prohibited the Games, and within a few generations even the site of Olympia had been lost.

1896
1st Summer Games

The resurgence of interest in Ancient Greece in the 17th and 18th centuries led to the inauguration of the Cotswold Olympic Games in 1636 and the foundation of the Much Wenlock Olympic Society in 1850, both in England. In Germany the famed founder of modern gymnastics, Johann Guts Muths, suggested the revival of the Olympic ideal at the end of the 18th century, and this was reiterated by his countryman, archaeologist Ernst Curtius in 1852.

The true founder of the modern Olympic Games is commonly acknowledged to be Pierre de Fredi, Baron de Coubertin, of France. In 1889 a government commission to study physical culture methods led him to meet with Dr Penny Brooke of Much Wenlock, and at the end of his travels he formed his concept of a revived Games, which he first propounded publicly at a lecture in the Sorbonne on 25 November 1892. In June 1894 he convened an international conference, also in the Sorbonne, at which 12 countries were represented and another 21 sent messages of support. A resolution on 23 June called for sports competitions along the lines of the Ancient Games to be held every fourth year. The International Olympic Committee (IOC) was inaugurated under the presidency of Demetrius Vikelas of Greece, with de Coubertin as secretary-general. The Frenchman had hoped to herald the new century with the new Games in Paris in 1900, but the delegates were impatient and Athens was selected for 1896. Although the Greek government were apparently not consulted, and were anyway beset with internal problems, public support in the country was enthusiastic and with the generosity of a Greek businessman, Georgios Averoff, the Panathenean Stadium was reconstructed on the site of an ancient stadium in Athens. The new track measured 333.33m, had very sharp turns, and the competitors had to run in a clock wise direction.

There were 40 000 spectators in the stadium for the opening with thousands more on the surrounding hills. The great bulk of the competitors were from Greece itself, but a strong American colleges team dominated. Many athletes entered privately, including holiday makers and Embassy staff.

Not for the last time a gymnast, Hermann Weingärtner (GER), was the most successful with three first places, two seconds and a third place. James Connolly (USA) became the first modern Olympic champion when he won the hop, step and jump event. Victors actually received a silver medal and a crown of olive leaves; runners-up were given bronze medals and a crown of laurel; no awards were made for third place.

The marathon race had been instituted to commemorate the legendary feat of a Greek courier, possibly Pheidippides, who was supposed to have run from the site

James Connolly, the first modern Olympic champion. (Dave Terry)

The 100m final in 1896 – note the crouch start of winner Thomas Burke. (GSL)

of the battle against the Persians at Marathon in 490 BC to Athens, and after crying out 'Rejoice! We have won' collapsed and died. To the delight of the hosts the race was won by a Greek shepherd, Spiridon 'Spryos' Louis, who was escorted into the stadium by Crown Prince Constantine and Prince George. The oldest gold medallist was 37-year-old shooter Georgios Orphanidis (GRE), while the youngest was swimmer Alfred Hajos (HUN) aged 18yr 70 days.

1896 Medals

	Gold	Silver	Bronze
United States	11	7	1
Greece	10	19	17
Germany	7	5	2
France	5	4	2
Great Britain	3	3	1
Hungary	2	1	2
Austria	2	–	3
Australia	2	–	–
Denmark	1	2	4
Switzerland	1	2	–

1900
IInd Summer Games

Despite strong Greek pressure for exclusive rights to organize future Games, Baron de Coubertin won agreement to hold the 1900 Games in Paris, but made a serious mistake in making it part of the Universal Exposition also being held there. In the event the Games became merely a sideshow to the fair, with the track and field events being held on uneven turf in the Bois de Boulogne. A multitude of events were held over a period of 5 months, including motorboating and fishing in the Seine – although these were thankfully denied official recognition, as were other events for professionals. The general air of confusion was such that even medal winners were not aware until much later that they had been competing at the

Olympic Games.

France, the host country, had a record-sized team numbering 884, the largest ever entered for the Games. The Americans were still represented by colleges and clubs, and the decision to have competition on Sunday upset many of those whose colleges were church controlled. Thus long jumper Myer Prinstein, a Jew but under the aegis of the strongly Methodist University of Syracuse, gained a silver medal with his Saturday qualifying round jump (such performances then counted for medals), but had to withdraw from the Sunday final. The eventual winner, Alvin Kraenzlein (USA) set a record of four individual gold medals, a feat never surpassed in track and field at one Games. Also much in evidence was America's Ray Ewry, the standing jump expert, at the start of his fabulous Olympic career.

Women were allowed to compete

for the first time, but only in golf and tennis, and the first female Olympic champion in history was Britain's Charlotte Cooper, a Wimbledon champion, who won the tennis singles title on 9 July. Another unique record was set in the coxed pairs rowing final, in which a small French boy was drafted in at the last moment to cox the winning Dutch crew. His name was never recorded and he disappeared without trace afterwards, but he was no more than 10 years old, and possibly as young as 7, in either case the youngest ever Olympic gold medallist. The oldest champion in Paris was Eugène Mougin (FRA) in archery, at 47 yr 193 days.

1900 Medals

	Gold	Silver	Bronze
France	27	35	34
United States	19	15	16
Great Britain	17	8	12
Belgium	5	6	3
Switzerland	5	3	1
Germany	4	2	2
Australia	2	–	4
Denmark	2	3	2
Italy	2	2	–
Netherlands	1	2	3
Hungary	1	2	2
Cuba	1	1	–
Canada	1	–	1
Sweden	1	–	1
Austria	–	3	3
Norway	–	2	3
Czechoslovakia	–	1	2
India	–	2	–

1904
IIIrd Summer Games

The IOC originally designated Chicago for these Games, but at the request of President Theodore Roosevelt, also president of the US Olympic Committee, the venue was changed to St Louis to coincide with the World's Fair, held to celebrate the centenary of the Louisiana Purchase. Thus again they became merely a sideshow. The problems of distance and travel meant few overseas entrants so that 85 per cent of the competitors were from the host country, and they won 84 per cent of the medals. In fact the Games were a virtual college and club tournament with the New York AC beating the Chicago Athletic Association for the track and field team title. In such circumstances the cycling events, which had no foreigners at all and included

Quadruple gold-medallist in 1900, Alvin Kraenzlein is the only athlete to win four individual titles at a single Games. (GSL)

a number of professional riders, were refused official Olympic status.

Under the rather loose controls imposed on most sports some strange things happened. In the 400m track race no heats were held and all 13 entrants ran in the final. Rowing events entailed making a turn, and swimming events were held over Imperial distances. The unfortunate Myer Prinstein redressed his grievance of four years previously by taking the long jump title as well as winning the hop, step and jump. The ever liberal Prinstein here was representing the Greater New York Irish AA. The 200m final, uniquely held on a straightaway (ie no turns), was won by Archie Hahn, with all three of his opponents given a one-yard 0.99m handicap under the rules then governing false starts.

Yet again it was a gymnast, Anton Heida (USA), who gained the record total of medals (five golds and one silver). There was a scandal in the marathon when the first man out of the stadium, Fred Lorz (USA) was also the first man back, looking remarkably fresh. It later transpired that he had received a lift in a car after suffering cramp, and when the car itself broke down near the stadium he resumed running – as a joke he claimed. He was banned for life, and the title awarded to Thomas Hicks who had finished in a daze due to the strychnine he had taken as a stimulant – a practice then common. In ninth place was Lentauw (SAF), the first black African distance runner to compete in the Olympics. The youngest gold medallist was heavyweight boxer Samuel Berger (USA) aged 19 yr 274 days, while the oldest was the Reverend Galen Spencer (USA), an archer, aged 64 yr 2 days.

1904 Medals

	Gold	Silver	Bronze
United States	70	74	67
Cuba	5	2	3
Germany	4	4	5
Canada	4	1	–
Hungary	2	1	1
Austria	2	1	1
Great Britain	1	1	–
Switzerland	1	–	1
Greece	1	–	1
France	–	1	–

1906
The Intercalated Summer Games

After two débâcles something was needed to revive the flagging Olympic movement and de Coubertin, with some misgivings, agreed a series of four-yearly meetings, interspersed with the main Games, to be held in Athens. Although these had the blessing of the IOC, it was decided that the Interim games would not be numbered in sequence. In the event only this meeting of the projected series was ever held.

Again the Greeks showed their enthusiasm and large crowds, missing for the past 10 years, were in evidence. The 20 countries included the first 'official' American team, and the first ever team from Finland with the doyen of the famous Järvinen family, Werner, gaining his country's first ever Olympic gold medal.

Despite the soft cinder track in the stadium, poor facilities for swimmers in the sea at Phaleron, and general complaints about food and judging decisions, these Interim Games put the whole Olympic concept back on the right path.

Harry Hillman's winning 400m and 400m hurdles double of 1904 is still unmatched. (GSL)

Paul Pilgrim (USA) beats Halswelle (GBR) and Barker (AUS) in the 400m at Athens. Note runners competed in a clockwise direction. (Dave Terry)

To protest competition on a Sunday, Forrest Smithson won the 1908 high hurdles carrying his bible. (GSL)

The oldest gold medallist was Maurice Lecoq (FRA) aged 52 yr 15 days when he won the rapid fire pistol event. The youngest was the coxswain of the Italian fours crew, Giorgio Cesana aged 14 yr 10 days.

1906 Medals

	Gold	Silver	Bronze
France	15	9	16
United States	12	6	5
Greece	8	13	13
Great Britain	8	11	6
Italy	7	6	3
Switzerland	5	4	2
Germany	4	6	4
Norway	4	1	–
Austria	3	3	2
Sweden	2	5	7
Hungary	2	5	3
Belgium	2	2	3
Denmark	2	2	1
Finland	2	–	1
Canada	1	1	–
Netherlands	–	1	2
Australia	–	–	3
Czechoslovakia	–	–	2
South Africa	–	–	1

1908
IVth Summer Games

Originally awarded to Rome the IVth Games were re-allocated to London when the Italian authorities had to withdraw only two years beforehand. Nevertheless, they were the most successful held so far and set the pattern for future Games. A 68 000 capacity stadium was build in West London, for a reported cost of £40 000. It contained an athletics track of three laps to the mile, inside a 660yd banked concrete cycle track. On the grass infield stood a giant pool for the swimming events. Rowing was at Henley and tennis at Wimbledon, with yachting at Ryde, Isle of Wight. The main competitions took place in July, although the overall programme lasted from April to October.

There were 21 sports in all, including four ice skating events. Entries only by nations, as opposed to individuals, fuelled the nationalism which undoubtedly caused some of the disputes which marred this first truly international sporting event. Sweden and the United States were upset that their flags had been inadvertently missed from those flying around the stadium, and the latter refused to dip the Stars and Stripes to King

Edward in the march past. The Finnish team would not march behind the flag of Czarist Russia and came in without any banner. There were numerous complaints, mainly from US officials, about 'fixed' heats, illegal coaching rule breaking and British chauvinism. The weather was also rather bad even by British standards.

All the rancour came to a head in the 400m event final, in which three of the four finalists were Americans. They were accused of impeding the sole British runner, Lieut Wyndham Halswelle, and a re-run was ordered for the next day, with the winner of the disputed race, Carpenter, being disqualified. The other Americans refused to appear and Halswelle gained the gold medal in the only walk-over in Games history. One of the runners involved was John Taylor who, as a member of the winning medley relay team, became the first black man to win an Olympic gold medal. The previous year the IOC had decided that medals should be awarded for the first three places in all events.

The skating events gave the opportunity to Russia to win its first Olympic title, courtesy of Nikolai Panin who four years later was in the shooting team. Another Olympic first came in the London shooting programme when Oscar and Alfred Swahn of Sweden became the first father and son to win gold medals, with Oscar being the oldest gold medallist at these Games aged 60yr 265 days. The youngest champion was William Foster, in Britain's 4 × 200m freestyle relay team, aged 18yr 6 days.

Undoubtedly the most famous event in the IVth Games was the marathon. Originally the distance was to be about 25 miles, but the start was moved to Windsor Castle, an exact 26 miles. Then at the request of Princess Mary it was moved again to start beneath the windows of the royal nursery in the Castle grounds, making a final distance of 26 miles 385yd *42 195m*. This arbitrarily arrived – at distance was later accepted worldwide as the standard marathon length. The race itself was run in intensely hot and humid conditions. The little Italian Dorando Pietri reached the stadium first in a state of collapse, and fell five times on the last part-lap of the track. Over-zealous officials, reputedly including the famous author Sir Arthur Conan Doyle, helped him over the finish line, thus leading to his disqualification. As an expression of sympathy Queen Alexandra gave Pietri a special gold cup.

1908 Medals

	Gold	Silver	Bronze
Great Britain	57	50	40
United States	23	12	11
Sweden	8	6	11
France	5	5	9
Germany	3	5	4
Hungary	3	4	2
Canada	3	3	8
Norway	2	3	3
Italy	2	2	–
Belgium	1	5	2
Australia*	1	2	1
Russia	1	2	–
Finland	1	1	3
South Africa	1	1	–
Greece	–	3	1
Denmark	–	2	3
Czechoslovakia	–	–	2
Austria	–	–	1
Netherlands	–	–	1
New Zealand*	–	–	1

*Australia and New Zealand combined as Australasia.

1912
Vth Summer Games

Stockholm finally attained the honour that Sweden had wanted from the very beginning, and Torben Grut designed and built a 31 000 capacity stadium, with a 383m track laid out under the direction of Charles Perry, the Englishman responsible for the 1896 and 1908 tracks. Baron de Coubertin had insisted that the number of sports be cut, and now with only 14 there were high standards of performance and sportsmanship, with few arguments or protests. One of the rare complaints was from the Finns again about competing under the Russian flag. Indeed the double gold medallist Kolehmainen stated that he almost wished he had not won rather than see the hated flag raised for his victories.

Various innovations included the first use of electrical timing and photo-finish equipment for the running events. Baron de Coubertin had asked for a new event to be introduced, the modern pentathlon, which consisted of five disciplines in different sports. It was dominated by the Swedes but in fifth place was one Lieut George S Patton (USA), later to become a controversial Second World War general. As previously, the American team lived on the liner that had brought them across the Atlantic, ironically named *Finland* – for this was the Games in which the first of the 'Flying Finns', Hannes Kolehmainen, made his appearance, winning the 5000m, 10 000m and 12 000m cross country races.

In the swimming pool the first of the great Hawaiian competitors, Duke Kahanamoku, won the 100m freestyle. He competed in three more Games before becoming a film star. The longest road race ever held in the Games was contested in the cycling programme with Rudolph Lewis (SAF), taking the 320km event in just short of 10¾ hours. In

One of the world's greatest athletes, Jim Thorpe, happily reinstated after 72 years in limbo. (GSL)

Checking the 10km walk in 1912, with Webb (GBR) and Goulding (CAN) in the lead. (GSL)

wrestling problems were caused by the extreme length of some of the bouts, one actually taking 11hr 40min, a record for the sport. The first known twins to win Olympic gold medals were the Carlberg brothers, Vilhelm(3) and Eric(2), in shooting, while an even rarer sibling combination came in the 6m class yachting when the French winner *Mac Miche* was crewed by the three Thubé brothers.

However the star of the Games was undoubtedly Jim Thorpe. Of Irish, French, but mainly American Indian ancestry, Thorpe won both of the newly constituted athletic pentathlon and decathlon events, with consummate ease. Additionally he was fifth in the individual high jump and seventh in the long jump. Presenting him with his medals King Gustav V called him 'the greatest athlete in the world'. Thorpe reportedly replied, 'Thanks King'. Some time later it was revealed that he had played minor baseball for money, and owing to the violent amateur/professional dichotomy of the time, perhaps reinforced by anti-Indian prejudice, Thorpe's medals were taken back

and his performances removed from Olympic annals. It seems almost certain that he was ignorant of the amateur laws of the time, and the amount involved was very small. Twenty years after his death in 1953 the American Athletic Union reinstated him as an amateur, but the IOC stubbornly refused all entreaties on his behalf. It has been suggested that his cause was not helped by the fact that the President of the IOC from 1952–72 was Avery Brundage, a team-mate of Thorpe's in 1912 who had placed fifth (or sixth depending on your view) in the pentathlon. Finally, in October 1982 Thorpe was pardoned by the IOC and the medals presented to his family.

The oldest gold medallist at these Games was the ubiquitous Oscar Swahn (SWE) now aged 64yr 258 days, while team-mate diver Greta Johansson was the youngest aged 17yr 186 days. The only unfortunate incident at the Games was the collapse and death of Francisco Lazzaro (POR) during the marathon – ironically it was the first Games that his country had attended.

1912 Medals

	Gold	Silver	Bronze
United States[1]	27	19	19
Sweden	24	24	17
Great Britain	10	15	16
Finland	9	8	9
France	7	4	3
Germany	5	13	7
South Africa	4	2	–
Norway	4	1	5
Canada	3	2	3
Hungary	3	2	3
Italy	3	1	2
Australia[2]	2	2	2
Belgium	2	1	3
Denmark	1	6	5
Greece	1	–	1
New Zealand[2]	1	–	1
Switzerland	1	–	–
Russia	–	2	3
Austria	–	2	2
Netherlands	–	–	3

[1]Adjusted by reinstatement of Jim Thorpe in 1982.
[2]Australia and New Zealand combined as Australasia.

1920
VIIth Summer Games

The VIth Games were allocated to Berlin in the vain hope such a decision might avert the imminent war, and even when hostilities broke out in 1914 the Germans still

Jack Beresford's illustrious Olympic career began at Antwerp. It ended at Amsterdam with three gold and two silver medals. (GSL)

continued with their preparations believing the war would not last long. However in 1920, although Antwerp was sorely affected by the human tragedy and economic ruin of the conflict, the organizing committee under Count Henri de Baillet-Latour, later IOC President, overcame all difficulties to put the Games on. Although the recent enemies, Germany, Austria, Hungary and Turkey were not invited, a record number of countries attended. The concept of the Olympic oath was introduced, as was the newly devised Olympic flag of five interlaced rings coloured blue, yellow, black, green and red. Designed by de Coubertin in 1913, based on an ancient Greek motif, it was meant to symbolize the friendship of mankind, with the colours representing all nations as every national flag contains at least one of these colours.

Unfortunately the track at the new 30 000-seat stadium was very poor and badly affected by the persistent rain, and crowds generally were small. For the first time Finland competed under its own flag, having gained independence in 1917, and they celebrated the occasion by halting the American track and field juggernaut by winning as many athletic gold medals as the Americans. Also outstanding was Albert Hill of Great Britain who gained a 800m/1500m double, not repeated for 44 years. Second in the 1500m was Philip Baker (GBR), who later in life as Philip Noel-Baker MP, was the recipient of the 1959 Nobel Peace Prize – a unique achievement for an Olympian. The most successful competitor was Willis Lee (USA) who won five golds, one silver and two bronzes in shooting. Another shooter, the phenomenal Oscar Swahn (SWE) became the oldest ever Olympic medallist with a silver at the age of 72yr 280 days. The oldest champion at these Games was archer Hubert van Innis (BEL) aged 54yr 187 days, while the youngest was diver Aileen Riggin (USA) at 14yr 119 days.

One serious incident occurred in the soccer final when Czechoslovakia were disqualified for leaving the field after 40 minutes play in protest at decisions by the British referee. Belgium were leading 2-0.

Two winter sports were also held, ice hockey and figure skating. The latter witnessed the first gold medals won by husband and wife, in the pairs champions, Ludowika and Walter Jakobsson of Finland. On this subject it may be that the first Olympic marriage was that of American diver Alice Lord and high jump champion Dick Landon soon after they returned home.

1920 Medals

	Gold	Silver	Bronze
United States	41	27	28
Sweden	19	20	26
Great Britain	15	15	13
Finland	15	10	9
Belgium	14	11	10
Norway	13	9	9
Italy	13	5	5
France	9	19	13
Netherlands	4	2	5
Denmark	3	9	1
South Africa	3	4	3
Canada	3	3	3
Switzerland	2	2	7
Estonia	1	2	–
Brazil	1	1	1
Australia	–	2	1
Japan	–	2	–
Spain	–	2	–
Greece	–	1	–
Luxembourg	–	1	–
Czechoslovakia	–	–	2
New Zealand	–	–	1

1924
Ist Winter Games

Although initially opposed by the Scandinavian countries, who felt that Winter Olympics would detract from their own Nordic Games, an 'International Winter Sports Week' was held at Chamonix, France. In 1926 it was accorded the title of Winter Games retrospectively. The first ever official Olympic Winter gold medallist was Charles Jewtraw (USA) who won the 500m speed skating on 26 January, which also made it the earliest gold medal ever won in an Olympic year. There was no Alpine skiing and Norway and Finland dominated the Games. The oldest champion was speed skater Julius Skutnabb (FIN) aged 34yr 229 days, and the youngest was Heinrich Schläppi, in Switzerland's 4-man bob, aged 18yr 279 days. Two days before the closing ceremony a meeting established the International Ski Federation (FIS).

1924 Medals (Winter)

	Gold	Silver	Bronze
Norway	4	7	6
Finland	4	3	3
Austria	2	1	–
United States	1	2	1
Switzerland	1	–	1
Canada	1	–	–
Sweden	1	–	–
Great Britain	–	1	2
Belgium	–	–	1
France	–	–	1

Triple gold medallist at Chamonix, Clas Thunberg (FIN) won a record seven Olympic medals in all. (GSL)

1924
VIIIth Summer Games

Originally scheduled for Amsterdam, de Coubertin requested that the Games be transferred to Paris in the hope that the bad image acquired in 1900 could be eradicated. The IOC had taken steps to impose its authority on the staging of the Olympics so that never again could a host country add events as it wished. The Colombes stadium was enlarged to hold 60 000 spectators, and competitors were housed in huts scattered around the main site. Germany was still not present due to the particularly frosty relations between them and France. The weather was good, in fact too good at times – for the 10 000m cross country event it was reported to be over 40°C and over half of the starters did not finish. Despite all sports being organized by their international governing bodies, and the instigation of Juries of Appeal, there were still many complaints of unfair decisions, notably in boxing. The track events were dominated by the resurgent Finns with their outstanding stars Paavo Nurmi and Ville Ritola. Nurmi won a then record five gold medals, and Ritola four golds and two silvers. The remarkable Nurmi won the 1500m and 5000m titles within 100 minutes on the same day – a unique performance. The statue of him which stands outside the Helsinki stadium was sculpted in 1925 to commemorate his Paris triumphs. Two Britons scored upset wins when Harold Abrahams became the first European to win an Olympic sprint and Eric Liddell

Lucy Morton (GBR) winning the inaugural 200m breaststroke title at Paris. (GSL)

set a world record in taking the 400m crown. Abrahams later recollected that there were no victory ceremonies and that he received his gold medal in the post some weeks later.

In the pool Johnny Weissmuller (USA) won three golds in freestyle swimming and a bronze at water polo. In the 1930s he became the most famous screen 'Tarzan' of them all. This Games was the first to introduce lane dividers. In rowing another American to gain fame elsewhere was Benjamin Spock, number 7 in the winning eight, who later gained renown as a writer and paediatrician. The incredible Oscar Swahn (SWE) had been picked for his team but at 76 was too ill. However his son Alfred won a medal to make the family total six golds, four silvers and five bronzes. Tennis made its last appearance prior to 1988, and one of the gold medallists, Norris Williams, had been a survivor of the *Titanic* disaster in 1912.

The oldest gold medallist at Paris was British shooter Allen Whitty

DSO aged 58yr 82 days (Britain's oldest ever champion), while the youngest winner was boxer Jackie Fields (USA) at 16yr 162 days.

1924 Medals (Summer)

	Gold	Silver	Bronze
United States	45	27	27
Finland	14	13	10
France	13	15	10
Great Britain	9	13	12
Italy	8	3	5
Switzerland	7	8	10
Norway	5	2	3
Sweden	4	13	12
Netherlands	4	1	5
Belgium	3	7	3
Australia	3	1	2
Denmark	2	5	2
Hungary	2	3	4
Yugoslavia	2	–	–
Czechoslovakia	1	4	5
Argentina	1	3	2
Estonia	1	1	4
South Africa	1	1	1
Luxembourg	1	1	–
Greece	1	–	–
Uruguay	1	–	–
Austria	–	3	1
Canada	–	3	1
Ireland	–	1	1
Poland	–	1	1
Haiti	–	–	1
Japan	–	–	1
New Zealand	–	–	1
Portugal	–	–	1
Romania	–	–	1

1928
IInd Winter Games

Unseasonal weather threatened the programme at St Moritz in Switzerland, and a speed skating event was cancelled and the bobsleigh had only two runs instead of four. The bobs, for the first and only time, were composed of 5-man teams. The event was won by the United States whose driver, William Fiske, aged only 16yr 260 days, was the youngest ever male Winter gold medallist. Also in the team was the oldest gold medallist at these Games, Clifford Gray, aged 36yr 21 days. The youngest was Sonja Henie (NOR) taking the first of her three titles aged 15yr 316 days. She was the 'star' of the Games with her interpretation of 'The Dying Swan', which began a whole new era for figure skating.

In ski jumping the defending champion Jacob Tullin-Thams (NOR) was nearly killed crashing at the end of a 73m jump on a hill

The ski jump at St Moritz for the first Olympic contest in the discipline in 1924. (GSL)

designed for jumps of considerably less. A true Olympian, he reappeared in 1936 to win a silver medal at yachting. The cancellation of the 10 000m speed skating event by the Norwegian referee caused a considerable amount of bad feeling as at that point an American, Irving Jaffee, was surprisingly in the lead.

1928 Medals (Winter)

	Gold	Silver	Bronze
Norway	6	4	5
United States	2	2	2
Sweden	2	2	1
Finland	2	1	1
Canada	1	–	–
France	1	–	–
Austria	–	3	1
Belgium	–	–	1
Czechoslovakia	–	–	1
Germany	–	–	1
Great Britain	–	–	1
Switzerland	–	–	1

1928
IXth Summer Games

After unsuccessfully applying for the Games of 1916, 1920 and 1924, the Dutch finally were rewarded, and built a new 40 000 capacity stadium on reclaimed land in Amsterdam. The size of the track, 400m, was then standardized for future Games. One innovation was the erection of a large results board; others included the release of pigeons at the opening ceremony – to symbolize peace – and the burning of an Olympic flame throughout the Games.

Germany returned to the competition in great strength. After much argument women were allowed to compete in track and field, albeit in only five events. World records were set in all five, although there were such harrowing scenes of distress in the 800m that it was then omitted from the programme until 1964. The Finns again dominated the athletics, and with the young Canadian Percy Williams taking the sprints, and Lord Burghley becoming the first member of the British House of Lords to win an Olympic athletic title, the Americans had a lean time. A pointer for the future was the victory in the marathon of Mohamed El Ouafi, representing France, but an Algerian and the pathfinder for future great African distance runners. The US team was under the control of Major-General Douglas MacArthur, later in command of the victorious Americans in the Pacific theatre of the Second World War.

The swimming pool saw the emergence of another threat to the United States in the form of the Japanese, while 50 000 people at the hockey final saw India inaugurate their run of six consecutive titles. Another first came in yachting when Crown Prince Olav, later King Olav V of Norway, gained a gold medal in the 6m class. A team-mate in the *Norna*, Johann Anker, was the oldest gold medallist in Amsterdam aged 57yr 44 days, while the youngest, also water-borne, was the Swiss pairs cox Hans Boúrquin aged 14yr.

1928 Medals (Summer)

	Gold	Silver	Bronze
United States	22	18	16
Germany	10	7	14
Finland	8	8	9
Sweden	7	6	12
Italy	7	5	7
Switzerland	7	4	4
France	6	10	5
Netherlands	6	9	4
Hungary	4	5	–
Canada	4	4	7
Great Britain	3	10	7
Argentina	3	3	1
Denmark	3	1	2
Czechoslovakia	2	5	2
Japan	2	2	1
Estonia	2	1	2
Egypt	2	1	1
Austria	2	–	1
Australia	1	2	1
Norway	1	2	1
Poland	1	1	3
Yugoslavia	1	1	3
South Africa	1	–	2
India	1	–	–
Ireland	1	–	–
New Zealand	1	–	–
Spain	1	–	–
Uruguay	1	–	–
Belgium	–	1	2
Chile	–	1	–
Haiti	–	1	–
Portugal	–	–	1
Philippines	–	–	1

Baron Carl von Langen (GER) won two gold medals in the 1928 dressage competition. He was fatally injured six years later. (GSL)

1932
IIIrd Winter Games

Snow had to be brought over to the United States from Canada for some of the venues at Lake Placid, and a thaw caused the 4-man bob event to be held after the closing ceremony. Incidentally, Eleanor, the redoubtable wife of the New York State Governor, Franklin D Roosevelt (later President of the United States), took a ride down the bob course. Innovatively, figure skating was held indoors, and three speed skating events for women were given demonstration status – 28 years later such events were on the programme proper. The men's speed skating caused an upset, due to the use of American 'mass start' rules which put the usually dominant Europeans at a distinct disadvantage.

The oldest ever Winter Games contestant was Joseph Savage (USA) aged 52yr 144 days in the pairs skating. The winners of that title, Pierre and Andrée Brunet (FRA), became the only pair to win both as an unmarried and married couple. In the ladies event Cecilia Colledge was Britain's youngest ever Olympic competitor, at any sport, aged 11yr 73 days. History of a different kind was made by Eddie Eagan (USA) in the 4-man bob as a late and virtually untried draftee. By winning he became the only man to win gold medals in both Summer and Winter celebrations – he was a 1920 boxing champion. The oldest

Sonja Henie (NOR) won the second of her three gold medals in 1932, before becoming a major Hollywood star. (Stan Greenberg)

gold medallist at Lake Placid was Eagan's bob team-mate Jay O'Brien aged 48yr 359 days, while Sonja Henie was again the youngest, now aged 19yr 308 days.

1932 Medals (Winter)

	Gold	Silver	Bronze
United States	6	4	2
Norway	3	4	3
Sweden	1	2	–
Canada	1	1	5
Finland	1	1	1
Austria	1	1	–
France	1	–	–
Switzerland	–	1	–
Germany	–	–	2
Hungary	–	–	1

1932
Xth Summer Games

Despite trepidations felt over the memory of the 1904 'farce' at St Louis, in 1923 Los Angeles was awarded the 1932 Games. Against further worries of distance and cost of travel were set the advantages of favourable weather and competitive conditions. The announcement by the organizing committee that they would subsidize transportation, housing and feeding costs helped greatly at a time of the Depression. The concept of an Olympic 'village' came to fruition with the construction of 550 specially designed small houses for male competitors – women were put up separately in the Chapman Park Hotel, and the strict rule preventing women in the village barred the Finnish team's lady cook. After journeys often lasting two weeks, the foreigners found excellent facilities awaiting them.

The Coliseum held 101 000 seated spectators, and a special wooden cycling track was erected in the Pasadena Rose Bowl. New ideas included the use of photo-finish equipment, the three-tiered victory stand, and in boxing the system of having the referee in the ring with the boxers. Most incidents were minor, but not all. The Finnish runner Lauri Lehtinen blocked the American Ralph Hill in the closing stages of the 5000m final – a not uncommon practice in Europe. Loud booing from the partisan crowd was quickly quietened by the announcer, Bill Henry, whose words 'Remember please, these people are our guests' have entered Olympic lore. More serious was the insulting of the referee by the Brazilian water polo team after their loss to Germany – they were disqualified from the tournament.

On the brighter side was the performance of Mildred 'Babe' Didrikson. Much to her annoyance she was only allowed to enter three events, winning the javelin and 80m hurdles, and gaining a silver in the high jump. She thus is the only athlete to win medals at running, jumping and throwing. Although clearing the same height as the winner in the high jump her style was declared illegal, but she was only 'demoted' to second place. Another strange happening was in the 400m hurdles where Irishman Bob Tisdall, who spent most of the preceding days in bed resting, won the gold medal, but because he knocked down a hurdle the world record was given to the runner-up Glenn Hardin (USA). In swimming the Japanese were superb with their 4 × 200m team breaking the world record by a remarkable 37.8sec.

The oldest gold medallist at Los Angeles was dressage champion Xavier Lesage (FRA) aged 46yr 290 days, while the youngest was

Juan Zabala (ARG) won the 1932 marathon two months short of his 21st birthday, the youngest ever winner. (GSL)

1500m freestyle champion Kusuo Kitamura (JPN) aged 14yr 309 days.

1932 Medals (Summer)

	Gold	Silver	Bronze
United States	41	32	30
Italy	12	12	12
France	10	5	4
Sweden	9	5	9
Japan	7	7	4
Hungary	6	4	5
Finland	5	8	12
Germany	4	12	5
Great Britain	4	7	5
Australia	3	1	1
Argentina	3	1	–
Canada	2	5	8
Netherlands	2	5	–
Poland	2	1	4
South Africa	2	–	3
Ireland	2	–	–
Czechoslovakia	1	2	1
Austria	1	1	3
India	1	–	–
Denmark	–	3	3
Mexico	–	2	–
Latvia	–	1	–
New Zealand	–	1	–
Switzerland	–	1	–
Philippines	–	–	3
Spain	–	–	1
Uruguay	–	–	1

1936
IVth Winter Games

Despite much discussion about non-attendance at these Games in protest at the racialist policies of the National Socialist government of Germany, there was a record number of countries at Garmisch-Partenkirchen. For the first time Alpine skiing was included, although the only event was a combination one, for both men and women. Birger Ruud (NOR) became the only ski jumper ever successfully to defend his title, and then caused a major surprise by winning the downhill segment of the men's Alpine combination.

The top medal winner was speed skater Ivar Ballangrud (NOR) with three golds and a silver. Sonja Henie (NOR) won her third consecutive figure skating title, and then went off to Hollywood, followed sometime later by the twelfth-placed British girl, Gladys Jepson-Turner, who gained cinematic fame as Belita. The British caused a major upset by winning the ice hockey, albeit their team was mainly composed of Anglo-Canadians. In this competition appeared Rudi Ball, one of only two athletes of Jewish origin

The gold medal Switzerland II bob at Garmisch-Partenkirchen. (GSL)

selected by Germany in 1936. He was especially requested to return from his exile in France – the hosts hoping to offset criticism of their attitude to Jewish sportsmen and women by this act.

A most unusual double nearly came the way of Ernst Baier (GER) who won the pairs skating, but only came second in the men's singles. His pairs partner, Maxi Herber was the youngest gold medallist aged 15yr 128 days, while the oldest was Alan Washbond (USA) aged 36yr 124 days in the 2-man bob.

1936 Medals (Winter)

	Gold	Silver	Bronze
Norway	7	5	3
Germany	3	3	–
Sweden	2	2	3
Finland	1	2	3
Austria	1	1	2
Switzerland	1	2	–
Great Britain	1	1	1
United States	1	–	3
Canada	–	1	–
France	–	–	1
Hungary	–	–	1

1936
XIth Summer Games

These Games were awarded to Berlin just prior to the rise to power of Adolf Hitler and the National Socialist (Nazi) Party. Abhorrence of Germany's policies under this government led many countries to propose a boycott, but the President of the US Olympic Committee, Avery Brundage, was strongly in favour of participation, and won the day. Political overtones overshadowed the Games until the last moment when Spain withdrew owing to the outbreak of the civil war there. Hitler had decreed that a brand new 100 000 capacity stadium be built to replace that built for the aborted 1916 Games. Other fine stadia and halls were erected, plus a magnificent 'village' for the competitors. At the instigation of Carl Diem, the main organizer, a torch relay was inaugurated to bring the sacred Olympic flame from the Temple of Zeus at Olympia – 3000 runners crossed seven countries in ten days.

The German team, with full government backing, was probably the best prepared team ever to compete in the Games. As a sop to

Jesse Owens won the 1936 long jump with a record leap that lasted for 24 years. (GSL)

foreign criticism it contained one athlete of Jewish origin, Helène Mayer, persuaded to return from America with the promise of full 'Aryan' classification. Ironically she placed second in the foil to the Hungarian Jewess, Ilona Elek.

For the first time there was television coverage, but only on closed circuit to 28 special halls. Very high standards were reached at these Games, and at the forefront of the record breaking were the ten black members of the US track and field team, dubbed the 'Black Auxiliaries' by the German propaganda machine. Between them they won seven gold, three silver and three bronze medals – more than any other national team. The outstanding member was Jesse Owens with four gold medals, but many consider the highlight of the athletics events the 1500m victory by Jack Lovelock of New Zealand.

In the pool Holland's Hendrika Mastenbroek won three golds and a silver, and the winner of the women's springboard diving, Marjorie Gestring (USA), became the youngest ever female gold medallist, and the youngest ever individual event champion, aged 13yr 268 days. The oldest gold medallist at Berlin was Friedrich Gerhard (GER) in the dressage team aged 52yr 20 days.

Canoeing and basketball made their official debuts, with the inventor of the latter, Dr James Naismith, on hand to see the US team begin its remarkable sequence of victories. At the end of the Games a magnificent film *Olympische Spiele* was produced by Leni Riefenstahl, which although criticized as propaganda, is still the best documentary record of an Olympic Games. One other innovation at Berlin was the use of two sentences attributed to Baron de Coubertin, but actually based on words by the Bishop of Pennsylvania at a service in St Paul's Cathedral, London in 1908, which are now displayed on the scoreboard at every opening ceremony: 'The most important thing in the Olympic Games is not to win but to take part, just as the most important thing in life is not the triumph but the struggle. The essential thing is not to have conquered but to have fought well.'

1936 Medals (Summer)

	Gold	Silver	Bronze
Germany	33	26	30
United States	24	20	12
Hungary	10	1	5
Italy	8	9	5
Finland	7	6	6
France	7	6	6
Sweden	6	5	9
Japan	6	4	8
Netherlands	6	4	7
Great Britain	4	7	3
Austria	4	6	3
Czechoslovakia	3	5	–
Argentina	2	2	3
Estonia	2	2	3
Egypt	2	1	2
Switzerland	1	9	5
Canada	1	3	5
Norway	1	3	2
Turkey	1	–	1
India	1	–	–
New Zealand	1	–	–
Poland	–	3	3
Denmark	–	2	3
Latvia	–	1	1
Romania	–	1	–
South Africa	–	1	–
Yugoslavia	–	1	–
Mexico	–	–	3
Belgium	–	–	2
Australia	–	–	1
Philippines	–	–	1
Portugal	–	–	1

Henri Oreiller (FRA) won the 1948 downhill race by the greatest margin ever in the Games. (GSL)

1948
Vth Winter Games

The 1940 Games were initially awarded to Sapporo, Japan, but as a consequence of the Sino–Japanese conflict they were reallocated to St Moritz. Due to some disagreements the IOC transferred them again in June 1939 to Garmisch-Partenkirchen, Germany, at the same time deciding that the 1944 meeting should be held at Cortina d'Ampezzo, Italy. The Second World War then upset these plans and in 1946 a postal vote of IOC members relocated the 1948 Games in St Moritz as neutral Switzerland was virtually untouched by the war. Germany and Japan were not invited, but Italy was present. There were now six Alpine events which attracted larger fields than Nordic skiing. Poor weather affected some of the competitions.

Medals were shared among a record number of countries (13). A new concept was brought to figure skating by the athletic Americans, and the men's winner, Dick Button, was the youngest champion aged 18yr 202 days. The oldest gold medallist was Francis Tyler, in the US 4-man bob aged 43yr 58 days, and the great Norwegian ski jumper Birger Ruud, now nearly 37 and a survivor of a concentration camp, ended his Olympic career with a silver medal to add to his two golds. He and his brother Sigmund had made the event a family preserve since 1928. In the skeleton toboggan, only held when the Games are at St Moritz, John Heaton (USA) won his second silver medal on the Cresta Run, twenty years after his first one.

1948 Medals (Winter)

	Gold	Silver	Bronze
Norway	4	3	3
Sweden	4	3	3
Switzerland	3	4	3
United States	3	4	2
France	2	1	2
Canada	2	–	1
Austria	1	3	4
Finland	1	3	2
Belgium	1	1	–
Italy	1	–	–
Czechoslovakia	–	1	–
Hungary	–	1	–
Great Britain	–	–	2

1948
XIVth Summer Games

The 1940 Games were supposed to have been in Tokyo but were then re-awarded to Helsinki. The Soviet invasion of Finland cancelled those plans and in June 1939 the IOC allocated the 1944 Games to London. A postal vote in 1946 gave the 1948 meeting to London. In the meantime, in 1936, Baron de Coubertin had died and his heart buried at Olympia.

These were the 'austerity' Games – after six years of war Britain still had rationing of food and clothing. Housing was very short due to wartime destruction, and competitors were housed at RAF and Army camps and colleges. A temporary running track was laid at the 83 000 capacity Wembley Stadium, and other buildings adapted. Germany and Japan were not invited but a record 59 countries attended. Some of the hottest weather for years occurred on the opening days, but later it rained.

The star of the Games was Francina 'Fanny' Blankers-Koen (HOL) who won four gold medals, a record for a woman. At 30 years of age she held seven world records including those in the high and long jumps, neither of which she contested in London. Bob Mathias (USA) became the youngest ever male Olympic individual athletics champion when he won the decathlon aged 17yr 263 days. He retained the title in 1952, made a film of his life, and later was elected a US Congressman. Another athlete to catch the eye was Emil Zatopek (TCH) by his running in the 5000m and 10 000m. An American, Harrison Dillard, acknowledged the world's best high hurdler, had failed to make their team in his best event. In London he won his 'second string' event, the 100m, and won another gold in the relay. The marathon provided its usual drama when Etienne Gailly, a Belgian paratrooper, entered the stadium first, but exhausted was passed by two runners prior to the tape. An outstanding competitor in the modern pentathlon was Willie Grut of Sweden who won three disciplines of the five-sport event, and placed fifth and eighth in the others.

The superlative Fanny Blankers-Koen (HOL), on the podium for one of her four gold medals, with Maureen Gardner (left), and Shirley Strickland.
(London & Wide World)

He was the son of the designer of the 1912 Olympic stadium.

A very strange incident occurred in the soccer tournament, when in the semifinal Sweden beat Denmark. The Swedish centre-forward Gunnar Nordahl, one of three brothers in the team, leapt into the Danish goalnet to avoid being offside during a Swedish attack. At the end of the move his inside-left headed the ball into the goal, where in the absence of the Danish keeper it was caught by Nordahl. Sweden went on to win the gold medal.

The oldest gold medallist in London was Paul Smart (USA) in the Star class yachting aged 56yr 212 days, and the youngest was Thelma Kalama (USA) in the swimming sprint relay for women aged 17yr 135 days. Yachting also witnessed the end of a long Olympic career when Ralph Craig (USA), the 1912 sprint champion, reappeared in the Dragon class. A Star class competitor for Britain was Durward Knowles, who then represented the Bahamas in the following six Olympics.

1948 Medals (Summer)

	Gold	Silver	Bronze
United States	38	27	19
Sweden	16	11	17
France	10	6	13
Hungary	10	5	12
Italy	8	12	9
Finland	8	7	5
Turkey	6	4	2
Czechoslovakia	6	2	3
Switzerland	5	10	5
Denmark	5	7	8
Netherlands	5	2	9
Great Britain	3	14	6
Argentina	3	3	1
Australia	2	6	5
Belgium	2	2	3
Egypt	2	2	1
Mexico	2	1	2
South Africa	2	1	1
Norway	1	3	3
Jamaica	1	2	–
Austria	1	1	3
India	1	–	–
Peru	1	–	–
Yugoslavia	–	2	–
Canada	–	1	2
Portugal	–	1	1
Uruguay	–	1	1
Ceylon (now Sri Lanka)	–	1	–
Cuba	–	1	–
Spain	–	1	–
Trinidad & Tobago	–	1	–
Korea	–	–	2
Panama	–	–	2
Brazil	–	–	1
Iran	–	–	1
Puerto Rico	–	–	1
Poland	–	–	1

Finnish skier Veikko Hakulinen won seven medals at three Games including the 50km gold in 1952. (GSL)

1952
VIth Winter Games

These Games, held in Oslo, are the only Winter Olympics to be held in a Nordic country even though Norway, Sweden and Finland between them have won 352 medals to date, including 115 golds. A feature of these Games was the enormous crowds at all venues, including a record for any Olympic event, at the ski jumping at Holmenkollen, estimated at 150 000. As the opening day coincided with the funeral of Britain's King George VI all the Commonwealth competitors wore black armbands. Back in the Olympic fold were Germany and Japan. For the first time there was a Nordic ski race for women, while in the men's Nordic events silver medallist Martin Stokken (NOR) finished the first part of his feat to become one of the few men ever to compete in Winter and Summer Games in the same year (he later competed in Helsinki).

The men's figure skating title was retained by Dick Button (USA) with some remarkable jumping. In seventh place was Alain Giletti, (FRA) at 12yr 5 months of age the youngest ever male competitor in the Winter Olympics, while just ahead of him, in sixth place, was Carlo Fassi (ITA), later coach of Britain's John Curry and Robin Cousins. The ladies skating champion Jeanette Altwegg (GBR) later disdained professionalism and worked at the famed village for orphan children at Pestalozzi in Switzerland.

The oldest gold medallist at Oslo was Franz Kemser in the German 4-man bob aged 41yr 103 days, and the youngest was slalom winner Andrea Mead-Lawrence (USA) aged 19yr 301 days.

1952 Medals (Winter)

	Gold	Silver	Bronze
Norway	7	3	6
United States	4	6	1
Finland	3	4	2
Germany	3	2	2
Austria	2	4	2
Italy	1	–	1
Canada	1	–	1
Great Britain	1	–	–
Netherlands	–	3	–
Sweden	–	–	4
Switzerland	–	–	2
France	–	–	1
Hungary	–	–	1

1952
XVth Summer Games

One of the greatest Olympian countries, Finland, finally hosted the Games, and the occasion was made particularly memorable when the runner to bring the flame into the Helsinki stadium turned out to be the immortal Paavo Nurmi. Included in the record 69 countries was the Soviet Union, competing for the first time – Czarist Russia had last competed in 1912. Unfortunately their presence led to the establishment of two Olympic villages, the Soviet bloc having their own, surprisingly with IOC approval.

The athlete of these Games was the Czech runner Emil Zatopek who won an unprecedented triple of the 5000m, 10 000m and marathon. To crown his achievements his wife Dana, born on the same day as Emil, also won a gold medal, in the javelin,

Emil Zatopek on his way to his first gold medal, in the 10km, at Helsinki, leads Mimoun (FRA), Pirie (GBR), Perry (AUS), Anufriev (URS), Sando (GBR) and Posti (FIN). (All-Sport)

within an hour of his 5000m victory. Australia's Marjorie Jackson set world records winning the 100m and 200m but dropped the baton when certain to win a third gold in the sprint relay. In the winning American relay team was Barbara Jones who became the youngest ever track and field gold medallist aged 15yr 123 days. However, the youngest gold medallist at Helsinki was French cox Bernard Malivoire at 14yr 94 days in the pairs event.

Small nations did well with Jamaican runners invincible over 400m, and Josy Barthel causing the band some problems as they tried to find the anthem of his native Luxembourg when he scored an upset win in the 1500m. When Horace Ashenfelter in the steeplechase scored America's first win in a distance run since 1908 the Press had great fun with the fact that Ashenfelter, an FBI agent, was here followed home by a Russian. However, the Soviet team came into its own in gymnastics with Viktor Chukarin winning four golds and two silvers, and his female counterpart Maria Gorokhovskaya taking two golds and five silvers.

The sole French victory in swimming, by Jean Boiteux, was celebrated rather unusually by his father who jumped fully clothed into the pool. Almost matching the Zatopeks were Éva Székely (HUN) who won the 200m breaststroke, and her husband Dezsö Gyarmati, a gold at water polo.

The oldest gold medallist was Everard Endt (USA) in the 6m yachting aged 59yr 112 days, but worthy of mention is André Jousseame (FRA) who won a bronze in dressage two days after his 58th birthday, and twenty years after his Los Angeles gold medal.

1952 Medals (Summer)

	Gold	Silver	Bronze
United States	40	19	17
Soviet Union	22	30	19
Hungary	16	10	16
Sweden	12	12	10
Italy	8	9	4
Czechoslovakia	7	3	3
France	6	6	6
Finland	6	3	13
Australia	6	2	3
Norway	3	2	–
Switzerland	2	6	6
South Africa	2	4	4
Jamaica	2	3	–
Belgium	2	2	–
Denmark	2	1	3
Turkey	2	–	1
Japan	1	6	2
Great Britain	1	2	8
Argentina	1	2	2
Poland	1	2	1
Canada	1	2	–
Yugoslavia	1	2	–
Romania	1	1	2
Brazil	1	–	2
New Zealand	1	–	2
India	1	–	1
Luxembourg	1	–	–
Germany	–	7	17
Netherlands	–	5	–
Iran	–	3	4
Chile	–	2	–
Austria	–	1	1
Lebanon	–	1	1
Ireland	–	1	–
Mexico	–	1	–
Spain	–	1	–
Korea	–	–	2
Trinidad & Tobago	–	–	2
Uruguay	–	–	2
Bulgaria	–	–	1
Egypt	–	–	1
Portugal	–	–	1
Venezuela	–	–	1

1956
VIIth Winter Games

Once again snow needed to be imported for some venues, but nevertheless facilities at Cortina d'Ampezzo, Italy, were excellent. The entry of the Soviet Union provided the first Russian competitors in Olympic 'Winter' events since 1908, and these were the first Winter Games to be televised. Most attention was gained by the Austrian plumber Toni Sailer who gained a grand slam of all three Alpine titles, each by outstanding margins. The most medals won was by Sixten Jernberg (SWE) with one gold, two silvers and a bronze in Nordic skiing. Using a new style the Finns dominated the ski jumping and the Norwegians, who had won 15 of the 18 medals available in the sport since 1924, failed to place in the first six. Though Germany competed as a single team the bronze, won by Harry Glass, is claimed by the GDR as its first Olympic medal. The speed skating surface, at an altitude of 1755m, was considered to be the fastest ever, and witnessed a wholesale attack on the record book. In figure skating Hayes (gold) and David (bronze) Jenkins were the first brothers to win medals in the same skating event.

A member of the winning Italian 2-man bob was Giacomo Conti, at 47yr 216 days the oldest ever Winter Games gold medallist. The youngest champion at Cortina d'Ampezzo was Elisabeth Schwartz (AUT) in pairs skating aged 19yr 199 days. The Soviet competitors won a total of 15 medals to head the unofficial medal table – a position they were rarely to lose in future Winter Games.

1956 Medals (Winter)

	Gold	Silver	Bronze
Soviet Union	7	3	6
Austria	4	3	4
Finland	3	3	1
Switzerland	3	2	1
Sweden	2	4	4
United States	2	3	2
Norway	2	1	1
Italy	1	2	–
Germany	1	–	1
Canada	–	1	2
Japan	–	1	–
Hungary	–	–	1
Poland	–	–	1

Toni Sailer won three gold medals at Cortina d'Ampezzo, becoming the youngest ever male Alpine skiing champion. (George Konig)

1956
XVIth Summer Games

Due to Australian quarantine regulations the equestrian events had to be allocated to a separate venue, Stockholm, and held at a different time of year. The Games proper, the first in the Southern Hemisphere, opened in Melbourne under a cloud of ill-will, occasioned by the Soviet invasion of Hungary, and the French and British intervention in the Suez Canal dispute between Israel and Egypt. Despite various withdrawals due to the above, 67 countries attended the opening ceremony in Melbourne Cricket Ground, where the final torch bearer was 19-year-old Ron Clarke, destined to become one of the world's greatest distance runners. The distance runs in Melbourne were dominated by the Soviet sailor Vladimir Kuts. Ireland won its first gold medal since 1932 with Ronnie Delaney's gold medal in the 1500m. After placing second to Emil Zatopek in three Olympic races since 1948, Frenchman Alain Mimoun finally beat him into sixth place, by taking the marathon only a month short of his 36th birthday.

In the pool Pat McCormick (USA) achieved a unique double 'double' retaining both her diving titles from Helsinki. László Papp did his bit to raise Hungarian spirits by gaining an unprecedented third gold medal at boxing. Not surprisingly bad feelings erupted in the water polo semi-final between Hungary and the Soviet Union. By a nice touch of irony the referee was from the perenially neutral Sweden. With Hungary leading 4-0 he ended the game as it had degenerated into a 'boxing match under water'. However, by beating Yugoslavia in the soccer final on the last day, December 8, the Soviet Union went into history as the winners of the latest gold medal ever won in an Olympic year.

The oldest gold medallist in Melbourne was Henri St. Cyr (SWE) in dressage aged 54yr 93 days, while the youngest was Sandra Morgan of Australia in the 4 × 100m freestyle relay aged 14yr 183 days. At the closing ceremony for the first time the athletes entered *en masse*, signifying the

Soviet sailor Vladimir Kuts won the 5km/10km double in Melbourne, destroying the opposition with his merciless front running tactics. (Planet News)

friendship of the Games. The idea for this had come from a Chinese-born Australian boy, John Wing, in a letter to the organizing committee.

A happy postscript to these Games occurred in Prague in March 1957 when the American hammer winner, Harold Connolly, married Olga Fikotova, the Czech Olympic discus champion. The best man at this 'Olympic' wedding was, appropriately, Emil Zatopek.

1956 Medals (Summer)

	Gold	Silver	Bronze
Soviet Union	37	29	32
United States	32	25	17
Australia	13	8	14
Hungary	9	10	7
Italy	8	8	9
Sweden	8	5	6
Germany	6	13	7
Great Britain	6	7	11
Romania	5	3	5
Japan	4	10	5
France	4	4	6
Turkey	3	2	2
Finland	3	1	11
Iran	2	2	1
Canada	2	1	3
New Zealand	2	–	–
Poland	1	4	4
Czechoslovakia	1	4	1
Bulgaria	1	3	1
Denmark	1	2	1
Ireland	1	1	3
Norway	1	–	2
Mexico	1	–	1
Brazil	1	–	–
India	1	–	–
Yugoslavia	–	3	–
Chile	–	2	2
Belgium	–	2	–
Argentina	–	1	1
Korea	–	1	1
Iceland	–	1	–
Pakistan	–	1	–
South Africa	–	–	4
Austria	–	–	2
Bahamas	–	–	1
Greece	–	–	1
Switzerland	–	–	1
Uruguay	–	–	1

1960
VIIIth Winter Games

When the IOC voted narrowly, 32–30, to give the Games to Squaw Valley, USA, instead of Innsbruck virtually nothing existed at the site. Due to the efforts of Alexander Cushing, who owned most of the area, it became the first purpose-built Winter Games venue. The official opening, by Richard Nixon, then Vice-President, was under the direction of Walt Disney.

Bobsledding was dropped as the organizers would not accept the cost

of building a run for what they considered would be a small entry. Concern was expressed over the altitude (over 1900m) at which the Nordic skiing events were held. East and West Germany competed as one entity with agreement reached on Beethoven's Ninth Symphony played for any victory ceremonies. A team from South Africa appeared, for the first and only time in Winter Games, as they were banned thereafter. The biathlon and speed skating for women made Olympic debuts. The speed skating times in general were excellent, while in figure skating David Jenkins kept the men's title in the family – his brother Hayes had won in 1956, and made the family even more Olympian by marrying Squaw Valley's lady champion Carol Heiss two months later.

In Alpine skiing metallic skis were used in the Games for the first time. The medals were more widespread than usual, with no skier winning more than one event. The oldest gold medallist was Veikko Hakulinen (FIN) in the Nordic relay aged 35yr 52 days, and the youngest Heidi Biebl (GER), the

downhill champion 3 days past her 19th birthday.

1960 Medals (Winter)

	Gold	Silver	Bronze
Soviet Union	7	5	9
Germany	4	3	1
United States	3	4	3
Norway	3	3	–
Sweden	3	2	2
Finland	2	3	3
Canada	2	1	1
Switzerland	2	–	–
Austria	1	2	3
France	1	–	2
Netherlands	–	1	1
Poland	–	1	1
Czechoslovakia	–	1	–
Italy	–	–	1

One of the great gymnasts of all time Boris Shakhlin (URS) won four gold medals at Rome.

Helmut Recknagel, an East German competing for the combined German team, was the first ski jumper to break the domination of the Nordic countries. (GSL)

1960
XVIIth Summer Games

After missing out in 1908 the Games finally went to Rome, the home city of the Emperor Theodosius, who had ended the Ancient Games 1567 years before. A number of old Roman sites were utilized as well as a brand-new 100 000 capacity stadium. These Games were the first to have world-wide television coverage. The extreme heat undoubtedly caused upsets but did nothing to hinder the successes of Australasians in the middle distance running events. An unknown runner, Abebe Bikila, won the marathon barefoot and signalled the entry of Ethiopia on to the world distance running scene. Incidentally, this was the first

Olympic marathon not to start or finish in the stadium – it began on Capitol Hill and finished near the Arch of Constantine.

The stadium was captured by sprinter Wilma Rudolph (USA) who won three gold medals – she was one of 19 children and had suffered from polio as a child. In the swimming pool the only one of the fifteen events not won by either Australia or the United States went to Anita Lonsbrough (GBR). The outstanding swimmer was America's Christine von Saltza, a descendant of Prussian/Swedish nobility, with three golds and a silver. An unfortunate incident occurred in the men's 100m freestyle when Lance Larson (USA) was timed at one-tenth faster

than John Devitt (AUS) but was placed second to him. In future Games full electronic timing was used.

Boris Shakhlin (URS) won seven medals in gymnastics, while Aladar Gerevich (HUN), at 50yr 178 days the oldest champion in Rome, won his sixth team sabre gold medal in as many Games – itself a record. The youngest gold medallist was Carolyn Wood (USA) in the freestyle relay aged 14yr 260 days. Crown Prince Constantine of Greece (later King Constantine II) won the second Royal gold medal in history in Dragon class yachting. The light-heavyweight boxing title went to Cassius Clay (USA), later Muhammad Ali who amassed a

record $68 million as a professional. India lost its first match ever in Olympic hockey since 1928, unfortunately in the final to Pakistan. The sad collapse and death of cyclist Knut Jensen (DEN), originally diagnosed as due to the heat, was later revealed as due to a drug overdose.

1960 Medals (Summer)

	Gold	Silver	Bronze
Soviet Union	43	29	31
United States	34	21	16
Italy	13	10	13
Germany	12	19	11
Australia	8	8	6
Turkey	7	2	–
Hungary	6	8	7
Japan	4	7	7
Poland	4	6	11
Czechoslovakia	3	2	3
Romania	3	1	6
Great Britain	2	6	12
Denmark	2	3	1
New Zealand	2	–	1
Bulgaria	1	3	3
Sweden	1	2	3
Finland	1	1	3
Austria	1	1	–
Yugoslavia	1	1	–
Pakistan	1	–	1
Ethiopia	1	–	–
Greece	1	–	–
Norway	1	–	–
Switzerland	–	3	3
France	–	2	3
Belgium	–	2	2
Iran	–	1	3
Netherlands	–	1	2
South Africa	–	1	2
Argentina	–	1	1
Egypt (UAR)	–	1	1
Canada	–	1	–
Ghana	–	1	–
India	–	1	–
Morocco	–	1	–
Portugal	–	1	–
Singapore	–	1	–
Taiwan	–	1	–
Brazil	–	–	2
Jamaica*	–	–	2
Iraq	–	–	1
Mexico	–	–	1
Spain	–	–	1
Venezuela	–	–	1

*Part of an Antilles team.

Soviet speed skater Lydia Skoblikova swept the board at Innsbruck. (Associated Press)

1964
IXth Winter Games

This very successful Games at Innsbruck, Austria had over a 1000 competitors from a record 36 countries, and total spectator attendance of over a million. However, weather again was a problem, and snow had to be manhandled to some venues by the Austrian Army. Computers were used to aid judging as well as provide electronic timing.

Korea was split into North and South teams, while India made its Winter debut. The Soviet husband and wife skating pair, Ludmila

Belousova and Oleg Protopopov brought a new concept, classical ballet, to the sport, and team-mate Lydia Skoblikova won all four women's speed skating titles. The first sisters to win gold medals at the same Games were Marielle and Christine Goitschel (FRA) who swapped first and second places in the Alpine slalom events. The victory by Tony Nash and Robin Dixon (GBR) in the 2-man bob, the first by a 'lowland' country, owed much to a replacement bolt supplied by an Italian adversary Eugenio Monti. He was later awarded the Pierre de Coubertin Fair Play Trophy.

The Games were dominated by the Soviet Union but, for the first time before or since, Switzerland failed to gain a single medal. The oldest gold medallist was Sixten Jernberg, winning his ninth Olympic medal two days after his 35th birthday, while the youngest was Manfred Stengl (AUT) aged 17yr 310 days in the 2-man luge.

1964 Medals (Winter)

	Gold	Silver	Bronze
Soviet Union	11	8	6
Austria	4	5	3
Norway	3	6	6
Finland	3	4	3
France	3	4	–
Sweden	3	3	1
Germany	3	2	3
United States	1	2	4
Canada	1	1	1
Netherlands	1	1	–
Great Britain	1	–	–
Italy	–	1	3
North Korea	–	1	–
Czechoslovakia	–	–	1

1964
XVIIIth Summer Games

Asia's first Games witnessed vast crowds and a tremendous assault on the record books. The Olympic flame was carried to the opening ceremony in Tokyo by a young runner born near Hiroshima the day that the atom bomb was dropped in 1945. The growth of the Games can be highlighted by distance runner Ron Clarke's remark after failing to gain the gold medal over 10 000m. Having dropped all the known opposition he looked over his shoulder and saw 'an Ethiopian, a North African Arab and an American Indian'. In the

1964 Medals (Summer)

	Gold	Silver	Bronze
United States	36	26	28
Soviet Union	30	31	35
Japan	16	5	8
Germany	10	22	18
Italy	10	10	7
Hungary	10	7	5
Poland	7	6	10
Australia	6	2	10
Czechoslovakia	5	6	3
Great Britain	4	12	2
Bulgaria	3	5	2
Finland	3	–	2
New Zealand	3	–	2
Romania	2	4	6
Netherlands	2	4	4
Turkey	2	3	1
Sweden	2	2	4
Denmark	2	1	3
Yugoslavia	2	1	2
Belgium	2	–	1
France	1	8	6
Canada	1	2	1
Switzerland	1	2	1
Bahamas	1	–	–
Ethiopia	1	–	–
India	1	–	–
South Korea	–	2	1
Trinidad & Tobago	–	1	2
Tunisia	–	1	1
Argentina	–	1	–
Cuba	–	1	–
Pakistan	–	1	–
Philippines	–	1	–
Iran	–	–	2
Brazil	–	–	1
Ghana	–	–	1
Ireland	–	–	1
Kenya	–	–	1
Mexico	–	–	1
Nigeria	–	–	1
Uruguay	–	–	1

marathon Bikila (ETH) became the first man to retain the title, this time wearing shoes, and Peter Snell (NZL) won the rare 800m/1500m double. Britain won its first ever gold in women's athletics when Mary Rand took the long jump – her room-mate Ann Packer added the 800m gold for good measure.

At the much admired pool Australia and the United States won all the titles bar one, and Don Schollander (USA) gained a unique four golds in a single Games. The most medals were won by gymnast Larissa Latynina (URS) with two golds, two silvers and two bronzes. Unusually wrestler Imre Polyak (HUN) finally won gold in his fourth Games after an unprecedented three silvers. The host country suffered a terrible shock when the Open class judo title went to the giant Dutchman Anton Geesink. Leading the United States basketball team to its sixth consecutive victory was Bill Bradley, now a senator.

The oldest gold medallist in Tokyo was Australian 5.5m yachtsman William Northam aged

59yr 23 days, and the youngest was swimmer 'Pokey' Watson (USA) aged 14yr 96 days in the freestyle relay. Interestingly, the 46-year-old cox of the winning American eight, Robert Zimonyi, had coxed the bronze medal Hungarian pairs in 1948.

1968
Xth Winter Games

There were complaints that venues at Grenoble were very widespread, with some 40km distant, but the new 12 000 seat indoor ice stadium delighted everyone. For the first time sex tests for female competitors were held. The political split between East and West Germany was finally acknowledged and separate teams accepted. The star of these Games was Jean-Claude Killy (FRA) who emulated Toni Sailer and won all three Alpine events. By winning the 30km race Franco Nones (ITA) became the first ever non-Scandinavian winner in Nordic skiing. Another upset was in the women's luge, where the GDR girls, in first, second and fourth places, were disqualified for illegally heating their sled runners. The good sport of Innsbruck, four years previously, Eugenio Monti (ITA), nine times a world champion bobsledder, finally won Olympic gold medals, and was the oldest champion in Grenoble aged 40yr 24 days. The youngest was skater Peggy Fleming (USA) aged 19yr 198 days. A remarkable three-way tie occurred for the silver medal in the women's 500m speed skating, made unique by the fact that all three girls were from the United States.

1968 Medals (Winter)

	Gold	Silver	Bronze
Norway	6	6	2
Soviet Union	5	5	3
France	4	3	2
Italy	4	–	–
Austria	3	4	4
Netherlands	3	3	3
Sweden	3	2	3
West Germany (FRG)	2	2	3
United States	1	5	1
Finland	1	2	2
East Germany (GDR)	1	2	2
Czechoslovakia	1	2	1
Canada	1	1	1
Switzerland	–	2	4
Romania	–	–	1

Bob Beamon setting the world long jump record at Mexico City – a performance which will probably survive the century. (All-Sport)

1968
XIXth Summer Games

The effects of altitude – Mexico City is 2240m above sea level – on competitors in endurance events was the major topic leading up to the Games, with some medical authorities forecasting possible deaths. This extreme view was, thankfully, overly pessimistic, but many cases of severe exhaustion occurred. When Australian distance runner, Ron Clarke, developed serious heart problems in 1981, there was speculation that his condition had been aggravated by his efforts in Mexico City. Certainly standards were low in events which required over three minutes of continuous effort. Equally there were startling performances from the 'explosive' events. Outstanding was the 8.90m *29ft 2½in* long jump by Bob Beamon (USA) – a performance of 21st-century quality. At the time of writing, some 18 years later, the world records set in that long jump, the 400m and 4 × 400m relay still stand.

A threatened boycott by Black African nations over the readmission of South Africa forced the IOC to reverse its decision. A few weeks prior to the Games there were serious student riots in Mexico City which were ruthlessly suppressed, and a proposed boycott of the American team by black athletes did not happen, but some demonstration was threatened. At the opening ceremony Enriqueta Basilio became the first woman to light an Olympic flame in the stadium.

Due to conditions the distance running events were dominated by athletes who lived and trained at high altitude. The high jump winner, Dick Fosbury (USA), used the 'flop' style which he had popularized and which was to revolutionize the event. Al Oerter (USA) won his record fourth consecutive discus title, and Wyomia Tyus (USA) was the first sprinter successfully to defend an Olympic 100m crown, other than Archie Hahn (USA) in the 1906 Intercalated Games. After the 200m final, Black Power supporters Tommie Smith and John Carlos (USA), first and third respectively, raised black-gloved fists during the playing of the American anthem, for which action they were suspended and expelled from the Olympic village. Gymnasts Mikhail Woronin (URS) with seven medals, and Vera Caslavska (TCH) with four golds and two silvers, were the main medal winners. Although eliminated in the fencing, Janice Romary (USA) was the first woman to compete in six consecutive Games.

The oldest gold medallist was Josef Neckarmann (FRG) in the dressage team aged 56yr 141 days, while the youngest was Günther Tiersch (GDR), cox of the winning eight aged 14yr 172 days. The oldest female champion was Liselott Linsenhoff (FRG), also in the dressage team aged 41yr 58 days, while the youngest female gold medallist was swimmer Susan Pedersen (USA) in the medley relay the day after her 15th birthday. A record 30 countries won at least one gold medal, a feat unsurpassed in Olympic history.

1968 Medals (Summer)

	Gold	Silver	Bronze
United States	45	28	34
Soviet Union	29	32	30
Japan	11	7	7
Hungary	10	10	12
East Germany (GDR)	9	9	7
France	7	3	5
Czechoslovakia	7	2	4
West Germany (FRG)	5	11	10
Australia	5	7	5
Great Britain	5	5	3
Poland	5	2	11
Romania	4	6	5
Italy	3	4	9
Kenya	3	4	2
Mexico	3	3	3
Yugoslavia	3	3	2
Netherlands	3	3	1
Bulgaria	2	4	3
Iran	2	1	2
Sweden	2	1	1
Turkey	2	–	–
Denmark	1	4	3
Canada	1	3	1
Finland	1	2	1
Ethiopia	1	1	–
Norway	1	1	–
New Zealand	1	–	2
Tunisia	1	–	1
Pakistan	1	–	–
Venezuela	1	–	–
Cuba	–	4	–
Austria	–	2	2
Switzerland	–	1	4
Mongolia	–	1	3
Brazil	–	1	2
Belgium	–	1	1
South Korea	–	1	1
Uganda	–	1	1
Cameroun	–	1	–
Jamaica	–	1	–
Argentina	–	–	2
Greece	–	–	1
India	–	–	1
Taiwan	–	–	1

1972
XIth Winter Games

Sapporo, Japan was the most populous city, with one million inhabitants, to host the Winter Games. Some $555 million was spent on facilities, not least for the media personnel who outnumbered competitors by two to one. Arguments between the IOC and sponsored skiers, which had caused problems in 1968, came to a head and led to Karl Schranz being expelled. Another aspect of the amateur/professional debate was highlighted by Canada's refusal to compete at ice hockey due to the state-sponsored players from the Eastern bloc.

slam in the 70m ski jump. In Alpine skiing the women's slalom was won by Barbara Cochran (USA) by the smallest margin ever in the Games. Galina Kulakova (URS) won three gold medals in Nordic skiing, and this total was matched in the speed skating by Ard Schenk of Holland. Austria's Trixie Schuba took the women's figure skating title despite a comparatively poor free skating segment – her compulsory figures were excellent and at the time the two segments scored on a 50-50 basis. Soon after the Games this method was changed in favour of free skating ability.

The oldest gold medallist was Jean Wicki (SUI) in the 4-man bob aged 38yr 239 days. The youngest was Anne Henning (USA) who won the 500m speed skating title aged 16yr 157 days. In all medals were won by a record 17 countries, with 14 of them gaining gold.

1972 Medals (Winter)

	Gold	Silver	Bronze
Soviet Union	8	5	3
East Germany (GDR)	4	3	7
Switzerland	4	3	3
Netherlands	4	3	2
United States	3	2	3
West Germany (FRG)	3	1	1
Norway	2	5	5
Italy	2	2	1
Austria	1	2	2
Sweden	1	1	2
Japan	1	1	1
Czechoslovakia	1	–	2
Poland	1	–	–
Spain	1	–	–
Finland	–	4	1
France	–	1	2
Canada	–	1	–

Nine canoes battle out the K2 1000m at Munich. (Gerry Cranham)

1972
XXth Summer Games

Awarded the Games in 1966, Munich built a magnificent complex on the rubble from the Second World War bombing. Just prior to the opening day the IOC expelled Rhodesia under intense pressure from Black African nations. New sports and additions to others made a total of 195 gold medals available, and the Soviet Union took over a quarter of them. There was an all-time live TV-viewing record of the opening ceremony of 1000 million people, who saw the oath taken by Heidi Schüller, the first woman ever to do so at the Summer Games. A record 122 countries and a record 7156 competitors were present.

The first week was dominated by swimmer Mark Spitz (USA) who smashed all records for a single Games by winning seven gold medals, four individual and three relays. With his medals from Mexico City he had a total of nine golds, one silver and a bronze. His female equivalent, Shane Gould (AUS) won three golds, a silver and a bronze, swimming in 12 races. The closest win in Olympic history came in the men's 400m medley when Gunnar Larsson (SWE) was given the decision over Tim McKee (USA) by two-thousandths of a second. This decision led to a change in the rules so that in future times and places would be decided in hundredths. Valeriy Borzov (URS) became the first European to win a men's sprint double on the track, and Ulrike Meyfarth (FRG) equalled the world high jump record to win the gold medal aged 16yr 123 days, the youngest ever individual athletics event champion. The outstanding attraction of the first few days was gymnast Olga Korbut (URS) whose gamine qualities stole the show from her more illustrious colleague, Ludmila Tourischeva (who later married Borzov). Virtually overnight Korbut became a 'superstar'.

On the morning of 5 September all the euphoria evaporated when a band of eight Arab terrorists broke into the Israeli team headquarters. Two Israelis were killed immediately, and another nine were murdered after an abortive rescue attempt at the airport. Some of the terrorists were also killed. The following morning the Games were suspended for a memorial service in a packed stadium, but, with the agreement of Israeli officials, competitions were resumed later in the day. The overall feeling was that the Games should go on, although a number of individuals withdrew. The Israeli team returned home immediately.

The Games continued with the

1972 Medals (Summer)

	Gold	Silver	Bronze
Soviet Union	50	27	22
United States	33	31	30
East Germany (GDR)	20	23	23
West Germany (FRG)	13	11	16
Japan	13	8	8
Australia	8	7	2
Poland	7	5	9
Hungary	6	13	16
Bulgaria	6	10	5
Italy	5	3	10
Sweden	4	6	6
Great Britain	4	5	9
Romania	3	6	7
Cuba	3	1	4
Finland	3	1	4
Netherlands	3	1	1
France	2	4	7
Czechoslovakia	2	4	2
Kenya	2	3	4
Yugoslavia	2	1	2
Norway	2	1	1
North Korea	1	1	3
New Zealand	1	1	1
Uganda	1	1	–
Denmark	1	–	–
Switzerland	–	3	–
Canada	–	2	3
Iran	–	2	1
Belgium	–	2	–
Greece	–	2	–
Austria	–	1	2
Colombia	–	1	2
Argentina	–	1	–
Lebanon	–	1	–
Mexico	–	1	–
Mongolia	–	1	–
Pakistan	–	1	–
South Korea	–	1	–
Tunisia	–	1	–
Turkey	–	1	–
Brazil	–	–	2
Ethiopia	–	–	2
Ghana	–	–	1
India	–	–	1
Jamaica	–	–	1
Niger	–	–	1
Nigeria	–	–	1
Spain	–	–	1

United States suffering an unusual number of misfortunes and reverses. Two prospective medallists had missed the 100m final due to a misreading of the starting time. The world 1500m record holder, Jim Ryun, fell in his heat and was eliminated. A pre-Games banning of the poles used by the American pole vaulters possibly ended a 13-time winning streak. Their gold and silver medallists in the 400m were banned from further competition for a 'Black Power' protest which meant that the United States could not field a 4 × 400m relay team. One of their swimmers, Rick DeMont, was disqualified after winning the 400m freestyle after a dope test proved positive. If the US team officials had notified the IOC beforehand that he had to take a certain drug, containing the prohibited substance, to alleviate an asthma condition it would have been allowed. Then to cap it all the Amer-

ican basketball team were controversially defeated by the Soviet Union – ending a remarkable 63 consecutive victories in the Games since 1936.

The oldest gold medallist at Munich was Hans Günter Winkler (FRG) aged 46yr 49 days in the show jumping team, and the youngest Deana Deardurff (USA) aged 15yr 118 days in the swimming medley relay. Britain's Lorna Johnstone set a record as the oldest ever female competitor in the Olympics when she reached the last 12 in the dressage five days over her 70th birthday.

1976
XIIth Winter Games

These Games were originally awarded to Denver, Colorado, but in 1972 a State referendum decided against providing the necessary finance. So in February 1973 Innsbruck was given the Games, for the second time. Most facilities were still available from 1964, and a total of 1½ million spectators watched the 37-event schedule. There were also 600 million television viewers around the world. An influenza outbreak affected some of the competitors, but not Rosi Mittermaier (FRG) who won two golds and a silver in the Alpine skiing. In the men's downhill Austria's Franz Klammer achieved the then highest speed ever recorded in an Olympic downhill race, 102.828km/h. In Nordic skiing Galina Kulakova (URS) was disqualified in the 5000m event when a banned drug was found present in a nasal spray she was using, but she was allowed to compete in other events and won a gold medal. Irina Rodnina (URS) successfully defended her pairs skating title, but this time with a different partner, while the men's champion John Curry (GBR) brought balletic art to his event just as the Protopopovs had to the pairs some years before.

The oldest gold medallist was Meinhard Nehmer (GDR) in the 2-man bob aged 35yr 25 days, and the youngest was Canada's Kathy Kreiner who won the giant slalom aged 18yr 285 days. Incidentally, a figure skating competitor, Yelena

Vodorezova (URS), was three months away from her 13th birthday.

1976 Medals (Winter)

	Gold	Silver	Bronze
Soviet Union	13	6	8
East Germany (GDR)	7	5	7
United States	3	3	4
Norway	3	3	1
West Germany (FRG)	2	5	3
Finland	2	4	1
Austria	2	2	2
Switzerland	1	3	1
Netherlands	1	2	3
Italy	1	2	1
Canada	1	1	1
Great Britain	1	–	–
Czechoslovakia	–	1	–
Liechtenstein	–	–	2
Sweden	–	–	2
France	–	–	1

1976
XXIst Summer Games

When the Games were initially awarded to Montreal, mainly due to the efforts of Mayor Jean Drapeau, it was estimated that they would cost $310 million. Because of planning errors, strikes, slowdowns, and, it has been suggested, widespread corruption, the final bill amounted to $1400 million – the stadium alone cost $485 million, and the projected 160m high tower and roof was never completed. After the Munich disaster security arrangements involving 16 000 police and soldiers cost $100 million. To add to these problems there was a last minute boycott by 20 Third World, mainly African, nations, protesting against the inclusion of New Zealand, whose Rugby Union team had visited South Africa. Also withdrawing was Taiwan because Canada refused to recognize them under the title of Republic of China. Although efforts had been made by the IOC to prune the programme, the addition of other events, especially for women, raised the total events to 198, three more than at Munich.

The star of Munich, gymnast Olga Korbut, was at Montreal, but she was overshadowed by a 14-year-old Romanian, Nadia Comaneci, who scored a first ever maximum 10.00 marks on the first day, and ended the Games with a total of seven maximums, having drawn a

1976 Medals (Summer)

	Gold	Silver	Bronze
Soviet Union	49	41	35
East Germany (GDR)	40	25	25
United States	34	35	25
West Germany (FRG)	10	12	17
Japan	9	6	10
Poland	7	6	13
Bulgaria	6	9	7
Cuba	6	4	3
Romania	4	9	14
Hungary	4	5	13
Finland	4	2	–
Sweden	4	1	–
Great Britain	3	5	5
Italy	2	7	4
France	2	3	4
Yugoslavia	2	3	3
Czechoslovakia	2	2	4
New Zealand	2	1	1
South Korea	1	1	4
Switzerland	1	1	2
Jamaica	1	1	–
North Korea	1	1	–
Norway	1	1	–
Denmark	1	–	2
Mexico	1	–	1
Trinidad & Tobago	1	–	–
Canada	–	5	6
Belgium	–	3	3
Netherlands	–	2	3
Portugal	–	2	–
Spain	–	2	–
Australia	–	1	4
Iran	–	1	1
Mongolia	–	1	–
Venezuela	–	1	–
Brazil	–	–	2
Austria	–	–	1
Bermuda	–	–	1
Pakistan	–	–	1
Puerto Rico	–	–	1
Thailand	–	–	1

Cuba's Alberto Juantorena, known affectionately as El Caballo (The Horse), achieved the elusive 400m/800m double in 1976. (Associated Press)

world record crowd for gymnastics of 18 000 to the finals of the women's events. In the swimming pool, Kornelia Ender (GDR) and John Naber (USA) each won four golds and a silver, with Ender and her team-mates only failing to win two of the thirteen women's swimming titles. The American men did better, only losing one of their thirteen events – David Wilkie won Britain's first men's swimming gold since 1908. In the main stadium Lasse Viren, the latest 'Flying Finn', completed his double 'double' by taking the 5000m and 10 000m, while the Cuban Alberto Juantorena, nicknamed 'The Horse', won a rare 400m/800m double. Irena Szewinska (POL) won the 400m in her fourth Games, to equal the record total of seven medals in athletics. The winner of the men's javelin, with a new world record, Miklos Nemeth (HUN), was the son of the 1948 hammer winner.

America's Margaret Murdock became the first woman to win a shooting medal, and twelfth-placed show jumper Raimondo d'Inzeo (ITA) set an unprecedented record by competing in his eighth Games.

The oldest gold medallist at Montreal was Harry Boldt (FRG) in the winning dressage team aged 46yr 157 days. The youngest was gymnast Maria Filatova (URS) who won a team gold on her 15th birthday. One of the youngest ever competitors in the Olympic Games was Spanish swimmer Antonia Real aged 12yr 310 days.

1980
XIIIth Winter Games

Most of the facilities used in 1932 at Lake Placid had to be rebuilt, and new ones constructed, so that the budget for these Games was nearly 80 times the $1.1 million spent then. Some complaints were voiced about the 'village', a building later to be used as a penal institution, but as a report noted 'at least security will not be a problem'. One worry which turned into a major problem was transport for spectators and Press. At times it was virtually impossible to reach and/or return from venues.

Eric Heiden (USA) stole all the headlines by gaining an unprecedented sweep of all five speed skating gold medals. In Nordic skiing Nikolai Simyatov (URS) won a unique three golds in one Games, while team-mate Galina Kulakova raised her total medals over four Games to eight. The closest ever result in Olympic skiing came in the men's 15km cross-country event when Thomas Wassberg (SWE) beat Juha Mieto (FIN) by one-hundredth of a second. Eight years previously the unlucky Finn had lost a bronze medal by only sixth-hundredths.

Irina Rodnina (URS) equalled the record of three gold medals by a

1980 Medals (Winter)

	Gold	Silver	Bronze
Soviet Union	10	6	6
East Germany (GDR)	9	7	7
United States	6	4	2
Austria	3	2	2
Sweden	3	–	1
Liechtenstein	2	2	–
Finland	1	5	3
Norway	1	3	6
Netherlands	1	2	1
Switzerland	1	1	3
Great Britain	1	–	–
West Germany (FRG)	–	2	3
Italy	–	2	–
Canada	–	1	1
Hungary	–	1	–
Japan	–	1	–
Bulgaria	–	–	1
Czechoslovakia	–	–	1
France	–	–	1

figure skater when she retained the pairs title with her husband Aleksandr Zaitsev, while Robin Cousins retained the men's singles title for Britain.

The oldest gold medallist was Meinhard Nehmer (GDR) in the 4-man bob aged 39yr 42 days, and the youngest was his team-mate Karin Enke who won the 500m speed skating title aged 18yr 240 days.

The most popular win was undoubtedly that of the American ice hockey team over the Soviet Union (unbeaten since 1964) on their way to the final against Finland which they also won. The following celebrations were described on American television as the biggest since the end of the Second World War.

1980
XXIInd Summer Games

There had been only a little dissent when the IOC awarded these Games to Moscow in 1974. However, in December 1979 the Soviet Union invaded Afghanistan, and much of the non-Communist world, led by the United States, tried to impose a boycott on the Games – although not, it should be noted, on trade or other economic activity. Not all countries supported the boycott, although sports within those countries sometimes did. Because a number of countries which were unlikely to go to Moscow anyway for financial reasons found it politic to 'jump on the bandwagon', it is difficult to complete a list of boycotting nations. The most reliable estimate is 45–50, of which the most important in sporting terms were the United States, the Federal Republic of Germany and Japan.

Facilities in Moscow were excellent, including the 103 000 capacity Lenin stadium, and large crowds attended most sports – there was now a total of 203 events.

For the first time for many years the star of gymnastics was a male, Aleksandr Ditiatin (URS) who won a record number of medals, eight, at one Games. He also was awarded a 10.00 in the horse vault, the first maximum ever to a male gymnast in the Games. East African athletes dominated the distance runs, led by Miruts Yifter (ETH) with a 5000m/10 000m double. The 100m was the closest for 28 years with Britain's Allan Wells given the verdict. Two other Britons each won the 'wrong' event, Steve Ovett and Sebastian Coe taking the 800m and 1500m respectively. In the triple jump Viktor Saneyev (URS) ended his remarkable career with a silver to add to his three golds since 1968. Although only winning the pentathlon silver medal Olga Rukavishnikova (URS) theoretically held the world record, albeit for only 0.4sec, as she finished first in the last discipline, 800m. That gave her the shortest reign of any world record holder ever.

Once more the GDR girls dominated the swimming events, winning 26 of the available 35 medals. Three lots of twins won gold medals: Jörg and Bernd Landvoigt (GDR) retained their coxless pairs rowing title; Ullrich and Walter Diessner (GDR) won theirs in the coxed fours; in wrestling both Anatoly and Sergey Beloglasov (URS) won titles.

The oldest gold medallist was Valentin Mankin (URS) in the Star yachting aged 41yr 346 days, while the youngest was swimmer Rica Reinisch (GDR) winning the first of her three golds aged 15yr 105 days. Despite the unfillable losses and gaps caused by the boycott the standard of performances was very high throughout the Games.

Eric Heiden won an unprecedented five gold medals at Lake Placid.
(All-Sport)

1980 Medals (Summer)

	Gold	Silver	Bronze
Soviet Union	80	69	46
East Germany (GDR)	47	37	42
Bulgaria	8	16	17
Cuba	8	7	5
Italy	8	3	4
Hungary	7	10	15
Romania	6	6	13
France	6	5	3
Great Britain	5	7	9
Poland	3	14	15
Sweden	3	3	6
Finland	3	1	4
Czechoslovakia	2	3	9
Yugoslavia	2	3	4
Australia	2	2	5
Denmark	2	1	2
Brazil	2	–	2
Ethiopia	2	–	2
Switzerland	2	–	–
Spain	1	3	2
Austria	1	2	1
Greece	1	–	2
Belgium	1	–	–
India	1	–	–
Zimbabwe	1	–	–
North Korea	–	3	2
Mongolia	–	2	2
Tanzania	–	2	–
Mexico	–	1	3
Netherlands	–	1	2
Ireland	–	1	1
Uganda	–	1	–
Venezuela	–	1	–
Jamaica	–	–	3
Guyana	–	–	1
Lebanon	–	–	1

1984
XIVth Winter Games

The first Winter Games held in Eastern Europe was awarded to Sarajevo in Yugoslavia, which previously was famous as the site of the assassination of Archduke Ferdinand in 1914 – an act which historians argue caused the First World War. There were a record 49 countries attending, and, though the weather was not too good, the enthusiasm of the organizers and the local populace overcame most difficulties. Even the transport system worked. One unfortunate happening just prior to the Games was the banning, as 'professionals', of the two defending champions in the men's and women's slalom races, Ingemar Stenmark (SWE) and Hanni Wenzel (LIE).

The outstanding competitor, unusually, was a female Nordic skier, Marja-Liisa Hämäläinen (FIN), who won all three individual events and a bronze in the relay. However, Britain's Jayne Torvill and Christoper Dean gained the most media attention with their

Everybody's happy on the podium after the 1500m at Moscow, (Jurgen Straub, Seb Coe and Steve Ovett. (Provincial Sports Photography)

superb ice dancing routines – their artistic interpretation of Ravel's *Bolero* was awarded nine perfect sixes. Alpine skiers from the United States made a major impact with Bill Johnson taking the first Olympic downhill title by an American, in a record average speed, and his twin team-mates Phil and Steve Mahre winning the gold and silver medals in the slalom. By winning the women's downhill race Michela Figini (SUI) became the youngest ever Alpine skiing gold medallist aged 17yr 314 days, as well as being the youngest champion at Sarajevo.

The oldest gold medallist there was the Soviet ice hockey goalminder Vladislav Tretyak, winning his third gold medal in four Games aged 31yr 300 days.

Competitors from the GDR dominated the bob events while their female speed skaters won 9 of the 12 medals available to them, including all four golds. Gaetan Boucher won Canada's first Olympic golds at speed skating, while there was confusion, once again, about the eligibility rules for ice hockey where the Soviet Union equalled Canada's record of six gold medals.

The scoreboard for Torvill and Dean's historic marks in the ice dancing at Sarajevo. (All-Sport)

1984 Medals (Winter)

	Gold	Silver	Bronze
East Germany (GDR)	9	9	6
Soviet Union	6	10	9
United States	4	4	–
Finland	4	3	6
Sweden	4	2	2
Norway	3	2	4
Switzerland	2	2	1
Canada	2	1	1
West Germany (FRG)	2	1	1
Italy	2	–	–
Great Britain	1	–	–
Czechoslovakia	–	2	4
France	–	1	2
Japan	–	1	–
Yugoslavia	–	1	–
Liechtenstein	–	–	2
Austria	–	–	1

1984
XXIIIrd Summer Games

The IOC awarded the Games to Los Angeles only after protracted negotiations about the financial guarantees usually required from a host city. Various innovations to protect the city from a Montreal-like deficit were implemented – not least widespread sponsorship by private corporations. Television rights alone amounted to $287 million – one of the largest TV audiences in history, some 2500 million, watched the Games – of which the great bulk came from the ABC network for US rights. The programme was expanded to 221 events, including an extra 12 for women, while baseball and tennis were demonstration sports.

The Memorial Coliseum, main site of the 1932 Games, was fully refurbished and had a seating capacity of 92 607, and many other venues, often famous in their own right, were utilized. There were complaints that some of these venues were too far-flung, but the overall good weather and the enthusiasm, at times overwhelming, of the American crowds offset most problems. Smog and traffic congestion did not materialize to anything like the degree predicted, although one unfortunate phenomenon, however, was the orgy of American chauvinism displayed – especially by the media. Attendances at all sports were quite remarkable with the highest single figure, 101 799, for the final of the soccer tourna-

Carl Lewis matched his hero Jesse Owens by winning the same events at Los Angeles. (All-Sport)

ment in the famed Rose Bowl at Pasadena.

The one, albeit major, disaster of these Games was the last-minute boycott by the Soviet Union and other Socialist countries, although of 159 official invitations sent out a record 140 countries accepted and competed – notably including Romania. Nevertheless a number of sports were very seriously affected, although standards were still generally high. One tremendous outlay at these Games was the cost of security – some 7000 personnel and ancillary equipment costing as

1984 Medals (Summer)

	Gold	Silver	Bronze
United States	83	61	31
Romania	20	16	17
West Germany (FRG)	17	19	23
China	15	8	9
Italy	14	6	12
Canada	10	18	16
Japan	10	8	14
New Zealand	8	1	2
Yugoslavia	7	4	7
Korea	6	6	7
Great Britain	5	11	21
France	5	7	16
Netherlands	5	2	6
Australia	4	8	12
Finland	4	2	6
Sweden	2	10	6
Mexico	2	3	1
Morocco	2	–	–
Brazil	1	5	2
Spain	1	2	2
Belgium	1	1	2
Austria	1	1	1
Kenya	1	–	2
Portugal	1	–	2
Pakistan	1	–	–
Switzerland	–	4	4
Denmark	–	3	3
Jamaica	–	1	2
Norway	–	1	2
Greece	–	1	1
Nigeria	–	1	1
Puerto Rico	–	1	1
Colombia	–	1	–
Egypt	–	1	–
Ireland	–	1	–
Ivory Coast	–	1	–
Peru	–	1	–
Syria	–	1	–
Thailand	–	1	–
Turkey	–	–	3
Venezuela	–	–	3
Algeria	–	–	2
Cameroun	–	–	1
Dominican Republic	–	–	1
Iceland	–	–	1
Taiwan (Taipei)	–	–	1
Zambia	–	–	1

much as $100 million. Nevertheless, at the end of the Games the organizers reported a profit of $215 million – prompting the suggestion that perhaps the pendulum had swung too far the other way since Montreal. After the opening ceremony, which was a three-hour Hollywood-style extravaganza with, among other things, marching bands and 85 pianos, the first gold medal was won by shooter Xu Haifeng with China's first ever Olympic title. Aided enormously by the absence of Soviet and East German opposition, the United States gained by far the lion's share of the medals. Leading their gold rush were sprinter/jumper Carl Lewis, who equalled Jesse Owens's feat of 1936, with four golds, and another athlete, Valerie Brisco-Hooks, and five swimmers, who all won three golds each. However, the most successful competitors were gymnasts Ecaterina Szabo (HUN) with four golds and a silver, and China's Li Ning with three golds, two silvers and a bronze.

The oldest gold medallist at Los Angeles was William Buchan (USA) in the Star yachting aged 49yr 91 days (his son William also won a gold medal on the same day in the Flying Dutchman class). The youngest was Romanian gymnast Simona Pauca in the team event aged 14yr 317 days.

1988
XVth Winter Games

Having had three unsuccessful bids previously, Calgary in Canada was finally awarded these Games in 1981. Most venues are close together except for Mount Allan and Kenmore, some 90km away, where the Alpine and Nordic skiing takes place. The programme has been stretched to 16 days to include three weekends, particularly favourable for television coverage – for which ABC paid $309 million for the North American rights, over three times the sum for Sarajevo. There are a number of new events; Nordic Combination, Team jumping, Alpine Combination, Super Giant Slalom, and a 5000m speed skating event for women. The demonstration sports at Calgary will be curling, short track speed skating, and freestyle skiing.

1988
XXIVth Summer Games

The capital of Korea, Seoul, has one of the largest populations of any city on earth – an estimated 9 000 000. Nearly all facilities for the Games were *in situ* by the end of 1986 when the Asian Games were held there. Most major installations are part of the sports complex on the banks of the Han River, and include a 100 000 stadium.

Once again the programme has been expanded, with the reintroduction of tennis (for the first time since 1924), the addition of table tennis, and the inclusion of a number of extra events, which bring the total to a record 237. Baseball, Taekwondo and women's judo will be demonstration sports. American television companies offered incredible sums (up to $750 million) for the US rights, providing that major sports finals take place during American prime time viewing. This would require that athletics finals be held between 9.00–11.00am Korean time. This was opposed by the International Amateur Athletic Federation, and indeed by the IOC, although some compromise has been made. The income from television sources will still be immense.

One interesting feature of the opening ceremony will be that as the Korean alphabet begins with 'G' the traditional first team Greece will be followed into the stadium by Gabon and Ghana.

Though there have been threats of possible boycotts, the most tenacious problem has been the claim of North Korea to host half of the Games. Against IOC rules, but with their blessing, some sports have been offered to them, but they continue to be intransigent.

Because the original 1920 Olympic flag has been fading away, a new one has been presented to the IOC by the Seoul Organizing Committee and will be flown for the first time on 17 September 1988.

THE FUTURE

After intense 'politicking' the 1992 Summer Games were awarded to Barcelona, Spain in October 1986. At the same time the 1992 Winter Games were awarded to Albertville, France. It has also been decided that in future the Winter Games will be held during the even-numbered years between the Summer Games, so that the next celebration will be in 1994. As the 1996 Summer Games will be the 100th anniversary of the rebirth of the Olympics, Athens is thought to be a strong contender.

Profiles

Paavo Johannes Nurmi

Before the second decade of the century Finnish runners had made little impact on the world athletics scene. Then in 1912 Hannes Kolehmainen burst upon the world at the Stockholm Olympic Games, winning three gold medals and launching a line of 'Flying Finns' which was to dominate distance running for nearly thirty years. Among those he inspired back in Finland was a young boy named Paavo Nurmi, who would become the greatest running machine the world had ever seen.

Born at Turku on 13 June 1897, he was the eldest of five children of a carpenter. He was 9 years old when he decided to become an athlete and a year later he clocked 5min 03.0sec for the 1500m. He started work early, at 13, because his father had died and perhaps because of this his progress was not particularly exciting. He had a scientific approach to his training and running, and experimented with training methods, pacing and diet – he became a vegetarian although this may have been because the family was too poor to afford much meat. He did not drink coffee, tea or alcohol, and did not smoke. A very introverted boy with few friends, he rarely smiled or showed emotion. On his way to and from his work with an engineering company he used to pace himself against trams and freight trains, sometimes holding on with one hand.

Then while serving in the Army in 1919 he won a route 'march' in full equipment by running most of the way – allowed but rarely practised – with a margin of victory so great that he was unjustly accused of taking a shortcut. His time in the Army, freed from the responsibilities and chores of his home life, seemed to be the turning point, and in 1920 he won his first Finnish title, at 1500m. He had developed the habit of running stopwatch in hand, pacing himself oblivious of the rest of the runners, to a time

that he had considered fast enough to win. Usually on the last lap he would discard it and sprint to the finish. As he was to say later in life, 'Time, not any man, was my opponent.'

He had a classic running style, with head upright, high arm action, elbows in to his sides, and a long – unusually long – smooth stride. A loner for most of his life, he was married, briefly, and had a son, but as he got older he was something of a recluse, his renowned short temper and impatience not endearing him to people.

In his first Olympic race, the 1920 5000m, he was beaten by Joseph Guillemot (FRA), a man who apparently had his heart on his right side. Three days later, Nurmi beat the Frenchman over 10 000m, and was never again beaten in the Olympics by other than his own team-mates. In 1924 he ran seven races in seven days and won a record five gold medals. To his annoyance Finnish officials would not let him run in the 10 000m as well. While his perennial rival Ville Ritola was winning in a world record 30min 23.2sec, it is said that Nurmi was on a training track running the distance in under 30 minutes. Certainly eight weeks later he smashed Ritola's record by 17 seconds with a time that lasted for thirteen years.

Before the Paris Games it had been decided by the organizers to allow only half an hour between the 1500m and 5000m finals, but after vigorous Finnish protests this was extended to 55 minutes. Nurmi had injured himself in training at Easter, but three weeks prior to the Games he tested himself at Helsinki and broke both world records, 3min 52.6sec and 14min 28.2sec respectively, with only an hour's rest. He knew he was ready. In Paris he ran the first 400m in 58.0sec, and having dropped the rest of the field with a lap to go, coasted to the finish. In the 5000m his opponents started very fast, hoping to capitalize on his lack of rest – the first 1000m was passed in an outstanding 2min 46.4sec, with Nurmi some 6m down. But he took the lead after halfway and was never passed. Two days later the 10 000m cross-country race was held in 40°C weather. Thirty-eight competitors started but only fifteen finished, with most

of them totally exhausted. Nurmi won easily, showing no distress, and the next day, with many of those runners still in hospital, he won the 3000m team race.

Probably his hardest Olympic race was the 10 000m in 1928 when he and Ritola fought out the last seven laps with Nurmi just holding on at the end. Also at Amsterdam he ran in the steeplechase, in which he was a virtual novice. In his heat he fell at the first water jump, and was helped up by a Frenchman Lucien Duquesne. Thereafter in the race Nurmi showed a rare glimpse of humanitarian concern and dropped back to encourage and pace the Frenchman and helped him make the final. In that final he was back to business and won a silver medal with the Frenchman back in sixth place.

In all Nurmi won a record nine gold medals and three silvers. He would almost certainly have added to that in 1932, when he was entered for the marathon as well as the 10 000m, but he was declared a professional for illegal expenses just prior to the Games.

In total he set 29 world records in 16 different events ranging from 1500m to 20 000m.

He retired in 1933 – after winning his last Finnish title at 1500m as a 'national amateur' – and started a construction business and later had a clothing shop, becoming quite well-off. On his death on 2 October 1973 he had a state funeral, with eight Olympic medallists as pall-bearers. His last running appearance had been 21 years earlier when he had carried the Olympic torch into the Olympic stadium at Helsinki and lit a flame by the trackside, before handing the torch to his great predecessor, Kolehmainen, who took it to the top of the stadium tower and lit the main flame. As always the name of the last runner had been kept secret and was only announced on the main scoreboard seconds before the runner entered the stadium. As the first letter 'N' came up the 80 000 spectators erupted in cheering and the teams of competitors, neatly lined up on the grass, rushed to get a look at a 'living legend'.

Paavo Nurmi (Radio Times Hulton Picture Library)

Jesse Owens

James Cleveland 'Jesse' Owens was not the first athlete to win four gold medals at an Olympic Games, but his achievements at the Berlin Games of 1936 have uniquely entered the realms of sports history.

He was born on 12 September 1913, at Oakville, Alabama, one of the eleven children of Henry and Emma Owens. His parents were poor sharecroppers whose own parents had been slaves, and Jesse, a sickly child, spent his early years picking cotton. At the age of 9 he and his family moved to Cleveland, where he came into contact with coach Charles Riley, at Cleveland's East Technical High School. Under Riley's tutelage Owens blossomed into a fine athlete and had been timed at 9.9sec for 100 yards by the time he was 15 years old. It was also at this school that he 'acquired' his first name; when his first teacher asked him what his name was, he answered 'J.C.', the nickname given to him by his family. She misheard and entered him as 'Jesse' and it stuck. One of his early inspirations was a visit to the school by the then 100 yards world record holder, and 1920 Olympic sprint champion, Charlie Paddock.

As was not uncommon in those days Jesse got married very young, at 16, to Ruth, and despite the many problems, both personal and financial, which beset them, they remained together for 49 years and had three daughters. With her support in those early days Jesse improved even beyond Riley's hopes and in 1932/1933 he set American high school records for the 100yd, 220yd and the long jump, and equalled the world record for 100yd of 9.4sec. On leaving high school 28 colleges wanted him to join them, but he chose Ohio State in order to stay close to home. There he came under the influence of one of the top coaches in America, Larry Snyder, and, although working as a lift operator in the State legislature to earn some money, continued to improve. On 25 May 1935 he competed for his university in the Big Ten conference championships at Ferry Field, Ann Arbor, Michigan, and became a sporting immortal. A few days prior to the meeting he badly hurt his back playing around with some friends, and coach Snyder did not want him to compete in case he really injured himself in what was a vital pre-Olympic year. Despite having to be helped off the team bus, he convinced Snyder that he could at least run in the 100yd, the first event. Thus began one of the most incredible afternoons in the history of sport. At 3.15pm he equalled the world record of 9.4sec in the 100yd, with some of the time-keepers recording a tenth faster. Ten minutes later he had his only long jump of the day – a record leap of 26ft 8¼in *8.13m*. In the 220yd, run twenty minutes after, he set another world mark of 20.3sec, and finally, about 50 minutes after he had started his afternoon's work, he bettered the record for the 220yd hurdles, then a popular event, with 22.6sec. As both of the 220yd races were longer than the metric equivalents at 200m the records were also allowed for them – thus he was credited with six world records on that outstanding day. It is reported that immediately after his last event the backache returned, worse than ever, and he had to be helped on to the bus again.

During the next twelve months he was beaten a number of times by Eulace Peacock and Ralph Metcalfe, but at the Olympic trials he won his three events and was on the team for Berlin. At the Games, despite a most virulent campaign by Dr Goebbels and his propaganda machine against the 'Black Auxiliaries' of the American team, tremendous interest was shown by the public in Owens and his comrades. He ran a total of ten races as well as competing in the long jump qualifying and final. At the end of the track and field programme he had won four gold medals and was world famous. It was commented that Adolf Hitler had snubbed Owens, and other black champions, by not congratulating them as he had German winners. In fact Hitler had been reprimanded by the President of the IOC, Henri Baillet Latour, for this highhanded practice on the first day, and thereafter refrained. However, it was highly unlikely that he would have greeted Owens anyway, but as Jesse said later 'perhaps Chancellor Hitler didn't

Jesse Owens (Mary Evans)

shake hands, but nor did President Roosevelt'. In fact Roosevelt didn't even send congratulations. Additionally, the AAU, the American governing body, suspended him for refusing an invitation to compete in Sweden after the Games, and did not give him the Sullivan Award as the Amateur Athlete of the Year. (He had not been awarded it the previous year either when it was given to a white golfer.) However, there were ticker-tape parades in New York and Cleveland. Watching the latter was a young boy to whom Owens later gave his gold medal shoes – his name was Harrison Dillard, and he became the greatest sprinter/hurdler in the world winning four gold medals himself in the Games of 1948 and 1952.

After the Games, with a family to support, Owens took various jobs, and raced against horses and greyhounds. He got into serious debt when a dry-cleaning business that he had invested in went bankrupt, and was in serious financial difficulties for many years. In the 1950s things got better and he went into public relations and public speaking on behalf of a number of corporations. He was often the target of militant black groups for not supporting their, often violent, aims, but he said he believed in trying to bring change by example, and was an avid supporter of men like Martin Luther King. In 1956 and again in 1972 he was sent to the Games as an official representative of the President of the United States, and was honoured wherever he went. In 1976 he was given the Silver Olympian Order by the IOC, and President Ford awarded him the Medal of Freedom.

On the 31 March 1980 he died of cancer, having been a heavy smoker for the last 30 years of his life. Prior to the 1984 Games a street outside the stadium in Berlin was named after him, and at the Los Angeles Games his granddaughter Gina Hemphill carried the Olympic flame into the stadium. As he told newspapermen in 1936, 'I went to Berlin to run – and I did.'

Dawn Fraser

One of the greatest swimmers the world has ever known, Dawn Fraser was born the youngest of eight children at Balmain, New South Wales on 4 September 1937. She began swimming at 6 years of age and had early coaching from Harry Gallagher, who deliberately kept her out of competition until she was 15. As a child she suffered from asthma and pleurisy. She had to face many problems in her career, including being banned from swimming due to official strictures on her club which had been giving cash incentives to some older members. This was not to be the last time that she was in conflict with officialdom.

She won her first Australian title, over 220yd freestyle, in 1955, and the following year set her first world record winning the national 100m freestyle in 64.5sec, beating a 20-year-old mark. In all she was to win 23 Australian titles, remain the world's top sprinter for ten years, and set a total of 27 individual world records plus another 12 in relays. Besides freestyle swimming she was also of champion class at 100m butterfly and 200m individual medley.

Just before her first Olympic Games in 1956 her brother died of leukaemia, and she dedicated herself to winning for him. She took the 100m freestyle title with another world record of 62.0sec just beating fellow Australian Lorraine Crapp. In the 400m she came second to Crapp, and then they joined forces with two team-mates to win the 4 × 100m freestyle relay. The night before the 100m final, her first major international appearance, she had a nightmare in which her feet were stuck to the starting blocks by honey. Then when she finally got loose and dived into the pool, it wasn't water but spaghetti in which she got hopelessly entangled. One can imagine her thoughts at the actual race start.

At the 1960 Games in Rome she had made herself very unpopular with some of her team-mates and the officials by disobeying orders. Despite winning the 100m again, comfortably beating the American Christine von Saltza, and gaining

Dawn Fraser (Sport & General)

Jean-Claude Killy

two silvers in the relays, she was omitted from tours to Japan and South Africa. In 1958 she had won two gold and two silver medals in the Commonwealth Games at Cardiff, and in 1962 she added another four gold medals to add another record to her illustrious career.

She became the first woman to swim faster than 60.0sec for the 100m freestyle in October 1962 and was to take the record down eventually to 58.9sec. She was the holder of the sprint record for 15 years in all.

By 1964 she was known as 'Granny' to the other swimmers as at 27 she was very old by world swimming standards. In March of that year she was involved in a car crash in which her mother was killed, a sister injured, and she herself suffered severe neck vertebrae damage. After many weeks in plaster she still was in deep depression. Nevertheless, seven months after the accident she competed at her third Games. Just to add to her troubles she had a bad cold which stopped her from doing her usual fast tumble turn, and necessitated a slow open turn losing precious time. She still beat Sharon Stouder (USA) for her record third consecutive victory in the 100m, gained fourth place in the 400m in a personal best of 4min 47.6sec, and

won another silver medal in the freestyle relay (in which her split was 58.6sec). This brought her Olympic medal haul to four gold and four silver medals, a record since only matched by Kornelia Ender (GDR) but never beaten.

Then came her most traumatic brush with the Australian Swimming Union. She had upset them at the start of the Games by disobeying their order not to march in the opening ceremony as she had races on the following day. But then she was involved with some high jinks which culminated in the 'appropriation' of a souvenir flag from the gardens of the Imperial Palace. She was caught by police, who incidentally dropped the charges and let her keep the flag, but the Australian authorities perhaps overreacted and banned her for ten years – virtually ending her career. Although she was reinstated four years later, and awarded the OBE in 1967, it was too late for the 1968 Games. She was a guest of the Mexican Organizing Committee and watched 'her title' go to Jan Henne (USA) in 60.0sec. As if to prove something while in Mexico City, while badly out of condition by her exacting standards, she swam an exhibition 100m in under 62.0sec. If things had been different she may have set an unattainable record in her fourth Games.

Who ever heard of an Irish Alpine skier? Well, Jean-Claude Killy is not quite that but was born into a family descended from Irish mercenaries who had fought in France – Killy being a corruption of Kelly. Jean-Claude was born at St Cloud on 30 August 1943, but at the end of the Second World War the family moved to Val d'Isere in the French Alps, and by the time he was 3 years old he had already begun to ski. Making good progress he was a member of the French national team by the age of 16, and was also beginning to acquire his other reputation as something of a playboy.

While serving in the French Army in Algeria he contracted a bad case of hepatitis, but despite this he was able to qualify for a place in the Olympic team at Innsbruck, Austria in 1964. Competing in all three events he placed fifth in the giant slalom, but failed to finish in the slalom and the downhill. The exposure obviously did him good and soon he was making his presence felt on the skiing circuit, and in 1966 he won the combined title and the downhill at the World Championships at Portillo, Chile. The following year he won the inaugural World Cup competition with the maximum possible points taking all three specialist disciplines, a unique feat which may never be equalled.

His intense determination to win found another outlet at this time when he toyed with motor racing, and some years later actually drove in the classic Targa Florio. The intensity of his will to win is perhaps demonstrated by a report that at the start of one of his ski races he made such an explosive exit from the start gate that both sets of ski bindings snapped. However, he started the pre-Olympic season of 1967–1968 rather poorly by his standards and had only won a single race, a giant slalom, before the start of the Games at Grenoble. With a predominantly French crowd present he was under tremendous pressure to do well, and there was much speculation as to whether he could emulate the Austrian Toni Sailer, who, at Cortina d'Ampezzo in 1956, had won all three titles, each by remarkable margins.

Prior to the Games he had made a number of deals with ski equipment manufacturers which caused the IOC to step in and warn him about violating the amateur code. There was further trouble when the IOC initially banned the practice of prominent display of trade names and trade marks on skis. It was pointed out to them that the sport could only exist with the financial support of the ski companies. Eventually a strange compromise was reached by which the trade marks could be left on the equipment, but officials would take the skis away immediately after use so that the skiers could not be photographed with them.

Killy's first event was the downhill race, and he had a bad draw with number 14 as the snow was soft. To add to his troubles just before his run he accidentally ruined the waxing on his skis, and his equipment adviser Michael Arpin desperately made crude repairs. Throwing caution to the winds he gave the run everything he had and made it down just 0.08sec faster than the previous leader Guy Perillat, his team-mate. After that the giant slalom was easy and he won by more than 2sec from Willy Favre of Switzerland, to the delight of the French spectators.

Five days later, on the day of the slalom, there was thick fog on the course, and there were some thoughts about postponing the competition. However, it was adjudged good enough to carry on and Killy was lying in first place after the first run. It was said that the only time the sun shone through that day was during that run by Killy. He then made the first run of the second round and had to wait to see if anyone could push him out of first place overall. The biggest threat came from the Austrian Karl Schranz, who was going very well when he stopped just past gate 21, claiming that someone had run across in front of him. The referee agreed to his request to be allowed a re-run and with an almost flawless performance snatched first place from Killy. Just prior to the prize-giving ceremony the French lodged a protest declaring that before Schranz had pulled up after gate 21 he had already missed gates 18 and 19. The Austrians argued that these errors had been caused by the mysterious figure appearing in front of him, while the French suggested that after missing the gates Schranz had made up the rest of the story. After long deliberation the Jury of Appeal decided against the Austrian and Killy was given the title as he was 0.09sec faster than the other Austrian Herbert Huber. So the Frenchman had equalled Sailer's record. Soon after the Games he signed public relations contracts with a number of companies, particularly in America, and also made a few movies. He married a French actress, Danielle Gaubert, and they had a daughter, Emily. In 1973 he reappeared to win the Grand Prix on the professional skiing circuit, while ten years later he competed in the New York marathon, for charity, clocking 3hr 58min.

In February 1987 he was appointed to the Presidency of the 1992 Olympic Winter Games Organizing Committee for Albertville, but only a few weeks later resigned after a disagreement with his colleagues.

Jean-Claude Killy

Vera Caslavska

Although her first love had been ice skating, Vera Caslavska turned to gymnastics at the unusually late age of 15, and within a very short while was in the national team. She was born in Prague on 3 May 1942, and came into the sport when it was totally dominated by the Soviet Union, with the leading individual being Larissa Latynina. Caslavska's first major international appearance was at the 1958 World Championships in Moscow, and she won her first medal, a silver, as a member of the Czechoslovakian team. She placed a respectable eighth in the individual competition. The following year the European Championships were held in Cracow, Poland, and she won her first important gold medal, winning the individual title on the balance beam.

Her first Olympic Games, only three years after taking up the sport, was in 1960 in Rome where she won a team silver medal, was again eighth in the individual overall contest, and placed sixth on the beam. The gymnastics world began to take notice of the blonde and glamorous Czech, although the 1961 European Championships did not live up to her hopes as she only took home two bronze medals. When the world titles were held in her hometown of Prague in 1962 she had begun to hone her skills, and before a cheering, partisan crowd gained the silver medal in the individual overall contest, and won the horse vault gold medal.

By the Tokyo Games in 1964 she was ready, and beat Latynina to win the individual gold medal, and lead her national team to within a hairbreadth of the Soviet team. She also won golds on the beam and in the vault, and would have assuredly won another in the asymmetrical bars if she had not attempted too daring a move and fallen.

The following year, at the European Championships in Sofia, she completed a clean sweep of all five available titles and in 1966 in Dortmund she lead the Czech team to a World Championship victory,

Vera Caslavska (UPI)

adding the individual title for good measure. In all she won four golds, four silvers and a bronze medal in World Championship competition.

She ended her European title assault in Amsterdam in 1967 by once again taking all five gold medals, and in the floor exercises and on the beam she was awarded the first ever 10.00 marks in major competition. Her total of European medals comprised eleven golds, one silver and two bronzes, from 1959 to 1967, which would have been more except that the Czech team did not compete in 1963.

Two months before the 1968 Olympic Games the Soviet Union sent its troops to occupy Czechoslovakia, and the ensuing upheaval caused tremendous problems with her training. Also, a great patriot, she was deeply disturbed with the situation. At 26 she was one of the oldest competitors in the Auditorio in Mexico City for her last Olympic Games. Once again she led her national team to the closest that they had ever got to the unbeatable Soviet team. In the individual competitions she was superb taking

the overall title plus further gold medals in the vault, asymmetrical bars and the floor exercises, as well as a silver on the beam. In the latter event she was initially only given a 9.60 by the judges, but amid uproar from the spectators it was changed to 9.80, with the excuse that there had been an error. Her floor routine to the music of 'Mexican Hat Dance' remains one of the great moments in Olympic gymnastic history. At the end of the Games she had won a total of seven Olympic golds and four silvers from three Games. Although her rival Latynina had won a remarkable 18 medals (including nine golds) from 1956 to 1964, all of Caslavska's gold medals had come in individual contests and not team ones.

The day before the Games ended at Mexico City Vera Caslavska married her countryman, Josef Odlozil, the 1964 silver medallist at 1500m, and 10 000 people waited to greet them outside the Cathedral in Zocalo Square. On returning home to an honourable retirement she presented her gold medals to the leaders of her country.

Mark Andrew Spitz

When he was quite young Mark Spitz's father told him that 'swimming isn't everything – winning is', and it seems that he took that credo to heart. Born in Modesto, California on 10 January 1950 he spent his early life in Hawaii, and set out to be a great swimmer. It is reasonable to agree that he succeeded. Unfortunately, on the way he gained a reputation of being a rather arrogant, brash young man, and committed the cardinal sin of being as good as, perhaps even better, than he said he was – a 'failing' the world never forgives.

He made his international debut at the age of 15 in the Maccabiah Games in Israel and won four gold medals, and two years later won five more in the Pan-American Championships in Winnipeg, Canada. Also in June 1967 he broke his first world record in the 400m freestyle, an event that he later forsook for the shorter distances. Such early success will undoubtedly affect a young man, but it seems that the boastful claims that he would win six gold medals at the Olympic Games of 1968 in Mexico City, came not from him, but from his then coach, George Haines. Much to Spitz's dismay, and, it must be said, the joy of many of his team-mates, he 'only' came away with two golds, a silver and a bronze – the golds were both in relays. He had received a hard lesson but now could he learn from it. Happily, after Mexico City he came under the tutelage of the famed James 'Doc' Counsilman when he attended the University of Indiana. Although he still had his own private coach, Sherman Chavoor, Counsilman helped to mature him as a person and as a competitor. During those days he paced his college to three NCAA championships and set numerous world marks. Incidentally, Counsilman later, in 1979, became the oldest man ever to swim the English Channel succeeding in his 59th year.

At Munich in 1972 Spitz wanted to better the record of five swimming gold medals held by his great rival in his early years, Don Schollander. In fact the greatest number of medals ever won at swimming was the five golds, one silver and two bronzes gained by fellow American, Charles Daniels, from 1904 to 1908. Rather fittingly his first race in Munich, the 200m butterfly, was the same event that had been his last race in Mexico City. In that he had been a bad last in the final, a dejected and exhausted boy. In his heat in Munich he smashed the Olympic record and then in the final improved on his own world mark. Over the eight days he had a total of thirteen races, winning a record seven gold medals with world records being set in all the finals of his events – 100m and 200m freestyle, 100m and 200m butterfly, 4 × 100m and 4 × 200m freestyle relays and the 4 × 100m medley relay, in which he swam the butterfly leg. It was rumoured that he had intended to withdraw from the 100m freestyle, but was told that it would seem to be a case of 'chickening out'. As he said to the world's Press when asked how he did it all, his answer was 'I swam my brains out.' There was one sour note during his run of successes when he was called before the IOC for waving his shoes at the crowd (and the TV cameras) during the 200m freestyle victory ceremony. He was able to convince them that the act was merely one of exuberance and not advertising. The day after his last gold medal the Games community awoke to the news of the Arab terrorist attack on the Israeli team, and the consequent murder of eleven of them. Spitz, being a Jew, was thought to be a likely target for any further outrage and was given special security. On advice he returned home immediately, before the Games ended.

He thus ended his swimming career, having won more Olympic gold medals than any other man bar athlete Ray Ewry, and having broken 26 world records in individual events plus another six in relays. In 1971 he was awarded the Sullivan Award, as top Amateur Sportsman in the United States, and in 1972 was named Swimmer of the Year by FINA, the sport's governing body, an honour he had already received in 1967 and 1971. He is reported to have made a fortune after the Games and has a successful real estate business.

Mark Spitz (All-Sport)

58

Olga Korbut

After the delightfully feminine charms and skills of Czechoslovakia's Vera Caslavska had aroused some interest in gymnastics among non-aficionados of the sport, there remained a gap left by her retirement which badly needed filling to raise the sport to a worldwide attraction. Perhaps surprisingly it was filled by almost the antithesis of the Czech girl – Olga Korbut.

Olga was born at Grodno, Byelorussia, near the Polish border, on 16 May 1955, the youngest of four daughters. She began gymnastics aged 10 and was a member of the national team, the strongest in the world, five years later. Coached by Renald Knysh, with whom she had a long stormy coach/athlete relationship, she won her first Soviet title, in the vault, in 1970. Though undoubtedly promising, she only made the 1972 Olympic team as a reserve, and got her chance due to the withdrawal of a team-mate because of injury. That she took her chance is now a matter of history.

Though she was far outshone technically by her compatriot, the world champion Ludmila Tourischeva, the elfin (1.49m *4ft 11in* 38kg *84lb*) Korbut caught the media and public imagination from her first appearance in Munich. She performed spectacularly in the initial team contest, especially on the asymmetrical bars, but it was her gamine quality that seemed to catch the eye. Strangely it was a poor performance on those same asymmetrical bars that brought her the most attention. Scoring only a very low 7.50 marks, which put her down to seventh in the individual overall competition, she burst into body-racking sobs which the TV cameras caught and beamed around the world, touching untold hearts. The following day in the individual apparatus finals she won gold medals on the beam, where she performed her innovative backward somersault, and in the floor exercises, where her pert finish has been repeated dozens of times on television screens worldwide. The individual champion, Tourischeva, a magnificent figure of a woman,

Olga Korbut (Ed Lacey)

who later married double sprint champion Valery Borzov, was almost ignored. It has often been suggested that the applause of the crowd caused the judges to mark Olga rather higher than she perhaps deserved.

After Munich the global interest in gymnastics in general and in Korbut in particular prompted the Soviet Union to send their team on international goodwill tours, but they were becoming embarrassed with the overwhelming interest shown in her every move and action. It also affected her, as she was still only 18, and there were reports of friction with her coach and officials. In 1973 at the European Championships held in London, she came second to Tourischeva in the overall but was then injured and did not compete in the individual apparatus finals. Thus that silver was the only European medal she ever won. The following year in Varna for the World Championships she was again second overall but won a gold medal in the team contest and the individual vault competition, as well as silvers in the other three disciplines.

The stress of media attention and training injuries began to take its toll and by the Montreal Olympics of 1976 she was a shadow of her former self – no longer the cute kid of four years previously. But she was just as popular to the Canadian fans and media prior to the Games, and was even made Soviet team captain, causing much ill-will in the Soviet camp, not least with Tourischeva. In the event the true stars of the Montreal gymnastics were 14-year-old Nadia Comaneci of Romania, as solemn as Korbut had been perky, and the attractive Nelli Kim (URS), both of whom earned maximum 10.00 marks during the competitions. Korbut won a team gold, with a solitary silver on the beam, and only placed fifth in the overall contest.

While on a last tour of the United States in 1976 she titillated the world's press by buying a wedding dress in St Louis, and rumours of marriage and retirement abounded. At the beginning of 1978 she married Leonid Bortkevich, a pop singer, at Minsk, and worked as a coach, until in March 1979 she gave birth to a baby boy.

Lasse Artturi Viren

When Lasse Viren stepped into the stadium at Munich for the 1972 Olympic 10 000 final, Finland, which had once so dominated the running events, had not won a track title for 36 years. Until only a month or so prior to the Games Viren did not seem to be the man to break that pattern. The previous year, in the European Championships in Helsinki, it was his compatriot Juha Vaatainen who had caused the big upset and won a stunning 5000m/ 10 000m double. Lasse had trailed in seventeenth in the longer race and seventh in the 5000m. It was only after winning a fast 5000m

against Great Britain and Spain, also in Helsinki, five weeks before the Olympics began that he loomed as a threat to the world's best.

Viren was born at Myrskyla on 22 July 1949. He did not begin training seriously until he was 16 and success came quite quickly when he won the national junior 3000m championship in 1967. Two years later he had broken the national junior record for 5000m with 13min 55.0sec and had achieved his first major victory, also at 5000m against the traditional 'enemy' Sweden. However, he failed to make the Finnish team for the 1969 European Championships in Athens, but an enlightened governing body sent him there to watch and learn. Prior to the championships he had gone to Brigham Young University in the United States, but decided to return home after only six months.

Lasse Viren (Keystone)

In 1970 he had poor results, but the following year he drastically improved on his times, but did not do well in the European Championships.

As preparation for the Olympics he spent much of the winter in South America and then Spain, and returning home in April began to show tremendous form, culminating in a world record 8min 14.0sec for 2 miles just three weeks before the Games. He and his coach, Ralf Haikkola, who was a former champion himself from Viren's home town, originally intended that Viren would only run in the 5000m at Munich, but his form seemed so outstanding that it was decided to try for the double. He was now a policeman, and sported a typical Nordic beard, although he was only 23 years old. For the first time since 1920 the Olympic 10 000m required heats, in which he easily qualified behind the reigning Olympic 5000m champion Mohamed Gammoudi (TUN). In the final, just before the halfway mark, Gammoudi fell bringing down Viren as well. The Finn was up quickly and back in contention before the end of the lap and taking the lead with about a lap and a half to go held on to take the gold medal, and, as a bonus, the world record with a 27min 38.4sec clocking. With his 'second string' event out of the way he could now concentrate on the 5000m, and despite a very determined thrust by the American Steve Prefontaine with four laps to go Viren completed only the fourth distance double in Games history. His predecessors had been the original 'Flying Finn' Hannes Kolehmainen (1912), Emil Zatopek of Czechoslovakia (1952) and the Soviet runner Vladimir Kuts (1956). The last mile of that Munich race was estimated at about 4min 01.0sec. Back in Helsinki after the Games he broke the world 5000m mark with 13min 16.4sec.

A combination of injuries and too many social engagements affected much of his running between Munich and Montreal, although he did gain a bronze medal in the 1974 European Championships 5000m (and seventh place in the 10 000m). In 1975 he had an operation on a thigh and hamstring, and early in 1976 he was badly affected by sinus trouble. Nevertheless, at Montreal he completed an unprecedented 'double double'. In the 10 000m final he was the only one able to keep up with the very fast pace set by Carlos Lopes of Portugal, and outkicked him on the last lap. The 5000m was much more difficult with about nine men still in contention at the bell. Viren was quoted as saying that 'it would have been a hell of a race to watch'. Then, having raced a total of 30 000m in the previous seven days, he attempted his first marathon, in the hope of equalling the immortal Zatopek's triple of 1952. Despite running out of energy with a third of the race yet to go he still managed to finish in fifth place in a creditable time of 2hr 13min 11sec.

It was now that rumours began to circulate that the reason for his exceptional running at the Olympics, but comparatively poor performances between Games, was that he was involved in the new practice of blood doping or boosting. This technique consists basically of taking some of the athlete's blood and storing it in a frozen state. When the body has made up the lost amount the previously withdrawn blood is reinjected thereby increasing the oxygen-carrying red blood cells. Viren and his supporters have always rejected the accusation, even though other Finnish runners have admitted to the practice. He was also in trouble at Montreal for allegedly advertising his shoe manufacturers when he ran his victory lap after the 10 000m waving them above his head. The furore died away when he stated that he had a blister and had to take them off. He also claimed that his Olympic successes, to the detriment of other races, came because to him only the Olympic gold medals were important. As he said, 'Your world records will be broken, but no one can take your gold medals away.'

Now married to Paivi, and with a son Tuomas, Viren tried to increase his collection in 1980, but injury and, perhaps, lack of incentive left him with only a fifth placing in the 10 000m. In the marathon he was caught by an attack of diarrhoea and dropped out of the race, but he had already done enough in his Olympic appearances to join the illustrious Pantheon of Finnish running greats which includes Kolehmainen, Ritola and Nurmi.

Eric Heiden

The grounds of the Lake Placid High School, the site of the 1980 Olympic speed skating, was the stage for one of the great Winter Games performers of all time. The United States had not had a clean sweep of all men's titles since the highly controversial Games of 1932, also held at Lake Placid. That was the occasion when the American 'mass start' system had been introduced, one with which the Europeans were totally unfamiliar. In 1980 there was no such excuse, as Eric Heiden showed his home crowd the talent that had been appreciated in Europe for a number of years. Born on 14 June 1958, he had previously competed in the Games in 1976, at Innsbruck, where, as a 17 year old he had placed seventh in the 1500m and nineteenth in the 5000m, creating little or no interest.

However, over the next twelve months he made tremendous improvement as he filled out – he developed 73cm $29in$ thighs – and in 1977 won the world overall speed skating title. To show the Dutch, Norwegian and Soviet experts that it was no fluke, he retained the title in 1978 and then again in 1979. In March 1978 he set his first world record, over 3000m, and in total set seven world marks – his last one over 10 000m at the 1980 Games.

Surprisingly in his run-up to Lake Placid he lost the world overall title to Hilbert Van Der Duim (HOL), but won the world sprint title, although even in this latter he was beaten over 500m by a teammate. Though he went into the Games as the favourite for all the events, it was the short race that posed the most problems. In that race he was perhaps lucky to be paired with the world record holder Yevgeny Kulikov (URS) who set a fast pace before making a slight error which Heiden was quick to take advantage of. He had another nasty moment during the 1500m when he nearly fell with half of the race gone. In the 5000m Kai Arne Stenshjemmet (NOR), the world record holder, was up on Heiden's best time for most of the way but couldn't quite keep up the pace and lost out by under a second. The night

Sebastian Newbold Coe

Eric Heiden (All-Sport)

Few men can have reached the depths of despair that Sebastian Coe experienced after the 800m final at Moscow in 1980, only to rise to the heights of ecstasy after victory in the 1500m, all within six days. Neither Coe nor his father/coach Peter will ever forget those extremes of feelings which were the culmination of some twelve years of joint effort.

Born in Chiswick, London on 29 September 1956, Seb, the oldest of the four children of Angela and Peter Coe, spent most of his early life in Sheffield, where his father was a production engineer with a cutlery firm. There was some sporting background in the family as his great grandfather, Robert Coe, had competed as a professional sprinter in the north-east of England, and Peter had achieved some success as a racing cyclist in his youth.

Initially more interested in football – he is still a strong supporter of Chelsea FC – Coe achieved early success in schools competitions, and joined Hallamshire Harriers when he was 12 years old. His father brought a clear analytical mind to his coaching, uncluttered by long-held attitudes and methods, and they began to build a background of great strength into Coe's deceptively frail frame. Even today he is only 1.77m *5ft 9½in* tall, weighing 54kg *119lb*, and as a boy was usually much smaller than his rivals. Early in 1972 he ran in the English Schools Intermediate cross-country championships and came tenth – an older boy named Ovett was second. Later that year he broke 2 minutes for 800m for the first time, but it was at 3000m that he won his first title, in the English Schools Championships. He followed that with a win in the AAA Youth 1500m.

In 1974 he had his first problem with injury followed by a frustrating season on the sidelines. But the following year, now 18, he won the AAA Junior 1500m title and was selected for the European Junior Championships, in which he placed third. His big breakthrough

before his last event, the 10 000m, Heiden watched the United States ice hockey team (in which he had some friends) beat the Soviet Union in a highly charged and emotional match which virtually gave the title to the Americans. Overly excited he had a restless night, and nearly overslept. Nevertheless, he went into this final event filled with determination and not only won his record fifth gold medal but smashed the world record held by Viktor Leskin (URS) by a massive 6sec. He thus became the first Olympic competitor, in any sport, summer or winter, to win five individual event gold medals at one celebration of the Games. To add a little more icing to the cake, his sister Beth, herself a world champion in 1979, won a bronze medal in the women's

3000m.

Almost 'overnight' Heiden – who with great foresight had been given the honour at the start of the Games of carrying the American flag in the opening ceremony – became a national hero. Unusually he did not like the intense publicity which resulted; as he said at the time, 'I really liked it best when I was a nobody.' He decided to retire and take up seriously his other love, cycling, following in the footsteps of previous Olympic champions Sheila Young (USA) and Yevgeniy Grischin (URS). However, although Beth won a world road race title, major success did not come to Eric Heiden in this new sport, but no doubt he enjoyed it all the more for the consequent lack of intrusion into his life.

came in the Olympic year of 1976 when he improved his times, particularly in the 800m, and came seventh in the Trials 1500m race.

During the 1977 indoor season he won his first international title over 800m at San Sebastian, Spain, in the European Indoor Champion-ships, barely missing the world's best time. Later in the year he was barged out of contention in the European Cup 800m race in Helsinki, by Willie Wulbeck (FRG), when poised to make his final effort. Back home he surprisingly won the Emsley Carr mile, beating world record holder Filbert Bayi (TAN). Early in 1978 he seriously damaged an ankle while training which gave him a lot of trouble throughout the season. At the European Championships that year he made the pace with a remarkably fast first 400m in 49.3sec, in an effort to take the sting from main rival Steve Ovett's finish, but was shunted back to third place as the unheralded Uwe Beyer (GDR) came through to beat both of them. It was 'back to the drawing board' for the father and son team, and in 1979 a new Sebastian Coe appeared, reaching an unsurpassed standard of performance during a 41 day period in mid-summer. It began on a perfect evening at Oslo when he set his first world record of 1min 42.33sec for 800m. Just over a week later, in the AAA championships, he was the fastest British runner in the 400m with a personal best of 46.87sec to place second. Next he was back in Oslo for a world record-breaking mile of 3min 49.0sec. Then at the beginning of August he settled old scores in the European Cup final 800m, winning the race easily with Wulbeck in third place, and Beyer in fifth. He ended this tremendous sequence with another world record, 1500m in 3min 32.1, at Zurich, and became the first athlete ever to hold the 800m, 1500, and mile records simultaneously.

Coe went to the Moscow Olympics in 1980 as firm favourite for the 800m title. The American-led boycott had nearly been joined by Great Britain but strong opposition from British sports bodies and athletes prevailed. As someone said to Coe after the 800m, 'There was no way you could lose, but you found a way.' Tactically, he had run like a novice, and it was remarkable

Sebastian Coe (All-Sport)

that he was able to salvage a silver medal – although that was little consolation to him or his father. The reaction from some of the media was almost savage, and it says much for the man that he was able to resurrect himself for the 1500m final, in which his perennial rival Ovett was now a 'sure thing'. In the event Coe did everything right, and when Jurgen Straub (GDR) injected pace into what began as a slow race (800m in 2min 04.9sec), he glided after him through a 54.6sec lap and then inserted two 'kicks' over the last 100m or so to take the gold medal, leaving Ovett in third place. It was one of the great comebacks of all time.

The following year he improved his world 800m mark down to 1min 41.73sec, and the mile record to 3min 47.33sec, and won the event in the European and World Cups. In 1982 he was part of a British team which broke the 4 × 800m world record with 7min 03.89sec at Crystal Palace. That, to date, is his last outdoor world record, but the following winter he set two more indoor marks, to bring his total to nine outdoor and three indoor world records. However, suffering from what was later diagnosed as a form of glandular fever, he again failed to win the European 800m title, placing second to a startled Hans-Peter Ferner (FRG). Despite patches of good form 1983 was a bad

year for Coe and it was evident that all was not well with his health. He withdrew from the track and did not race for eight months, his comeback being a road relay race at the end of March 1984 for his new club, Haringey AC. The trail back was hard and even six weeks prior to the Games Coe lost to Peter Elliott in the AAA 1500m championship, the race considered to be a decider for the vacant 1500m Olympic place. In fact, the British selectors chose Coe to double – Elliott was also in the 800m for Los Angeles – basing their decision more on past than current form. That they were vindicated is now history. As Peter Coe had inti-mated, Sebastian ran into form with four rounds of the 800m, coming second to the outstanding and worthy Brazilian winner, Joachim Cruz. Then in his seventh race of the Games he became the first man successfully to defend an Olympic 1500m title since James Lightbody (USA) in 1906, in one of the fastest ever races at champion-ship level.

After a year of training, Coe approached 1986 with a firm goal in mind, to win a major title over 800m. An influenza virus destroyed his Commonwealth Games hopes, but at his third European Cham-pionships, in Stuttgart, he finally achieved his ambition in his last championship race at the distance. The future is to be at 5000m.

Greg Louganis

Possibly the greatest diver the world has ever known, Greg Louganis was born to Samoan and Scots/English parents on 29 January 1960. At the age of 9 months he was adopted by Francis and Peter Louganis and grew up in a suburb of San Diego, California. From an early age he showed ability as an acrobat and a dancer, and studied dance from the age of 2. He began diving at the age of 9 and at 16 he was on the American Olympic team of 1976. At Montreal the coaching that he had been receiving for about a year from the 1948 and 1952 Olympic highboard champion, Dr Sammy Lee, came to fruition with a silver medal in the highboard and sixth place in the springboard.

In 1978 he won his first world title, in highboard diving. He won the same event in the 1979 FINA World Cup, and was gold medallist in the 1979 Pan-American Games in both diving events. At the start of Olympic year, 1980, he was favourite for both titles but the American boycott ended his hopes. Louganis made up for that disappointment by winning both diving events at the 1982 World Championships in Guayaquil, Ecuador, and it was during those championships that he became the first diver ever to be awarded the maximum marks by all seven judges for an inward 1½ somersault piked. He was now beginning completely to dominate world diving and in 1983 consolidated his position by double victories at both the Pan-American Games and the FINA World Cup. In the same year he graduated in drama from the University of California at Irvine, and had his appendix removed.

At the American Olympic Trials he won both dives, as he had in 1976 and 1980, and approached the Games at Los Angeles as one of the hottest favourites in any sport. He did not disappoint his fans, as he won both events by record margins with scores of 754.41 points in the springboard, and 710.91 points in the highboard. He was probably the most dominant champion at the 1984 Olympic Games, and as Klaus Dibiasi – his only rival for the 'best

Greg Louganis (All-Sport)

ever accolade' – said, 'I'm just glad that I don't have to compete against him, I'd have no chance.' The highboard/springboard double in the Olympics had not been achieved since 1928, but Louganis made it look easy. Although he appears to be extraordinarily calm during competition, he admits that 'they don't know what is going on inside', and he confesses to singing to himself on the board while waiting to perform his dives. He made a dramatic last dive at the Games – a reverse tuck 3½ somersault (with a 3.5 degree of difficulty) – a desperately difficult dive which had already claimed one life, that of 21-year-old Soviet diver Sergei Shalib-

ashvili at the 1983 World University Games, when he had smashed his head against the board.

Presented with the Sullivan Award for the best amateur sportsman in the United States in 1985, he has, at the time of writing, won a record 38 national diving titles, indoors and outdoors. In the World Championships of 1986 he again won both titles by big margins and thus equalled Dibiasi's record of three consecutive wins in the same event. His next target is the XXIV Olympic Games in Seoul in 1988 when he hopes to take his tally to a record five gold medals, thus ending a career of superlative achievement.

Francis Morgan 'Daley' Thompson

An Olympic decathlon champion is traditionally considered to be the best athlete in the world. By that criterion alone Daley Thompson may be the greatest athlete who ever lived. By the end of 1986, he had won two Olympic titles, the World Championship, two European Championships and three Commonwealth Games gold medals. Of 28 decathlon competitions he had won 19 and, more particularly, was unbeaten since his second place in the 1978 European title meeting. Additionally he is a top class sprinter/long jumper, and an above average hurdler and pole vaulter.

Thompson was born in the Notting Hill district of London on 30 July 1958, of a Scottish mother and Nigerian father. The name Daley is a corruption of Dele – short for the African name Ayodele. His father died when he was only 12 years of age. While at a boarding school in Sussex he joined an athletics club, and found a ready outlet for his highly competitive sporting drive, and in 1974 won the County 200m title. Returning to London the following year he joined the Essex Beagles club and met coach Bob Mortimer. He won the 1975 AAA junior indoor 60m championship, and aged 16 won his first decathlon at Cwmbran, Wales. He followed this with a win in the AAA junior decathlon championship, and ended the season as the third best in Britain. The following year he was selected for the Montreal Olympics, and, though placed eighteenth, learned much from the other competitors. In 1977 he set world junior records for the event and won the European Junior Championship in the Soviet Union. At the Commonwealth Games of 1978, in Edmonton, Alberta, he won by a remarkable margin, setting a Games long jump record during the decathlon discipline. But in the European Championships he lost to the Soviet athlete Aleksandr Grebenyuk.

The season of 1979 was highlighted by winning the long jump in the United Kingdom Championships, as he did not finish his only decathlon competition of the year. In May 1980, realizing that his main Olympic opposition, Guido Kratschmer (FRG), would not be at Moscow due to the boycott, he took him on and beat him setting a new world record of 8648 points (new tables). At the Olympics he had little trouble winning, and only rain on the second day stopped him bettering the world mark again.

The following year was a quiet one, but in 1982 he was in magnificent form, setting a world record of 8730 points at Götzis, Austria (one of his favourite places) in May, and then improving on it, to 8774 points, at the European Championships in Athens. At the end of the year he won the Commonwealth Games title in Brisbane. In 1983 he won the inaugural World Championship title, once again beating his perennial rival Jürgen Hingsen (FRG), even though he was not fully recovered from an injury. In the circumstance, his performance at Helsinki of 8666 points must rank as one of the greatest competitive exploits of all time.

Prior to the Los Angeles Olympic Games Hingsen improved the world mark again, to 8798 points (old tables), and seemed capable of finally getting the better of Thompson. Some people thought that the German second string Siggi Wentz would also be a serious threat. But Thompson, having spent most of the summer training just outside Los Angeles, was quite confident and told the press that,

Daley Thompson (All-Sport)

'The only way that Hingsen will go home with a gold medal is to steal mine or switch to another event.' The contest began with the 100m in which he clocked 10.44sec. Then he jumped a personal best legal jump of 8.01m *26ft 3½in*, and had a shot putt of 15.72m *51ft 7in*. A high jump of 2.03m *6ft 8in* and a 400m run of 46.97sec gave him a first day record score of 4633 points. He started the second day with a 14.34sec hurdles time and threw the discus 46.56m *152ft 9in*. Hingsen had now pulled back the deficit to only 32 points, but Thompson's pole vault of 5.00m *16ft 4¾in* reopened the gap, and with a javelin throw of 65.24m *214ft* he was virtually unassailable. Easing off at the end of the 1500m (the only decathlon event that he hates) Thompson ended the day with 8797 points, just one short of the world record. In fact, when the photo-finish pictures were re-examined some weeks later, it was found that his 110m hurdle time should have been given as 14.33sec, adding one point to his total, and thus equalling Hingsen's record. However, by then new scoring tables had been brought into being, and Thompson was the new record holder anyway. His new score was 8847 points. At Los Angeles he also ran the first leg of the British sprint relay team which finished seventh.

Ever the humorist, Daley both delighted and offended people with his comments and actions after the competition. He is a very complex man, a mixture of arrogance and humility, bonhomie with a nasty streak, extreme strong will and immaturity. He provokes intense loyalty in his friends, and equal dislike in others. He annoyed many of the crowd at the 1986 Commonwealth Games when he declined to put everything he had into the final 1500m when easily winning the whole competition. But most of those same critics were praising him to the skies at the European Championships, later in the year, when, finding himself behind Hingsen after seven events, his real competitiveness shone through. Despite another 'scare' from Wentz going into the 1500m at Stuttgart, Thompson recorded one of his best ever times to prove once again that there is only one 'best in the world'. Daley Thompson intends to go on proving it for many years to come.

Marja-Liisa Hämäläinen

Two years before the 1984 Winter Olympic Games at Sarajevo Marja-Liisa had seriously considered retiring from the sport of Nordic skiing, following a series of poor results. Happily she did not retire, and indeed went on the following two years to win the World Cups of her sport. But nothing had prepared her for the successes of those ten days in February 1984, when she totally dominated the women's cross-country skiing races as nobody had ever done before.

The tall, slim blonde had been born on 10 September 1955 in Simpole, Finland, and had begun skiing at the age of 5. Only a year later she was entering competitions, and in 1971 competed in the European Junior Championships. She gained only a sixth place in the individual competitions, but was a member of the winning Finnish relay team.

Her father and brothers were members of the national team and she was never short of subjects for her physiotherapy studies. She also took up athletics with some little success. Her first taste of Olympic

Marja-Liisa Hämäläinen (All-Sport)

competition came in 1976 at Innsbruck when she finished 22nd in the 10 000m event. At the World Championships held two years later in the Finnish town of Lahti she was a place further back, 23rd, in the 10 000m, but was sixteenth over 20 000m. However, she again won a gold medal as a member of the winning 4 × 5000m relay team. Her hoped-for breakthrough at the 1980 Olympics did not materialize as she placed eighteenth and nineteenth in the 10 000m and 5000m races respectively, and this time the Finnish relay team could only finish fifth.

Although she was winning national titles quite regularly – she won nine in all – her performances in the 1982 World Championships left much to be desired, with her best placing only an eleventh in the 10 000m, as well as a fourth in the relay. It was at this point that she had serious doubts about her future. However, she persevered and in the following two seasons was very successful, winning the World Cups, twice at 5000m and twice at 10 000m.

Her third Games, at Sarajevo, must have seemed like a fairy tale. Firstly, she won the 10 000m title by 18 seconds from the redoubtable Soviet skier Raisa Smetanina. Three days later she beat Norway's Berit Aunli by 10 seconds in the 5000m, with Kvetoslava Jeriova (TCH) in third place. Another three days later, in the 4 × 5000m relay, she had a hard-fought duel on the last leg with Jeriova for the silver medal placing – the Norwegian team was well in the lead. After a tremendous tussle, during which they left the Soviet skier well behind them, the Czech girl just managed to get in front, and Hämäläinen had to be content with a bronze. Then, yet another three days after that, she took the lead well before halfway and again beat Smetanina in the inaugural 20 000m event, winning by some 41sec. No Nordic skier, male or female, had ever won three individual gold medals at one Games.

After Sarajevo she married her team-mate, Harri Kirvesniemi, himself a three-time bronze medallist in 1980 and 1984, and in 1985 won two silver medals at the World Championships held in Seefeld, Austria.

Michael Gross

He gets a lot of fun from his swimming and will continue 'until the fun stops' – this is the credo of perhaps the finest swimmer that Germany has produced. Spectacularly built at 2.01m *6ft 7in* and 84kg *186lb*, Michael Gross has a remarkable span, from finger-tip to finger-tip, of 2.25m *7ft 4¾in*, a characteristic which has certainly not been a handicap in his swimming.

Born on 17 June 1964 at Frankfurt on Main, he began swimming at 4 years of age, but his early ambition, and one he still cherishes secretly, was to be a *Lufthansa* pilot. His current interest, outside swimming, is journalism, but, providing the 'fun' remains, his lean, bony body should be breaking records for a number of years yet. The child of a well-to-do family, he won his first German Junior title in 1979 (in fact he won four that year), and he would probably have been in two events at the 1980 Olympic Games but for the boycott by his country and others. In fact, the day before the Olympic 100m butterfly final in Moscow, Gross, in Canada, swam faster than the eventual gold medal winner.

His international career started in earnest at the 1981 European Championships in Split, Yugoslavia, where he won the 200m butterfly (setting a European record) and gained silver and bronze medals in relays. He also finished third in the 100m butterfly final but was disqualified for an irregular touch. The following year at the World Championships in Guayaquil, Ecuador, he won the 200m freestyle and 200m butterfly titles, beating the reigning world record holders in both events. Additionally he won silver medals in the 100m butterfly and 4 × 200m relay.

A very reserved and introverted individual, Gross was awarded the Sportsman of the Year trophy in Germany in 1982 and again in 1983. He has set nearly 50 German records in various events, and his first world mark came in June 1983 over 200m freestyle. That same year, in the European Championships in Rome, he set another world record, this time over 200m butterfly, to become the first male swimmer since Mark Spitz to hold world marks at two different strokes.

Although he had suffered a bad bout of influenza only two weeks before those European Championships he added three more gold

Michael Gross (All-Sport)

medals, over 200m freestyle, 100m butterfly and a relay, to his tally. Despite the approach of the Olympic Games he enrolled in the German Army to do his compulsory National Service. He was now saddled with a nickname 'The Albatross' which he did not like – it was probably referring to that enormous armspan that enabled him to take fewer strokes than most swimmers. Contrary to his nature he found himself the centre of media attention in Los Angeles, but this did not deter him and he started his programme auspiciously by winning the 200m freestyle in a new world record of 1min 47.44sec. The following day he added the 100m butterfly title with another world mark of 53.08sec, but about an hour later just failed to create an upset for his national 4 × 200m relay team by beating the United States quartet. In that race he entered the water on the last leg about 2 metres (1.56sec) behind the last American, Bruce Hayes. He tried to make up the deficit too quickly and tired towards the end losing by only 0.04sec (perhaps 7cm *3in*). The time for his 200m split was 1min 46.89sec, the fastest ever swum, and in recognition of his efforts the Americans refer to the race as the 'Gross relay'. Perhaps that race took more out of him than he thought as the rest of his swimming was almost anti-climactic. In the 4 × 100m freestyle and 4 × 100m medley relays his German team only came fourth, while the biggest surprise of the Games came in the 200m butterfly when Gross was beaten by the unheralded Jon Sieben of Australia. However, it should be noted that Sieben had to break Gross's world record to beat him. At the end of the season he was awarded the FINA Prize Eminence for 1984.

In 1985, at the European Championships in Sofia, he won a record six gold medals, in the 200m freestyle, 100m and 200m butterfly, and three relays, setting the only world mark of the meeting in the 200m butterfly. Also in 1985 he broke his first world record over 400m freestyle. At the World Championships the following year in Madrid he retained his titles in the 200m freestyle and 200m butterfly and again won silver medals in the medley and 4 × 200m freestyle relays.

Valerie Ann Brisco-Hooks

Like many another female athletes, Brisco-Hooks found that her performances improved dramatically after she became a mother, although even she could hardly have dreamed to what level that improvement would take her. In the sixth month of her pregnancy she had been a member of a sprint relay team that broke the American record. In many respects, it was the highlight of her career to that date. Her previous benchmark was when she had been a member of the US team at the 1979 Pan-American Games, after coming second in the

TAC championships 400m. At San Juan, Puerto Rico, she was fourth in the 400m, but had then won a gold medal in the 4 × 100m relay. That same year, while still in high school, she had run 400m in a surprising 52.08sec – it was to remain her personal best until the US Olympic Trials of 1984.

Brisco-Hooks was born in Greenwood, Mississippi on 6 July 1960, and in 1981 had married Alvin Hooks, a professional football player, who had himself been a reasonably successful sprinter. Her first performances of note came in 1977 when she was timed in 54.19sec for 400m. Missing the 1982 season because of her baby son, Alvin Jr, she made a comeback in 1983 and ended the pre-Olympic season with best times of 11.39sec for 100m and 23.10sec for 200m.

Valerie Brisco-Hooks (All-Sport)

Trained by Bob Kersee, her coach in 1979, she went through a hard programme of weight-training and distance runs, intended to build up her strength for the goals that they had set out for her. Unlike most of the top US athletes in 1984 she ran in the TAC championships, held only a week before the US Olympic Trials. She sent shock waves around the world with a new American record of 49.83sec for the 400m. A week later at the Trials she won the 200m with a personal best of 22.16sec, and bettered her 400m time with 49.79sec, but only came second as Chandra Cheeseborough set a new American record of 49.28sec. At the Games Valerie ran nine races in seven days and became the first athlete, male or female, to win the 200m and 400m titles at the same Olympic celebration.

She set Olympic and American records in all her finals. After the first one, the 400m in which she clocked an outstanding 48.83sec, her coach leapt the barrier on to the track and in front of 85,000 people they hugged and cried and wrestled each other to the ground in a moving display of uninhibited joy. The 200m final witnessed another superb performance of 21.81sec, raising the question of whether the absence of the crack East German women made much difference to the outcome of these races after all. Lastly she ran a 49.23sec third leg in the 4 × 400m relay, which the American team won easily in 3min 18.29sec.

After the Games, in Europe she was well beaten by the GDR sprinters over 200m, but the media gave that much more significance than it deserved. Brisco-Hooks had really passed her peak for the year, whereas the East German athletes had just reached theirs. However, in 1985, at the Weltklasse meeting in Zurich in August, she was ready for them and caused quite an upset, especially in the 100m in which she beat Marlies Gohr with a personal best time of 11.01sec. Later she also beat Marita Koch over 200m. Since then she has shown flashes of brilliance at all three distances, improving her 100m time to 10.99sec in 1986. She intends to defend her titles at Seoul in 1988, and has stated that she will still be around for 1992. By then Alvin Jr will probably be training with her.

Tracy Caulkins

To win five gold medals, as well as a silver, in the World Championships at the age of 15 would be sufficient achievement for most people. To be presented with the Sullivan Award, as the best amateur athlete in the United States, the youngest athlete ever to be given the award, would be honour enough for most people. To win a record 48 national swimming titles, 12 more than the legendary Johnny Weissmuller, would be enough for most people. But all of the above could not banish a feeling of loss in Tracy Caulkins, the greatest female swimmer produced by America. The particular loss that rankled was caused by the US boycott of the Moscow Olympics, at which she was expected to win as many as five gold medals.

Caulkins was born in Nashville, Tennessee, on 11 January 1963, and really started swimming to be with her older sister, Amy, and her brother, Tim. She won her first US national title in 1977, aged 14, taking the 100yd and 200yd events in the short-course championships. Later that same year she won the long-course 200m and 400m individual medley titles. Over the years she has won championships at all four strokes as well as in the medley events, and in total has broken over 60 US records. She originally preferred the backstroke, as it kept her face out of the water, but that soon changed. Later in her career she invented what is known as the 'Caulkins flutter' in breaststroke swimming, which caused some argument at first as to its legality.

Her outstanding 1978 season culminated in her record-breaking efforts in the World Championships in West Berlin. Her gold medals came in the 200m butterfly, 200m and 400m individual medleys, and the 4 × 100m freestyle and 4 × 100m medley relays, with an additional silver in the 100m breaststroke. She was making the individual medley races her own, and the following year won both of them at the Pan-American Games, as well as winning silver medals in the 100m breaststroke and 400m freestyle. She would have been in

Tracy Caulkins (All-Sport)

five individual events plus a relay in Moscow, and could well have bettered Kornelia Ender's single Games record of four golds, but international politics never gave her a chance.

In 1981 she swept all before her and started the 1982 World Championship season in the same vein. But a mix-up by the American swimming authorities over the dates of their trials, and the team's late arrival in Guayaquil leaving insufficient time to acclimatize, plus the effects of the local bugs, left Tracy a pale shadow of her normal self. She came away with only two bronze medals, in the individual medleys. Nevertheless, she was awarded the Broderick Cup for the top women's Collegiate athlete in America for that year.

The Los Angeles Olympic Games were now beckoning, renewing her dream of Olympic glory. In the run-up to them in 1983, she again won both individual medley titles at the Pan-American Games, and took a silver in the 200m butterfly. During Olympic year she raised to 12 the number of NCAA titles she had won for the University of Florida, and in the US Trials competed in six finals, winning three. It was an ironic twist of fate that at Los Angeles her biggest rivals, the GDR girls, were missing, as she had been when they had virtually swept the pool at Moscow in 1980. Caulkins won her first event, the 400m individual medley, by a huge margin of over 9 seconds. After that excitement she had to wait four days for the 100m breaststroke, in which she nearly didn't make the final. She was far too leisurely in her heat and was only advanced to the final, as the slowest qualifier, because the Italian Manuela Dalla Valle was disqualified for an improper kick. In that final she placed fourth. The following day, her last in major competition, provided the perfect swansong to an illustrious career. Firstly, she won the 200m individual medley by 2.53 seconds in a new Olympic record, and then, swimming the second, breaststroke, leg in the medley relay, she helped her team (incidentally she was the captain of the US women's swimming team) to win yet another gold medal. She hopes to make a career in radio and television broadcasting.

Frederick Carlton 'Carl' Lewis

Many men may dream of being a sporting hero, but very few dream of equalling the achievements of a legend. Only a rare few realize such a dream. One of those was Carl Lewis in the 1984 Olympic Games, where he matched the four gold medals achieved by the late, great, Jesse Owens 48 years earlier. As in Owens' case politics intruded into the 1984 celebration, with the Soviet-led boycott, but it is true to say that his events were not among those particularly affected by the absentees. In eight memorable days he raced eleven times and also competed in the qualifying round and final of the long jump. At the end of it all he had won gold medals in the 100m, 200m, long jump and 4 × 100m relay, exactly matching those won by Owens at Berlin, and as in Owens's case, nobody was really surprised.

The two athletes' lives began in a similar vein as Lewis was born in Alabama, as was Owens, on 1 July 1961. His family were very sports-orientated, as his mother Evelyn (neé Lawler) had been the US 80m hurdles champion in 1950, while his father had played football (the American variety) and run the 880yd at college. While he was still young the family moved to New Jersey, and his early interest was soccer, although he also competed in athletics at the club run by his parents. At this point, aged 12, he met his future hero, Jesse Owens. Initially his two elder brothers and his younger sister, Carol, showed more promise than he did. One problem was that he was quite small until he was about 15 years old — he is now a superbly built athlete standing 1.88m *6ft 2in* tall and weighing 80kg *176lb*.

He did not cause any interest until 1978 when he was timed in a wind-assisted 9.3sec for 100yd and jumped 7.85m *25ft 9in*, also with the wind helping. The following season he made dramatic improvements in all his events including a jump of 8.13m *26ft 8¼in*, which equalled the world record of Jesse Owens which had stood from 1935 to 1960. That same year, 1979, he placed second in the TAC long jump, and then won a bronze medal at the Pan-American Games. At the end of the year he went to the University of Houston and came under the guidance of Tom Tellez, who took over his coaching. Tellez changed his long jumping style to such advantage that he won the NCAA Championship with a leap of 8.35m *27ft 4¾in*. Winning the 100m and 200m in the American Junior Championships, he went on to place second in the Olympic Trials long jump and fourth in the 100m, thereby gaining election to the mythical US Olympic team of 1980 in the long jump and the 4 × 100m relay. Later in the year he won both sprints in the Pan-American Junior Championships.

Gaining strength from weight-training he broke the world indoor long jump mark with 8.49m *27ft 10¼in* in 1981, while outdoors at the TAC titles meeting he jumped the second best ever of 8.62m *28ft 3½in* (plus a windy 8.72m *28ft 7½in*), as well as winning the 100m. At the end of the year he was awarded the Sullivan Award as the best Amateur Sportsman in America. In 1982 he again won the 100m/long jump double at the TAC championships, and then improved his long jump best to 8.76m *28ft 9in*. He was now being likened to Owens, which he took as a great compliment, but he did say that, 'instead of being a second Owens, I'd like to be the first Carl Lewis'.

The year 1983 gave Lewis his first real international challenge with the inaugural World Championships in Helsinki. At the US Trials he won the 100m, then set another personal best in the long jump with 8.79m *28ft 10¼in*, and finally won the 200m in a US record of 19.75sec although he relaxed at the end losing a probable world record. He and Tellez decided not to go for the longer race at Helsinki, and so he 'only' won gold medals in the 100m, long jump and the 4 × 100m relay (in which he gained his first world record outdoors as the US team recorded 37.86sec). To add to the excitement his sister, Carol, won a bronze medal in the long jump for women. It was then that a goal of four golds at Los Angeles was seen as a strong possibility.

Beginning indoors with a new best of 8.79m, he tuned up for the Games with a series of excellent performances, culminating in the US Trials in which he qualified for his four events by winning the 100m, 200m and long jump. By now the show business bug had got him and prior to Los Angeles he made his first record *Going for the Gold*. At a Games with the greatest media coverage of almost any event in history, he was the centre of attention. But he proved he could deal with this well and still compete to the highest level. Firstly, he won the 100m in 9.99sec by a margin of 0.20sec, the biggest in Olympic 100m history. Then in the long jump, after leading the qualifying competition, he made his winning jump of 8.54m *28ft 0¹/₄in* in his first effort in the final. After a foul with his second jump he withdrew, to conserve his energies, a decision that was not at all popular with many spectators or the media. He then won the 200m with a new Olympic record of 19.80m, which, with a wind against him in the final straight, is considered to be intrinsically superior to the world record of 19.72sec set at altitude. Then, lastly, he anchored the US team to a new world mark of 37.83sec in the 4 × 100m relay, being timed for his leg in a breathtaking 8.94sec.

Since then injuries and other commitments have kept his performances low-key (but only by his standards), and in 1986 he had arthoscopic surgery on his left knee. So far he steadfastly refuses to go to altitude to attempt to beat Bob Beamon's fabulous long jump record of 8.90m *29ft 2¹/₂in* – Lewis maintains that on the right day he can beat it at sea level. Similarly with the 100m in which his 9.97sec at sea level compares favourably with the world mark of 9.93sec at altitude.

To the end of 1986 he had won 48 consecutive long jump competitions, a remarkable record in an event so prone to injury and error. As Lewis has said, 'I want to get every inch out of my life', and one cannot have a better ambition than that.

Carl Lewis (All-Sport)

The Sports

ARCHERY

The sport made its first appearance in the 1900 Games in Paris with six events on the programme. Some Olympic historians consider that another, live pigeon shooting, was an official event, but the majority think not, and this book follows that opinion. The eligibility of the 1904 archery competitions is also disputed by some, particularly as only American archers took part. However the majority of historians and the author accept them as Olympic events. The competitors in the 1904 women's contests were among the first women to compete in the Olympics, only the 1900 tennis players having a prior claim. The competitions of 1908 were accorded a much higher status than before, although only three nations took part. The men's York Round was won by William Dod (GBR) and

his remarkable sister, Charlotte, took the silver behind Queenie Newall in the women's event. Lottie Dod, then over 36 years old, was one of the greatest sportswomen of her, or any other, generation. She had won the Wimbledon tennis singles five times, the British Ladies golf crown in 1904, and had represented England at hockey. She also excelled at skating and tobogganing.

Archery was not included in the 1912 Games but, reflecting Belgium's great interest in the sport, there were ten events at Antwerp in 1920, all in the Belgian style of shooting. With only three countries present again, Hubert van Innis (BEL), now 54, brought his total medals to a record six golds and three silvers. The sport was dropped from the Games until 1972 when events were standardized into contests over Double FITA Rounds for men and women. A FITA (Fédération Internationale de Tir à l'Arc)

Round consists of 144 arrows, comprising 36 each over distances of 90m, 70m, 50m and 30m for men, and 70m, 60m, 50m and 30m for women. In 1988 there will also be team competitions.

The oldest gold medallist was the Rev Galen Spencer (USA) in the winning 1904 team two days past his 64th birthday. The youngest champion was Seo Hyang-Soon (KOR) aged 17yr 34 days winning the 1984 women's title. The youngest male winner was John Williams (USA) in 1972 aged 18yr 355 days, while the oldest female champion was his team-mate Doreen Wilber aged 42yr 246 days. The oldest ever medallist was Samuel Harding Duvall (USA) aged 68yr 194 days winning a silver in the 1904 team contest, while the youngest medallist was Henry Richardson (USA) with a team bronze in 1904 aged 15yr 126 days.

Archery

	Gold	Silver	Bronze
1900	*Au cordon doré – 50m* Henri Herouin (FRA)	Hubert van Innis (BEL)	Emile Fisseux (FRA)
	Au cordon doré – 33m Hubert van Innis (BEL)	Victor Thibaud (FRA)	Charles Petit (FRA)
	Au chapelet – 50m Eugène Mougin (FRA)	Henri Helle (FRA)	Emile Mercier (FRA)
	Au chapelet – 33m Hubert van Innis (BEL)	Victor Thibaud (FRA)	Charles Petit (FRA)
	Sur la perche à la herse Emmanuel Foulon (FRA)	Serrurier (FRA) Druat Jr (FRA)	–
	Sur la perche à la pyramide Emile Grumiaux (FRA)	Louis Glineux (FRA)	–
1904	**Men** *Double York Round* Phillip Bryant (USA)	Robert Williams (USA)	William Thompson (USA)
	Double American Round Phillip Bryant (USA)	Robert Williams (USA)	William Thompson (USA)
	Team Round Potamac Archers (USA)	Cincinatti Archery Club (USA)	Boston AA (USA)
	Women *Double National Round* Lida Howell (USA)	Jessie Pollack (USA)	Emma Cooke (USA)
	Double Columbia Round Lida Howell (USA)	Emma Cooke (USA)	Jessie Pollack (USA)
	Team Round Cincinatti Archery Club (USA)	Potamac Archers (USA)	–
1908	**Men** *York Round* William Dod (GBR)	R B Brooks-King (GBR)	Henry Richardson (USA)
	Continental Style E G Grisot (FRA)	Louis Vernet (FRA)	Gustave Cabaret (FRA)
	Women *National Round* Queenie Newall (GBR)	Charlotte Dod (GBR)	Hill-Lowe (GBR)
1920	*Fixed bird target – small birds – individual* Edmond van Moer (BEL)	Louis van de Perck (BEL)	Joseph Hermans (BEL)
	Fixed bird target – small birds – team Belgium	–	–
	Fixed bird target – large birds – individual Edouard Cloetens (BEL)	Louis van de Perck (BEL)	Firmin Flamand (BEL)

Darrell Pace (USA) won back the title he lost by default in 1980. (All-Sport)

Gold	Silver	Bronze
Fixed bird target – large birds – team Belgium	–	–
Moving bird target – 28m – individual Hubert van Innis (BEL)	Léonce Quentin (FRA)	–
Moving bird target – 28m – team Netherlands	Belgium	France
Moving bird target – 33m – individual Hubert van Innis (BEL)	Julien Brulé (FRA)	–
Moving bird target – 33m – team Belgium	France	–
Moving bird target – 50m – individual Julien Brulé (FRA)	Hubert van Innis (BEL)	–
Moving bird target – 50m – team Belgium	France	–

DOUBLE FITA ROUND (maximum possible score 2880 points)

Men

	Gold	Silver	Bronze
1972	John Williams (USA) 2528pts	Gunnar Jarvil (SWE) 2481pts	Kyösti Laasonen (FIN) 2467pts
1976	Darrell Pace (USA) 2571pts	Hiroshi Michinaga (JPN) 2502pts	Giancarlo Ferrari (ITA) 2495pts
1980	Tomi Poikolainen (FIN) 2455pts	Boris Isachenko (URS) 2452pts	Aleksandr Gazov (URS) 2449pts
1984	Darrell Pace (USA) 2616pts*	Richard McKinney (USA) 2564pts	Hiroshi Yamamoto (JPN) 2563pts

Women

	Gold	Silver	Bronze
1972	Doreen Wilber (USA) 2424pts	Irena Szydlowska (POL) 2407pts	Emma Gapchenko (URS) 2403pts
1976	Luann Ryon (USA) 2499pts	Valentina Kovpan (URS) 2460pts	Zebeniso Rustamova (URS) 2407pts
1980	Keto Losaberidze (URS) 2491pts	Natalya Butuzova (URS) 2477pts	Päivi Meriluoto (FIN) 2449pts
1984	Hyang-Soon Seo (KOR) 2568pts*	Lingjuan Li (CHN) 2559pts	Jin-Ho Kim (KOR) 2555pts

*Olympic record

Archery – Medals

	Men			Women			
	G	S	B	G	S	B	Total
United States	6	4	4	5	3	2	24
France	6	9	6	–	–	–	21
Belgium	10	7	2	–	–	–	19
Soviet Union	–	1	–	1	2	2	6
Great Britain	1	1	–	1	1	1	5
Finland	1	–	1	–	–	1	3
Korea	–	–	–	1	–	1	2
Japan	–	1	1	–	–	–	2
Italy	–	–	2	–	–	–	2
Netherlands	1	–	–	–	–	–	1
China	–	–	–	–	1	–	1
Poland	–	–	–	–	1	–	1
Sweden	–	1	–	–	–	–	1
	25[1]	24[2]	16[3]	8	8	7[4]	88

[1]Only a gold medal awarded in two 1920 events.
[2]Two silvers awarded in a 1900 event.
[3]No bronze medals in two 1900 events and six 1920 events.
[4]No bronze medal in 1904 team event.

BASKETBALL

The game made its official Olympic debut in 1936, although it was demonstrated in 1904, and the analogous Dutch game Korfball was demonstrated in 1928. The 1936 tournament was uniquely played outdoors, and one of the referees was Avery Brundage (USA), later to become President of the IOC, while the man who had devised the modern game, Dr James Naismith, presented the medals. The tournament was won by the United States, beginning a winning streak of seven titles and 63 victories until they were beaten by the Soviet Union 51-50 in the 1972 final. That final was much disputed, the Americans claiming that too much overtime was played during which the Soviet Aleksandr Belov (who tragically died six years later) scored the winning basket. With one second to go, and the USA in the lead 50-49, the Soviet inbounds pass had been deflected and everyone thought the game over. However, the Soviet team was given another inbounds chance, but did not score. Again the game seemed to be over. But Dr William Jones (GBR), Secretary-General of FIBA (Fédération Internationale de Basketball Amateur), stated that play was incorrectly restarted at one second and that there should have been three seconds allowed. The clock was then reset to three seconds and the Soviet team scored. The US team protested vigorously and refused to accept the silver medals. With their 1984 win the USA brought its overall Olympic tally to 77-1.

After various changes and qualifying conditions since 1976 the IOC has accepted 18 teams in basketball so allowing FIBA to allocate 12 places to the men's competition and six to the women. The Palacia de los Deportes in Mexico City in 1968 had a record capacity for an Olympic basketball game of 22 370 seats. A member of the star-studded US team of 1960, Burdette Haldorson, is the only player to win two gold medals, in 1956 and 1960. Sergey Belov (URS) is the only one to win medals in four Games, with a gold and three bronzes between 1968 and 1980 (at the latter Games he brought the torch into the stadium

United States confronts the Soviet Union in the controversial 1972 basketball final. (All-Sport)

and lit the Olympic flame). The oldest gold medallist was Gennadiy Volnov (URS) in 1972 aged 32yr 286 days, while the youngest was Spencer Haywood (USA) aged 19yr 186 days in 1968.

The highest aggregate score in a game is 221 points when the Soviet Union beat Spain 119-102, and when Brazil beat India 137-64, both in 1980. The Brazilian score is the highest ever by a team in Olympic contests. The biggest margin of victory is 100 points, when Korea beat Iraq 120-20, and when China beat Iraq 125-25, both in 1948.

In the women's game Japan beat Canada 121-89 for an aggregate record of 210 points, while the highest total was 122 by the Soviet Union against Bulgaria (83) in 1980. The biggest margin was 66 points when the Soviet Union beat Italy 119-53 in 1980. The tallest ever player in Olympic basketball, and the tallest ever medallist in any sport, was Tommy Burleson (USA) at 2.23m *7ft 4in* in 1972. The tallest female player, and the tallest Olympic female gold medallist ever, was Iuliana Semenova (URS) at 2.18m *7ft 1¾in* in 1976 and 1980. She was also the heaviest female gold medallist ever at 129kg *284lb*.

Basketball

	Gold	Silver	Bronze
Men			
1936	United States	Canada	Mexico
1948	United States	France	Brazil
1952	United States	Soviet Union	Uruguay
1956	United States	Soviet Union	Uruguay
1960	United States	Soviet Union	Brazil
1964	United States	Soviet Union	Brazil
1968	United States	Yugoslavia	Soviet Union
1972	Soviet Union	United States	Cuba
1976	United States	Yugoslavia	Soviet Union
1980	Yugoslavia	Italy	Soviet Union
1984	United States	Spain	Yugoslavia

1896–1932 Event not held

	Gold	Silver	Bronze
Women			
1976	Soviet Union	United States	Bulgaria
1980	Soviet Union	Bulgaria	Yugoslavia
1984	United States	Korea	China

1896–1972 Event not held

Basketball – Medals

	Men			Women			
	G	S	B	G	S	B	Total
United States	9	1	–	1	1	–	12
Soviet Union	1	4	3	2	–	–	10
Yugoslavia	1	2	1	–	–	1	5
Brazil	–	–	3	–	–	–	3
Bulgaria	–	–	–	–	1	1	2
Uruguay	–	–	2	–	–	–	2
Canada	–	1	–	–	–	–	1
France	–	1	–	–	–	–	1
Italy	–	1	–	–	–	–	1
Korea	–	–	–	–	1	–	1
Spain	–	1	–	–	–	–	1
China	–	–	–	–	–	1	1
Cuba	–	–	1	–	–	–	1
Mexico	–	–	1	–	–	–	1
	11	11	11	3	3	3	42

London policeman Harry Mallin, the first man successfully to defend an Olympic boxing title. (GSL)

BOXING

Contests were included in the ancient Games in 688 BC, when competitors wore leather straps on their hands. As the status of the Games deteriorated in Roman times, metal studs were added. The last known champion before the Games were abolished was Varazdetes (or Varastades), the winner in AD 369, who later became King of Armenia. This type of boxing should not be confused with the *pankration* event, which was a brutal combination of boxing and wrestling in which virtually anything was permitted. It is recorded that Arrachion of Phigalia was awarded the title in 564 BC, as his opponent 'gave up' – although Arrachion was by then lying dead in the arena.

Boxing was included in the modern Games in 1904 when the USA won all the titles. A pattern was set by the first heavyweight champion, Samuel Berger, when he turned professional after his victory. Incidentally he was a member of the San Francisco Olympic Club which had also produced 'Gentleman Jim' Corbett who had won the world title in 1892. Over the years the weight limits for the various classes have changed, and new classes added. Bronze medals for losing semi-finalists were not awarded until 1952.

Two men have won three golds. László Papp (HUN), a southpaw, won the middleweight division in 1948 and the light-middleweight class in 1952 and 1956, while Teofilo

Stevenson (CUB) won the same class, heavyweight, from 1972 to 1980. In 1904 Oliver Kirk (USA) won two events at the same Games, also unique. The first boxer to defend successfully a title was Harry Mallin (GBR) with the middleweight crown in 1920 and 1924. In those 1924 Games the standard of refereeing was highly suspect, not least because the European custom of seating the referees outside the ring was followed. Mallin was continually fouled by his French opponent in a preliminary bout, and ended the fight with teeth marks on his chest. Despite this the outclassed Frenchman was declared the winner of the bout. An immediate appeal, backed by the threatened withdrawal of all the English-speaking countries, was upheld. A strange occurrence was the disqualification of Ingemar Johansson (SWE) in the 1952 heavyweight final, and the withholding of the silver medal due to 'inactivity in the ring'. Thirty years

later he was presented with his medal. In 1984 protective headgear was introduced as a safety measure, and again there was a number of controversial decisions.

The oldest gold medallist was Richard Gunn (GBR), the 1908 featherweight champion, aged 37yr 254 days. The youngest was Jackie Fields (USA) winning the 1924 featherweight crown aged 16yr 162 days. Floyd Patterson (USA) won the 1952 middleweight title aged 17yr 211 days, and four years later was the youngest ever world professional heavyweight champion.

Olympic boxing champions who have won world professional titles include (alphabetically); Nino Benvenuti (ITA), Mark Breland (USA), Cassius Clay (later Muhammad Ali) (USA), Jackie Fields (USA), George Foreman (USA), Joe Frazier (USA), Frankie Genaro (USA), Fidel LaBarba (USA), Ray Leonard (USA), Patrizio Oliva (ITA), Mate Parlov

(YUG), Floyd Patterson (USA), Pascual Perez (ARG), Leon and Michael Spinks (USA).

The Val Barker Cup is presented by the International Amateur Boxing Association (AIBA) to the competitor adjudged the best stylist at the Games. First awarded in 1936, the winners have been:

1936	Louis Laurie (USA)
	Bronze – flyweight
1948	George Hunter (SAF)
	Gold – light-heavyweight
1952	Norvel Lee (USA)
	Gold – light-heavyweight
1956	Dick McTaggart (GBR)
	Gold – lightweight
1960	Giovanni Benvenuti (ITA)
	Gold – welterweight
1964	Valery Popentschenko (URS)
	Gold – middleweight
1968	Philip Waruinge (KEN)
	Bronze – featherweight
1972	Teofilo Stevenson (CUB)
	Gold – heavyweight
1976	Howard Davis (USA)
	Gold – lightweight
1980	Patrizio Oliva (ITA)
	Gold – light-welterweight
1984	Paul Gonzales (USA)
	Gold – light-flyweight

Boxing

Gold	Silver	Bronze

Light-Flyweight
Weight up to 48kg *105.8lb*

	Gold	Silver	Bronze
1968	Francisco Rodriguez (VEN)	Yong-ju Jee (KOR)	Harlan Marbley (USA)
			Hubert Skrzypczak (POL)
1972	György Gedo (HUN)	U Gil Kim (PRK)	Ralph Evans (GBR)
			Enrique Rodriguez (ESP)
1976	Jorge Hernandez (CUB)	Byong Uk Li (PRK)	Payao Pooltarat (THA)
			Orlando Maldonado (PUR)
1980	Shamil Sabirov (URS)	Hipolito Ramos (CUB)	Byong Uk Li (PRK)
			Ismail Moustafov (BUL)
1984	Paul Gonzales (USA)	Salvatore Todisco (ITA)	Keith Mwila (ZAM)
			Jose Bolivar (VEN)

1896–1964 Event not held.

Flyweight
From 1948 the weight limit has been 51kg *112½lb*. In 1904 it was *105lb* 47.6kg. From 1920 to 1936 it was *112lb* 50.8kg.

	Gold	Silver	Bronze
1904	George Finnegan (USA)	Miles Burke (USA)	–*
1920	Frank De Genaro (USA)	Anders Petersen (DEN)	William Cuthbertson (GBR)
1924	Fidel LaBarba (USA)	James McKenzie (GBR)	Raymond Fee (USA)
1928	Antal Kocsis (HUN)	Armand Appel (FRA)	Carlo Cavagnoli (ITA)
1932	István Énekes (HUN)	Francisco Cabanas (MEX)	Louis Salica (USA)
1936	Willi Kaiser (GER)	Gavino Matta (ITA)	Louis Laurie (USA)
1948	Pascual Perez (ARG)	Spartaco Bandinelli (ITA)	Soo-Ann Han (KOR)
1952	Nathan Brooks (USA)	Edgar Basel (GER)	Anatoliy Bulakov (URS)
			William Toweel (SAF)
1956	Terence Spinks (GBR)	Mircea Dobrescu (ROM)	John Caldwell (IRL)
			René Libeer (FRA)
1960	Gyula Török (HUN)	Sergey Sivko (URS)	Kyoshi Tanabe (JPN)
			Abdelmoneim Elguindi (EGY)
1964	Fernando Atzori (ITA)	Artur Olech (POL)	Robert Carmody (USA)
			Stanislav Sorokin (URS)
1968	Ricardo Delgado (MEX)	Artur Olech (POL)	Servilio Oliveira (BRA)
			Leo Rwabwogo (UGA)
1972	Gheorghi Kostadinov (BUL)	Leo Rwabwogo (UGA)	Leszek Blazynski (POL)
			Douglas Rodriguez (CUB)
1976	Leo Randolph (USA)	Ramon Duvalon (CUB)	Leszek Blazynski (POL)
			David Torosyan (URS)
1980	Petar Lessov (BUL)	Viktor Miroshnichenko (URS)	Hugh Russell (IRL)
			Janos Varadi (HUN)
1984	Steve McCrory (USA)	Redzep Redzepovski (YUG)	Eyup Can (TUR)
			Ibrahim Bilali (KEN)

1896–1900, 1906–1912 Event not held. *No third place.

Gold	Silver	Bronze

Bantamweight
From 1948 the weight limit has been 54kg *119lb*. In 1904 it was *115lb* 52.16kg. In 1908 it was *116lb* 52.62kg. From 1920 to 1936 *118lb* 53.52kg.

	Gold	Silver	Bronze
1904	Oliver Kirk (USA)	George Finnegan (USA)	–*
1908	Henry Thomas (GBR)	John Condon (GBR)	W Webb (GBR)
1920	Clarence Walker (SAF)	Christopher Graham (CAN)	James McKenzie (GBR)
1924	William Smith (SAF)	Salvatore Tripoli (USA)	Jean Ces (FRA)
1928	Vittorio Tamagnini (ITA)	John Daley (USA)	Harry Isaacs (SAF)
1932	Horace Gwynne (CAN)	Hans Ziglarski (GER)	José Villanueva (PHI)
1936	Ulderico Sergo (ITA)	Jack Wilson (USA)	Fidel Ortiz (MEX)
1948	Tibor Csik (HUN)	Giovanni Zuddas (ITA)	Juan Venegas (PUR)
1952	Pentti Hämäläinen (FIN)	John McNally (IRL)	Gennadiy Garbuzov (URS)
			Joon-Ho Kang (KOR)
1956	Wolfgang Behrendt (GER)	Soon-Chun Song (KOR)	Frederick Gilroy (IRL)
			Claudio Barrientos (CHI)
1960	Oleg Grigoryev (URS)	Primo Zamparini (ITA)	Brunoh Bendig (POL)
			Oliver Taylor (AUS)
1964	Takao Sakurai (JPN)	Shin Cho Chung (KOR)	Juan Fabila Mendoza (MEX)
			Washington Rodriguez (URU)
1968	Valeriy Sokolov (URS)	Eridadi Mukwanga (UGA)	Eiji Morioka (JPN)
			Kyou-Chull Chang (KOR)
1972	Orlando Martinez (CUB)	Alfonso Zamora (MEX)	George Turpin (GBR)
			Ricardo Carreras (USA)
1976	Yong Jo Gu (PRK)	Charles Mooney (USA)	Patrick Cowdell (GBR)
			Chulsoon Hwang (KOR)
1980	Juan Hernandez (CUB)	Bernardo Pinango (VEN)	Dumitru Cipere (ROM)
			Michael Anthony (GUY)
1984	Maurizio Stecca (ITA)	Hector Lopez (MEX)	Dale Walters (CAN)
			Pedro Nolasco (DOM)

1896–1900, 1906, 1912 Event not held. *No third place.

Featherweight
From 1952 the weight limit has been 57kg *126lb*. In 1904 it was *125lb* 56.70kg. From 1908 to 1936 it was *126lb* 57.15kg. In 1948 it was 58kg *127¾lb*.

	Gold	Silver	Bronze
1904	Oliver Kirk (USA)	Frank Haller (USA)	Fred Gilmore (USA)
1908	Richard Gunn (GBR)	C W Morris (GBR)	Hugh Roddin (GBR)
1920	Paul Fritsch (FRA)	Jean Gachet (FRA)	Edoardo Garzena (ITA)
1924	John Fields (USA)	Joseph Salas (USA)	Pedro Quartucci (ARG)
1928	Lambertus van Klaveren (HOL)	Victor Peralta (ARG)	Harold Devine (USA)
1932	Carmelo Robledo (ARG)	Josef Schleinkofer (GER)	Carl Carlsson (SWE)
1936	Oscar Casanovas (ARG)	Charles Catterall (SAF)	Josef Miner (GER)
1948	Ernesto Formenti (ITA)	Denis Shepherd (SAF)	Aleksey Antkiewicz (POL)
1952	Jan Zachara (TCH)	Sergio Caprari (ITA)	Joseph Ventaja (FRA)
			Leonard Leisching (SAF)
1956	Vladimir Safronov (URS)	Thomas Nicholls (GBR)	Henryk Niedzwiedzki (POL)
			Pentti Hämäläinen (FIN)
1960	Francesco Musso (ITA)	Jerzy Adamski (POL)	William Meyers (SAF)
			Jorma Limmonen (FIN)
1964	Stanislav Stepashkin (URS)	Antony Villaneuva (PHI)	Charles Brown (USA)
			Heinz Schultz (GER)
1968	Antonio Roldan (MEX)	Albert Robinson (USA)	Philip Waruinge (KEN)
			Ivan Michailov (BUL)
1972	Boris Kuznetsov (URS)	Philip Waruinge (KEN)	Clemente Rojas (COL)
			András Botos (HUN)
1976	Angel Herrera (CUB)	Richard Nowakowski (GDR)	Juan Paredes (MEX)
			Leszek Kosedowski (POL)
1980	Rudi Fink (GDR)	Adolfo Horta (CUB)	Viktor Rybakov (URS)
			Krzysztof Kosedowski (POL)
1984	Meldrick Taylor (USA)	Peter Konyegwachie (NGR)	Turgut Aykac (TUR)
			Omar Peraza (VEN)

1896–1900, 1906, 1912 Event not held.

Lightweight
From 1952 the weight has been 60kg *132lb*. In 1904 and from 1920 to 1936 it was *135lb* 61.24kg. In 1908 it was *140lb* 63.50kg. In 1948 it was 62kg *136½lb*.

	Gold	Silver	Bronze
1904	Harry Spanger (USA)	James Eagan (USA)	Russell Van Horn (USA)
1908	Frederick Grace (GBR)	Frederick Spiller (GBR)	H H Johnson (GBR)
1920	Samuel Mosberg (USA)	Gotfred Johansen (DEN)	Clarence Newton (CAN)
1924	Hans Nielsen (DEN)	Alfredo Coppello (ARG)	Frederick Boylstein (USA)
1928	Carlo Orlandi (ITA)	Stephen Halaiko (USA)	Gunnar Berggren (SWE)
1932	Lawrence Stevens (SAF)	Thure Ahlqvist (SWE)	Nathan Bor (USA)
1936	Imre Harangi (HUN)	Nikolai Stepulov (EST)	Erik Agren (SWE)
1948	Gerald Dreyer (SAF)	Joseph Vissers (BEL)	Svend Wad (DEN)
1952	Aureliano Bolognesi (ITA)	Aleksey Antkiewicz (POL)	Gheorghe Fiat (ROM)
			Erkki Pakkanen (FIN)
1956	Richard McTaggart (GBR)	Harry Kurschat (GER)	Anthony Byrne (IRL)
			Anatoliy Lagetko (URS)
1960	Kazimierz Pazdzior (POL)	Sandro Lopopoli (ITA)	Richard McTaggart (GBR)
			Abel Laudonio (ARG)
1964	Józef Grudzien (POL)	Vellikton Barannikov (URS)	Ronald Harris (USA)
			James McCourt (IRL)
1968	Ronald Harris (USA)	Józef Grudzien (POL)	Calistrat Cutov (ROM)
			Zvonimir Vujin (YUG)
1972	Jan Szczepanski (POL)	László Orban (HUN)	Samuel Mbugua (KEN)
			Alfonso Perez (COL)
1976	Howard Davis (USA)	Simion Cutov (ROM)	Ace Rusevski (YUG)
			Vasiliy Solomin (URS)

	Gold	Silver	Bronze
1980	Angel Herrera (CUB)	Viktor Demianenko (URS)	Kazimierz Adach (POL)
			Richard Nowakowski (GDR)
1984	Pernell Whitaker (USA)	Luis Ortiz (PUR)	Martin Ebanga (CMR)
			Chi-Sung Chun (KOR)

1896–1900, 1906, 1912 Event not held.

Light-Welterweight
Weight up to 63.5kg *140lb.*

	Gold	Silver	Bronze
1952	Charles Adkins (USA)	Viktor Mednov (URS)	Erkki Mallenius (FIN)
			Bruno Visintin (ITA)
1956	Vladimir Yengibaryan (URS)	Franco Nenci (ITA)	Henry Loubscher (SAF)
			Constantin Dumitrescu (ROM)
1960	Bohumil Nemecek (TCH)	Clement Quartey (GHA)	Quincy Daniels (USA)
			Marian Kasprzyk (POL)
1964	Jerzy Kulej (POL)	Yegeniy Frolov (URS)	Eddie Blay (GHA)
			Habib Galhia (TUN)
1968	Jerzy Kulej (POL)	Enrique Regueiferos (CUB)	Arto Nilsson (FIN)
			James Wallington (USA)
1972	Ray Seales (USA)	Anghel Anghelov (BUL)	Zvonimir Vujin (YUG)
			Issaka Daborg (NIG)
1976	Ray Leonard (USA)	Andres Aldama (CUB)	Vladimir Kolev (BUL)
			Kazimierz Szczerba (POL)
1980	Patrizio Oliva (ITA)	Serik Konakbayev (URS)	Jose Aguilar (CUB)
			Anthony Willis (GBR)
1984	Jerry Page (USA)	Dhawee Umponmaha (THA)	Mircea Fuger (ROM)
			Mirko Puzovic (YUG)

1896–1948 Event not held.

Welterweight
From 1948 the weight limit has been 67kg *148lb.* In 1904 it was *143¾lb* 65.27kg. From 1920 to 1936 it was *147lb* 66.68kg.

	Gold	Silver	Bronze
1904	Albert Young (USA)	Harry Spanger (USA)	Joseph Lydon (USA)
			James Eagan (USA)
1920	Albert Schneider (CAN)	Alexander Ireland (GBR)	Frederick Colberg (USA)
1924	Jean Delarge (BEL)	Héctor Mendez (ARG)	Douglas Lewis (CAN)
1928	Edward Morgan (NZL)	Raul Landini (ARG)	Raymond Smillie (CAN)
1932	Edward Flynn (USA)	Erich Campe (GER)	Bruno Ahlberg (FIN)
1936	Sten Suvio (FIN)	Michael Murach (GER)	Gerhard Petersen (DEN)
1948	Julius Torma (TCH)	Horace Herring (USA)	Alessandro D'Ottavio (ITA)
1952	Zygmunt Chychla (POL)	Sergey Schtsherbakov (URS)	Victor Jörgensen (DEN)
			Günther Heidemann (GER)
1956	Nicholae Lince (ROM)	Frederick Tiedt (IRL)	Kevin Hogarth (AUS)
			Nicholas Gargano (GBR)
1960	Giovanni Benvenuti (ITA)	Yuriy Radonyak (URS)	Leszek Drogosz (POL)
			James Lloyd (GBR)
1964	Marian Kasprzyk (POL)	Ritschardas Tamulis (URS)	Pertti Purhonen (FIN)
			Silvano Bertini (ITA)
1968	Manfred Wolke (GDR)	Joseph Bessala (CMR)	Vladimir Musalinov (URS)
			Mario Guilloti (ARG)
1972	Emilio Correa (CUB)	Janos Kajdi (HUN)	Dick Murunga (KEN)
			Jesse Valdez (USA)
1976	Jochen Bachfeld (GDR)	Pedro Gamarro (VEN)	Reinhard Skricek (GER)
			Victor Zilberman (ROM)
1980	Andres Aldama (CUB)	John Mugabi (UGA)	Karl-Heinz Krüger (GDR)
			Kazimierz Szczerba (POL)
1984	Mark Breland (USA)	Young-Su An (KOR)	Joni Nyman (FIN)
			Luciano Bruno (ITA)

1896–1900, 1906–1912 Event not held.

Light-Middleweight
Weight up to 71kg *157lb.*

	Gold	Silver	Bronze
1952	László Papp (HUN)	Theunis van Schalkwyk (SAF)	Boris Tishin (URS)
			Eladio Herrera (ARG)
1956	László Papp (HUN)	José Torres (USA)	John McCormack (GBR)
			Zbigniew Pietrzkowski (POL)
1960	Wilbert McClure (USA)	Carmelo Bossi (ITA)	Boris Lagutin (URS)
			William Fisher (GBR)
1964	Boris Lagutin (URS)	Josef Gonzales (FRA)	Nojim Maiyegun (NGR)
			Jozef Grzesiak (POL)
1968	Boris Lagutin (URS)	Rolando Garbey (CUB)	John Baldwin (USA)
			Günther Meier (FRG)
1972	Dieter Kottysch (GER)	Wieslaw Rudkowski (POL)	Alan Minter (GBR)
			Peter Tiepold (GDR)
1976	Jerzy Rybicki (POL)	Tadija Kacar (YUG)	Rolando Garbey (CUB)
			Viktor Savchenko (URS)
1980	Armando Martinez (CUB)	Aleksandr Koshkin (URS)	Jan Franck (TCH)
			Detlef Kastner (GDR)
1984	Frank Tate (USA)	Shawn O'Sullivan (CAN)	Manfred Zielonka (FRG)
			Christophe Tiozzo (FRA)

1896–1948 Event not held.

Middleweight
From 1952 the weight limit has been 75kg *165lb.* From 1904 to 1908 it was *158lb* 71.68kg. From 1920 to 1936 it was *160lb* 72.57kg. In 1948 it was 73kg *161lb.*

	Gold	Silver	Bronze
1904	Charles Mayer (USA)	Benjamin Spradley (USA)	–*
1908	John Douglas (GBR)	Reginald Baker (AUS/NZL)	W Philo (GBR)
1920	Harry Mallin (GBR)	Georges Prud'homme (CAN)	Moe Herscovitch (CAN)
1924	Harry Mallin (GBR)	John Elliott (GBR)	Joseph Beecken (BEL)

	Gold	*Silver*	*Bronze*
1928	Piero Toscani (ITA)	Jan Hermánek (TCH)	Léonard Steyaert (BEL)
1932	Carmen Barth (USA)	Amado Azar (ARG)	Ernest Pierce (SAF)
1936	Jean Despeaux (FRA)	Henry Tiller (NOR)	Raúl Villareal (ARG)
1948	László Papp (HUN)	John Wright (GBR)	Ivano Fontana (ITA)
1952	Floyd Patterson (USA)	Vasile Tita (ROM)	Boris Nikolov (BUL)
			Stig Sjolin (SWE)
1956	Gennadiy Schatkov (URS)	Ramón Tapia (CHI)	Gilbert Chapron (FRA)
			Victor Zalazar (ARG)
1960	Edward Crook (USA)	Tadeusz Walasek (POL)	Ion Monea (ROM)
			Evgeniy Feofanov (URS)
1964	Valeriy Popentschenko (URS)	Emil Schultz (GER)	Franco Valle (ITA)
			Tadeusz Walasek (POL)
1968	Christopher Finnegan (GBR)	Aleksey Kisselyov (URS)	Agustin Zaragoza (MEX)
			Alfred Jones (USA)
1972	Vyatcheslav Lemechev (URS)	Reima Virtanen (FIN)	Prince Amartey (GHA)
			Marvin Johnson (USA)
1976	Michael Spinks (USA)	Rufat Riskiev (URS)	Alec Nastac (ROM)
			Luis Martinez (CUB)
1980	Jose Gomez (CUB)	Viktor Savchenko (URS)	Jerzy Rybicki (POL)
			Valentin Silaghi (ROM)
1984	Joon-Sup Shin (KOR)	Virgil Hill (USA)	Mohamed Zaoui (ALG)
			Aristides Gonzalez (PUR)

1896–1900, 1906, 1912 Event not held. *No third place.

Light-Heavyweight
From 1952 the weight limit has been 81kg *178½lb*. From 1920 to 1936 it was *175lb* 79.38kg. In 1948 it was 80kg *186¼lb*.

	Gold	Silver	Bronze
1920	Edward Eagan (USA)	Sverre Sörsdal (NOR)	H Franks (GBR)
1924	Harry Mitchell (GBR)	Thyge Petersen (DEN)	Sverre Sörsdal (NOR)
1928	Victor Avendano (ARG)	Ernst Pistulla (GER)	Karel Miljon (HOL)
1932	David Carstens (SAF)	Gino Rossi (ITA)	Peter Jörgensen (DEN)
1936	Roger Michelot (FRA)	Richard Vogt (GER)	Francisco Risiglione (ARG)
1948	George Hunter (SAF)	Donald Scott (GBR)	Maurio Cla (ARG)
1952	Norvel Lee (USA)	Antonio Pacenza (ARG)	Anotiliy Perov (URS)
			Harri Siljander (FIN)
1956	James Boyd (USA)	Gheorghe Negrea (ROM)	Carlos Lucas (CHI)
			Romualdas Murauskas (URS)
1960	Cassius Clay (USA)	Zbigniew Pietrzykowski (POL)	Anthony Madigan (AUS)
			Giulio Saraudi (ITA)
1964	Cosimo Pinto (ITA)	Aleksey Kisselyov (URS)	Aleksandr Nikolov (BUL)
			Zbigniew Pietrzykowski (POL)
1968	Dan Poznyak (URS)	Ion Monea (ROM)	Georgy Stankov (BUL)
			Stanislav Gragan (POL)
1972	Mate Parlov (YUG)	Gilberto Carrillo (CUB)	Isaac Ikhouria (NGR)
			Janusz Gortat (POL)
1976	Leon Spinks (USA)	Sixto Soria (CUB)	Costica Danifoiu (ROM)
			Janusz Gortat (POL)
1980	Slobodan Kacar (YUG)	Pavel Skrzecz (POL)	Herbert Bauch (GDR)
			Ricardo Rojas (CUB)
1984	Anton Josipovic (YUG)	Kevin Barry (NZL)	Mustapha Moussa (ALG)
			Evander Holyfield (USA)

1896–1912 Event not held.

Heavyweight
From 1984 the weight limit has been 91kg *200½lb*. From 1904 to 1908 it was over *158lb* 71.67kg. From 1920 to 1936 it was over *175lb* 79.38kg. In 1948 it was over 80kg *176¼lb*. From 1952 to 1980 it was over 81kg *178½lb*.

	Gold	Silver	Bronze
1904	Samuel Berger (USA)	Charles Mayer (USA)	William Michaels (USA)
1908	A L Oldham (GBR)	S C H Evans (GBR)	Frederick Parks (GBR)
1920	Ronald Rawson (GBR)	Sören Petersen (DEN)	Xavier Eluère (FRA)
1924	Otto von Porat (NOR)	Sören Petersen (DEN)	Alfredo Porzio (ARG)
1928	Arturo Rodriguez Jurado (ARG)	Nils Ramm (SWE)	Jacob Michaelsen (DEN)
1932	Santiago Lovell (ARG)	Luigi Rovati (ITA)	Frederick Feary (USA)
1936	Herbert Runge (GER)	Guillermo Lovvell (ARG)	Erling Nilsen (NOR)
1948	Rafael Iglesias (ARG)	Gunnar Nilsson (SWE)	John Arthur (SAF)
1952	Hayes Edward Sanders (USA)	Ingemar Johansson* (SWE)	Andries Nieman (SAF)
			Ilkka Koski (FIN)
1956	Peter Rademacher (USA)	Lev Mukhin (URS)	Daniel Bekker (SAF)
			Giacomo Bozzano (ITA)
1960	Franco de Piccoli (ITA)	Daniel Bekker (SAF)	Josef Nemec (TCH)
			Günter Siegmund (GER)
1964	Joe Frazier (USA)	Hans Huber (GER)	Guiseppe Ros (ITA)
			Vadim Yemelyanov (URS)
1968	George Foreman (USA)	Ionas Tschepulis (URS)	Giorgio Bambini (ITA)
			Joaquin Rocha (MEX)
1972	Teofilo Stevenson (CUB)	Ion Alexe (ROM)	Peter Hussing (GER)
			Hasse Thomsen (SWE)
1976	Teofilo Stevenson (CUB)	Mircea Simon (ROM)	Johnny Tate (USA)
			Clarence Hill (BER)
1980	Teofilo Stevenson (CUB)	Pyotr Zayev (URS)	Jurgen Fanghanel (GDR)
			Istvan Levai (HUN)
1984	Henry Tillman (USA)	Willie Dewit (CAN)	Angelo Musone (ITA)
			Arnold Vanderlijde (HOL)

1896–1900, 1906, 1912 Event not held. *Originally silver medal not awarded; Johansson disqualified but reinstated in 1982.

Super-Heavyweight
From 1984 the class has been for those over 91kg *200½lb*.

	Gold	Silver	Bronze
1984	Tyrell Biggs (USA)	Francesco Damiani (ITA)	Robert Wells (GBR)
			Salihu Azis (YUG)

1896–1980 Event not held.

Boxing – Medals

	G	S	B	Total
United States	42	17	26	85
Soviet Union	13	18	15	46
Great Britain	12	10	19	41
Italy	13	12	13	38
Poland	8	9	21	38
Cuba	12	8	5	25
Argentina	7	7	9	23
Germany (FRG)	4	10	8	22
South Africa	6	4	9	19
Romania	1	7	10	18
Hungary	9	2	3	14
Finland	2	1	10	13
France	3	3	6	12
Canada	2	4	5	11
Denmark	1	5	5	11
Yugoslavia	3	2	5	10
GDR	3	1	6	10
Mexico	2	3	5	10
Korea	1	4	5	10
Bulgaria	2	1	6	9
Sweden	–	4	5	9
Ireland	–	2	5	7
Czechoslovakia	3	1	2	6
Norway	1	2	2	5
Venezuela	1	2	2	5
Kenya	–	1	4	5
N. Korea (PRK)	1	2	4	4
Belgium	1	1	2	4
Uganda	–	3	1	4
Australia	–	1	3	4
Puerto Rico	–	1	3	4
Japan	1	–	2	3
Netherlands	1	–	2	3
Chile	–	1	2	3
Ghana	–	1	2	3
Nigeria	–	1	2	3
New Zealand	1	1	–	2
Cameroun	–	1	1	2
Philippines	–	1	1	2
Algeria	–	–	2	2
Colombia	–	–	2	2
Turkey	–	–	2	2
Estonia	–	1	–	1
Thailand	–	1	–	1
Bermuda	–	–	1	1
Brazil	–	–	1	1
Dominican Rep.	–	–	1	1
Egypt	–	–	1	1
Guyana	–	–	1	1
Niger	–	–	1	1
Spain	–	–	1	1
Trinidad	–	–	1	1
Tunisia	–	–	1	1
Uruguay	–	–	1	1
Zambia	–	–	1	1
	156	156	250[1]	562

[1] From 1952 each losing semi-finalist was awarded a bronze medal.

CANOEING

Official canoeing competitions were first held in 1936, although kayak and Canadian events were demonstrated in 1924. The most successful competitor has been Gert Fredriksson (SWE) with six golds, one silver and one bronze from 1948 to 1960, all in kayaks. The most medals won by a woman is three golds and a bronze by Ludmila Pinayeva (née Khvedosyuk) (URS) from 1964 to 1972. Two men, Vladimir Parfenovich in 1980, and Ian Ferguson (NZL) in 1984, have won three gold medals at one Games. The best by a woman at one Games is by Agneta Andersson (SWE) with two golds and a silver in 1984.

The higest speed achieved in the Games over the standard 1000m course is 19.74 km/h when the New Zealand K4 clocked 3 min 02.28 sec in 1984.

The oldest ever canoeing gold medallist was Gert Fredriksson (SWE) aged 40yr 292 days in the 1960 K2 at 1000m. The youngest was Bent Peter Rasch (DEN) in the 1952 C2 at 1000m aged 18yr 58 days. The youngest female champion was Brigit Fischer (GDR) aged 18yr 158 days in the 1980 K1, while the oldest was Sylvi Saimo (FIN) in the 1952 K1 aged 37yr 259 days.

The first Canadian to win a Canadian *event was Francis Amyot in 1936.* (Alexandra Studio)

Canoeing

Men

Gold	Silver	Bronze

500 Metres Kayak Singles (K1)

	Gold	Silver	Bronze
1976	Vasile Diba (ROM) 1:46.41	Zoltan Szytanity (HUN) 1:46.95	Rüdiger Helm (GDR) 1:48.30
1980	Vladimir Parfenovich (URS) 1:43.43	John Sumegi (AUS) 1:44.12	Vasile Diba (ROM) 1:44.90
1984	Ian Ferguson (NZL) 1:47.84	Lars-Erik Möberg (SWE) 1:48.18	Bernard Bregeon (FRA) 1:48.41

1896–1972 Event not held.

1000 Metres Kayak Singles (K1)

	Gold	Silver	Bronze
1936	Gregor Hradetzky (AUT) 4:22.9	Helmut Cämmerer (GER) 4:25.6	Jacob Kraaier (HOL) 4:35.1
1948	Gert Fredriksson (SWE) 4:33.2	Johan Kobberup (DEN) 4:39.9	Henri Eberhardt (FRA) 4:41.4
1952	Gert Fredriksson (SWE) 4:07.9	Thorvald Strömberg (FIN) 4:09.7	Louis Gantois (FRA) 4:20.1
1956	Gert Fredriksson (SWE) 4:12.8	Igor Pissaryev (URS) 4:15.3	Lajor Kiss (HUN) 4:16.2
1960	Erik Hansen (DEN) 3:53.00	Imre Szöllösi (HUN) 3:54.02	Gert Fredriksson (SWE) 3:55.89
1964	Rolf Peterson (SWE) 3:57.13	Mihály Hesz (HUN) 3:57.28	Aurel Vernescu (ROM) 4:00.77
1968	Mihály Hesz (HUN) 4:02.63	Aleksandr Shaparenko (URS) 4:03.58	Erik Hansen (DEN) 4:04.39
1972	Aleksandr Shaparenko (URS) 3:48.06	Rolf Peterson (SWE) 3:48.35	Geza Csapo (HUN) 3:49.38
1976	Rüdiger Helm (GDR) 3:48.20	Geza Csapo (HUN) 3:48.84	Vasile Diba (ROM) 3:49.65
1980	Rüdiger Helm (GDR) 3:48.77	Alain Lebas (FRA) 3:50.20	Ion Birladeanu (ROM) 3:50.49
1984	Alan Thompson (NZL) 3:45.73	Milan Janic (YUG) 3:46.88	Greg Barton (USA) 3:47.38

1896–1932 Event not held.

10 000 Metres Kayak Singles (K1)

	Gold	Silver	Bronze
1936	Ernst Krebs (GER) 46:01.6	Fritz Landertinger (AUT) 46:14.7	Ernest Riedel (USA) 47:23.9
1948	Gert Fredriksson (SWE) 50:47.7	Kurt Wires (FIN) 51:18.2	Ejvind Skabo (NOR) 51:35.4
1952	Thorvald Strömberg (FIN) 47:22.8	Gert Fredriksson (SWE) 47:34.1	Michel Scheuer (GER) 47:54.5
1956	Gert Fredriksson (SWE) 47:43.4	Ferenc Hatlaczky (HUN) 47:53.3	Michel Scheuer (GER) 48:00.3

1896–1932, 1960–1984 Event not held.

500 Metres Kayak Pairs (K2)

	Gold	Silver	Bronze
1976	GDR 1:35.87	Soviet Union 1:36.81	Romania 1:37.43
1980	Soviet Union 1:32.38	Spain 1:33.65	GDR 1:34.00
1984	New Zealand 1:34.21	Sweden 1:35.26	Canada 1:35.41

1896–1972 Event not held.

1000 Metres Kayak Pairs (K2)

	Gold	Silver	Bronze
1936	Austria 4:03.8	Germany 4:08.9	Netherlands 4:12.2
1948	Sweden 4:07.3	Denmark 4:07.5	Finland 4:08.7
1952	Finland 3:51.1	Sweden 3:51.1	Austria 3:51.4
1956	Germany 3:49.6	Soviet Union 3:51.4	Austria 3:55.8
1960	Sweden 3:34.7	Hungary 3:34.91	Poland 3:37.34
1964	Sweden 3:38.4	Netherlands 3:39.30	Germany 3:40.69
1968	Soviet Union 3:37.54	Hungary 3:38.44	Austria 3:40.71
1972	Soviet Union 3:31.23	Hungary 3:32.00	Poland 3:33.83
1976	Soviet Union 3:29.01	GDR 3:29.33	Hungary 3:30.56
1980	Soviet Union 3:26.72	Hungary 3:28.49	Spain 3:28.66
1984	Canada 3:24.22	France 3:25.97	Australia 3:26.80

1896–1932 Event not held.

10 000 Metres Kayak Pairs (K2)

	Gold	Silver	Bronze
1936	Germany 41:45.0	Austria 42:05.4	Sweden 43:06.1
1948	Sweden 46:09.4	Norway 46:44.8	Finland 46:48.2
1952	Finland 44:21.3	Sweden 44:21.7	Hungary 44:26.6
1956	Hungary 43:37.0	Germany 43:40.6	Australia 43:43.2

1896–1932, 1960–1984 Event not held.

1000 Metres Kayak Fours (K4)

	Gold	Silver	Bronze
1964	Soviet Union 3:14.67	Germany 3:15.39	Romania 3:15.51
1968	Norway 3:14.38	Romania 3:14.81	Hungary 3:15.10
1972	Soviet Union 3:14.02	Romania 3:15.07	Norway 3:15.27
1976	Soviet Union 3:08.69	Spain 3:08.95	GDR 3:10.76
1980	GDR 3:13.76	Romania 3:15.35	Bulgaria 3:15.46
1984	New Zealand 3:02.28	Sweden 3:02.81	France 3:03.94

1896–1960 Event not held.

500 Metres Canadian Singles (C1)

	Gold	Silver	Bronze
1976	Aleksandr Rogov (URS) 1:59.23	John Wood (CAN) 1:59.58	Matija Ljubek (YUG) 1:59.60
1980	Sergey Postrekhin (URS) 1:53.37	Lubomir Lubenov (BUL) 1:53.49	Olaf Heukrodt (GDR) 1:54.38
1984	Larry Cain (CAN) 1:57.01	Henning Jakobsen (DEN) 1:58.45	Costica Olaru (ROM) 1:59.86

1896–1972 Event not held.

1000 Metres Canadian Singles (C1)

	Gold	Silver	Bronze
1936	Francis Amyot (CAN) 5:32.1	Bohuslav Karlik (TCH) 5:36.9	Erich Koschik (GER) 5:39.0
1948	Josef Holeček (TCH) 5:42.0	Douglas Bennett (CAN) 5:53.3	Robert Boutigny (FRA) 5:55.9
1952	Josef Holeček (TCH) 4:56.3	János Parti (HUN) 5:03.6	Olavi Ojanperä (FIN) 5:08.5
1956	Leon Rotman (ROM) 5:05.3	István Hernek (HUN) 5:06.2	Gennadiy Bukharin (URS) 5:12.7
1960	János Parti (HUN) 4:33.93	Aleksandr Silayev (URS) 4:34.41	Leon Rotman (ROM) 4:35.87
1964	Jürgen Eschert (GER) 4:35.14	Andrei Igorov (ROM) 4:37.89	Yevgeny Penyayev (URS) 4:38.31
1968	Tibor Tatai (HUN) 4:36.14	Detlef Lewe (FRG) 4:38.31	Vitaly Galkov (URS) 4:40.42
1972	Ivan Patzaichin (ROM) 4:08.94	Tamas Wichmann (HUN) 4:12.42	Detlef Lewe (GER) 4:13.63
1976	Matija Ljubek (YUG) 4:09.51	Vasiliy Urchenko (URS) 4:12.57	Tamas Wichmann (HUN) 4:14.11
1980	Lubomir Lubenov (BUL) 4:12.38	Sergey Postrekhin (URS) 4:13.53	Eckhard Leue (GDR) 4:15.02
1984	Ulrich Eicke (FRG) 4:06.32	Larry Cain (CAN) 4:08.67	Henning Jakobsen (DEN) 4:09.51

1896–1932 Event not held.

Gold	Silver	Bronze

10 000 Metres Canadian Singles (C1)

Gold	Silver	Bronze
1948 Frantisek Capek (TCH) 62:05.2	Frank Havens (USA) 62:40.4	Norman Lane (CAN) 64:35.3
1952 Frank Havens (USA) 57:41.1	Gabor Novak (HUN) 57:49.2	Alfred Jindra (TCH) 57:53.1
1956 Leön Rotman (ROM) 56:41.0	János Parti (HUN) 57:11.0	Gennadiy Bukharin (URS) 57:14.5
1896–1936, 1960–1984 Event not held.		

500 Metres Canadian Pairs (C2)

Gold	Silver	Bronze
1976 Soviet Union 1:45.81	Poland 1:47.77	Hungary 1:48.35
1980 Hungary 1:43.39	Romania 1:44.12	Bulgaria 1:44.83
1984 Yugoslavia 1:43.67	Romania 1:45.68	Spain 1:47.71
1896–1972 Event not held.		

1000 Metres Canadian Pairs (C2)

Gold	Silver	Bronze
1936 Czechoslovakia 4:50.1	Austria 4:53.8	Canada 4:56.7
1948 Czechoslovakia 5:07.1	United States 5:08.2	France 5:15.2
1952 Denmark 4:38.3	Czechoslovakia 4:42.9	Germany 4:48.3
1956 Romania 4:47.4	Soviet Union 4:48.6	Hungary 4:54.3
1960 Soviet Union 4:17.94	Italy 4:20.77	Hungary 4:20.89
1964 Soviet Union 4:04.64	France 4:06.52	Denmark 4:07.48
1968 Romania 4:07.18	Hungary 4:08.77	Soviet Union 4:11.30
1972 Soviet Union 3:52.60	Romania 3:52.63	Bulgaria 3:58.10
1976 Soviet Union 3:52.76	Romania 3:54.28	Hungary 3:55.66
1980 Romania 3:47.65	GDR 3:49.93	Soviet Union 3:51.28
1984 Romania 3:40.60	Yugoslavia 3:41.56	France 3:48.01
1896–1932 Event not held.		

10 000 Metres Canadian Pairs (C2)

Gold	Silver	Bronze
1936 Czechoslovakia 50:33.5	Canada 51:15.8	Austria 51:28.0
1948 United States 55:55.4	Czechoslovakia 57:38.5	France 58:00.8
1952 France 54:08.3	Canada 54:09.9	Germany 54:28.1
1956 Soviet Union 54:02.4	France 54:48.3	Hungary 55:15.6
1896–1932, 1960–1984 Event not held.		

4 × 500 Metres Kayak Singles (K1) Relay

Gold	Silver	Bronze
1960 Germany 7:39.43	Hungary 7:44.02	Denmark 7:46.09
1896–1956, 1964–1984 Event not held.		

10 000 Metres Folding Kayak Singles (K1)

Gold	Silver	Bronze
1936 Gregor Hradetzky (AUT) 50:01.2	Henri Eberhardt (FRA) 50:04.2	Xaver Hörmann (GER) 50:06.5
1896–1932, 1948–1984 Event not held		

10 000 Metres Folding Kayak Pairs (K2)

Gold	Silver	Bronze
1936 Sweden 45:48.9	Germany 45:49.2	Netherlands 46:12.4
1896–1932, 1948–1984 Event not held.		

Slalom Racing
(Only held in 1972)

Kayak Singles (K1)

Gold	Silver	Bronze
Siegbert Horn (GDR) 268.56	Norbert Sattler (AUT) 270.76	Harald Gimpel (GDR) 277.95

Canadian Singles (C1)

Gold	Silver	Bronze
Reinhard Eiben (GDR) 315.84	Reinhold Kauder (FRG) 327.89	Jamie McEwan (USA) 335.95

Canadian Pairs (C2)

Gold	Silver	Bronze
GDR 310.68	FRG 311.90	France 315.10

Women

500 Metres Kayak Singles (K1)

Gold	Silver	Bronze
1948 Karen Hoff (DEN) 2:31.9	Alide Van de Anker-Doedans (HOL) 2:32.8	Fritzi Schwingl (AUT) 2:32.9
1952 Sylvi Saimo (FIN) 2:18.4	Gertrude Liebhart (AUT) 2:18.8	Nina Savina (URS) 2:21.6
1956 Elisaveta Dementyeva (URS) 2:18.9	Therese Zenz (GER) 2:19.6	Tove Söby (DEN) 2:22.3
1960 Antonina Seredina (URS) 2:08.08	Therese Zenz (GER) 2:08.22	Daniel Walkowiak (POL) 2:10.46
1964 Ludmila Khvedosyuk (URS) 2:12.87	Hilde Lauer (ROM) 2:15.35	Marcia Jones (USA) 2:15.68
1968 Ludmila Pinayeva (URS) 2:11.09	Renate Breuer (FRG) 2:12.71	Viorica Dumitru (ROM) 2:13.22
1972 Yulia Ryabchinskaya (URS) 2:03.17	Mieke Jaapies (HOL) 2:04.03	Anna Pfeffer (HUN) 2:05.50
1976 Carola Zirzow (GDR) 2:01.05	Tatyana Korshunova (URS) 2:03.07	Klara Rajnai (HUN) 2:05.01
1980 Birgit Fischer (GDR) 1:57.96	Vanya Ghecheva (BUL) 1:59.48	Antonina Melnikova (URS) 1:59.66
1984 Agneta Andersson (SWE) 1:58.72	Barbara Schuttpelz (FRG) 1:59.93	Annemiek Derckx (HOL) 2:00.11
1896–1936 Event not held.		

500 Metres Kayak Pairs (K2)

Gold	Silver	Bronze
1960 Soviet Union 1:54.76	Germany 1:56.66	Hungary 1:58.22
1964 Germany 1:56.95	United States 1:59.16	Romania 2:00.25
1968 FRG 1:56.44	Hungary 1:58.60	Soviet Union 1:58.61
1972 Soviet Union 1:53.50	GDR 1:54.30	Romania 1:55.01
1976 Soviet Union 1:51.15	Hungary 1:51.69	GDR 1:51.81
1980 GDR 1:43.88	Soviet Union 1:46.91	Hungary 1:47.95
1984 Sweden 1:45.25	Canada 1:47.13	FRG 1:47.32
1896–1956 Event not held.		

Gold	Silver	Bronze

500 Metres Kayak Fours (K4)
1984   Romania 1:38.34 — Sweden 1:38.87 — Canada 1:39.40
1896–1980 Event not held.

Slalom Racing
(Only held in 1972)

Kayak Singles (K1)
Angelika Bahmann (GDR) 364.50 — Gisela Grothaus (FRG) 398.15 — Magdalena Wunderlich (FRG) 400.50

Canoeing – Medals

	Men			Women			Total			Total
	G	S	B	G	S	B	G	S	B	Medals
Soviet Union	18	8	6	8	2	3	26	10	9	45
Hungary	5	16	11	–	2	4	5	18	15	38
Germany (FRG)	6	8	8	2	6	2	8	14	10	32
Romania	8	8	8	1	1	3	9	9	11	29
Sweden	11	7	2	2	1	–	13	8	2	23
GDR	7	2	6	4	1	1	11	3	7	21
France	1	5	9	–	–	–	1	5	9	15
Canada	3	5	3	–	1	1	3	6	4	13
Austria	3	4	4	–	1	1	3	5	5	13
Denmark	2	3	4	1	–	1	3	3	5	11
Czechoslovakia	6	3	1	–	–	–	6	3	1	10
Finland	3	2	3	1	–	–	4	2	3	9
United States	2	2	3	–	1	1	2	3	4	9
Netherlands	–	1	3	–	2	1	–	3	4	7
Bulgaria	1	1	3	–	1	–	1	2	3	6
Yugoslavia	2	2	1	–	–	–	2	2	1	5
New Zealand	4	–	–	–	–	–	–	–	–	4
Norway	1	1	2	–	–	–	1	1	2	4
Spain	–	2	2	–	–	–	–	2	2	4
Poland	–	1	2	–	–	1	–	1	3	4
Australia	–	1	2	–	–	–	–	1	2	3
Italy	–	1	–	–	–	–	–	1	–	1
	83	83	83	19	19	19	102	102	102	306

CYCLING

The first Olympic cycling champion was Léon Flameng (FRA), winner of the 100km race in 1896, which was held on a 333.33m cement track and involved 300 circuits.

Four men have won three gold medals: Paul Masson (FRA) in 1896, Francisco Verri (ITA) in 1906, Robert Charpentier (FRA) in 1936, and Daniel Morelon (FRA) in 1968 (two) and 1972. Of these only Morelon won a bronze as well. He also won a record seven world amateur titles. Although the 1904 cycling events were not considered official it should be noted that Marcus Hurley (USA) won four of them.

The greatest family performance in Olympic cycling was by the Pettersson brothers of Sweden, Gösta, Sture, Erik, and Tomas. The first three with Sten Hamrin won a bronze in the 1964 team road race, and then, in 1968 with their younger brother, won the silver. One of the first modern sporting drug abuse cases occurred in the 1960 100km race when two Danish cyclists collapsed, and one, Knut Jensen, died from what was originally thought to be sunstroke. It transpired that they had both taken overdoses of a blood-circulation stimulant. Two other extremes of sportsmanship have highlighted the cycling at the Games. In 1936 Charpentier beat his team-mate Guy Lapébie by 0.2sec at the end of the 100km, the latter inexplicably slowing down just before the line. A photograph showed that Charpentier had pulled his rival back by his shirt. More credit-worthy was another Frenchman, Flameng, who, when far ahead of his only opposition, a Greek, in 1896, stopped when the man's cycle broke down. Waiting for it to be replaced, Flameng still won by six laps.

The greatest speed ever achieved in Olympic cycling was in the altitude of Mexico City in 1968 when Daniel Morelon and Pierre Trentin (FRA) clocked 9.83sec for the last 200m in the tandem race, an average of 73.24km/h *45.51mph*. The greatest speed by an individual rider was 68.76km/h *42.73mph* by Sergey Kopylov (URS) in Moscow, 1980, when he clocked 10.47sec for the last 200m in the 1000m time-trial.

Few top professionals competed at the Games successfully as amateurs – the most notable being Patrick Sercu (BEL) who won the 1964 time-trial and later won a record 86 professional six-day events. The two co-record holders in the Tour de France (five wins each), Eddy Merckx (BEL) and Jacques Anquetil (FRA), both finished twelfth in the Olympic road race, in 1964 and 1952 respectively.

The youngest gold medallist was Franco Giorgetti (ITA) in the 1920 team pursuit aged 17yr 304 days, while the oldest was Maurice Peeters (HOL) aged 38yr 99 days in the 1920 1000m sprint. Winning a bronze four years later in the tandem Peeters, at 42yr 83 days, was the oldest ever medallist as well. In 1984 a road race for women was added and was won by Connie Carpenter-Phinney (USA), whose husband Davis won a bronze in the 100km team event.

Cycling

Men

Gold	Silver	Bronze

1000 Metres Time-Trial

Gold	Silver	Bronze
1896[1] Paul Masson (FRA) 24.0	Stamatios Nikolopoulos (GRE) 25.4	Adolf Schmal (AUT) 26.6
1906[1] Francesco Verri (ITA) 22.8	Herbert Crowther (GBR) 22.8	Menjou (FRA) 23.2
1928 Willy Falck-Hansen (DEN) 1:14.4	Gerard Bosch van Drakestein (HOL) 1:15.2	Edgar Gray AUS) 1:15.6
1932 Edgar Gray (AUS) 1:13.0	Jacobus van Egmond (HOL) 1:13.3	Charles Rampelberg (FRA) 1:13.4
1936 Arie van Vliet (HOL) 1:12.0	Pierre Georget (FRA) 1:12.8	Rudolf Karsch (GER) 1:13.2
1948 Jacques Dupont (FRA) 1:13.5	Pierre Nihant (BEL) 1:14.5	Thomas Godwin (GBR) 1:15.0
1952 Russell Mockridge (AUS) 1:11.1	Marino Morettini (ITA) 1:12.7	Raymond Robinson (SAF) 1:13.0
1956 Leandro Faggin (ITA) 1:09.8	Ladislav Foucek (TCH) 1:11.4	J Alfred Swift (SAF) 1:11.6
1960 Sante Gaiardoni (ITA) 1:07.27	Dieter Gieseler (GER) 1:08.75	Rotislav Vargashkin (URS) 1:08.86
1964 Patrick Sercu (BEL) 1:09.59	Giovanni Pettenella (ITA) 1:10.09	Pierre Trentin (FRA) 1:10.42
1968 Pierre Trentin (FRA) 1:03.91	Niels-Christian Fredborg (DEN) 1:04.61	Janusz Kierzkowski (POL) 1:04.63
1972 Niels-Christian Fredborg (DEN) 1:06.44	Daniel Clark (AUS) 1:06.87	Jürgen Schuetze (GDR) 1:07.02
1976 Klaus-Jürgen Grunke (GDR) 1:05.93	Michel Vaarten (BEL) 1:07.52	Niels-Christian Fredborg (DEN) 1:07.62
1980 Lothar Thoms (GDR) 1:02.955*	Aleksandr Pantilov (URS) 1:04.845	David Weller (JAM) 1:05.241
1984 Fredy Schmidtke (FRG) 1:06.10	Curtis Harnett (CAN) 1:06.44	Fabrice Colas (FRA) 1:06.65

[1]Held over 333.33 metres. 1908–1924 Event not held. *Olympic record

1000 Metres Sprint

Gold	Silver	Bronze
1896[1] Paul Masson (FRA) 4:56.0	Stamatios Nikolopoulas (GRE)	Léon Flemeng (FRA)
1900[1] Georges Taillandier (FRA) 2:52.0	Fernand Sanz (FRA)	John Lake (USA)
1906 Francesco Verri (ITA) 1:42.2	H C Bouffler (GBR)	Eugène Debougnie (BEL)
1920 Maurice Peeters (HOL) 1:38.3	H Thomas Johnson (GBR)	Harry Ryan (GBR)
1924[3] Lucien Michard (FRA) 12.8	Jacob Meijer (HOL)	Jean Cugnot (FRA)
1928 René Beaufrand (FRA) 13.2	Antoine Mazairac (HOL)	Willy Falck-Hansen (DEN)
1932 Jacobus van Egmond (HOL) 12.6	Louis Chaillot (FRA)	Bruno Pellizzari (ITA)
1936 Toni Merkens (GER) 11.8	Arie van Vliet (HOL)	Louis Chaillot (FRA)
1948 Mario Ghella (ITA) 12.0	Reginald Harris (GBR)	Axel Schandorff (DEN)
1952 Enzo Sacchi (ITA) 12.0	Lionel Cox (AUS)	Werner Potzernheim (GER)
1956 Michel Rousseau (FRA) 11.4	Guglielmo Pesenti (ITA)	Richard Ploog (AUS)
1960 Sante Gaiardoni (ITA) 11.1	Leo Sterckx (BEL)	Valentino Gasparella (ITA)
1964 Giovanni Pettenella (ITA) 13.69	Sergio Bianchetto (ITA)	Daniel Morelon (FRA)
1968 Daniel Morelon (FRA) 10.68	Giordano Turrini (ITA)	Pierre Trentin (FRA)
1972 Daniel Morelon (FRA) 11.25	John Nicholson (AUS)	Omari Phakadze (URS)
1976 Anton Tkac (TCH) 10.78	Daniel Morelon (FRA)	Hans-Jurgen Geschke (GDR)
1980 Lutz Hesslich (GDR) 11.40	Yave Cahard (FRA)	Sergey Kopylov (URS)
1984 Mark Gorski (USA) 10.49	Nelson Vails (USA)	Tsutomu Sakamoto (JPN)

1904, 1908[2]–1912 Event not held. [1]Held over 2000 metres. In 1900 Taillander's last 200 was 13.0 sec. [2]There was a 1000 metres sprint event in the 1908 Games, but it was declared void because 'the riders exceeded the time limit, in spite of repeated warnings.' [3]Since 1924 only times over the last 200 metres of the event have been recorded.

4000 Metres Individual Pursuit

Note: Bronze medal times are set in a third place race, so can be faster than those set in the race for first and second place.

Gold	Silver	Bronze
1964 Jiři Daler (TCH) 5:04.75	Giorgio Ursi (ITA) 5:05.96	Preben Isaksson (DEN) 5:01.90
1968 Daniel Rebillard (FRA) 4:41.71	Mogens Frey Jensen (DEN) 4:42.43	Xaver Kurmann (SUI) 4:39.42
1972 Knut Knudsen (NOR) 4:45.74	Xaver Kurmann (SUI) 4:51.96	Hans Lutz (FRG) 4:50.80
1976 Gregor Braun (GDR) 4:47.61	Herman Ponsteen (HOL) 4:49.72	Thomas Huschke (GDR) 4:52.71
1980 Robert Dill-Bundi (SUI) 4:35.66*	Alain Bondue (FRA) 4:42.96	Hans-Henrik Orsted (DEN) 4:36.54
1984 Steve Hegg (USA) 4:39.35	Rolf Golz (FRG) 4:43.82	Leonard Nitz (USA) 4:44.03

1896–1960 Event not held. *Olympic record 4:34.92 in heats.

Gold	Silver	Bronze

4000 Metres Team Pursuit

Note: Bronze medal times are set in a third place race, so can be faster than those set in the race for first and second place.

Gold	Silver	Bronze
1908[1] Great Britain 2:18.6	Germany 2:28.6	Canada 2:29.6
1920 Italy 5:20.0	Great Britain n.t.a.	South Africa n.t.a.
1924 Italy 5:15.0	Poland n.t.a.	Belgium n.t.a.
1928 Italy 5:01.8	Netherlands 5:06.2	Great Britain n.t.a.
1932 Italy 4:53.0	France 4:55.7	Great Britain 4:56.0
1936 France 4:45.0	Italy 4:51.0	Great Britain 4:52.6
1948 France 4:57.8	Italy 4:36.7	Great Britain 4:55.8
1952 Italy 4:46.1	South Africa 4:53.6	Great Britain 4:51.5
1956 Italy 4:37.4	France 4:39.4	Great Britain 4:42.2
1960 Italy 4:30.90	Germany 4:35.78	Soviet Union 4:34.05
1964 Germany 4:35.67	Italy 4:35.74	Netherlands 4:38.99
1968 Denmark 4:22.44[2]	FRG 4:18.94	Italy 4:18.35
1972 FRG 4:22.14	GDR 4:25.25	Great Britain 4:23.78
1976 FRG 4:21.06	Soviet Union 4:27.15	Great Britain 4:22.41
1980 Soviet Union 4:15.70*	GDR 4:19.67	Czechoslovakia[3]
1984 Australia 4.25.99	United States 4:29.85	FRG 4:25.60

1896–1906, 1912 Event not held.
[1]Held over 1810.5 metres. [2]Federal Republic of Germany finished first but were disqualified for illegal assistance. After the Games ended the International Cycling Federation awarded them the silver medal. [3]Italy disqualified in third place race. *Olympic record 4:14.64 in heats.

	Gold	*Silver*	*Bronze*

2000 Metres Tandem

1906	Great Britain 2:57.0	Germany 2:57.2	Germany n.t.a.
1908	France 3:07.8	Great Britain n.t.a.	Great Britain n.t.a.
1920	Great Britain 2:49.4	South Africa n.t.a.	Netherlands n.t.a.
1924[1]	France 12.6	Denmark	Netherlands
1928	Netherlands 11.8	Great Britain	Germany
1932	France 12.0	Great Britain	Denmark
1936	Germany 11.8	Netherlands	France
1948	Italy 11.3	Great Britain	France
1952	Australia 11.0	South Africa	Italy
1956	Australia 10.8	Czechoslovakia	Italy
1960	Italy 10.7	Germany	Soviet Union
1964	Italy 10.75	Soviet Union	Germany
1968	France 9.83	Netherlands	Belgium
1972	Soviet Union 10.52	GDR	Poland

[1]Since 1924 only times over last 200m have been recorded.
1896–1904, 1912, 1976–1984 Event not held

Individual Points Race

1984	Roger Ilegems (BEL)	Uwe Messerschmidt (FRG)	Jose Youshimatz (MEX)

1896–1980 Event not held.

Team Road Race

(Consisting of the combined times of the best three – four 1912–20 – riders from each country in the individual race. In 1956 based on placings).

1912	Sweden 44h 35:33.6	Great Britain 44h 44:39.2	United States 44h 47:55.5
1920	France 19h 16:43.2	Sweden 19h 23:10.0	Belgium 19h 28:44.4
1924	France 19h 30:14.0	Belgium 19h 46:55.4	Sweden 19h 59:41.6
1928	Denmark 15h 09:14.0	Great Britain 15h 14:49.0	Sweden 15h 27:49.0
1932	Italy 7h 27:15.2	Denmark 7h 38:50.2	Sweden 7h 39:12.6
1936	France 7h 39:16.2	Switzerland 7h 39:20.4	Belgium 7h 39:21.0
1948	Belgium 15h 58:17.4	Great Britain 16h 03:31.6	France 16h 08:19.4
1952	Belgium 15h 20:46.6	Italy 15h 33:27.3	France 15h 38:58.1
1956	France 22 points	Great Britain 23 points	Germany 27 points

Road Team Time-Trial

Over 100km except in 1964 (108.89km), 1968 (102km), 1980 (101km).

1960	Italy 2h 14:33.53	Germany 2h 16:56.31	Soviet Union 2h 18:41.67
1964	Netherlands 2h 26:31.19	Italy 2h 26:55.39	Sweden 2h 27:11.52
1968	Netherlands 2h 07:49.06	Sweden 2h 09:26.60	Italy 2h 10:18.74
1972	Soviet Union 2h 11:17.8	Poland 2h 11:47.5	*
1976	Soviet Union 2h 08:53.0	Poland 2h 09:13.0	Denmark 2h 12:20.0
1980	Soviet Union 2h 01:21.7	GDR 2h 02:53.2	Czechoslovakia 2h 02:53.9
1984	Italy 1h 58:28.0	Switzerland 2h 02:38.0	United States 2h 02:46.0

*Netherlands finished in third place but their bronze medal was withdrawn following a dope test. 1896–1908 Event not held.

	Gold	*Silver*	*Bronze*

Individual Road Race

1896	Aristidis Konstantinidis (GRE) 3h 22:31.0	August Goedrich (GER) 3h 42:18.0	F Battel (GBR) d.n.a.
1906	Fernand Vast (FRA) 2h 41:28.0	Maurice Bardonneau (FRA) 2h 41:28.4	Edmund Lugnet (FRA) 2h 41:28.6
1912	Rudolph Lewis (SAF) 10h 42:39.0	Frederick Grubb (GBR) 10h 51:24.2	Carl Schutte (USA) 10h 52:38.8
1920	Harry Stenqvist (SWE) 4h 40:01.8	Henry Kaltenbrun (SAF) 4h 41:26.6	Fernand Canteloube (FRA) 4h 42:54.4
1924	Armand Blanchonnet (FRA) 6h 20:48.0	Henry Hoevenaers (BEL) 6h 30:27.0	René Hamel (FRA) 6h 40:51.6
1928	Henry Hansen (DEN) 4h 47:18.0	Frank Southall (GBR) 4h 55:06.0	Gösta Carlsson (SWE) 5h 00:17.0
1932	Attilio Pavesi (ITA) 2h 28:05.6	Guglielmo Segato (ITA) 2h 29:21.4	Bernhard Britz (SWE) 2h 29:45.2
1936	Robert Charpentier (FRA) 2h 33:05.0	Guy Lapébie (FRA) 2h 33:05.2	Ernst Nievergelt (SUI) 2h 33:05.8
1948	José Beyaert (FRA) 5h 18:12.6	Gerardus Voorting (HOL) 5h 18:16.2	Lode Wouters (BEL) 5h 18:16.2
1952	André Noyelle (BEL) 5h 06:03.4	Robert Grondelaers (BEL) 5h 06:51.2	Edi Ziegler (GER) 5h 07:47.5
1956	Ercole Baldini (ITA) 5h 21:17.0	Arnaud Geyre (FRA) 5h 23:16.0	Alan Jackson (GBR) 5h 23:16.0
1960	Viktor Kapitonov (URS) 4h 20:37.0	Livio Trapè (ITA) 4h 20:37.0	Willy van den Berghen (BEL) 4h 20:57.0
1964	Mario Zanin (ITA) 4h 39:51.63	Kjell Rodian (DEN) 4h 39:51.65	Walter Godefroot (BEL) 4h 39:51.74
1968	Pierfranco Vianelli (ITA) 4h 41:25.24	Leif Mortensen (DEN) 4h 42:49.71	Gösta Pettersson (SWE) 4h 43:15.24
1972	Hennie Kuiper (HOL) 4h 14:37.0	Kevin Sefton (AUS) 4h 15:04.0	*
1976	Bernt Johansson (SWE) 4h 46:52.0	Giuseppe Martinelli (ITA) 4h 47:23.0	Mieczyslaw Nowicki (POL) 4h 47:23.0
1980	Sergey Sukhoruchenkov (URS) 4h 48:28.9	Czeslaw Lang (POL) 4h 51:26.9	Yuriy Barinov (URS) 4h 51:26.9
1984	Alexi Grewal (USA) 4h 59:57.0	Steve Bauer (CAN) 4h 59:57.0	Dag Otto Lauritzen (NOR) 5h 00:18.0

This event has been held over the following distances: 1896 – 87km; 1906 – 84km; 1912 – 320km; 1920 – 175km; 1924 – 188km; 1928 – 168km; 1932 and 1936 – 100km; 1948 – 194.63km; 1952 – 190.4km; 1956 – 187.73km; 1960 – 175.38km; 1968 – 196.2km; 1972 – 182.4km; 1976 – 175km; 1980 – 189km; 1984 – 190km. 1900–1904, 1908 Event not held. *Jaime Huelamo (ESP) finished third but medal withdrawn following a drug test.

Discontinued Events

660 Yards (603.5 Metres) Track

1908	Victor Johnson (GBR) 51.2	Emile Demangel (FRA) close	Karl Neumer (GER) 1 length

5000 Metres Track

1906	Francesco Verri (ITA) 8:35.0	Herbert Crowther (GBR) 2 lengths	Fernand Vast (FRA) 5 lengths
1908	Benjamin Jones (GBR) 8:36.2	Maurice Schilles (FRA) close	André Auffray (FRA)

Gold	Silver	Bronze

10 000 Metres Track
1896   Paul Masson (FRA) 17:54.2   Léon Flameng (FRA)   Adolf Schmal (AUT)

20 000 Metres Track
1906   William Pett (GBR) 29:00.0   Maurice Bardonneau (FRA) 29:30.0   Fernand Vast (FRA) 29:32.0
1908   Charles Kingsbury (GBR) 34:13.6   Benjamin Jones (GBR) close   Joseph Werbrouck (BEL)

50 000 Metres Track
1920   Henry George (BEL) 1h 16:43.2   Cyril Alden* (GBR) close   Petrus Ikelaar (HOL) close
1924   Jacobus Willems (HOL) 1h 18:24.0   Cyril Alden (GBR) 1 length   Frederick Wyld (GBR) 1 length

*Most eyewitnesses considered Ikelaar (HOL) finished in second place

100km Track
1896   Léon Flameng (FRA) 3h 08:19.2   G Kolettis (GRE) 6 laps   *
1908   Charles Bartlett (GBR) 2h 41:48.6   Charles Denny (GBR) 1 length   Octave Lapize (FRA)

*Only two riders finished.

12 Hours Track
1896   Adolf Schmal (AUT) 314.997km   F Keeping (GBR) 314.664km   Georgios Paraskevopoulos (GRE) 313.330km

Women

Individual Road Race (79.2km)
1984   Connie Carpenter-Phinney (USA) 2h 11:14.0   Rebecca Twigg (USA) 2h 11:14.0   Sandra Schumacher (FRG) 2h 11:14.0

1896–1980 Event not held.

Cycling – Medals

	G	S	B	Total
France	27	15	20	62
Italy	26	14	6	46
Great Britain	8	21	14	43
Germany (FRG)	6	10	11	27
Netherlands	8	10	4	22
Belgium	6	6	9	21
Denmark	5	6	7	18
Soviet Union	7	3	7	17
United States	4	3	5	12
Sweden	3	2	7	12
Australia	5	4	2	11
GDR	4	4	3	11
South Africa	1	4	3	8
Poland	–	4	3	7
Czechoslovakia	2	2	2	6
Switzerland	1	3	2	6
Greece	1	3	1	5
Austria	1	–	2	3
Canada	–	2	1	3
Norway	1	–	1	2
Jamaica	–	–	1	1
Japan	–	–	1	1
Mexico	–	–	1	1
	116	116	113[1]	345

[1]No bronzes in 1896 100km, 1972 road team trial and individual road race.

World and Olympic time-trial champion in 1936 Arie Van Vliet. (GSL)

EQUESTRIANISM

In the ancient Games the first event using horses was a chariot race in 680 BC. Horses with riders came into the Games in 648 BC. The first equestrian gold medallist of the modern Olympics was Aimé Haegeman (BEL) on *Benton II* in the 1900 show jumping. In 1956 the equestrian events were held separately, at Stockholm, from the main Games due to the strict Australian quarantine laws. The most gold medals by a rider is five (one individual and four team events) by Hans-Günter Winkler (FRG) 1956–1972, and also by Reiner Klimke (FRG) 1964–1984. Winkler's total of seven medals, including a silver and a bronze, is also a record.

The oldest gold medallist was Josef Neckarmann (FRG) in the 1968 dressage team aged 56yr 141 days. The oldest individual winner was Ernst Lindner (SWE) in the 1924 dressage aged 56yr 91 days. The youngest champion was Edmund Coffin (USA) in the 1976 three-day event aged 21yr 77 days.

Raimondo d'Inzeo (ITA) competed in a record eight Games, 1948–1976, winning a gold, two silver and three bronze medals. No other Olympic competitor in any sport has matched this number of appearances. A Bulgarian, Kroum Lekarski, competed in the three-day event for a record period of 36 years between 1924 and 1960, but only competed in four Games. Gustav-Adolf Boltenstern Jr (SWE) won dressage medals over a record 24-year period, 1932–1956. Of competitors who have competed in two different equestrian disciplines, the most successful was Åge Lundström (SWE) with a gold in the 1920 three-day event and another in the 1924 show jumping. Women first competed in 1952, and Lis Hartel (DEN) won the first female medal with a silver in the dressage, which she repeated in 1956.

The only horse to be ridden to medals in three Games was *Absent* in the Soviet dressage team, with a gold and two bronze under Sergey Filatov in 1960 and 1964, and a silver with Ivan Kalita in 1968.

In 1936 Germany completed the only six gold medal 'clean sweep' in Games equestrian history. In the

The Flying Finn wins again as Capt Stubbendorff rides Nurmi *to victory in the three-day event in 1936.* (Dave Terry)

1912 and 1920 dressage Sweden took the first three places both times, a unique occurrence.

Show Jumping

From 1924 until 1968 teams comprised three members, all counting for the final score. This led to many teams not finishing, as in 1932 when no team medals were awarded at all, and 1948 when only four of the 14 competing teams finished. Since 1972 teams have consisted of four riders with the best three scoring. The most gold medals won are five by Winkler (see above). Only Pierre Jonquères d'Oriola (FRA) has won the individual title twice. The first woman to win a medal was Pat Smythe (GBR) in the 1956 team event, while the first individual medallist was Marion Coakes (GBR) in 1968.

The oldest gold medallist was Winkler in 1976 aged 46yr 49 days, while the oldest individual champion was Jonquères d'Oriola aged 44yr 266 days in 1964. Bill Steinkraus (USA) won medals over a twenty-year period 1952–1972, a

record matched by Winkler 1956–1976. The youngest gold medallist was Jim Day (CAN) in the 1968 team aged 22yr 117 days.

The lowest score obtained by a winner is no faults by Frantisek Ventura (TCH) on *Eliot* in 1928, Jonquères d'Oriola (FRA) on *Ali Baba* in 1952, and Alwin Schockemöhle (FRG) on *Warwick Rex* in 1976. The most successful horse was Winkler's *Halla* with three golds in 1956 and 1960.

Dressage

The most successful rider was Reiner Klimke (see above) but only Henri St Cyr (SWE) won the individual title twice. In all he won four golds, which would have been more but his team was disqualified in 1948, having finished first, because one of its members, Gehnäll Persson, was not a fully commissioned officer – a requirement at that time. With the rules changed Persson was in the 1952 and 1956 winning teams. This Swedish team of St Cyr, Persson and Gustav-Adolf Boltenstern, Jr, uniquely finished in first place three times in a row, and can claim to be the most successful combination in Olympic history.

The first woman to win a medal was Lis Hartel (see above), while the first female gold medallist was Liselott Linsenhoff (FRG) in 1972. The oldest gold medallist was Josef Neckarmann (see above), who was also the oldest medallist in 1972 aged 60yr 96 days. Incidentally the oldest competitor in Olympic equestrian history was General Arthur von Pongracz (AUT) who began in 1924 aged 60yr and ended it in 1936, just missing a bronze medal, aged 72 – one of the oldest ever Olympians. The oldest woman ever to compete in the Olympic Games was Lorna Johnstone (GBR) who placed twelfth in the 1972 dressage five days after her 70th birthday. The youngest rider to win a gold medal was Elisabeth Theurer (AUT) in 1980 aged 23yr 316 days. Four men have won medals at four Games, while the most successful horse was *Dux* ridden by Reiner Klimke (FRG) to two golds and a bronze in 1964 and 1968.

Three-Day Event

Competitions actually last four days as the dressage segment occupies two days.

Only Charles Pahud de Mortanges (HOL) has won the individual title twice, 1928 and 1932, and he also won a record total of four golds and a silver from 1924 to 1932. His Dutch team, including Gerard de Kruyff and Adolph van der Voort van Zijp, uniquely won two team titles with the same team members. The longest span of competition by a medal winner is 20 years by Mickey Plumb (USA) 1964–1984. The first female competitor was Helena Dupont (USA), 33rd in 1964, while the first female gold medallists were Mary Gordon-Watson and Bridget Parker (both GBR) in 1972. The first individual medals won by women were in 1984 by Karen Stives (USA) and Virginia Holgate (GBR)

The oldest gold medallist was Derek Allhusen (GBR) aged 54yr 286 days in 1968, while the youngest was Edmund Coffin (see above). The oldest medallist was William Roycroft (AUS) with a bronze in 1976 aged 61yr 129 days in the same team as his son, Wayne. The most successful horse was *Marcroix* ridden by Charles Pahud de Mortanges (HOL) to three golds and a silver in 1928 and 1932. *Silver Piece* ridden by Voort van Zijp (HOL) also won three golds in 1924 and 1928.

The 1936 cross-country course was so tough that only four teams out of 14 finished. In 1920 the dressage was excluded with two cross-country runs, at 20km and 50km, added to the jumping.

Equestrianism

	Gold	Silver	Bronze
	Grand Prix (Jumping)		
1900	Aimé Haegeman (BEL) *Benton II*	Georges van de Poele (BEL) *Winds or Squire*	M de Champsavin (FRA) *Terpsichore*
1912	Jean Cariou (FRA) 186pts *Mignon*	Rabod von Kröcher (GER) 186 *Dohna*	Emanuel de Blomaert de Soye (BEL) 185 *Clonmore*
1920	Tommaso Lequio (ITA) 2 faults *Trebecco*	Alessandro Valerio (ITA) 3 *Cento*	Gustaf Lewenhaupt (SWE) 4 *Mon Coeur*
1924	Alphonse Gemuseus (SUI) 6 faults *Lucette*	Tommaso Lequio (ITA) *Trebecco*	Adam Krolikiewicz (POL) 10 *Picador*
1928	Frantisek Ventura (TCH) no faults *Eliot*	Pierre Bertrand de Balanda (FRA) 2 *Papillon*	Charles Kuhn (SUI) 4 *Pepita*
1932	Takeichi Nishi (JPN) 8pts *Uranus*	Harry Chamberlin (USA) 12 *Show Girl*	Clarence von Rosen Jr (SWE) 16 *Empire*
1936	Kurt Hasse (GER) 4 faults *Tora*	Henri Rang (ROM) 4 *Delius*	József von Platthy (HUN) 8 *Sellö*
1948	Humberto Mariles Cortés (MEX) 6.25 faults *Arete*	Rubén Uriza (MEX) 8 *Harvey*	Jean d'Orgeix (FRA) 8 *Sucre de Pomme*
1952	Pierre Jonquères d'Oriola (FRA) no faults *Ali Baba*	Oscar Cristi (CHI) 4 *Bambi*	Fritz Thiedemann (GER) 8 *Meteor*
1956	Hans Günter Winkler (GER) 4 faults *Halla*	Raimondo d'Inzeo (ITA) 8 *Merano*	Piero d'Inzeo (ITA) 11 *Uruguay*
1960	Raimondo d'Inzeo (ITA) 12 faults *Posillipo*	Piero d'Inzeo (ITA) 16 *The Rock*	David Broome (GBR) 23 *Sunsalve*
1964	Pierre Jonquères d'Oriola (FRA) 9 faults *Lutteur*	Hermann Schridde (GER) 13.75 *Dozent*	Peter Robeson (GBR) 16 *Firecrest*
1968	William Steinkraus (USA) 4 faults *Snowbound*	Marian Coakes (GBR) 8 *Stroller*	David Broome (GBR) 12 *Mister Softee*
1972	Graziano Mancinelli (ITA) 8 faults *Ambassador*	Ann Moore (GBR) 8 *Psalm*	Neal Shapiro (USA) 8 *Sloopy*
1976	Alwin Schockemöhle (FRG) no faults *Warwick Rex*	Michael Vaillancourt (CAN) 12 *Branch County*	Francois Mathy (BEL) 12 *Gai Luron*
1980	Jan Kowalczyk (POL) 8 faults *Artemor*	Nikolai Korolkov (URS) 9.50 *Espadron*	Joaquin Perez Heras (MEX) 12 *Alymony*
1984	Joe Fargis (USA) 4 faults *Touch of Class*	Conrad Homfeld (USA) 4 *Abdullah*	Heidi Robbiani (SUI) 8 *Jessica V*

1896, 1904–1908 Event not held.

	Gold	Silver	Bronze
	Grand Prix (Jumping) Team		
1912	Sweden 545pts	France 538	Germany 530
1920	Sweden 14 faults	Belgium 16.25	Italy 18.75
1924	Sweden 42.25pts	Switzerland 50	Portugal 53
1928	Spain 4 faults	Poland 8	Sweden 10
1932[1]	–	–	–
1936	Germany 44 faults	Netherlands 51.5	Portugal 56
1948	Mexico 34.25 faults	Spain 56.50	Great Britain 67
1952	Great Britain 40.75 faults	Chile 45.75	United States 52.25
1956	Germany 40 faults	Italy 66	Great Britain 69
1960	Germany 46.50 faults	United States 66	Italy 80.50
1964	Germany 68.50 faults	France 77.75	Italy 88.50
1968	Canada 102.75 faults	France 110.50	FRG 117.25
1972	FRG 32 faults	United States 32.25	Italy 48
1976	France 40 faults	FRG 44	Belgium 63
1980	Soviet Union 16 faults	Poland 32	Mexico 39.25
1984	United States 12 faults	Great Britain 36.75	FRG 39.25

[1]There was a team competition but no nation had three riders complete the course. 1896–1908 Event not held.

Gold	Silver	Bronze

Grand Prix (Dressage)

Gold	Silver	Bronze
1912 Carl Bonde (SWE) 15pts *Emperor*	Gustaf-Adolf Boltenstern Sr (SWE) 21 *Neptun*	Hans von Blixen-Finecke (SWE) 32 *Maggie*
1920 Janne Lundblad (SWE) 27 237pts *Uno*	Bertil Sandström (SWE) 26 312 *Sabel*	Hans von Rosen (SWE) 25 125 *Running Sister*
1924 Ernst Linder (SWE) 276.4pts *Piccolo-mini*	Bertil Sandström (SWE) 275.8 *Sabel*	Xavier Lesage (FRA) 265.8 *Plumard*
1928 Carl von Langen (GER) 237.42pts *Draüfgänger*	Charles Marion (FRA) 231.00 *Linon*	Ragnar Olsson (SWE) 229.78 *Günstling*
1932 Xavier Lesage (FRA) 1031.25pts *Taine*	Charles Marion (FRA) 916.25 *Linon*	Hiram Tuttle (USA) 901.50 *Olympic*
1936 Heinz Pollay (GER) 1760pts *Kronos*	Friedrich Gerhard (GER) 1745.5 *Absinth*	Alois Podhajsky (AUT) 1721.5 *Nero*
1948 Hans Moser (SUI) 492.5pts *Hummer*	André Jousseaume (FRA) 480.0 *Harpagon*	Gustaf-Adolf Boltenstern Jr (SWE) 477.5 *Trumpf*
1952 Henri St Cyr (SWE) 561pts *Master Rufus*	Lis Hartel (DEN) 541.5 *Jubilee*	André Jousseaume (FRA) 541.0 *Harpagon*
1956 Henri St Cyr (SWE) 860pts *Juli*	Lis Hartel (DEN) 850 *Jubilee*	Liselott Linsenhoff (GER) 832 *Adular*
1960 Sergey Filatov (URS) 2144pts *Absent*	Gustav Fischer (SUI) 2087 *Wald*	Josef Neckermann (GER) 2082 *Asbach*
1964 Henri Chammartin (SUI) 1504pts *Woermann*	Harry Boldt (GER) 1503 *Remus*	Sergey Filatov (URS) 1486 *Absent*
1968 Ivan Kizimov (URS) 1572pts *Ikhov*	Josef Neckermann (FRG) 1546 *Mariano*	Reiner Klimke (FRG) 1537 *Dux*
1972 Liselott Linsenhoff (FRG) 1229pts *Piaff*	Elena Petuchkova (URS) 1185 *Pepel*	Josef Neckermann (FRG) 1177 *Venetia*
1976 Christine Stückelberger (SUI) 1486pts *Granat*	Harry Boldt (FRG) 1435 *Woycek*	Reiner Klimke (FRG) 1395 *Mehmed*
1980 Elisabeth Theurer (AUT) 1370pts Mon Cherie	Yuriy Kovshov (URS) 1300 *Igrok*	Viktor Ugryumov (URS) 1234 *Shkval*
1984 Reiner Klimke (FRG) 1504pts *Ahlerich*	Anne Grethe Jensen (DEN) 1442 *Marzog*	Otto Hofer (SUI) 1364 *Limandus*

1896–1908 Event not held.

Gold	Silver	Bronze

Grand Prix (Dressage) Team

Gold	Silver	Bronze
1928 Germany 669.72pts	Sweden 650.86	Netherlands 642.96
1932 France 2818.75pts	Sweden 2678	United States 2576.75
1936[1] Germany 5074pts	France 4846	Sweden 4660.5
1948[1] France 1269pts	United States 1256	Portugal 1182
1952 Sweden 1597.5pts	Switzerland 1759	Germany 1501
1956 Sweden 2475pts	Germany 2346	Switzerland 2346
1964 Germany 2558pts	Switzerland 2526	Soviet Union 2311
1968 FRG 2699pts	Soviet Union 2657	Switzerland 2547
1972 Soviet Union 5095pts	FRG 5083	Sweden 4849
1976 FRG 5155pts	Switzerland 4684	United States 4670
1980 Soviet Union 4383pts	Bulgaria 3580	Romania 3346
1984 FRG 4955pts	Switzerland 4673	Sweden 4630

[1]Sweden were originally declared winners with 1366pts but were subsequently disqualified one year later. 1896–1924, 1960 Event not held.

Gold	Silver	Bronze

Three-day Event

Gold	Silver	Bronze
1912 Axel Nordlander (SWE) 46.59pts *Lady Artist*	Friedrich von Rochow (GER) 46.42 *Idealist*	Jean Cariou (FRA) 46.32 *Cocotte*
1920 Helmer Mörner (SWE) 1775pts *Germania*	Åge Lundström (SWE) 1738.75 *Yrsa*	Ettore Caffaratti (ITA) 1733.75 *Traditore*
1924 Adolph van der Voort van Zijp (HOL) 1976pts *Silver Piece*	Fröde Kirkebjerg (DEN) 1853.5 *Meteor*	Sloan Doak (USA) 1845.5 *Pathfinder*
1928 Charles Pahud de Mortanges (HOL) 1969.82pts *Marcroix*	Gerard de Kruyff (HOL) 1967.26 *Va-t-en*	Bruno Neumann (GER) 1944.42 *Ilja*
1932 Charles Pahud de Mortanges (HOL) 1813.83pts *Marcroix*	Earl Thomson (USA) 1811 *Jenny Camp*	Clarence von Rosen Jr (SWE) 1809–42 *Sunnyside Maid*
1936 Ludwig Stubbendorff (GER) 37.7 faults *Nurmi*	Earl Thomson (USA) 99.9 *Jenny Camp*	Hans Mathiesen-Lunding (DEN) 102.2 *Jason*
1948 Bernard Chevallier (FRA) +4pts *Aiglonne*	Frank Henry (USA) −21 *Swing Low*	Robert Selfelt (SWE) −25 *Claque*
1952 Hans von Blixen-Finecke (SWE) 28.33 faults *Jubal*	Guy Lefrant (FRA) 54.50 *Verdun*	Wilhelm Büsing (GER) 55.50 *Hubertus*
1956 Petrus Kastenman (SWE) 66.53 faults *Iluster*	August Lütke-Westhues (GER) 84.87 *Trux von Kamax*	Frank Weldon (GBR) 85.48 *Kilbarry*
1960 Lawrence Morgan (AUS) +7.15pts *Salad Days*	Neale Lavis (AUS) −16.50 *Mirrabooka*	Anton Bühler (SUI) −51.21 *Gay Spark*
1964 Mauro Checcoli (ITA) 64.40pts *Surbean*	Carlos Moratorio (ARG) 56.40 *Chalan*	Fritz Ligges (GER) 49.20 *Donkosak*
1968 Jean-Jacques Guyon (FRA) 38.86pts *Pitou*	Derek Allhusen (GBR) 41.61 *Lochinvar*	Michael Page (USA) 53.31 *Faster*
1972 Richard Meade (GBR) 57.73pts *Laurieston*	Alessa Argenton (ITA) 43.33 *Woodland*	Jan Jonsson (SWE) 39.67 *Sarajevo*
1976 Edmund Coffin (USA) 114.99pts *Bally-Cor*	Michael Plumb (USA) 125.85 *Better & Better*	Karl Schultz (FRG) 129.45 *Madrigal*
1980 Federico Roman (ITA) 108.60pts *Rossinan*	Aleksandr Blinov (URS) 120.80 *Galzun*	Yuriy Salnikov (URS) 151.60 *Pintset*
1984 Mark Todd (NZL) 51.60pts *Charisma*	Karen Stives (USA) 54.20 *Ben Arthur*	Virginia Holgate (GBR) 56.80 *Priceless*

1896–1908 Event not held.

Gold	Silver	Bronze

Three-day Event Team

Gold	Silver	Bronze
1912 Sweden 139.06pts	Germany 138.48	United States 137.33
1920 Sweden 5057.5pts	Italy 4735	Belgium 4560
1924 Netherlands 5297.5pts	Sweden 4743.5	Italy 4512.5
1928 Netherlands 5865.68pts	Norway 5395.68	Poland 5067.92
1932 United States 5038.08pts	Netherlands 4689.08	–[1]
1936 Germany 676.75pts	Poland 991.70	Great Britain 9195.50
1948 United States 161.50 faults	Sweden 165.00	Mexico 305.25

	Gold	Silver	Bronze
1952	Sweden 221.49pts	Germany 235.49	United States 587.16
1956	Great Britain 355.48pts	Germany 475.61	Canada 572.72
1960	Australia 128.18pts	Switzerland 386.02	France 515.71
1964	Italy 85.80pts	United States 65.86	Germany 56.73
1968	Great Britain 175.93pts	United States 245.87	Australia 331.26
1972	Great Britain 95.53pts	United States 10.81	FRG −18.00
1976	United States 441.00pts	FRG 584.60	Australia 599.54
1980	Soviet Union 457.00pts	Italy 656.20	Mexico 1172.85
1984	United States 186.00pts	Great Britain 189.20	FRG 234.00

[1]No other teams finished.   1896–1908 Event not held.

	Gold	Silver	Bronze

Discontinued Events

Equestrian High Jump
1900	Dominique Gardères (FRA) 1.85m *Canela*	–	A Moreau (FRA) 1.70 *Ludlow*
	Gian Giorgio Trissino (ITA) 1.85m *Oreste*		

Equestrian Long Jump
1900	Constant van Langhendonck (BEL) 6.10m *Extra Dry*	Gian Giorgio Trissino (ITA) 5.70 *Oreste*	de Prunelle (FRA) 5.30 *Tolla*

Figure Riding
(Only open to soldiers below the rank of NCO)

1920	Bouckaert (BEL) 30.5pts	Fiel (FRA) 29.5	Finet (BEL) 29.0
	Teams		
	Belgium	France	Sweden

Equestrianism – Medals

	G	S	B	Total
Germany (FRG)	20	15	17	52
Sweden	17	8	14	39
United States	8	13	9	30
France	10	11	8	29
Italy	7	9	7	23
Great Britain	5	5	8	18
Switzerland	4	7	6	17
Soviet Union	6	5	4	15
Belgium	4	2	5	11
Netherlands	5	3	1	9
Mexico	2	1	4	7
Poland	1	3	2	6
Australia	2	1	2	5
Denmark	–	4	1	5
Canada	1	1	1	3
Portugal	–	–	3	3
Spain	1	1	–	2
Austria	1	–	1	2
Chile	–	2	–	2
Romania	–	1	1	2
Czechoslovakia	1	–	–	1
Japan	1	–	–	1
New Zealand	1	–	–	1
Argentina	–	1	–	1
Bulgaria	–	1	–	1
Norway	–	1	–	1
Hungary	–	–	1	1
	97[1]	95	95[2]	287

[1]Two golds in 1900 high jump.
[2]No bronze in 1932 Three-day team event.

FENCING

One of the original sports held in 1896, when the first Olympic champion was Emile Gravelotte (FRA) in the foil. It is the only sport in which professionals have openly competed in the Games, as special events for fencing masters were held in 1896 and 1900. At the latter Games they even competed against the other competitors so that Albert Ayat (FRA) beat his pupil Ramón Fonst (CUB) in the épée. A foil competition for women was introduced in 1924 and a team contest for them in 1960. Electronic scoring equipment was used for épée in 1936, and for foil in 1956.

Aladar Gerevich (HUN) won a record seven gold medals in the sabre between 1932 and 1960. The record for most medals is 13 by Edoardo Mangiarotti (ITA) in foil and épée 1936–1960, comprising six golds, five silvers and two bronzes, while his elder brother Dario won a gold and two silvers in 1948 and 1952. Nedo Nadi (ITA) won an unequalled five golds at one Games in 1920, and his younger brother Aldo added three more golds and a silver – a family record total at a Games. The most individual event gold medals is three achieved by Ramón Fonst (CUB) in 1900 and

1904 (two), and by Nedo Nadi (ITA) in 1912 and 1920 (two). The only man, in any sport, to win Olympic gold medals at six consecutive Games was Aladar Gerevich (see above); his medal winning span of 28 years is also a record. Britain's Bill Hoskyns also competed at six Games, 1956–1976, but only won two silver medals. The equal longest span of competition by any Olympic competitor is 40 years by Ivan Osiier (DEN) who fenced from 1908 to 1948, during which time he won a silver medal in 1912, and became the oldest Olympic fencer in 1948 aged 59yr 240 days. His wife Ellen won a gold medal in 1924.

Only two fencers have won individual medals in all three disciplines at one Games. Outstanding was Roger Ducret (FRA) with foil and épée golds and a sabre silver in 1924. In the sparsely supported 1904 events American-born Albertson Van Zo Post (CUB) won a foil silver and bronzes in the other two disciplines. The oldest gold medallist was Aladar Gerevich (HUN) in 1960 aged 50yr 178 days, while the youngest was Ramón Fonst (CUB) aged 16yr 289 days in 1900. The family of Gerevich has a unique position in Olympic fencing as he won seven golds, one silver and two bronzes, his wife Erna Bogen won a bronze in 1932, his father-in-law Albert Bogen won a

silver in 1912, and Aladar's son Pal won bronze medals in 1972 and 1980.

Foil
Only Nedo Nadi (ITA) in 1912 and 1920, and Christian d'Oriola (FRA) in 1952 and 1956 have won two individual titles. In addition d'Oriola won two team golds and two silvers for a record six medals. The oldest gold medallist was Henri Jobier (FRA) who was over 44 years old in the winning 1924 team, while the youngest was Nedo Nadi (ITA) in 1912 aged 18yr 29 days.

Épée
Ramón Fonst (CUB) was the only double winner of the individual title, but the most successful was Edoardo Mangiarotti (ITA) with five gold, one silver and two bronze medals 1936–1960. The oldest gold medallist was Fiorenzo Marini (ITA) aged 46yr 179 days in the 1960 team, and the youngest was Fonst (see above).

Sabre
Jean Georgiadis (GRE), Jenö Fuchs (HUN), Rudolf Karpati (HUN) and Viktor Krovopouskov (URS) have all won two individual titles. Gerevich (see above) won a record seven gold medals (only one individual) and was also the oldest gold medallist. The youngest was

Mikhail Burtsev (URS) aged 20yr 36 days in the 1976 team event. Hungarians have dominated the sport to an unparalleled extent, winning eleven gold, six silver and eight bronze individual medals. They have won the team title nine times, placed second once and third on three occasions. Their 1960 team included Gerevich, Karpati and Pal Kovacs, who between them amassed a total of 19 gold medals. The winning Hungarian teams of 1948 and 1952 comprised the same members.

Women's Foil

Only Ilona Elek (HUN) has won two individual titles, in 1936 and 1948, but Elena Novikova-Belova (URS) won a record four golds from 1968 to 1976. The record for most medals is seven by Ildikó Sagi-Retjö (formerly Ujlaki-Rejtö) of Hungary in a record five Games, 1960–1976. Ellen Müller-Preis (AUT) competed over a record period of 24 years, 1932–1956, and this is a record span for any female Olympian.

The oldest gold medallist was Elek aged 41yr 77 days in 1948, while the youngest was Romanian-born Zita Funkenhauser (FRG) in the 1984 team aged 18yr 31 days.

Gold medallist in 1928 Helène Mayer (GER) also won a silver in 1936. (Mary Evans)

Fencing

	Gold	Silver	Bronze

Foil (Individual)

Wins are assessed on both wins (2pts) *and* draws (1pt) so, as in 1928, the winner does not necessarily have most wins.

Year	Gold	Silver	Bronze
1896	Emile Gravelotte (FRA) 4 wins	Henri Callott (FRA) 3	Perikles Mavromichalis-Pierrakos (GRE) 2
1900	Emile Coste (FRA) 6 wins	Henri Masson (FRA) 5	Jacques Boulenger (FRA) 4
1904	Ramón Fonst (CUB) 3 wins	Albertson Van Zo Post[1] (CUB) 2	Charles Tatham[1] (CUB) 1
1906	Georges Dillon-Kavanagh (FRA) d.n.a.	Gustav Casmir (GER) d.n.a.	Pierre d'Hugues (FRA) d.n.a.
1912	Nedo Nadi (ITA) 7 wins	Pietro Speciale (ITA) 5	Richard Verderber (AUT) 4
1920	Nedo Nadi (ITA) 10 wins	Philippe Cattiau (FRA) 9	Roger Ducret (FRA) 9
1924	Roger Ducret (FRA) 6 wins	Philippe Cattiau (FRA) 5	Maurice van Damme (BEL) 4
1928	Lucien Gaudin (FRA) 9 wins	Erwin Casmir (GER) 9	Giulio Gaudini (ITA) 9
1932	Gustavo Marzi (ITA) 9 wins	Joseph Levis (USA) 6	Giulio Gaudini (ITA) 5
1936	Giulio Gaudini (ITA) 7 wins	Edouard Gardère (FRA) 6	Giorgio Bocchino (ITA) 4
1948	Jean Buhan (FRA) 7 wins	Christian d'Oriola (FRA) 5	Lajos Maszlay (HUN) 4
1952	Christian d'Oriola (FRA) 8 wins	Edoardo Mangiarotti (ITA) 6	Manlio di Rosa (ITA) 5
1956	Christian d'Oriola (FRA) 6 wins	Giancarlo Bergamini (ITA) 5	Antonio Spallino (ITA) 5
1960	Viktor Zhdanovich (URS) 7 wins	Yuriy Sissikin (URS) 4	Albert Axelrod (USA) 3
1964	Egon Franke (POL) 3 wins	Jean-Claude Magnan (FRA) 2	Daniel Revenu (FRA) 1
1968	Ion Drimba (ROM) 4 wins	Jenö Kamuti (HUN) 3	Daniel Revenu (FRA) 3
1972	Witold Woyda (POL) 5 wins	Jenö Kamuti (HUN) 4	Christian Nöel (FRA) 2
1976	Fabio Dal Zotto (ITA) 4 wins	Aleksandr Romankov (URS) 4	Bernard Talvard (FRA) 3
1980	Vladimir Smirnov (URS) 5 wins	Paskal Jolyot (FRA) 5	Aleksandr Romankov (URS) 5
1984	Mauro Numa (ITA)	Matthias Behr (FRG)	Stefano Cerioni (ITA)

[1]Van Zo Post and Tatham were American citizens but competed for Cuba. 1908 Event not held.

	Gold	Silver	Bronze
Foil (Team)			
1904	Cuba	United States	Cuba[1]
1920	Italy	France	United States
1924	France	Belgium	Hungary
1928	Italy	France	Argentina
1932	France	Italy	United States
1936	Italy	France	Germany
1948	France	Italy	Belgium
1952	France	Italy	Hungary
1956	Italy	France	Hungary
1960	Soviet Union	Italy	Germany
1964	Soviet Union	Poland	France
1968	France	Soviet Union	Poland
1972	Poland	Soviet Union	France
1976	FRG	Italy	France
1980	France	Soviet Union	Poland
1984	Italy	FRG	France

[1]No other teams entered.   1896–1900, 1906–1912 Event not held.

	Gold	Silver	Bronze
Épée (Individual)			
1900	Ramón Fonst (CUB)	Louis Perree (FRA)	Léon Sée (FRA)
1904	Ramón Fonst (CUB) 3 wins	Charles Tatham (CUB) 2	Albertson Van Zo Post (CUB) 1
1906	Georges de la Falaise (FRA) d.n.a.	Georges Dillon-Kavanagh (FRA) d.n.a.	Alexander van Blijenburgh (HOL) d.n.a.
1908	Gaston Alibert (FRA) 5 wins	Alexandre Lippmann (FRA) 4	Eugène Olivier (FRA) 4
1912	Paul Anspach (BEL) 6 wins	Ivan Osiier (DEN) 5	Philippe Le Hardy de Beaulieu (BEL) 4
1920	Armand Massard (FRA) 9 wins	Alexandre Lippmann (FRA) 7	Gustave Buchard (FRA) 6
1924	Charles Delporte (BEL) 8 wins	Roger Ducret (FRA) 7	Nils Hellsten (SWE) 7
1928	Lucien Gaudin (FRA) 8 wins	Georges Buchard (FRA) 7	George Calnan (USA) 6
1932	Giancarlo Cornaggia-Medici (ITA) 8 wins	Georges Buchard (FRA) 7	Carlo Agostini (ITA) 7
1936	Franco Riccardi (ITA) 5 wins	Saverio Ragno (ITA) 6	Giancarlo Cornaggia-Medici (ITA) 6
1948	Luigi Cantone (ITA) 7 wins	Oswald Zappelli (SUI) 5	Edoardo Mangiarotti (ITA) 5
1952	Edoardo Mangiarotti (ITA) 7 wins	Dario Mangiarotti (ITA) 6	Oswald Zappelli (SUI) 6
1956	Carlo Pavesi (ITA) 5 wins	Giuseppe Delfino (ITA) 5	Edoardo Mangiarotti (ITA) 5
1960	Giuseppe Delfino (ITA) 5 wins	Allan Jay (GBR) 5	Bruno Khabarov (URS) 4
1964	Grigoriy Kriss (URS) 2 wins	William Hoskyns (GBR) 2	Guram Kostava (URS) 1
1968	Gyözö Kulcsár (HUN) 4 wins	Grigoriy Kriss (URS) 4	Gianluigi Saccaro (ITA) 4
1972	Csaba Fenyvesi (HUN) 4 wins	Jacques la Degaillerie (FRA) 3	Gyözö Kulcsár (HUN) 3
1976	Alexander Pusch (FRG) 3 wins	Jürgen Hehn (FRG) 3	Gyözö Kulcsár (HUN) 3
1980	Johan Harmenberg (SWE) 4 wins	Ernö Kolczonay (HUN) 3	Philippe Riboud (FRA) 3
1984	Philippe Boisse (FRA)	Bjorne Vaggo (SWE)	Philippe Riboud (FRA)

1896 Event not held.

	Gold	Silver	Bronze
Épée (Team)			
1906	France	Great Britain	Belgium
1908	France	Great Britain	Belgium
1912	Belgium	Great Britain	Netherlands
1920	Italy	Belgium	France
1924	France	Belgium	Italy
1928	Italy	France	Portugal
1932	France	Italy	United States
1936	Italy	Sweden	France
1948	France	Italy	Sweden
1952	Italy	Sweden	Switzerland
1956	Italy	Hungary	France
1960	Italy	Great Britain	Soviet Union
1964	Hungary	Italy	France
1968	Hungary	Soviet Union	Poland
1972	Hungary	Switzerland	Soviet Union
1976	Sweden	FRG	Switzerland
1980	France	Poland	Soviet Union
1984	FRG	France	Italy

1896–1904 Event not held.

	Gold	Silver	Bronze
Sabre (Individual)			
1896	Jean Georgiadis (GRE) 4 wins	Telemachos Karakalos (GRE) 3	Holger Nielsen (DEN) 2
1900	Georges de la Falaise (FRA) d.n.a.	Léon Thiébaut (FRA) d.n.a.	Siegfried Flesch (AUT) d.n.a.
1904	Manuel Diaz (CUB) 4 wins	William Grebe (USA) 3	Albertson Van Zo Post (CUB) 2
1906	Jean Georgiadis (GRE) d.n.a.	Gustav Casmir (GER) d.n.a.	Federico Cesarano (ITA) d.n.a.
1908	Jenö Fuchs (HUN) 6 wins	Béla Zulavsky (HUN) 6	Vilem Goppold von Lobsdorf (BOH) 4
1912	Jenö Fuchs (HUN) 6 wins	Béla Békéssy (HUN) 5	Ervin Mészáros (HUN) 5
1920	Nedo Nadi (ITA) 11 wins	Aldo Nadi (ITA) 9	Adrianus E W de Jong (HOL) 7
1924	Şándor Posta (HUN) 5 wins	Roger Ducret (FRA) 5	János Garai (HUN) 5
1928	Ödön Tersztyánszky (HUN) 9 wins	Attila Petschauer (HUN) 9	Bino Bini (ITA) 8
1932	György Piller (HUN) 8 wins	Giulio Gaudini (ITA) 7	Endre Kabos (HUN) 5
1936	Endre Kabos (HUN) 7 wins	Gustavo Marzi (ITA) 6	Aladár Gerevich (HUN) 6
1948	Aladár Gerevich (HUN) 7 wins	Vicenzo Pinton (ITA) 5	Pál Kovács (HUN) 5
1952	Pál Kovács (HUN) 8 wins	Aladár Gerevich (HUN) 7	Tibor Berczelly (HUN) 5
1956	Rudolf Kárpáti (HUN) 6 wins	Jerzy Pawlowski (POL) 5	Lev Kuznyetsov (URS) 4
1960	Rudolf Kárpáti (HUN) 5 wins	Zoltán Horvath (HUN) 4	Wladimiro Calarese (ITA) 4
1964	Tibor Pézsa (HUN) 2 wins	Claude Arabo (FRA) 2	Umar Mavlikhanov (URS) 1

Gold		Silver	Bronze
1968	Jerzy Pawlowski (POL) 4 wins	Mark Rakita (URS) 4	Tibor Pézsa (HUN) 3
1972	Viktor Sidiak (URS) 4 wins	Peter Maroth (HUN) 3	Vladimir Nazlimov (URS) 3
1976	Victor Krovopouskov (URS) 5 wins	Vladimir Nazlimov (URS) 4	Viktor Sidiak (URS) 3
1980	Viktor Krovopouskov (URS) 5 wins	Mikhail Burtsev (URS) 4	Imre Gedovari (HUN) 3
1984	Jean Francois Lamour (FRA)	Marco Marin (ITA)	Peter Westbrook (USA)

Gold		Silver	Bronze

Sabre (Team)

	Gold	Silver	Bronze
1906	Germany	Greece	Netherlands
1908	Hungary	Italy	Bohemia
1912	Hungary	Austria	Netherlands
1920	Italy	France	Netherlands
1924	Italy	Hungary	Netherlands
1928	Hungary	Italy	Poland
1932	Hungary	Italy	Poland
1936	Hungary	Italy	Germany
1948	Hungary	Italy	United States
1952	Hungary	Italy	France
1956	Hungary	Poland	Soviet Union
1960	Hungary	Poland	Italy
1964	Soviet Union	Italy	Poland
1968	Soviet Union	Italy	Hungary
1972	Italy	Soviet Union	Hungary
1976	Soviet Union	Italy	Romania
1980	Soviet Union	Italy	Hungary
1984	Italy	France	Romania

1896–1904 Event not held.

Gold		Silver	Bronze

Women's Foil (Individual)

	Gold	Silver	Bronze
1924	Ellen Osiier (DEN) 5 wins	Gladys Davis (GBR) 4	Grete Heckscher (DEN) 3
1928	Helène Mayer (GER) 7 wins	Muriel Freeman (GBR) 6	Olga Oelkers (GER) 4
1932	Ellen Preis (AUT) 9 wins	Heather Guinness (GBR) 8	Ena Bogen (HUN) 7
1936	Ilona Elek (HUN) 6 wins	Helène Mayer (GER) 5	Ellen Preis (AUT) 5
1948	Ilona Elek (HUN) 6 wins	Karen Lachmann (DEN) 5	Ellen Müller-Preis (AUT) 5
1952	Irene Camber (ITA) 5 wins	Ilona Elek (HUN) 5	Karen Lachmann (DEN) 4
1956	Gillian Sheen (GBR) 6 wins	Olga Orban (ROM) 6	Renée Garilhe (FRA) 5
1960	Heidi Schmid (GER) 6 wins	Valentina Rastvorova (URS) 5	Maria Vicol (ROM) 4
1964	Ildikó Ujlaki-Rejtö (HUN) 2 wins	Helga Mees (GER) 2	Antonella Ragno (ITA) 2
1968	Elena Novikova (URS) 4 wins	Pilar Roldan (MEX) 3	Ildikó Ujlaki-Rejtö (HUN) 3
1972	Antonella Ragno-Lonzi (ITA) 4 wins	Ildikó Bóbis (HUN) 3	Galina Gorokhova (URS) 3
1976	Ildikó Schwarczenberger (HUN) 4 wins	Maria Collino (ITA) 4	Elena Novikova-Belova (URS) 3
1980	Pascale Trinquet (FRA) 4 wins	Magda Maros (HUN) 3	Barbara Wysoczanska (POL) 3
1984	Jujie Luan (CHN)	Cornelia Hanisch (FRG)	Dorina Vaccaroni (ITA)

1896–1920 Event not held.

Gold		Silver	Bronze

Women's Foil (Team)

	Gold	Silver	Bronze
1960	Soviet Union	Hungary	Italy
1964	Hungary	Soviet Union	Germany
1968	Soviet Union	Hungary	Romania
1972	Soviet Union	Hungary	Romania
1976	Soviet Union	France	Hungary
1980	France	Soviet Union	Hungary
1984	FRG	Romania	France

1896–1956 Event not held.

Gold		Silver	Bronze

Discontinued Events

Foil for Fencing Masters

	Gold	Silver	Bronze
1896	Léon Pyrgos (GRE)	M Perronnet (FRA)	–
1900	Lucien Mérignac (FRA)	Alphonse Kirchhoffer (FRA)	Jean-Baptiste Mimiague (FRA)

Épée for Fencing Masters

	Gold	Silver	Bronze
1900	Albert Ayat (FRA)	Emile Bougnol (FRA)	Henri Laurent (FRA)
1906	Cyrille Verbrugge (BEL)	Mario Gubiani (ITA)	Ioannis Raissis (GRE)

Épée for Amateurs and Fencing Masters

	Gold	Silver	Bronze
1900	Albert Ayat (FRA)	Ramón Fonst (CUB)	Léon Sée (FRA)

Sabre for Fencing Masters

	Gold	Silver	Bronze
1900	Antonio Conte (ITA)	Italo Santelli (ITA)	Milan Neralic (AUT)
1906	Cyrille Verbrugge (BEL)	Ioannis Raissis (GRE)	–

Three Cornered Sabre

	Gold	Silver	Bronze
1906	Gustav Casmir (GER)	George van Rossem (HOL)	Péter Tóth (HUN)

Single Sticks

	Gold	Silver	Bronze
1904	Albertson Van Zo Post[1] (CUB)	William Grebe (USA)	William O'Connor (USA)

[1] Van Zo Post was an American citizen competing for Cuba.

Fencing – Medals

	G	S	B	Total
France	32	31	26	89
Italy	31	32	20	83
Hungary	30	17	22	69
Soviet Union	17	13	13	43
Germany (FRG)	8	10	5	23
Poland	4	5	7	16
Cuba	6	4	3	13
Belgium	5	3	5	13
United States	–	4	8	12
Great Britain	1	9	–	10
Greece	3	3	3	9
Romania	1	2	5	8
Netherlands	–	1	7	8
Sweden	2	3	2	7
Austria	1	1	5	7
Denmark	1	2	3	6
Switzerland	–	2	3	5
Bohemia (Czechoslovakia)	–	–	2	2
China	1	–	–	1
Mexico	–	1	–	1
Argentina	–	–	1	1
Portugal	–	–	1	1
	143	143	141[1]	427

[1]No bronze in one event in 1904 and another in 1906.

GYMNASTICS

In artistic gymnastics there are eight interlinked events for men and six for women. A team competition comes first comprising one compulsory and one optional exercise for each separate discipline. For men these are: floor exercises, side horse, rings, horse vault, parallel bars and horizontal bar. For women they are: floor exercises, asymmetrical bars, horse vault and balance beam. Each competitor is marked out of 10.00 for both the compulsory and optional exercises at each discipline. The best total of five gymnasts per country decides the team competition. The best 36 individuals then qualify for the individual all-round competition, and they each complete a further optional exercise for each discipline and are awarded new marks which are added to the average of their previous total from the team competition. The best six in each discipline go forward to the individual final for that event. A new mark for a further optional exercise is added to the average of their previous marks from the team competition. With the exception of 1948, when scores were marked out of 20.00, points since 1936 are of some comparative value. In 1984 a modern rhythmic event for women was introduced.

The first gymnastics gold medal was won by the German team on the parallel bars event in 1896, and the first individual champion was Carl Schuhmann of that team in the horse vault. Due to the large number of disciplines, each with

Attractive Nelli Kim (URS) won five gold and a silver at Montreal and Moscow. (George Herringshaw)

their own medals awarded, gymnasts are among the greatest collectors of Olympic medals. The most successful was Larissa Latynina (URS) who won a record 18 medals from 1956 to 1964, comprising nine golds (the most by any female Olympian), five silvers and four bronzes – unsurpassed in any sport. The most individual gold medals is seven won by Vera Caslavska (TCH) in 1964 and 1968. The male record for individual golds is six by Boris Shakhlin (URS) and Nikolai Andrianov (URS). The latter also holds the absolute Olympic record for most medals by a male competitor, in any sport, with a total of fifteen. In 1980 Aleksandr Ditiatin (URS) became the only male gymnast to gain medals in all eight categories open to him at one Games.

In recent years the sport has caught the imagination of the public due to a tremendous increase in media, especially television, coverage. In 1968 it was the attractive blonde Czech Vera Caslavska who caught the attention by defeating the Soviet girls only two months after the invasion of her country. At Munich it was elfin Olga Korbut (URS) who was the focus of all even though she was outshone, technically, by her illustrious team-mate Ludmila Tourischeva. In 1976 the unsmiling Nadia Comaneci (ROM) deserved the adulation as she scored the ultimate 10.00 on six occasions, while the photogenic Nelli Kim (URS) scored that figure twice. Aleksandr Ditiatin stole the show from the girls in 1980, but at Los Angeles the television cameras made a superstar of Mary Lou Retton (USA) in the absence of the East Europeans.

The oldest gold medallist was Masao Takemoto (JPN) aged 40yr 344 days in the 1960 team event. Only 24 days younger was Heikki Savolainen (FIN) in the 1948 team event, who in 1952 became the oldest medallist, with a bronze, aged 44yr 297 days. He also competed in a record five Games over a record span of 24 years from 1928 to 1952. The youngest champion was Nadia Comaneci (ROM) aged 14yr 313 days in 1976, while the oldest female champion was Agnes Keleti (HUN) in 1956 aged 35yr 171 days.

The closest margin of victory in the individual all-round contest was 0.025 of a point in 1984 when Koji Gushiken (JPN) beat Peter Vidmar (USA). The closest in the women's competition was also in 1984 when Mary Lou Retton (USA) beat Ecaterina Szabo (HUN) by 0.050 of a point.

The largest crowd to watch an Olympic gymnastic event was the 18000 at the Montreal Forum in 1976 for the final of the women's individual apparatus contests.

Gymnastics (Men)

Team

	Gold	Silver	Bronze
1904	United States 374.43pts	United States 356.37	United States 349.69
1906	Norway 19.00pts	Denmark 18.00	Italy 16.71
1908	Sweden 438pts	Norway 425	Finland 405
1912	Italy 265.75pts	Hungary 227.25	Great Britain 184.50
1920	Italy 359.855pts	Belgium 346.745	France 340.100
1924	Italy 839.058pts	France 820.528	Switzerland 816.661
1928	Switzerland 1718.625pts	Czechoslovakia 1712.250	Yugoslavia 1648.750
1932	Italy 541.850pts	United States 522.275	Finland 509.995
1936	Germany 657.430pts	Switzerland 654.802	Finland 638.468
1948	Finland 1358.3pts	Switzerland 1356.7	Hungary 1330.35
1952	Soviet Union 575.4pts	Switzerland 567.5	Finland 564.2
1956	Soviet Union 568.25pts	Japan 566.40	Finland 555.95
1960	Japan 575.20pts	Soviet Union 572.70	Italy 559.05
1964	Japan 577.95pts	Soviet Union 575.45	Germany 565.10
1968	Japan 575.90pts	Soviet Union 571.10	GDR 557.15
1972	Japan 571.25pts	Soviet Union 564.05	GDR 559.70
1976	Japan 576.85pts	Soviet Union 576.45	GDR 654.65
1980	Soviet Union 589.60pts	GDR 581.15	Hungary 575.00
1984	United States 591.40pts	China 590.80	Japan 586.70

1896–1900 Event not held.

Individual Combined Exercises

	Gold	Silver	Bronze
1900	Gustave Sandras (FRA) 302pts	Noël Bas (FRA) 295	Lucien Démanet (FRA) 293
1904	Julius Lenhart[1] (AUT) 69.80pts	Wilhelm Weber (GER) 69.10	Adolf Spinnler (SUI) 67.99
1906[2]	Pierre Payssé (FRA) 97pts	Alberto Braglia (ITA) 95	Georges Charmoille (FRA) 94
1906	Pierre Payssé (FRA) 116pts	Alberto Braglia (ITA) 115	Georges Charmoille (FRA) 113
1908	Alberto Braglia (ITA) 317.0pts	S W Tysal (GBR) 312.0	Louis Ségura (FRA) 297.0
1912	Alberto Braglia (ITA) 135.0pts	Louis Ségura (FRA) 132.5	Adolfo Tunesi (ITA) 131.5
1920	Giorgio Zampori (ITA) 88.35pts	Marco Torrés (FRA) 87.62	Jean Gounot (FRA) 87.45
1924	Leon Stukelj (YUG) 110.340pts	Robert Prazák (TCH) 110.323	Bedrich Supcik (TCH) 106.930
1928	Georges Miez (SUI) 247.500pts	Hermann Hänggi (SUI) 246.625	Leon Stukelj (YUG) 244.875
1932	Romeo Neri (ITA) 140.625pts	István Pelle (HUN) 134.925	Heikki Savolainen (FIN) 134.575
1936	Alfred Schwarzmann (GER) 113.100pts	Eugen Mack (SUI) 112.334	Konrad Frey (GER) 111.532
1948	Veikko Huhtanen (FIN) 229.7pts	Walter Lehmann (SUI) 229.0	Paavo Aaltonen (FIN) 228.8
1952	Viktor Chukarin (URS) 115.70pts	Grant Shaginyan (URS) 114.95	Josef Stalder (SUI) 114.75
1956	Viktor Chukarin (URS) 114.25pts	Takashi Ono (JPN) 114.20	Yuriy Titov (URS) 113.80
1960	Boris Shakhlin (URS) 115.95pts	Takashi Ono (JPN) 115.90	Yuriy Titov (URS) 115.60
1964	Yukio Endo (JPN) 115.95pts	Shuji Tsurumi (JPN) 115.40	–
		Viktor Lisitsky (URS) 115.40	
1968	Sawao Kato (JPN) 115.90pts	Mikhail Voronin (URS) 115.85	Akinori Nakayama (JPN) 115.65
1972	Sawao Kato (JPN) 114.650pts	Eizo Kenmotsu (JPN) 114.575	Akinori Nakayama (JPN) 114.325
1976	Nikolai Andrianov (URS) 116.650pts	Sawao Kato (JPN) 115.650	Mitsuo Tsukahara (JPN) 115.575
1980	Aleksandr Ditiatin (URS) 118.650pts	Nikolai Andrianov (URS) 118.225	Stoyan Deltchev (BUL) 118.000
1984	Koji Gushiken (JPN) 118.700pts	Peter Vidmar (USA) 118.675	Li Ning (CHN) 118.575

[1]Lenhart was a member of the Philadelphia Club, USA, which won the team event. [2]Two competitions in 1906, one of five events and one of six. 1896 Event not held.

	Gold	*Silver*	*Bronze*

Floor Exercises

	Gold	Silver	Bronze
1932	István Pelle (HUN) 9.60	Georges Miez (SUI) 9.47	Mario Lertora (ITA) 9.23
1936	Georges Miez (SUI) 18.666	Josef Walter (SUI) 18.5	Konrad Frey (GER) 18.466
			Eugen Mack (SUI) 18.466
1948	Ferenc Pataki (HUN) 38.7	János Mogyorósi-Klencs (HUN) 38.4	Zdenek Ružička (TCH) 38.1
1952	William Thoresson (SWE) 19.25	Tadao Uesako (JPN) 19.15	–
		Jerzy Jokiel (POL) 19.15	
1956	Valentin Muratov (URS) 19.20	Nobuyuki Aihara (JPN) 19.10	–
		William Thoresson (SWE) 19.10	
1960	Nobuyuki Aihara (JPN) 19.450	Yuriy Titov (URS) 19.325	Franco Menichelli (ITA) 19.275
1964	Franco Menichelli (ITA) 19.45	Viktor Lisitsky (URS) 19.35	–
		Yukio Endo (JPN) 19.35	
1968	Sawao Kato (JPN) 19.475	Akinori Nakayama (JPN) 19.400	Takeshi Kato (JPN) 19.275
1972	Nikolai Andrianov (URS) 19.175	Akinori Nakayama (JPN) 19.125	Shigeru Kasamatsu (JPN) 19.025
1976	Nikolai Andrianov (URS) 19.450	Vladimir Marchenko (URS) 19.425	Peter Kormann (USA) 19.300
1980	Roland Brückner (GDR) 19.750	Nikolai Andrianov (URS) 19.725	Aleksandr Ditiatin (URS) 19.700
1984	Li Ning (CHN) 19.925	Yun Lou (CHN) 19.775	Koji Sotomura (JPN) 19.700
			Philippe Vatuone (FRA) 19.700

1896–1928 Event not held.

Parallel Bars

	Gold	Silver	Bronze
1896	Alfred Flatow (GER) d.n.a.		Hermann Weingärtner (GER)
1904	George Eyser (USA) 44	Jules Zutter (SUI)	John Duha (USA) 40
1924	August Güttinger (SUI) 21.63	Anton Heida (USA) 43	Giorgio Zampori (ITA) 21.45
1928	Ladislav Vácha (TCH) 18.83	Robert Pražák (TCH) 21.61	Hermann Hänggi (SUI) 18.08
1932	Romeo Neri (ITA) 18.97	Josip Primožič (YUG) 18.50	Heikki Savolainen (FIN) 18.27
1936	Konrad Frey (GER) 19.067	István Pelle (HUN) 18.60	Alfred Schwarzmann (GER) 18.967
1948	Michael Reusch (SUI) 39.5	Michael Reusch (SUI) 19.034	Christian Kipfer (SUI) 39.1
		Veikkö Huhtanen (FIN) 39.3	Josef Stalder (SUI) 39.1
1952	Hans Eugster (SUI) 19.65	Viktor Chukarin (URS) 19.60	Josef Stalder (SUI) 19.50
1956	Viktor Chukarin (URS) 19.20	Masami Kubota (JPN) 19.15	Takashi Ono (JPN) 19.10
			Masao Takemoto (JPN) 19.10
1960	Boris Shakhlin (URS) 19.400	Giovanni Carminucci (ITA) 19.375	Takashi Ono (JPN) 19.350
1964	Yukio Endo (JPN) 19.675	Shuji Tsurumi (JPN) 19.450	Franco Menichelli (ITA) 19.350
1968	Akinori Nakayama (JPN) 19.475	Mikhail Voronin (URS) 19.425	Vladimir Klimenko (URS) 19.225
1972	Sawao Kato (JPN) 19.475	Shigeru Kasamatsu (JPN) 19.375	Eizo Kenmotsu (JPN) 19.250
1976	Sawao Kato (JPN) 19.675	Nikolai Andrianov (URS) 19.500	Mitsuo Tsukahara (JPN) 19.475
1980	Aleksandr Tkachev (URS) 19.775	Aleksandr Ditiatin (URS) 19.750	Roland Brückner (GDR) 19.650
1984	Bart Conner (USA) 19.950	Nobuyuki Kajitani (JPN) 19.925	Mitchell Gaylord (USA) 19.850

1900, 1906–1920 Event not held.

Pommel Horse

	Gold	Silver	Bronze
1896	Jules Zutter (SUI) d.n.a.	Hermann Weingärtner (GER)	–
1904	Anton Heida (USA) 42	George Eyser (USA) 33	William Merz (USA) 29
1924	Josef Wilhelm (SUI) 21.23	Jean Gutweiniger (SUI) 21.13	Antoine Rebetez (SUI) 20.73
1928	Hermann Hänggi (SUI) 19.75	Georges Miez (SUI) 19.25	Heikki Savolainen (FIN) 18.83
1932	István Pelle (HUN) 19.07	Omero Bonoli (ITA) 18.87	Frank Haubold (USA) 18.57
1936	Konrad Frey (GER) 19.333	Eugen Mack (SUI) 19.167	Albert Bachmann (SUI) 19.067
1948	Paavo Aaltonen (FIN) 38.7	Luigi Zanetti (ITA) 38.3	Guido Figone (ITA) 38.2
	Veikkö Huhtanen (FIN) 38.7		
	Heikki Savolainen (FIN) 38.7		
1952	Viktor Chukarin (URS) 19.50	Yevgeniy Korolkov (URS) 19.40	–
		Grant Shaginyan (URS) 19.40	
1956	Boris Shakhlin (URS) 19.25	Takashi Ono (JPN) 19.20	Viktor Chukarin (URS) 19.10
1960	Eugen Ekman (FIN) 19.375	–	Shuji Tsurumi (JPN) 19.150
	Boris Shaklin (URS) 19.375		
1964	Miroslav Cerar (YUG) 19.525	Shuji Tsurumi (JPN) 19.325	Yuriy Tsapenko (URS) 19.200
1968	Miroslav Cerar (YUG) 19.325	Olli Laiho (FIN) 19.225	Mikhail Voronin (URS) 19.200
1972	Viktor Klimenko (URS) 19.125	Sawao Kato (JPN) 19.000	Eizo Kenmotsu (JPN) 18.950
1976	Zoltan Magyar (HUN) 19.700	Eizo Kenmotsu (JPN) 19.575	Nikolai Andrianov (URS) 19.525
1980	Zoltan Magyar (HUN) 19.925	Aleksandr Ditiatin (URS) 19.800	Michael Nikolay (GDR) 19.775
1984	Li Ning (CHN) 19.950		Timothy Daggett (USA) 19.825
	Peter Vidmar (USA) 19.950		

1900, 1906–1920 Event not held.

Rings

	Gold	Silver	Bronze
1896	Ioannis Mitropoulos (GRE) d.n.a.	Hermann Weingärtner (GER)	Petros Persakis (GRE)
1904	Herman Glass (USA) 45	William Merz (USA) 35	Emil Voight (USA) 32
1924	Franco Martino (ITA) 21.553	Robert Pražák (TCH) 21.483	Ladislav Vácha (TCH) 21.430
1928	Leon Skutelj (YUG) 19.25	Ladislav Vácha (TCH) 19.17	Emanuel Löffler (TCH) 18.83
1932	George Gulack (USA) 18.97	William Denton (USA) 18.60	Giovanni Lattuada (ITA) 18.50
1936	Alois Hudec (TCH) 19.433	Leon Skutelj (YUG) 18.867	Matthias Volz (GER) 18.667
1948	Karl Frei (SUI) 39.60	Michael Reusch (SUI) 39.10	Zdenek Ružička (TCH) 38.30
1952	Grant Shaginyan (URS) 19.75	Viktor Chukarin (URS) 19.55	Hans Eugster (SUI) 19.40
			Dimitriy Leonkin (URS) 19.40
1956	Albert Azaryan (URS) 19.35	Valentin Muratov (URS) 19.15	Masao Takemoto (JPN) 19.10
			Masami Kubota (JPN) 19.10
1960	Albert Azaryan (URS) 19.725	Boris Shakhlin (URS) 19.500	Velik Kapsazov (BUL) 19.425
			Takashi Ono (JPN) 19.425
1964	Takuji Hayata (JPN) 19.475	Franco Menichelli (ITA) 19.425	Boris Shakhlin (URS) 19.400
1968	Akinori Nakayama (JPN) 19.450	Mikhail Voronin (URS) 19.325	Sawao Kato (JPN) 19.225
1972	Akinori Nakayama (JPN) 19.350	Mikhail Voronin (URS) 19.275	Mitsuo Tsukahara (JPN) 19.225
1976	Nikolai Andrianov (URS) 19.650	Aleksandr Ditiatin (URS) 19.550	Danut Grecu (ROM) 19.500
1980	Aleksandr Ditiatin (URS) 19.875	Aleksandr Tkachev (URS) 19.725	Jiri Tabak (TCH) 19.600
1984	Koji Gushiken (JPN) 19.850	–	Mitchell Gaylord (USA) 19.825
	Li Ning (CHN) 19.850		

1900, 1906–1920 Event not held.

The American 4 × 400m gold medallists: Sherri Howard, Chandra Cheeseborough, Valerie Brisco-Hooks, Lillie Leatherwood. (All-Sport)

1984 double gold medallist Evelyn Ashford, here anchoring the sprint relay. (All-Sport)

Britain's first ever Olympic throwing champion, Tessa Sanderson. (All-Sport)

(previous page) Sebastian Coe (GBR) successfully retains his 1500m title in 1984. (All-Sport)

The remarkable span of Michael Gross (FRG), nicknamed 'The Albatross'. (All-Sport)

One of the least surprising results at Los Angeles, Said Aouita wins the 5000m. (All-Sport)

ald Reagan ope

Joe Fargis on Touch of Class *leads the US show jumping team to the gold medal in Los Angeles.* (All-Sport)

The GDR 4-man bob on the way to winning the gold medal at Sarajevo. (All-Sport)

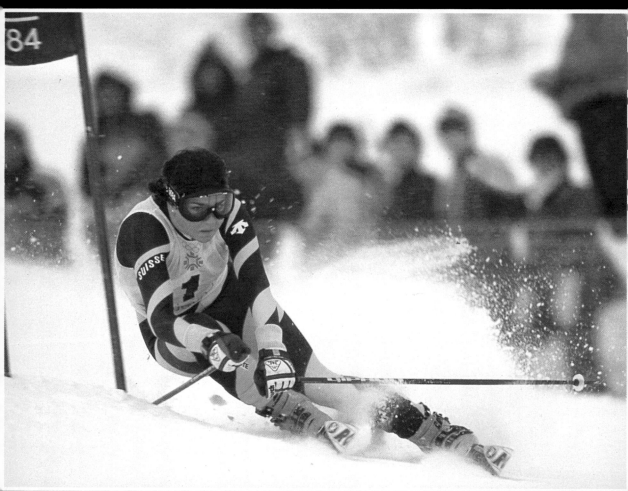

The youngest ever winner of an Olympic Alpine skiing title, Michela Figini of Switzerland. (All-Sport)

The end of a magnificent amateur career. Torvill and Dean dominating the ice dancing competition at Sarajevo. (All Sport)

The dynamic Mary Lou Retton (USA) won the individual all-around title before her home crowd. (All Sport)

Gold	*Silver*	*Bronze*

Horizontal Bar

	Gold	*Silver*	*Bronze*
1896	Hermann Weingärtner (GER) d.n.a.	Alfred Flatow (GER)	–
1904	Anton Heida (USA) 40	–	George Eyser (USA) 39
	Edward Hennig (USA) 40		
1924	Leon Štrukelj (YUG) 19.730	Jean Gutweniger (SUI) 19.236	André Higelin (FRA) 19.163
1928	Georges Miez (SUI) 19.17	Romeo Neri (ITA) 19.00	Eugen Mack (SUI) 18.92
1932	Dallas Bixler (USA) 18.33	Heikki Savolainen (FIN) 18.07	Einari Teräsvirta (FIN) 18.07[1]
1936	Aleksanteri Saarvala (FIN) 19.367	Konrad Frey (GER) 19.267	Alfred Schwarzmann (GER) 19.233
1948	Josef Stalder (SUI) 39.7	Walter Lehmann (SUI) 39.4	Veikkö Huhtanen (FIN) 39.2
1952	Jack Günthard (SUI) 19.55	Josef Stalder (SUI) 19.50	–
		Alfred Schwarzmann (GER) 19.50	
1956	Takashi Ono (JPN) 19.60	Yuriy Titov (URS) 19.40	Masao Takemoto (JPN) 19.30
1960	Takashi Ono (JPN) 19.60	Masao Takemoto (JPN) 19.525	Boris Shakhlin (URS) 19.475
1964	Boris Shakhlin (URS) 19.625	Yuriy Titov (URS) 19.55	Miroslav Cerar (YUG) 19.50
1968	Mikhail Voronin (URS) 19.550	–	Eizo Kenmotsu (JPN) 19.375
	Akinori Nakayama (JPN) 19.550		
1972	Mitsuo Tsukahara (JPN) 19.725	Sawao Kato (JPN) 19.525	Shigeru Kasamatsu (JPN) 19.450
1976	Mitsuo Tsukahara (JPN) 19.675	Eizo Kenmotsu (JPN) 19.500	Eberhard Gienger (GER) 19.475
1980	Stoyan Deltchev (BUL) 19.825	Aleksandr Ditiatin (URS) 19.750	Nikolai Andrianov (URS) 19.675
1984	Shinje Morisue (JPN) 20.00	Tong Fei (CHN) 19.955	Koji Gushiken (JPN) 19.950

[1]Teräsvirta conceded second place to Savolainen. 1900, 1906–1920 Event not held.

Horse Vault

	Gold	*Silver*	*Bronze*
1896	Carl Schuhmann (GER) d.n.a.	Jules Zutter (SUI)	–
1904	Anton Heida (USA) 36	–	William Merz (USA) 31
	George Eyser (USA) 36		
1924	Frank Kriz (USA) 9.98	Jan Koutny (TCH) 9.97	Bohumil Mořkovsky (TCH) 9.93
1928	Eugen Mack (SUI) 9.58	Emanuel Löffler (TCH) 9.50	Stane Derganc (YUG) 9.46
1932	Savino Guglielmetti (ITA) 18.03	Alfred Jochim (GER) 17.77	Edward Carmichael (USA) 17.53
1936	Alfred Schwarzmann (GER) 19.200	Eugen Mack (SUI) 18.967	Matthias Volz (GER) 18.467
1948	Paavo Aaltonen (FIN) 39.10	Olavi Rove (FIN) 39.00	János Mogyorósi-Klencs (HUN) 38.50
			Ferenc Pataki (HUN) 38.50
			Leos Sotornik (TCH) 38.50
1952	Viktor Chukarin (URS) 19.20	Masao Takemoto (JPN) 19.15	Tadao Uesako (JPN) 19.10
			Takashi Ono (JPN) 19.10
1956	Helmuth Bantz (GER) 18.85	–	Yuriy Titov (URS) 18.75
	Valentin Muratov (URS) 18.85		
1960	Takashi Ono (JPN) 19.350	–	Vladimir Portnoi (URS) 19.225
	Borish Shakhlin (URS) 19.350		
1964	Haruhiro Yamashita (JPN) 19.600	Viktor Lisitsky (URS) 19.325	Hannu Rantakari (FIN) 19.300
1968	Mikhail Voronin (URS) 19.000	Yukio Endo (JPN) 18.950	Sergey Diomidov (URS) 18.925
1972	Klaus Köste (GDR) 18.850	Viktor Klimenko (URS) 18.825	Nikolai Andrianov (URS) 18.800
1976	Nikolai Andrianov (URS) 19.450	Mitsuo Tsukahara (JPN) 19.375	Hiroshi Kajiyama (JPN) 19.275
1980	Nikolai Andrianov (URS) 19.825	Aleksandr Ditiatin (URS) 19.800	Roland Brückner (GDR) 19.775
1984	Yun Lou (CHN) 19.950	Li Ning (CHN) 19.825	–
		Koji Gushiken (JPN) 19.825	
		Mitchell Gaylord (USA) 19.825	
		Shinje Morisue (JPN) 19.825	

1900, 1906–1920 Event not held.

Gymnastics (Women)

	Gold	*Silver*	*Bronze*

Team

	Gold	*Silver*	*Bronze*
1928	Netherlands 316.75pts	Italy 289.00	Great Britain 258.25
1936	Germany 506.50pts	Czechoslovakia 503.60	Hungary 499.00
1948	Czechoslovakia 445.45pts	Hungary 440.55	United States 422.63
1952	Soviet Union 527.03pts	Hungary 520.96	Czechoslovakia 503.32
1956	Soviet Union 444.80pts	Hungary 443.50	Romania 438.20
1960	Soviet Union 382.320pts	Czechoslovakia 373.323	Romania 372.053
1964	Soviet Union 380.890pts	Czechoslovakia 379.989	Japan 377.889
1968	Soviet Union 382.85pts	Czechoslovakia 382.20	GDR 379.10
1972	Soviet Union 380.50pts	GDR 376.55	Hungary 368.25
1976	Soviet Union 390.35pts	Romania 387.15	GDR 385.10
1980	Soviet Union 394.90pts	Romania 393.50	GDR 392.55
1984	Romania 392.20pts	United States 391.20	China 388.60

1896–1924, 1932 Event not held.

Individual Combined Exercises

	Gold	*Silver*	*Bronze*
1952	Maria Gorokhovskaya (URS) 76.78	Nina Bocharova (URS) 75.94	Margit Korondi (HUN) 75.82
1956	Larissa Latynina (URS) 74.933	Ágnes Keleti (HUN) 74.633	Sofia Muratova (URS) 74.466
1960	Larissa Latynina (URS) 77.031	Sofia Muratova (URS) 76.696	Polina Astakhova (URS) 76.164
1964	Vera Caslavska (TCH) 77.564	Larissa Latynina (URS) 76.998	Polina Astakhova (URS) 76.965
1968	Vera Caslavska (TCH) 78.25	Zinaida Voronina (URS) 76.85	Natalya Kuchinskaya (URS) 76.75
1972	Ludmila Tourischeva (URS) 77.025	Karin Janz (GDR) 76.875	Tamara Lazakovitch (URS) 76.850
1976	Nadia Comaneci (ROM) 79.275	Nelli Kim (URS) 78.675	Ludmila Tourischeva (URS) 78.625
1980	Elena Davydova (URS) 79.150	Maxi Gnauck (GDR) 79.075	–
		Nadia Comaneci (ROM) 79.075	
1984	Mary Lou Retton (USA) 79.175	Ecaterina Szabo (ROM) 79.125	Simona Pauca (ROM) 78.675

1896–1948 Event not held.

Asymmetrical Bars

	Gold	*Silver*	*Bronze*
1952	Margit Korondi (HUN) 19.40	Maria Gorokhovskaya (URS) 19.26	Ágnes Keleti (HUN) 19.16
1956	Ágnes Keleti (HUN) 18.966	Larissa Latynina (URS) 18.833	Sofia Muratova (URS) 18.800

Gold	*Silver*	*Bronze*
1960 Polina Astakhova (URS) 19.616	Larissa Latynina (URS) 19.416	Tamara Lyukhina (URS) 19.399
1964 Polina Astakhova (URS) 19.332	Katalin Makray (HUN) 19.216	Larissa Latynina (URS) 19.199
1968 Vera Caslavska (TCH) 19.650	Karin Janz (GDR) 19.500	Zinaida Voronina (URS) 19.425
1972 Karin Janz (GDR) 19.675	Olga Korbut (URS) 19.450	
	Erika Zuchold (GDR) 19.450	
1976 Nadia Comaneci (ROM) 20.000	Teodora Ungureanu (ROM) 19.800	Marta Egervari (HUN) 19.775
1980 Maxi Gnauck (GDR) 19.875	Emila Eberle (ROM) 19.850	Steffi Kräker (GDR) 19.775
		Melita Rühn (ROM) 19.775
		Maria Filatova (URS) 19.775
1984 Ma Yanhong (CHN) 19.950	–	Mary Lou Retton (USA) 19.800
Julianne McNamara (USA) 19.950		

1896–1948 Event not held.

Balance Beam

1952 Nina Bocharova (URS) 19.22	Maria Gorokhovskaya (URS) 19.13	Margit Korondi (HUN) 19.02
1956 Ágnes Keleti (HUN) 18.80	Eva Bosáková (TCH) 18.63	–
	Tamara Manina (URS) 18.63	
1960 Eva Bosakova (TCH) 19.283	Larissa Latynina (URS) 19.233	Sofia Muratova (URS) 19.232
1964 Vera Caslavska (TCH) 19.449	Tamara Manina (URS) 19.399	Larissa Latynina (URS) 19.382
1968 Natalya Kuchinskaya (URS) 19.650	Vera Caslavska (TCH) 19.575	Larissa Petrik (URS) 19.250
1972 Olga Korbut (URS) 19.575	Tamara Lazakovitch (URS) 19.375	Karin Janz (GDR) 18.975
1976 Nadia Comaneci (ROM) 19.950	Olga Korbut (URS) 19.725	Teodora Ungureanu (ROM) 19.700
1980 Nadia Comaneci (ROM) 19.800	Elena Davydova (URS) 19.750	Natalya Shaposhnikova (URS) 19.725
1984 Simona Pauca (ROM) 19.800	–	Kathy Johnson (USA) 19.650
Ecaterina Szabo (ROM) 19.800		

1896–1948 Event not held.

Floor Exercises

1952 Agnes Keleti (HUN) 19.36	Maria Gorokhovskaya (URS) 19.20	Margit Korondi (HUN) 19.00
1956 Larissa Latynina (URS) 18.733	–	Elena Leustean (ROM) 18.70
Ágnes Keleti (HUN) 18.733		
1960 Larissa Latynina (URS) 19.583	Polina Astakhova (URS) 19.532	Tamara Lyukhina (URS) 19.449
1964 Larissa Latynina (URS) 19.599	Polina Astakhova (URS) 19.500	Anikó Jánosi (HUN) 19.300
1968 Larissa Petrik (URS) 19.675	–	Natalya Kuchinskaya (URS) 19.650
Vera Caslavska (TCH) 19.675		
1972 Olga Korbut (URS) 19.575	Ludmila Tourischeva (URS) 19.550	Tamara Lazakovitch (URS) 19.450
1976 Nelli Kim (URS) 19.850	Ludmila Tourischeva (URS) 19.825	Nadia Comaneci (ROM) 19.750
1980 Nelli Kim (URS) 19.875		Natalya Shaposhnikova (URS) 19.825
Nadia Comaneci (ROM) 19.875		Maxi Gnauck (GDR) 19.825
1984 Ecaterina Szabo (ROM) 19.975	Julianne McNamara (USA) 19.950	Mary Lou Retton (USA) 19.775

1896–1948 Event not held.

Horse Vault

1952 Yekaterina Kalinchuk (URS) 19.20	Maria Gorokhovskaya (URS) 19.19	Galina Minaitscheva (URS) 19.16
1956 Larissa Latynina (URS) 18.833	Tamara Manina (URS) 18.800	Ann-Sofi Colling (SWE) 18.733
		Olga Tass (HUN) 18.733
1960 Margarita Nikolayeva (URS) 19.316	Sofia Muratova (URS) 19.049	Larissa Latynina (URS) 19.016
1964 Vera Caslavska (TCH) 19.483	Larissa Latynina (URS) 19.283	–
	Birgit Radochla (GER) 19.283	
1968 Vera Caslavska (TCH) 19.775	Erika Zuchold (GDR) 19.625	Zinaida Voronina (URS) 19.500
1972 Karin Janz (GDR) 19.525	Erika Zuchold (GDR) 19.275	Ludmila Tourischeva (URS) 19.250
1976 Nelli Kim (URS) 19.800	Ludmila Tourischeva (URS) 19.650	
	Carola Dombeck (GDR) 19.650	
1980 Natalya Shaposhnikova (URS) 19.725	Steffi Kräker (GDR) 19.675	Melita Rühn (ROM) 19.650
1984 Ecaterina Szabo (ROM) 19.875	Mary Lou Retton (USA) 19.850	Lavinia Agache (ROM) 19.750

1896–1948 Event not held.

Modern Rhythmic

1984 Lori Fung (CAN) 57.950	Doina Staiculescu (ROM) 57.900	Regina Weber (FRG) 57.700

1896–1980 Event not held.

Discontinued Events

Parallel Bars (Men's Teams)

1896 Germany	Greece	Greece

Horizontal Bars (Men's Teams)

1896 Germany[1]	–	–

[1]Walk-over.

Rope Climbing (Men)

1896 Nicolaos Andriakopoulos (GRE) 23.4 sec	Thomas Xenakis (GRE)	Fritz Hofmann (GER)
1904 George Eyser (USA) 7.0sec	Charles Krause (USA) 7.8	Emil Voigt (USA) 9.8
1906 Georgios Aliprantis (GRE) 11.4sec	Béla Erödy (HUN) 13.8	Konstantinos Kozanitas (GRE) 13.8
1924 Bedrich Supcik (TCH) 7.2sec	Albert Séguin (FRA) 7.4	August Güttinger (SUI) 7.8
		Ladislav Vácha (CZE) 7.8
1932 Raymond Bass (USA) 6.7sec	William Galbraith (USA) 6.8	Thomas Connelly (USA) 7.0

Club Swinging (Men)

1904 Edward Hennig (USA) 13pts	Emil Voigt (USA) 9	Ralph Wilson (USA) 5
1932 George Roth (USA) 8.97pts	Philip Erenberg (USA) 8.90	William Kuhlmeier (USA) 8.63

Gold	Silver	Bronze

Tumbling (Men)
1932 Rowland Wolfe (USA) 18.90pts — Edward Gross (USA) 18.67 — William Herrmann (USA) 18.37

Nine Event Competition (Men)
1904 Adolf Spinnler (SUI) 43.49pts — Julius Lenhart (AUT) 43.00 — Wilhelm Weber (GER) 41.60

Triathlon (Men)
(Comprised 100 yards, long jump and shot put)
1904 Max Emmerich (USA) 35.70pts — John Grieb (USA) 34.00 — William Merz (USA) 33.90

Four Event Competition (Men)
1904 Anton Heida (USA) 161pts — George Eyser (USA) 152 — William Merz (USA) 135

Sidehorse Vault (Men)
1924 Albert Séguin (FRA) 10.00pts — Jean Gounot (FRA) 9.93 / Francois Gangloff (FRA) 9.93 — –

234717

Swedish System (Men's Teams)
1912 Sweden 937.46pts — Denmark 898.84 — Norway 857.21
1920 Sweden 1364pts — Denmark 1325 — Belgium 1094

Free System (Men's Teams)
1912 Norway 114.25pts — Finland 109.25 — Denmark 106.25
1920 Denmark — Norway — –1

1Only two teams competed.

Portable Apparatus (Women's Teams)
1952 Sweden 74.20pts — Soviet Union 73.00 — Hungary 71.60
1956 Hungary 75.20pts — Sweden 74.20 — Poland 74.00

Gymnastics – Medals

| | Men | | | Women | | | |
	G	S	B	G	S	B	Total
Soviet Union	31	35	16	30	26	23	161
Japan	27	27	26	–	–	1	81
United States	21	15	19	2	3	4	64
Switzerland	15	19	13	–	–	–	47
Czechoslovakia	3	7	9	9	6	1	35
Hungary	6	5	5	5	5	9	35
Germany (FRG)	11	7	10	1	1	1	31
Italy	12	7	9	–	1	–	29
Romania	–	–	1	10	7	9	27
GDR	2	1	6	3	9	6	27
Finland	8	5	12	–	–	–	25
France	4	7	8	–	–	–	19
China	4	4	1	1	–	1	11
Yugoslavia	5	2	4	–	–	–	11.
Sweden	5	2	–	–	–	1	8
Greece	3	2	3	–	–	–	8
Norway	2	2	1	–	–	–	5
Denmark	1	3	1	–	–	–	5
Bulgaria	1	–	2	–	–	–	3
Great Britain	–	1	1	–	–	1	3
Austria	1	1	–	–	–	–	2
Belgium	–	1	1	–	–	–	2
Poland	–	1	1	–	–	–	2
Canada	–	–	–	1	–	–	1
Netherlands	–	–	–	1	–	–	1
	162	154	149	63	58	57	643

Sixteen years after his gold medals at Berlin Alfred Schwarzmann (GER) won a silver at Helsinki. (Mary Evans)

HANDBALL

In 1936 handball was played as an outdoor eleven-a-side game, but when reintroduced in 1972 it was as an indoor seven-a-side competition. Four players, all Romanians, have gained medals in three Games, but none of them were gold. Six members of the Soviet women's team won gold medals in 1976 and 1980: Lubov Odinokova, Zinaida Turchina, Tatyana Kochergina, Ludmila Poradnik, Aldona Nenenene and Larissa Karlova.

The oldest gold medallist was Yuriy Klimov (URS) aged 36yr 6 days in 1976, while the oldest female was Ludmila Poradnik (URS) in 1980 aged 34yr 200 days.

A member of the German Democratic Republic winning team in 1980 was Hans-Georg Beyer, the brother of 1976 shot put champion, Udo. Roswitha Krause (GDR) who won a silver in 1976 and a bronze in 1980, had been a swimming silver medallist in 1968.

Handball

	Gold	Silver	Bronze
Handball (Men)			
1936[1]	Germany	Austria	Switzerland
1972	Yugoslavia	Czechoslovakia	Romania
1976	Soviet Union	Romania	Poland
1980	GDR	Soviet Union	Romania
1984	Yugoslavia	FRG	Romania

[1]Field handball played outdoors. 1896–1932, 1948–1968 Event not held.

	Gold	Silver	Bronze
Handball (Women)			
1976	Soviet Union	GDR	Hungary
1980	Soviet Union	Yugoslavia	GDR
1984	Yugoslavia	Korea	China

1896–1972 Event not held.

Handball – Medals

	Men G	S	B	Women G	S	B	Total
Soviet Union	1	1	–	2	–	–	4
Yugoslavia	2	–	–	1	1	–	4
Romania	–	1	3	–	–	–	3
GDR	1	–	–	–	1	1	3
Germany (FRG)	1	1	–	–	–	–	2
Austria	–	1	–	–	–	–	1
Czechoslovakia	–	1	–	–	–	–	1
Korea	–	–	–	–	1	–	1
China	–	–	–	–	–	1	1
Hungary	–	–	–	–	–	1	1
Poland	–	–	1	–	–	–	1
Switzerland	–	–	1	–	–	–	1
	5	5	5	3	3	3	24

HOCKEY

The first Olympic hockey game was won by Scotland who beat Germany 4-0 in 1908, with the first goal scored by Ian Laing only two minutes after the start. In those Games four of the six teams competing represented England, Ireland, Scotland and Wales. Since 1928 Olympic hockey has been dominated by teams from the Indian sub-continent with India winning eight times and Pakistan three. However, it should be noted that Great Britain, probably the world's strongest team at the time, did not participate from 1932 to 1936. The long-awaited meeting between them, the masters, and India, the pupils, came in the 1948 final which India won 4-0.

Interestingly, after years of decline, in 1984 the Great Britain team was a last-minute replacement for the boycotting Soviet Union, and they won the bronze – their first medal for 32 years.

Several members of Indian teams have won a record three gold medals: Richard Allen 1928–36, Dhyan Chand 1928–36, Randhir Singh 1948–56, Balbir Singh 1948–56, Leslie Claudius 1948–56, Ranganandhan Francis 1948–56, and Udham Singh 1952, 1956 and 1964. Of these only Claudius and Udham Singh also won a silver each in 1960. The oldest gold medallist was Abdul Rashid (PAK) aged 38yr 100 days in 1960. Stanley Shoveller (IND) was also over 38 in 1920, while Dharam Singh (IND) was reputed to be 45 years old in 1964. The youngest champion was Mehmood Ayaz (PAK) in 1984 aged 19yr 79 days, although Arlene Boxhall was under 19 as a member of the 1980 Zimbabwe women's team, but she did not actually play in the tournament. The oldest female was the Zimbabwe coach/ player Anthea Stewart aged 35yr 253 days.

The highest score ever achieved in international hockey was when India beat the United States 24-1 in 1932. The highest score in a final was also in 1932 when India beat Japan 11-1. Roop Singh (IND) scored a record 12 goals in that match versus the USA in 1932. The Indian goalkeepers did not concede a single goal during the 1928 tournament (five games), and only a total of three in 1932 (two matches) and 1936 (five matches). In that time the Indians scored a total of 102 goals.

The longest game in Olympic hockey lasted 2hr 25min (into the sixth period of extra time) when the Netherlands beat Spain 1-0 in Mexico on 25 October 1968.

Hockey

	Gold	Silver	Bronze
Men			
1908[1]	England	Ireland	Scotland[2] Wales[2]
1920	England[3]	Denmark	Belgium
1928	India	Netherlands	Germany
1932	India	Japan	United States
1936	India	Germany	Netherlands
1948	India	Great Britain	Netherlands
1952	India	Netherlands	Great Britain
1956	India	Pakistan	Germany
1960	Pakistan	India	Spain
1964	India	Pakistan	Australia
1968	Pakistan	Australia	India
1972	FRG	Pakistan	India
1976	New Zealand	Australia	Pakistan
1980	India	Spain	Soviet Union
1984	Pakistan	FRG	Great Britain

[1]Great Britain had four teams entered. [2]Tie for third place. [3]Great Britain represented by England team.
1896–1906, 1912, 1924 Event not held.

	Gold	Silver	Bronze
Women			
1980	Zimbabwe	Czechoslovakia	Soviet Union
1984	Netherlands	FRG	United States

1896–1976 Event not held.

Hockey – Medals

	Men G	S	B	Total
India	8	1	2	11
Great Britain	2	2	4	8
Pakistan	3	3	1	7
Germany (FRG)	1	2	2	5
Netherlands	–	2	2	4
Australia	–	2	1	3
Spain	–	1	1	2
New Zealand	1	–	–	1
Denmark	–	1	–	1
Japan	–	1	–	1
Belgium	–	–	1	1
Soviet Union	–	–	1	1
United States	–	–	1	1
	14	14	15[1]	43

[1]Two bronzes in 1908.

	Women G	S	B	Total
Netherlands	1	–	–	1
Zimbabwe	1	–	–	1
Czechoslovakia	–	1	–	1
Germany (FRG)	–	1	–	1
Soviet Union	–	–	1	1
United States	–	–	1	1
	2	2	2	6

JUDO

This sport was introduced in 1964 and appropriately the first gold medal was won by Japan's Takehide Nakatani in the lightweight class. However, one of the greatest upsets to a nation's sporting pride occurred in Tokyo's Nippon Budokan Hall in 1964 when the giant Dutchman Anton Geesink (1.98m *6ft 6in*) beat the Japanese favourite for the Open category title in front of 15 000 home supporters. Another Dutchman, Wilhelm Ruska, is the only man to win two gold medals, the 93kg plus and Open classes in 1972. Italian-born Angelo Parisi won a record four medals, with a bronze in 1972 representing Great Britain, and then gold and two silvers in 1980 and 1984 representing France. The oldest gold medallist was Ruska when he won the 1972 Open class aged 32yr 11 days, and the youngest was Isao Okano (JPN) in the 1964 middleweight division aged 20yr 275 days.

The biggest of many big men in Olympic judo was Jong Gil Pak (PRK) who was 2.13m *7ft 0in* tall and weighed 163kg *359lb* in the 1976 Games.

In 1972 the Mongolian lightweight silver medallist, Bakhaavaa Buidaa, became the first competitor ever disqualified for failing a dope test in any international judo competition. Women's judo will be a demonstration sport at the 1988 Games with hopes of it being added to the official programme at later Games.

Judo – Medals

	G	S	B	Total
Japan	13	2	3	18
Soviet Union	5	4	9	18
France	2	2	7	11
Korea	2	4	4	10
Great Britain	–	4	6	10
Germany (FRG)	1	3	4	8
GDR	1	–	5	6
Netherlands	3	–	1	4
Cuba	1	3	–	4
Brazil	–	1	3	4
United States	–	1	3	4
Italy	1	1	1	3
Switzerland	1	1	1	3
Poland	–	1	2	3
Hungary	–	–	3	3
Austria	1	–	1	2
Bulgaria	–	1	1	2
Canada	–	1	1	2
Mongolia	–	1	1	2
Romania	–	–	2	2
Yugoslavia	–	–	2	2
Belgium	1	–	–	1
Egypt	–	1	–	1
Australia	–	–	1	1
Czechoslovakia	–	–	1	1
Iceland	–	–	1	1
North Korea (PRK)	–	–	1	1
	32	31[1]	64	127

[1]1972 Silver withheld due to disqualification

Judo

	Gold	Silver	Bronze
Open Category, No Weight Limit			
1964	Antonius Geesink (HOL)	Akio Kaminaga (JPN)	Theodore Boronovskis (AUS) Klaus Glahn (GER)
1972	Wilhelm Ruska (HOL)	Vitaliy Kuznetsov (URS)	Jean-Claude Brondani (FRA) Angelo Parisi (GBR)
1976	Haruki Uemura (JPN)	Keith Remfry (GBR)	Shota Chochoshvili (URS) Jeaki Cho (KOR)
1980	Dietmar Lorenz (GDR)	Angelo Parisi (FRA)	András Ozsvar (HUN) Arthur Mapp (GBR)
1984	Yasuhiro Yamashita (JPN)	Mohamed Rashwan (EGY)	Mihai Cioc (ROM) Arthur Schnabel (FRG)
1968 Event not held.			
Over 95kg			
1980	Angelo Parisi (FRA)	Dimitar Zaprianov (BUL)	Vladimir Kocman (TCH) Radomir Kovacevic (YUG)
1984	Hitoshi Saito (JPN)	Angelo Parisi (FRA)	Yong-Chul Cho (KOR) Mark Berger (CAN)
Up to 95kg			
1980	Robert Van de Walle (BEL)	Tengiz Khubuluri (URS)	Dietmar Lorenz (GDR) Henk Numan (HOL)
1984	Hyoung-Zoo Ha (KOR)	Douglas Vieira (BRA)	Bjarni Fridriksson (ISL) Gunther Neureuther (FRG)
Up to 86kg			
1980	Jürg Röthlisberger (SUI)	Isaac Azcuy Oliva (CUB)	Detlef Ultsch (GDR) Aleksandr Yatskevich (URS)
1984	Peter Seisenbacher (AUT)	Robert Berland (USA)	Seiki Nose (JPN) Walter Carmona (BRA)
Up to 78kg			
1980	Shota Khabaleri (URS)	Juan Ferrer La Hera (CUB)	Harald Heinke (GDR) Bernard Tchoullouyan (FRA)
1984	Frank Wieneke (FRG)	Neil Adams (GBR)	Michel Nowak (FRA) Mircea Fratica (ROM)
Up to 71kg			
1980	Ezio Gamba (ITA)	Neil Adams (GBR)	Karl-Heinz Lehmann (GDR) Ravdan Davaadalai (MGL)
1984	Byeong-Keun Ahn (KOR)	Ezio Gamba (ITA)	Luis Onmura (BRA) Kerrith Brown (GBR)
Up to 65kg			
1980	Nikolai Solodukhin (URS)	Tsendying Damdin (MGL)	Ilian Nedkov (BUL) Janusz Pawlowski (POL)
1984	Yoshiyuki Matsuoka (JPN)	Jung-Oh Hwang (KOR)	Josef Reiter (AUT) Marc Alexandre (FRA)
Up to 60kg			
1980	Thierry Rey (FRA)	Rafael Carbonell (CUB)	Tibor Kincses (HUN) Aramby Emizh (URS)
1984	Shinji Hosokawa (JPN)	Jae-Yup Kim (KOR)	Edward Liddie (USA) Neil Eckersley (GBR)

Previous Winners
(categories changed in 1980)

	Gold	Silver	Bronze
Over 93kg			
1964	Isao Inokuma (JPN)	A H Douglas Rogers (CAN)	Parnaoz Chikviladze (URS) Anzor Kiknadze (URS)
1972	Wilhelm Ruska (HOL)	Klaus Glahn (FRG)	Givi Onashvili (URS) Motoki Nishimura (JPN)
1976	Sergey Novikov (URS)	Gunther Neureuther (FRG)	Sumio Endo (JPN) Allen Coage (USA)
1968 Event not held.			
80kg to 93kg			
1972	Shota Chochoshvili (URS)	David Starbrook (GBR)	Chiaki Ishii (BRA) Paul Barth (FRG)
1976	Kazuhiro Ninomiya (JPN)	Ramaz Harshiladze (URS)	David Starbrook (GBR) Jürg Röthlisberger (SUI)
1964–1968 Event not held.			

Gold	Silver	Bronze
70kg to 80kg		
1964 Isao Okano (JPN)	Wolfgang Hofmann (GER)	James Bergman (USA)
		Eui Tae Kim (KOR)
1972 Shinobu Sekine (JPN)	Seung-Lip Oh (KOR)	Brian Jacks (GBR)
		Jean-Paul Coche (FRA)
1976 Isamu Sonoda (JPN)	Valeriy Dvoinikov (URS)	Slavko Obadov (YUG)
		Youngchul Park (KOR)
1968 Event not held.		
63kg to 70kg		
1964 Takehide Nakatani (JPN)	Eric Haenni (SUI)	Oleg Stepanov (URS)
		Aron Bogulubov (URS)
1972 Toyokazu Nomura (JPN)	Anton Zajkowski (POL)	Dietmar Hötger (GDR)
		Anatoliy Novikov (URS)
1976 Vladimir Nevzorov (URS)	Koji Kuramoto (JPN)	Patrick Vial (FRA)
		Marian Talaj (POL)
1964–1968 Event not held.		
Up to 63kg		
1972 Takao Kawaguchi (JPN)	–[1]	Yong Ik Kim (PRK)
		Jean-Jacques Mounier (FRA)
1976 Hector Rodriguez (CUB)	Eunkyung Chang (KOR)	Felice Mariani (ITA)
		Jozsef Tuncsik (HUN)

[1]Bakhaavaa Buidaa (MGL) disqualified after positive drug test. 1964–8 Event not held.

MODERN PENTATHLON

The five events constituting the modern pentathlon are: riding (over an 800m course); fencing (with épée); swimming (300m freestyle); shooting (pistol at 25m); cross-country running (4000m). The order of events has differed over the years, as has the points system. Prior to 1956 competitors were given points according to their placings in each event, but since 1956 points have been allocated according to an international scoring table. It is therefore difficult to compare performers under the two systems, but it is generally accepted that the margin of victory by Willie Grut (SWE) in 1948 was the greatest ever. In that competition he placed first in riding, fencing and swimming, fifth in shooting, and eighth in running.

The most successful was András Balczó (HUN) with three gold medals in 1960 (team), 1968 (team) and 1972 (individual). Only Lars Hall (SWE) has won two individual titles, in 1952 and 1956. Pavel Lednev (URS) won a record seven medals (two golds, two silvers, three bronzes) from 1968 to 1980. He was the oldest gold medallist in 1980 aged 37yr 121 days, while the youngest was Aladár Kovácsi (HUN) in 1952 aged 19yr 227 days.

George Patton (USA), later the famous Second World War general, was fifth in 1912, with results that indicated that he was not very good at shooting. Three men have scored maximums of 200 hits in shooting; Charles Leonard (USA) 1936, Daniel Massala (ITA) 1976 and George Horvath (SWE) in 1980. In the only other measurable or comparable discipline, swimming, the fastest time ever recorded was 3min 10.856sec by Ivar Sisniega (MEX) in 1980.

In 1984 the competition was held, experimentally, over four days, but it will return to the traditional five days in 1988. One of the biggest scandals in Olympic history occurred in the 1976 fencing segment when Boris Onischenko (URS), previous winner of a gold and two silver medals, was disqualified for using an illegal weapon. He had tampered with his épée so that it registered a hit even when contact had not taken place. There has been speculation about whether he had used the implement in the 1972 Games, where his victory over Britain's Jim Fox (his opponent in Montreal when the incident came to light) cost the Briton the individual bronze medal.

Modern Pentathlon

Gold	Silver	Bronze
Individual		
1912 Gustaf Lilliehöök (SWE) 27	Gösta Asbrink (SWE) 28	Georg de Laval (SWE) 30
1920 Gustaf Orzyssen (SWE) 18	Erik de Laval (SWE) 23	Gösta Rüno (SWE) 27
1924 Bo Lindman (SWE) 18	Gustaf Orzyssen (SWE) 39.5	Bertil Uggla (SWE) 45
1928 Sven Thofelt (SWE) 47	Bo Lindman (SWE) 50	Helmuth Kahl (GER) 52
1932 Johan Gabriel Oxenstierna (SWE) 32	Bo Lindman (SWE) 35.5	Richard Mayo (USA) 38.5
1936 Gotthard Handrick (GER) 31.5	Charles Leonard (USA) 39.5	Silvano Abba (ITA) 45.5
1948 Willie Grut (SWE) 16	George Moore (USA) 47	Gösta Gärdin (SWE) 49
1952 Lars Hall (SWE) 32	Gábor Benedek (HUN) 39	István Szondi (HUN) 41
1956 Lars Hall (SWE) 4843	Olavi Nannonen (FIN) 4774.5	Väinö Korhonen (FIN) 4750
1960 Ferenc Németh (HUN) 5024	Imre Nagy (HUN) 4988	Robert Beck (USA) 4981
1964 Ferenc Török (HUN) 5116	Igor Novikov (URS) 5067	Albert Mokeyev (URS) 5039
1968 Björn Ferm (SWE) 4964	András Balczó (HUN) 4953	Pavel Lednev (URS) 4795
1972 András Balczó (HUN) 5412	Boris Onischenko (URS) 5335	Pavel Lednev (URS) 5328
1976 Janusz Pyciak-Peciak (POL) 5520	Pavel Lednev (URS) 5485	Jan Bartu (TCH) 5466
1980 Anatoliy Starostin (URS) 5568	Tamás Szombathelyi (HUN) 5502	Pavel Lednev (URS) 5282
1984 Daniel Massala (ITA) 5469	Svante Rasmuson (SWE) 5456	Carlo Massullo (ITA) 5406

1896–1908 Event not held.

	Gold	Silver	Bronze
Team			
1952	Hungary 116	Sweden 182	Finland 213
1956	Soviet Union 13 690.5	United States 13 482	Finland 13 185.5
1960	Hungary 14 863	Soviet Union 14 309	United States 14 192
1964	Soviet Union 14 961	United States 14 189	Hungary 14 173
1968	Hungary 14 325	Soviet Union 14 248	France 13 289[1]
1972	Soviet Union 15 968	Hungary 15 348	Finland 14 812
1976	Great Britain 15 559	Czechoslovakia 15 451	Hungary 15 395
1980	Soviet Union 16 126	Hungary 15 912	Sweden 15 845
1984	Italy 16 060	United States 15 568	France 15 565

[1]Sweden finished third in 1968 but were disqualified when a doping test indicated that a member of the team had an excessive level of alcohol. 1896–1948 Event not held.

Modern Pentathlon – Medals

	G	S	B	Total
Sweden	9	7	5	21
Hungary	6	6	3	15
Soviet Union	5	5	4	14
United States	–	5	3	8
Finland	–	1	4	5
Italy	2	–	2	4
Germany (FRG)	1	–	1	2
Czechoslovakia	–	1	1	2
France	–	–	2	2
Great Britain	1	–	–	1
Poland	1	–	–	1
	25	25	25	75

ROWING

Men's rowing was first held on the Seine in 1900 over a 1750m course. In 1904 the course measured 2 miles *3219m*, in 1908 it was 1½ miles *2414m* and in 1948 1 mile 300 yards *1883m*. Women's rowing was introduced in 1976 over a 1000m course, but from 1988 they will race over the same distance, 2000m, as the men. Even though recent Games rowing has been held on still water, as opposed to flowing rivers as in the past, water and weather conditions vary too much to allow official Olympic records. However, it is noteworthy that the fastest average speed achieved by a men's eight over the full course was 21.67km/h when the GDR crew clocked 5min 32.17sec in 1976. That same year

One of the closest finishes in Olympic rowing, the 1932 eights. From the top, Italy 2nd, Great Britain 4th, Canada 3rd, United States 1st. (Dave Terry)

the New Zealand crew averaged 22.48km/h for the first 500m in a heat. The 1984 American women's eight averaged 20.02km/h clocking 2min 59.80sec for the 1000m distance, but the 1976 Soviet eight had achieved an average speed of 20.78km/h over the second 250m in a heat.

One of the first winning crews in the Games, the 1900 German four, contained three brothers, Oskar, Gustav and Carl Gossler, the latter as coxswain. This started a tradition of sibling · participation and success which reached a peak at Moscow in 1980 when the Landvoigt twins (GDR) beat the Pimenov twins (URS) in the coxless pairs final. The most famous father/son successes are the Beresfords (GBR), Julius with a silver in 1912, and Jack with five medals (see below); the Costellos (USA), Paul winning three golds and son Bernard a silver

in 1956; the Kellys (USA), John Sr with three golds (see below) and John Jr a bronze in 1956; the Nickalls (GBR), Guy Sr with a gold in 1908 and Guy Jr with two silvers in 1920 and 1928. However, the Burnells (GBR), Charles (1908) and Richard (1948), are the only father and son oarsmen both to win Olympic gold medals. Six oarsmen have won a record three golds: John Kelly (USA) 1920–1924; his cousin Paul Costello (USA) 1920–1928; Jack Beresford (GBR) 1924, 1932–1936; Vyacheslav Ivanov (URS) 1956–1964; Siegfried Brietzke (GDR) 1972–1980; Pertti Karppinen (FIN) 1976–1984. Of these only Beresford also won two silvers making him the most successful rower of all time. Ivanov and Karppinen are the only men to win three individual golds, while Beresford, again, is the only oarsman to win medals at five

Games, 1920–1936.

The oldest gold medallist was Robert Zimonyi who coxed the United States eight in 1964 aged 46yr 180 days. In 1948 he had won a bronze coxing a pair from his native Hungary. The oldest oarsman to win a gold medal was Guy Nickalls (GBR) in the 1908 eight aged 42yr 170 days. The youngest gold medallist was the unknown French boy who coxed the winning Dutch pair in 1900. Believed to have been between 7 and 10 years of age he was recruited at the last moment to replace Hermanus Brockmann, their cox in the heats, who was considered to be too heavy. Of the many other young winning coxes over the years, the youngest known for certain was another French boy, Noël Vandernotte, in the 1936 pairs and fours aged 12yr 233 days. The latter crew included his father and uncle.

Rowing (Men)

Gold	Silver	Bronze

Single Sculls

	Gold	Silver	Bronze
1900	Henri Barrelet (FRA) 7:35.6	André Gaudin (FRA) 7:41.6	St. George Ashe (GBR) 8:15.6
1904	Frank Greer (USA) 10:08.5	James Juvenal (USA) 2 lengths	Constance Titus (USA) 1 length
1906	Gaston Delaplane (FRA) 5:53.4	Joseph Larran (FRA) 6:07.2	–
1908	Harry Blackstaffe (GBR) 9:26.0	Alexander McCulloch (GBR) 1 length	Bernhard von Gaza (GER) d.n.a.
			Károly Levitzky (HUN) d.n.a.
1912	William Kinnear (GBR) 7:47.6	Potydore Veirman (BEL) 1 length	Everard Butter (CAN) d.n.a.
			Mikhail Kusik (URS) d.n.a.
1920	John Kelly (USA) 7:35.0	Jack Beresford (GBR) 7:36.0	Clarence Hadfield d'Arcy (NZL) 7:48.0
1924	Jack Beresford (GBR) 7:49.2	William Garrett-Gilmore (USA) 7:54.0	Josef Schneider (SUI) 8:01.1
1928	Henry Pearce (AUS) 7:11.0	Kenneth Myers (USA) 7:20.8	David Collet (GBR) 7:19.8
1932	Henry Pearce (AUS) 7:44.4	William Miller (USA) 7:45.2	Guillermo Douglas (URU) 8:13.6
1936	Gustav Schäfer (GER) 8:21.5	Josef Hasenöhrl (AUT) 8:25.8	Daniel Barrow (USA) 8:28.0
1948	Mervyn Wood (AUS) 7:24.4	Eduardo Risso (URU) 7:38.2	Romolo Catasta (ITA) 7:51.4
1952	Yuriy Tyukalov (URS) 8:12.8	Mervyn Wood (AUS) 8:14.5	Teodor Kocerka (POL) 8:19.4
1956	Vyacheslav Ivanov (URS) 8:02.5	Stuart Mackenzie (AUS) 8:07.7	John Kelly (USA) 8:11.8
1960	Vyacheslav Ivanov (URS) 7:13.96	Achim Hill (GER) 7:20.21	Teodor Kocerka (POL) 7:21.26
1964	Vyacheslav Ivanov (URS) 8:22.51	Achim Hill (GER) 8:26.34	Gottfried Kottmann (SUI) 8:29.68
1968	Henri Jan Wienese (HOL) 7:47.80	Jochen Meissner (FRG) 7:52.00	Alberto Demiddi (ARG) 7:57.19
1972	Yuriy Malishev (URS) 7:10.12	Alberto Demiddi (ARG) 7:11.53	Wolfgang Gueldenpfennig (GDR) 7:14.45
1976	Pertti Karppinen (FIN) 7:29.03	Peter Kolbe (FRG) 7:31.67	Joachim Dreifke (GDR) 7:38.03
1980	Pertti Karppinen (FIN) 7:09.61	Vasiliy Yakusha (URS) 7:11.66	Peter Kersten (GDR) 7:14.88
1984	Pertti Karppinen (FIN) 7:00.24	Peter Kolbe (FRG) 7:02.19	Robert Mills (CAN) 7:10.38

1896 Event not held.

	Gold	Silver	Bronze

Double Sculls

	Gold	Silver	Bronze
1904	United States 10:03.2	United States d.n.a.	United States d.n.a.
1920	United States 7:09.0	Italy 7:19.0	France 7:21.0
1924	United States 7:45.0	France 7:54.8	Switzerland d.n.a.
1928	United States 6:41.4	Canada 6:51.0	Austria 6:48.8
1932	United States 7:17.4	Germany 7:22.8	Canada 7:27.6
1936	Great Britain 7:20.8	Germany 7:26.2	Poland 7:36.2
1948	Great Britain 6:51.3	Denmark 6:55.3	Uruguay 7:12.4
1952	Argentina 7:32.2	Soviet Union 7:38.3	Uruguay 7:43.7
1956	Soviet Union 7:24.0	United States 7:32.2	Australia 7:37.4
1960	Czechoslovakia 6:47.50	Soviet Union 6:50.49	Switzerland 6:50.59
1964	Soviet Union 7:10.66	United States 7:13.16	Czechoslovakia 7:14.23
1968	Soviet Union 6:51.82	Netherlands 6:52.80	United States 6:54.21
1972	Soviet Union 7:01.77	Norway 7:02.58	GDR 7:05.55
1976	Norway 7:13.20	Great Britain 7:15.26	GDR 7:17.45
1980	GDR 6:24.33	Yugoslavia 6:26.34	Czechoslovakia 6:29.07
1984	United States 6:36.87	Belgium 6:38.19	Yugoslavia 6:39.59

1896–1900, 1906–1912 Event not held.

	Gold	Silver	Bronze

Coxless Quadruple Sculls

	Gold	Silver	Bronze
1976	GDR 6:18.65	Soviet Union 6:19.89	Czechoslovakia 6:21.77
1980	GDR 5:49.81	Soviet Union 5:51.47	Bulgaria 5:52.38
1984	FRG 5:57.55	Australia 5:57.98	Canada 5:59.07

1896–1972 Event not held.

Coxless Pairs

	Gold	Silver	Bronze
1908	Great Britain 9:41.0	Great Britain 2½ lengths	–
1924	Netherlands 8:19.4	France 8:21.6	–
1928	Germany 7:06.4	Great Britain 7:08.8	United States 7:20.4
1932	Great Britain 8:00.0	New Zealand 8:02.4	Poland 8:08.2
1936	Germany 8:16.1	Denmark 8:19.2	Argentina 8:23.0
1948	Great Britain 7:21.1	Switzerland 7:23.9	Italy 7:31.5
1952	United States 8:20.7	Belgium 8:23.5	Switzerland 8:32.7
1956	United States 7:55.4	Soviet Union 8:03.9	Austria 8:11.8
1960	Soviet Union 7:02.01	Austria 7:03.69	Finland 7:03.80
1964	Canada 7:32.94	Netherlands 7:33.40	Germany 7:38.63
1968	GDR 7:26.56	United States 7:26.71	Denmark 7:31.84
1972	GDR 6:53.16	Switzerland 6:57.06	Netherlands 6:58.70
1976	GDR 7:23.31	United States 7:26.73	FRG 7:30.03
1980	GDR 6:48.01	Soviet Union 6:50.50	Great Britain 6:51.47
1984	Romania 6:45.39	Spain 6:48.47	Norway 6:51.81

1896–1906, 1912–1920 Event not held.

Coxed Pairs

	Gold	Silver	Bronze
1900	Netherlands 7:34.2	France I 7:34.4	France II 7:57.2
1906[1]	Italy I 4:23.0	Italy II 4:30.0	France d.n.a.
1906[2]	Italy 7:32.4	Belgium 8:03.0	France 8:08.6
1920	Italy 7:56.0	France 7:57.0	Switzerland d.n.a.
1924	Switzerland 8:39.0	Italy 8:39.1	United States 3m
1928	Switzerland 7:42.6	France 7:48.4	Belgium 7:59.4
1932	United States 8:25.8	Poland 8:31.2	France 8:41.2
1936	Germany 8:36.9	Italy 8:49.7	France 8:54.0
1948	Denmark 8:00.5	Italy 8:12.2	Hungary 8:25.2
1952	France 8:28.6	Germany 8:32.1	Denmark 8:34.9
1956	United States 8:26.1	Germany 8:29.2	Soviet Union 8:31.0
1960	Germany 7:29.14	Soviet Union 7:30.17	United States 7:34.58
1964	United States 8:21.23	France 8:23.15	Netherlands 8:23.42
1968	Italy 8:04.81	Netherlands 8:06.80	Denmark 8:08.
1972	GDR 7:17.25	Czechoslovakia 7:19.57	Romania 7:2
1976	GDR 7:58.99	Soviet Union 8:01.82	Czechoslov 3:03.28
1980	GDR 7:02.54	Soviet Union 7:03.35	Yugoslavia 92
1984	Italy 7:05.99	Romania 7:11.21	United State 12.81

[1]Over 1000m.　[2]Over 1600m.　1896, 1904, 1908–1912 Event not held.

Coxless Fours

	Gold	Silver	Bronze
1904	United States 9:53.8	United States d.n.a.	–
1908	Great Britain 8:34.0	Great Britain 1½ lengths	–
1924	Great Britain 7:08.6	Canada 7:18.0	Switzerland 2 lengths
1928	Great Britain 6:36.0	United States 6:37.0	Italy 6:31.6
1932	Great Britain 6:58.2	Germany 7:03.0	Italy 7:04.0
1936	Germany 7:01.8	Great Britain 7:06.5	Switzerland 7:10.6
1948	Italy 6:39.0	Denmark 6:43.5	United States 6:47.7
1952	Yugoslavia 7:16.0	France 7:18.9	Finland 7:23.3
1956	Canada 7:08.8	United States 7:18.4	France 7:20.9
1960	United States 6:26.26	Italy 6:28.78	Soviet Union 6:29.62
1964	Denmark 6:59.30	Great Britain 7:00.47	United States 7:01.37
1968	GDR 6:39.18	Hungary 6:41.64	Italy 6:44.01
1972	GDR 6:24.27	New Zealand 6:25.64	FRG 6:28.41
1976	GDR 6:37.42	Norway 6:41.22	Soviet Union 6:42.52
1980	GDR 6:08.17	Soviet Union 6:11.81	Great Britain 6:16.58
1984	New Zealand 6:03.48	United States 6:06.10	Denmark 6:07.72

1896–1900, 1906, 1912–1920 Event not held.

Coxed Fours

	Gold	Silver	Bronze
1900[1]	Germany 5:59.0	Netherlands 6:33.0	Germany 6:35.0
1900[1]	France 7:11.0	France 7:18.0	Germany 7:18.2
1906	Italy 8:13.0	France d.n.a.	France d.n.a.
1912	Germany 6:59.4	Great Britain 2 lengths	Norway d.n.a.
			Denmark d.n.a.
1920	Switzerland 6:54.0	United States 6:58.0	Norway 7:02.0
1924	Switzerland 7:18.4	France 7:21.6	United States 1 length
1928	Italy 6:47.8	Switzerland 7:03.4	Poland 7:12.8
1932	Germany 7:19.0	Italy 7:19.2	Poland 7:26.8
1936	Germany 7:16.2	Switzerland 7:24.3	France 7:33.3
1948	United States 6:50.3	Switzerland 6:53.3	Denmark 6:58.6
1952	Czechoslovakia 7:33.4	Switzerland 7:36.5	United States 7:37.0
1956	Italy 7:19.4	Sweden 7:22.4	Finland 7:30.9
1960	Germany 6:39.12	France 6:41.62	Italy 6:43.72
1964	Germany 7:00.44	Italy 7:02.84	Netherlands 7:06.46
1968	New Zealand 6:45.62	GDR 6:48.20	Switzerland 6:49.04
1972	FRG 6:31.85	GDR 6:33.30	Czechoslovakia 6:35.64
1976	Soviet Union 6:40.22	GDR 6:42.70	FRG 6:46.96
1980	GDR 6:14.51	Soviet Union 6:19.05	Poland 6:22.52
1984	Great Britain 6:20.28	United States 6:23.68	New Zealand 6:26.44

[1]Two separate finals were held in 1900.　1896, 1904, 1908 Event not held.

Gold	Silver	Bronze

Eights

	Gold	Silver	Bronze
1900	United States 6:09.8	Belgium 6:13.8	Netherlands 6:23.0
1904	United States 7:50.0	Canada d.n.a.	–
1908	Great Britain I 7:52.0	Belgium 2 lengths	Great Britain II d.n.a.
1912	Great Britain I 6:15.0	Great Britain II 6:19.0	Germany d.n.a.
1920	United States 6:02.6	Great Britain 6:05.0	Norway 6:36.0
1924	United States 6:33.4	Canada 6:49.0	Italy ¾ length
1928	United States 6:03.2	Great Britain 6:05.6	Canada 6:03.8
1932	United States 6:37.6	Italy 6:37.8	Canada 6:40.4
1936	United States 6:25.4	Italy 6:26.0	Germany 6:26.4
1948	United States 5:56.7	Great Britain 6:06.9	Norway 6:10.3
1952	United States 6:25.9	Soviet Union 6:31.2	Australia 6:33.1
1956	United States 6:35.2	Canada 6:37.1	Australia 6:39.2
1960	Germany 5:57.18	Canada 6:01.52	Czechoslovakia 6:04.84
1964	United States 6:18.23	Germany 6:23.29	Czechoslovakia 6:25.11
1968	FRG 6:07.00	Australia 6:07.98	Soviet Union 6:09.11
1972	New Zealand 6:08.94	United States 6:11.61	GDR 6:11.67
1976	GDR 5:58.29	Great Britain 6:00.82	New Zealand 6.03.51
1980	GDR 5:49.05	Great Britain 5:51.92	Soviet Union 5:52.66
1984	Canada 5:41.32	United States 5:41.74	Australia 5:42.40

1896, 1906 Event not held.

Discontinued Events

Naval Rowing Boats (2000m)

	Gold	Silver	Bronze
1906	Italy 10:45.0	Greece d.n.a.	Greece d.n.a.

16-Man Naval Rowing Boats (3000m)

	Gold	Silver	Bronze
1906	Greece 16:35.0	Greece 17:09.5	Italy d.n.a.

Coxed Fours (Inriggers)

	Gold	Silver	Bronze
1912	Denmark 7:47.0	Sweden 1 length	Norway d.n.a.

Rowing (Women)

Women's rowing was introduced in 1976 over a course of 1000 metres. From 1988, it will be over 2000m.

Single Sculls

	Gold	Silver	Bronze
1976	Christine Scheiblich (GDR) 4:05.56	Joan Lind (USA) 4:06.21	Elena Antonova (URS) 4:10.24
1980	Sandra Toma (ROM) 3:40.69	Antonina Makhina (URS) 3:41.65	Martina Schröter (GDR) 3:43.54
1984	Valeria Racila (ROM) 3:40.68	Charlotte Geer (USA) 3:43.89	Ann Haesebrouck (BEL) 3:45.72

Double Sculls

	Gold	Silver	Bronze
1976	Bulgaria 3:44.36	GDR 3:47.86	Soviet Union 3:49.93
1980	Soviet Union 3:16.27	GDR 3:17.63	Romania 3:18.91
1984	Romania 3:26.75	Netherlands 3:29.13	Canada 3:29.82

Coxless Pairs

	Gold	Silver	Bronze
1976	Bulgaria 4:01.22	GDR 4:01.64	FRG 4:02.35
1980	GDR 3:30.49	Poland 3:30.95	Bulgaria 3:32.39
1984	Romania 3:32.60	Canada 3:36.06	FRG 3:40.50

Coxed Quadruple Sculls

	Gold	Silver	Bronze
1976	GDR 3:29.99	Soviet Union 3:32.49	Romania 3:32.76
1980	GDR 3:15.32	Soviet Union 3:15.73	Bulgaria 3:16.10
1984	Romania 3:14.11	United States 3:15.57	Denmark 3:16.02

Coxed Fours

	Gold	Silver	Bronze
1976	GDR 3:45.08	Bulgaria 3:48.24	Soviet Union 3:49.38
1980	GDR 3:19.27	Bulgaria 3:20.75	Soviet Union 3:20.92
1984	Romania 3:19.30	Canada 3:21.55	Australia 3:23.29

Eights

	Gold	Silver	Bronze
1976	GDR 3:33.32	Soviet Union 3:36.17	United States 3:38.68
1980	GDR 3:03.32	Soviet Union 3:04.29	Romania 3:05.63
1984	United States 2:59.80	Romania 3:00.87	Netherlands 3:02.92

Rowing – Medals

	Men G	S	B	Women G	S	B	Total		Men G	S	B	Women G	S	B	Total
United States	29	15	13	1	3	1	62	Norway	1	2	6	–	–	–	9
Soviet Union	11	13	6	1	5	4	40	Poland	–	1	7	–	1	–	9
GDR	17	3	6	8	3	1	38	New Zealand	3	2	3	–	–	–	8
Germany (FRG)	16	11	9	–	–	2	38	Belgium	–	6	1	–	–	1	8
Great Britain	15	15	5	–	–	–	35	Bulgaria	–	–	1	2	2	2	7
Italy	10	10	8	–	–	–	28	Finland	3	–	3	–	–	–	6
France	4	13	9	–	–	–	26	Greece	1	2	1	–	–	–	4
Switzerland	4	6	9	–	–	–	19	Argentina	1	1	2	–	–	–	4
Canada	3	6	7	–	2	1	19	Yugoslavia	1	1	2	–	–	–	4
Romania	1	1	1	6	1	3	13	Austria	–	2	2	–	–	–	4
Netherlands	3	4	4	–	1	1	13	Uruguay	–	1	3	–	–	–	4
Denmark	3	3	6	–	–	1	13	Hungary	–	1	2	–	–	–	3
Australia	3	4	3	–	–	1	12	Sweden	–	2	–	–	–	–	2
Czechoslovakia	2	1	7	–	–	–	10	Spain	–	1	–	–	–	–	1
									129	129	127	18	18	18	439

SHOOTING

Baron de Coubertin, the founder of the modern Olympic games, was a pistol shooter of note in his youth and this undoubtedly led to the sport being included in the first Games held in 1896. The first champion was Pantelis Karasevdas (GRE) in the free rifle event. The number of events has varied considerably from 21 in 1920 to only two in 1932, while there were none at all in 1928. Since 1952 there has been some standardization, and in 1984 three events for women were introduced.

The most successful competitor was Carl Osburn (USA) who won a record eleven medals (five golds, four silvers, two bronzes) from 1912 to 1924. The only man to win three individual golds was Gudbrand Skatteboe (NOR) in 1906. Women first competed, in men's events, in 1968 when three countries, Poland, Peru and Mexico entered one each. The Mexican lady, Nuria Ortiz, was

the first to compete and finished thirteenth in the skeet event. The first woman to win a medal was Margaret Murdock (USA) in the 1976 small-bore rifle (three positions).

The oldest gold medallist in Olympic history was the remarkable Oscar Swahn (SWE) in the 1912 running deer team aged 64yr 258 days (his son Alfred was also in the team). At Antwerp in 1920 he became the oldest medallist and, indeed, competitor at any sport ever when he won a silver in the same event. He qualified for the 1924 Games in his 77th year, but illness prevented him from competing. The youngest champion was George Généreux (CAN) in the 1952 trap shooting aged 17yr 147 days. The youngest medallist was Ulrike Holmer (FRG) in the 1984 women's standard rifle aged 16yr 305 days.

John and Sumner Paine (USA) were the first brothers to win gold medals in the Olympic Games, in 1896, while the first twins to do so were Vilhelm and Eric Carlberg (SWE) in 1912. Károly Tákacs

(HUN) was a European pistol champion in the 1930s using his right hand. In 1938 while on army training a grenade blew up in his hand destroying his right arm. After the war he won the rapid fire pistol event with his left hand at the 1948 and 1952 Games, one of only five shooters who have successfully defended an Olympic title. The 1960 rapid fire pistol champion William McMillan (USA) competed in his record sixth Games in 1976.

Gerald Ouellette (CAN) won the 1956 small-bore (prone) with a world record maximum possible score of 600, but it was not accepted as the range was found to be 1½m short of the regulation 50m distance. When Ho Jun Li (PRK) won the same event in 1972 with 599 he was asked his secret and he replied that he was 'aiming at a capitalist'.

In the 1976 trap shooting event 65 year old Paul Cerutti of Monaco was disqualified for using drugs even though he had finished 43rd out of 44 competitors; probably the oldest ever so penalized.

Shooting

	Gold	Silver	Bronze
Free Pistol (50 metres)			
1896	Sumner Paine (USA) 442	Viggo Jensen (DEN) 285	Holger Nielsen (DEN) d.n.a.
1900	Karl Röderer (SUI) 503	Achille Paroche (FRA) 466	Konrad Stäheli (SUI) 453
1906	Georgios Orphanidis (GRE) 221	Jean Fouconnier (FRA) 219	Aristides Rangavis (GRE) 218
1912	Alfred Lane (USA) 499	Peter Dolfen (USA) 474	Charles Stewart (GBR) 470
1920	Karl Frederick (USA) 496	Afranio da Costa (BRA) 489	Alfred Lane (USA) 481
1936	Torsten Ullmann (SWE) 559	Erich Krempel (GER) 544	Charles des Jammonières (FRA) 540
1948	Edwin Vazquez Cam (PER) 545	Rudolf Schnyder (SUI) 539	Torsten Ullmann (SWE) 539
1952	Huelet Benner (USA) 553	Angel Léon de Gozalo (ESP) 550	Ambrus Balogh (HUN) 549
1956	Pentti Linnosvuo (FIN) 556	Makhmud Oumarov (URS) 556	Offutt Pinion (USA) 551
1960	Aleksey Gushchin (URS) 560	Makhmud Oumarov (URS) 552	Yoshihisa Yoshikawa (JPN) 552
1964	Väinö Markkanen (FIN) 560	Franklin Green (USA) 557	Yoshihisa Yoshikawa (JPN) 554
1968	Grigory Kossykh (URS) 562	Heinz Mertel (FRG) 562	Harald Vollmar (GDR) 560
1972	Ragnar Skanakar (SWE) 567	Dan Iuga (ROM) 562	Rudolf Dollinger (AUT) 560
1976	Uwe Potteck (GDR) 573	Harald Vollmar (GDR) 567	Rudolf Dollinger (AUT) 560
1980	Aleksandr Melentyev (URS) 581	Harald Vollmar (GDR) 568	Lubcho Diakov (URS) 565
1984	Haifeng Xu (CHN) 566	Ragnar Skanakar (SWE) 565	Yifu Wang (CHN) 564

1904, 1908, 1924–1932 Event not held.

Rapid-Fire Pistol			
1896	Jean Phrangoudis (GRE) 344	Georgios Orphanidis (GRE) 249	Holger Nielsen (DEN) d.n.a.
1900	Maurice Larrouy (FRA) 58	Léon Moreaux (FRA) 57	Eugene Balme (FRA) 57
1906	Maurice Lecoq (FRA) 250	Léon Moreaux (FRA) 249	Aristides Rangavis (GRE) 245
1908	Paul van Asbroeck (BEL) 490	Réginald Storms (BEL) 487	James Gorman (USA) 485
1912	Alfred Lane (USA) 287	Paul Palén (SWE) 286	Johan von Holst (SWE) 283
1920	Guilherme Paraense (BRA) 274	Raymond Bracken (USA) 272	Fritz Zulauf (SUI) 269
1924	Paul Bailey (USA) 18	Vilhelm Carlberg (SWE) 18	Lennart Hannelius (FIN) 18
1932	Renzo Morigi (ITA) 36	Heinz Hax (GER) 36	Domenico Matteucci (ITA) 36
1936	Cornelius van Oyen (GER) 36	Heinz Hax (GER) 35	Torsten Ullmann (SWE) 34
1948	Károly Takács (HUN) 580	Carlos Diaz Sáenz Valiente (ARG) 571	Sven Lundqvist (SWE) 569
1952	Károly Takács (HUN) 579	Szilárd Kun (HUN) 578	Gheorghe Lichiardopol (ROM) 578
1956	Stefan Petrescu (ROM) 587	Evgeniy Shcherkasov (URS) 585	Gheorghe Lichiardopol (ROM) 581
1960	William McMillan (USA) 587	Pentti Linnosvuo (FIN) 587	Aleksandr Zabelin (URS) 587
1964	Pentti Linnosvuo (FIN) 592	Ion Tripsa (ROM) 591	Lubomir Nacovsky (TCH) 590
1968	Jozef Zapedzki (POL) 593	Marcel Rosca (ROM) 591	Renart Suleimanov (URS) 591
1972	Jozef Zapedzki (POL) 593	Ladislav Faita (TCH) 594	Victor Torshin (URS) 593
1976	Norbert Klaar (GDR) 597	Jürgen Wiefel (GDR) 596	Roberto Ferraris (ITA) 595
1980	Corneliu Ion (ROM) 596	Jürgen Wiefel (GDR) 596	Gerhard Petrisch (AUT) 596
1984	Takeo Kamachi (JPN) 595	Corneliu Ion (ROM) 593	Rauno Bies (FIN) 591

1904, 1928 Event not held.

	Gold	Silver	Bronze

Small-Bore Rifle (Prone)[1]

	Gold	Silver	Bronze
1908	A A Carnell (GBR) 387	Harry Humby (GBR) 386	George Barnes (GBR) 385
1912	Frederick Hird (USA) 194	William Milne (GBR) 193	Harry Burt (GBR) 192
1920	Lawrence Nuesslein (USA) 391	Arthur Rothrock (USA) 386	Dennis Fenton (USA) 385
1924	Pierre Coquelin de Lisle (FRA) 398	Marcus Dinwiddie (USA) 396	Josias Hartmann (SUI) 394
1932	Bertil Rönnmark (SWE) 294	Gustavo Huet (MEX) 294	Zoltán Hradetsky-Soós (HUN) 293
1936	Willy Rögeberg (NOR) 300	Ralph Berzsenyi (HUN) 296	Wladyslaw Karás (POL) 296
1948	Arthur Cook (USA) 599	Walter Tomsen (USA) 599	Jonas Jonsson (SWE) 597
1952	Josif Sarbu (ROM) 400	Boris Andreyev (URS) 400	Arthur Jackson (USA) 399
1956	Gerald Ouellette (CAN) 600[2]	Vasiliy Borissov (URS) 599	Gilmour Boa (CAN) 598
1960	Peter Kohnke (GER) 590	James Hill (USA) 589	Enrico Pelliccione (VEN) 587
1964	László Hammerl (HUN) 597	Lones Wigger (USA) 597	Tommy Pool (USA) 596
1968	Jan Kurka (TCH) 598	László Hammerl (HUN) 598	Ian Ballinger (NZL) 597
1972	Ho Jun Li (PRK) 599	Victor Auer (USA) 598	Nicolae Rotaru (ROM) 598
1976	Karlheinz Smieszek (FRG) 599	Ulrich Lind (FRG) 597	Gennadiy Lushchikov (URS) 595
1980	Karoly Varga (HUN) 599	Hellfried Heilfort (GDR) 599	Petar Zapianov (BUL) 598
1984	Edward Etzel (USA) 599	Michel Bury (FRA) 596	Michael Sullivan (GBR) 596

[1]In 1908 and 1912 any position allowed; in 1920 it was a standing position. [2] Range found to be marginally short – record not allowed. 1896–1906, 1928 Event not held.

Small-Bore Rifle – Three Positions (Prone, Kneeling, Standing)

1952	Erling Kongshaug (NOR) 1164	Viho Ylönen (FIN) 1164	Boris Andreyev (URS) 1163
1956	Anatoliy Bogdanov (URS) 1172	Otakar Hořínek (TCH) 1172	Nils Sundberg (SWE) 1167
1960	Viktor Shamburkin (URS) 1149	Marat Niyasov (URS) 1145	Klaus Zähringer (GER) 1139
1964	Lones Wigger (USA) 1164	Velitchko Khristov (BUL) 1152	László Hammerl (HUN) 1151
1968	Bernd Klingner (FRG) 1157	John Writer (USA) 1156	Vitaly Parkhimovich (URS) 1154
1972	John Writer (USA) 1166	Lanny Bassham (USA) 1157	Werner Lippoldt (GDR) 1153
1976	Lanny Bassham (USA) 1162	Margaret Murdock (USA) 1162	Werner Seibold (FRG) 1160
1980	Viktor Vlasov (URS) 1173	Bernd Hartstein (GDR) 1166	Sven Johansson (SWE) 1165
1984	Malcolm Cooper (GBR) 1173	Daniel Nipkow (SUI) 1163	Alister Allan (GBR) 1162

1896–1948 Event not held.

Running Game Target

1900	Louis Debray (FRA) 20	P Nivet (FRA) 20	Comte de Lambert (FRA) 19
1972	Iakov Zhelezniak (URS) 569	Hanspeter Bellingrodt (COL) 565	John Kynoch (GBR) 562
1976	Aleksandr Gazov (URS) 579	Aleksandr Kedyarov (URS) 576	Jerzy Greszkiewicz (POL) 571
1980	Igor Sokolov (URS) 589	Thomas Pfeffer (GDR) 589	Aleksandr Gasov (URS) 587
1984	Yuwei Li (CHN) 587	Helmut Bellingrodt (COL) 584	Shiping Huang (CHN) 581

1896, 1904–1968 Event not held.

Olympic Trap Shooting

1900	Roger de Barbarin (FRA) 17	René Guyot (FRA) 17	Justinien de Clary (FRA) 17
1906[1]	Gerald Merlin (GBR) 24	Ioannis Peridis (GRE) 23	Sidney Merlin (GBR) 21
1906[2]	Sidney Merlin (GBR) 15	Anastasios Metaxas (GRE) 13	Gerald Merlin (GBR) 12
1908	Walter Ewing (CAN) 72	George Beattie (CAN) 60	Alexander Maunder (GBR) 57
			Anastasios Metaxas (GRE) 57
1912	James Graham (USA) 96	Alfred Goeldel-Bronikowen (GER) 94	Harry Blau (URS) 91
1920	Mark Arie (USA) 95	Frank Troeh (USA) 93	Frank Wright (USA) 87
1924	Gyula Halasy (HUN) 98	Konrad Huber (FIN) 98	Frank Hughes (USA) 97
1952	George Généreux (CAN) 192	Knut Holmquist (SWE) 191	Hans Liljedahl (SWE) 191
1956	Galliano Rossini (ITA) 195	Adam Smelczynski (POL) 190	Alessandro Ciceri (ITA) 188
1960	Ion Dumitrescu (ROM) 192	Galliano Rossini (ITA) 191	Sergey Kalinin (URS) 190
1964	Ennio Mattarelli (ITA) 198	Pavel Senichev (URS) 194	William Morris (USA) 194
1968	Robert Braithwaite (GBR) 198	Thomas Garrigus (USA) 196	Kurt Czekalla (GDR) 196
1972	Angelo Scalzone (ITA) 199	Michel Carrega (FRA) 198	Silvano Basagni (ITA) 195
1976	Don Haldeman (USA) 190	Armando Marques (POR) 189	Ubaldesco Baldi (ITA) 189
1980	Luciano Giovanetti (ITA) 198	Rustam Yambulatov (URS) 196	Jörg Damme (GDR) 196
1984	Luciano Giovanetti (ITA) 192	Francisco Boza (PER) 192	Daniel Carlisle (USA) 192

[1]Single shot. [2] Double shot. 1896, 1904, 1928–1948 Event not held.

Skeet Shooting

1968	Evgeny Petrov (URS) 198	Romano Garagnani (ITA) 198	Konrad Wirnhier (FRG) 198
1972	Konrad Wirnhier (FRG) 195	Evgeny Petrov (URS) 195	Michael Buchheim (GDR) 195
1976	Josef Panacek (TCH) 198	Eric Swinkels (HOL) 198	Wieslaw Gawlikowski (POL) 196
1980	Hans Kjeld Rasmussen (DEN) 196	Lars-Goran Carlsson (SWE) 196	Roberto Garcia (CUB) 196
1984	Matthew Dryke (USA) 198	Ole Rasmussen (DEN) 196	Luca Scribani Rossi (ITA) 196

1896–1964 Event not held.

Air Rifle

1984	Philippe Herberle (FRA) 589	Andreas Kronthaler (AUT) 587	Barry Dagger (GBR) 587

1896–1980 Event not held.

Discontinued Events

Free Rifle (3 positions)

1896	Georgios Orphanidis (GRE) 1583	Jean Phrangoudis (GRE) 1312	Viggo Jensen (DEN) 1305
1906	Gudbrand Skatteboe (NOR) 977	Konrad Stäheli (SUI) 943	Jean Reich (SUI) 933
1908	Albert Helgerud (NOR) 909	Harry Simon (USA) 887	Ole Saether (NOR) 883
1912	Paul Colas (FRA) 987	Lars Madsen (DEN) 981	Niels Larsen (DEN) 962
1920	Morris Fisher (USA) 997	Niels Larsen (DEN) 985	Östen Östensen (NOR) 980
1924	Morris Fisher (USA) 95	Carl Osburn (USA) 95	Niels Larsen (DEN) 93
1948	Emil Grunig (SUI) 1120	Pauli Janhonen (FIN) 1114	Willy Rögeberg (NOR) 1112
1952	Anatoliy Bogdanov (URS) 1123	Robert Bürchler (SUI) 1120	Lev Vainschtein (URS) 1109
1956	Vasiliy Borissov (URS) 1138	Allan Erdman (URS) 1137	Vilho Ylönen (FIN) 1128

The remarkable Oscar Swahn (with beard) in 1912, with (from left) his son Alfred, Ake Lundeberg and Per Arvidsson. (Dave Terry)

Gold	Silver	Bronze
1960 Hubert Hammerer (AUT) 1129	Hans Spillmann (SUI) 1127	Vasiliy Borissov (URS) 1127
1964 Gary Anderson (USA) 1153	Shota Kveliashvili (URS) 1144	Martin Gunnarsson (USA) 1136
1968 Gary Anderson (USA) 1157	Vladimir Kornev (URS) 1151	Kurt Müller (SUI) 1148
1972 Lones Wigger (USA) 1155	Boris Melnik (URS) 1155	Lajos Papp (HUN) 1149

1900–1904, 1928–1936 Event not held.

Free Rifle

1896[1] Pantelis Karasevdas (GRE) 2320	Paulas Pavlidis (GRE) 1978	Nicolaos Tricoupes (GRE) 1718
1906[2] Marcel de Stadelhofen (SUI) 243	Konrad Stäheli (SUI) 238	Léon Moreaux (FRA) 234
1906[3] Gudbrand Skatteboe (NOR)	–	–
1906[4] Konrad Stäheli (SUI)	–	–
1906[5] Gudbrand Skatteboe (NOR)	–	–
1908[6] Jerry Millner (GBR) 98	Kellogg Casey (USA) 93	Maurice Blood (GBR) 92

[1]Over 200m. [2]Any position (300m). [3]Prone (300m). [4]Kneeling (300m). [5]Standing (300m). [6]Over 1000 yards. 1900–1904 Event not held.

Free Rifle (Team)

1906	Switzerland 4596	Norway 4534	France 4511
1908	Norway 5055	Sweden 4711	France 4652
1912	Sweden 5655	Norway 5605	Denmark 5529
1920	United States 4876	Norway 4741	Switzerland 4698
1924	United States 676	France 646	Haiti 646

1896–1904 Event not held.

Military Rifle

1900[1] Emil Kellenberger (SUI) 930	Anders Nielsen (DEN) 921	Ole Östmo (NOR) 917
1900[2] Lars Madsen (DEN) 305	Ole Östmo (NOR) 299	Charles du Verger (BEL) 298
1900[3] Konrad Stäheli (SUI) 324	Emil Kellenberger (SUI) 314	–
	Anders Nielsen (DEN) 314	
1900[4] Achille Paroche (FRA) 332	Anders Nielsen (DEN) 330	Ole Östmo (NOR) 329
1906[5] Léon Moreaux (FRA) 187	Louis Richardet (SUI) 187	Jean Reich (SUI) 183
1906[6] Louis Richardet (SUI) 238	Jean Reich (SUI) 234	Raoul de Boigne (FRA) 232
1912[1] Sándor Prokopp (HUN) 97	Carl Osburn (USA) 96	Embret Skogen (NOR) 95
1912[7] Paul Colas (FRA) 94	Carl Osburn (USA) 94	Joseph Jackson (USA) 93
1920[4] Otto Olsen (NOR) 60	Léon Johnson (FRA) 59	Fritz Kuchen (SUI) 59
1920[2] Carl Osburn (USA) 56	Lars Madsen (DEN) 55	Lawrence Nuesslein (USA) 54
1920[8] Hugo Johansson (SWE) 58	Mauritz Eriksson (SWE) 56	Lloyd Spooner (USA) 56

1908 Event not held.

Military Rifle (Team)

1900	Switzerland 4399	Norway 4290	France 4278
1908	United States 2531	Great Britain 2497	Canada 2439
1912	United States 1687	Great Britain 1602	Sweden 1570
1920[2]	Denmark 266	United States 255	Sweden 255
1920[4]	United States 289	France 283	Finland 281
1920[8]	United States 287	South Africa 287	Sweden 287
1920[9]	United States 573	Norway 565	Switzerland 563

[1]Three positions (300m). [2]Standing (300m). [3]Kneeling (300m). [4]Prone (300m). [5]Standing or kneeling (200m). [6]Standing or kneeling (300m). [7]Any position (600m). [8]Prone (600m). [9]Prone (300m and 600m). 1896, 1904 Event not held.

Gold	Silver	Bronze
Small Bore Rifle		
1908[1] A F Fleming (GBR) 24	M K Matthews (GBR) 24	W B Marsden (GBR) 24
1908[2] William Styles (GBR) 45	H I Hawkins (GBR) 45	Edward Amoore (GBR) 45
1912[2] Wilhelm Carlberg (SWE) 242	Johan von Holst (SWE) 233	Gustaf Ericsson (SWE) 231

[1]Moving target. [2]Disappearing target.

Small Bore Rifle (Team)		
1908 Great Britain 771	Sweden 737	France 710
1912[1] Sweden 925	Great Britain 917	United States 881
1912[2] Great Britain 762	Sweden 748	United States 744
1920 United States 1899	Sweden 1873	Norway 1866

[1]Over 25m. [2]Over 50m.

Live Pigeon Shooting		
1900 Léon de Lunden (BEL) 21	Maurice Faure (FRA) 20	Donald MacIntosh (AUS) 18
		Crittenden Robinson (GBR) 18

Clay Pigeons (Team)		
1908 Great Britain 407	Canada 405	Great Britain 372
1912 United States 532	Great Britain 511	Germany 510
1920 United States 547	Belgium 503	Sweden 500
1924 United States 363	Canada 360	Finland 360

Running Deer Shooting		
1908[1] Oscar Swahn (SWE) 25	Ted Ranken (GBR) 24	Alexander Rogers (GBR) 24
1908[2] Walter Winans (USA) 46	Ted Ranken (GBR) 46	Oscar Swahn (SWE) 38
1912[1] Alfred Swahn (SWE) 41	Ake Lundeberg (SWE) 41	Nestori Toivonen (FIN) 41
1912[2] Ake Lundeberg (SWE) 79	Edvard Benedicks (SWE) 74	Oscar Swahn (SWE) 72
1920[1] Otto Olsen (NOR) 43	Alfred Swahn (SWE) 41	Harald Natwig (NOR) 41
1920[2] Ole Lilloe-Olsen (NOR) 82	Fredrik Landelius (SWE) 77	Einar Liberg (NOR) 71
1924[1] John Boles (USA) 40	Cyril Mackworth-Praed (GBR) 39	Otto Olsen (NOR) 39
1924[2] Ole Lilloe-Olsen (NOR) 76	Cyril Mackworth-Praed (GBR) 72	Alfred Swahn (SWE) 72

[1]Single shot [2]Double shot

Running Deer Shooting (Team)		
1908 Sweden 86	Great Britain 85	—
1912 Sweden 151	United States 132	Finland 123
1920[1] Norway 178	Finland 159	United States 158
1920[2] Norway 343	Sweden 336	Finland 284
1924[1] Norway 160	Sweden 154	United States 158
1924[2] Great Britain 263	Norway 262	Sweden 250

[1]Single shot. [2] Double shot.

Running Deer Shooting (Single & Double Shot)		
1952 John Larsen (NOR) 413	Per Olof Sköldberg (SWE) 409	Tauno Mäki (FIN) 407
1956 Vitaliy Romanenko (URS) 441	Per Olof Sköldberg (SWE) 432	Vladimir Sevrugin (URS) 429

Military Revolver		
1896 John Paine (USA) 442	Sumner Paine (USA) 380	Nikolaos Morakis (GRE) 205
1906 Louis Richardet (SUI) 253	Alexandros Theophilakis (GRE) 250	Georgios Skotadis (GRE) 240
1906[1] Jean Fouconnier (FRA) 219	Raoul de Boigne (FRA) 219	Hermann Martin (FRA) 215

[1]Model 1873. 1900–1904 Event not held.

Duelling Pistol		
1906[1] Léon Moreaux (FRA) 242	Cesare Liverziani (ITA) 233	Maurice Lecoq (FRA) 231
1906[2] Konstantinos Skarlatos (GRE) 133	Johann von Holst (SWE) 115	Wilhelm Carlberg (SWE) 115

[1]Over 20m. [2]Over 25m. 1896–1904 Event not held.

Team Event		
1900 Switzerland 2271	France 2203	Netherlands 1876
1908 United States 1914	Belgium 1863	Great Britain 1817
1912[1] United States 1916	Sweden 1849	Great Britain 1804
1912[2] Sweden 1145	Russia d.n.a.	Great Britain d.n.a.
1920[1] United States 2372	Sweden 2289	Brazil 2264
1920[2] United States 1310	Greece 1285	Switzerland 1270

[1]Over 50m. [2] Over 30m. 1904–1906 Event not held.

Shooting (Women) (Introduced in 1984)

Sport Pistol		
1984 Linda Thom (CAN) 585	Ruby Fox (USA) 585	Patricia Dench (AUS) 583

Standard Rifle		
1984 Xiaoxuan Wu (CHN) 581	Ulrike Holmer (FRG) 578	Wanda Jewell (USA) 578

Air Rifle		
1984 Pat Spurgin (USA) 393	Edith Gufler (ITA) 391	Xiaoxuan Wu (CHN) 389

Great Britain beat Denmark 4–2 to win its third gold medal in 1912. They have won no medals since. (Dave Terry)

Shooting – Medals

| | Men | | | |
	G	S	B	Total
United States	42	22	18	82
Sweden	13	22	18	53
Great Britain	12	13	19	44
Soviet Union	13	15	13	41[1]
France	12	14	12	38
Norway	15	7	10	32
Switzerland	11	9	10	30
Greece	5	7	6	18
Denmark	3	8	6	17
Finland	3	5	9	17
Italy	6	3	6	15
Germany (FRG)	5	6	4	15
GDR	2	7	5	14
Hungary	6	3	4	13
Romania	4	4	3	11
Canada	3	3	2	8
Belgium	2	3	1	6
Poland	2	1	3	6
Czechoslovakia	2	2	1	5
Austria	1	1	3	5
China	2	–	2	4
Brazil	1	1	1	3
Japan	1	–	2	3
Peru	1	1	–	2
Colombia	–	2	–	2
Bulgaria	–	1	1	2
Netherlands	–	1	1	2
North Korea (PRK)	1	–	–	1
Argentina	–	1	–	1
Mexico	–	1	–	1
Portugal	–	1	–	1
South Africa	–	1	–	1
Spain	–	1	–	1
Australia	–	–	1	1
Cuba	–	–	1	1
Haiti	–	–	1	1
New Zealand	–	–	1	1
Venezuela	–	–	1	1
	168	166	165	499

[1]Including a silver and a bronze for Russia in 1912.

| | Women | | | |
	G	S	B	Total
United States	1	1	1	3
China	1	–	1	2
Canada	1	–	–	1
FRG	–	1	–	1
Italy	–	1	–	1
Australia	–	–	1	1
	3	3	3	9

SOCCER

There were two unofficial matches at Athens in the first Games of 1896 when after two Greek towns had played an eliminator, the winner, Smyrna, was defeated by a Danish side 15-0. Although sometimes considered unofficial as well, the tournaments of 1900, 1904 and 1906 are usually counted in medal tables. Therefore soccer was the first team game in the Olympics. The first goal was scored by Great Britain (represented by Upton Park FC) versus France (4-0) in 1900. In 1906 a Danish team again beat Smyrna, this time representing Greece. In that team were five Britons named Whittal, who, if they were brothers as seems likely, set some sort of Olympic record. With the founding of FIFA in 1904 Olympic soccer came under their control, and from 1908 the competition grew in stature so that by 1924 there were 22 countries competing. That tournament and the next was won by Uruguay – who surprisingly never took part in Olympic soccer again. Two years after their Amsterdam victory Uruguay won the inaugural World Cup in 1930 with nine of their Olympic team playing. Only three other players, all Italian, have been in both Olympic and World Cup winning sides.

There has been considerable disillusionment with the interpret-ation of the term 'amateur' as applied to the Games, similar to the troubles in ice hockey. These arguments about pseudo-amateurs have been exacerbated with the entry of the Eastern European powers into the game after 1948. Great Britain, after three gold medals in the early days, did not enter in 1924 or 1928 due to disagreements between the Foot-ball Association (FA) and FIFA about broken time payments to amateurs. For the 1984 tournament players who had taken part in the 1982 World Cup were not eligible, and FIFA is considering imposing an age limit of 23 years for players in 1988.

The highest team score was by Denmark (17) against France (1) in 1908, during which the Danish centre-forward Sophus Nielsen scored 10 goals. His record was equalled by Gottfried Fuchs for Germany when they beat Russia 16-0 in 1912. The most goals scored by an individual in one tournament is 12 by Ferenc Bene (HUN) in 1964. The most scored in Olympic soccer is 13 by Sophus Nielsen 1908–1912, and by Antal Dunai (HUN) 1968–1972.

Hungary is the only country to win three times, 1952, 1964 and 1968. Their 1952 team was virtu-ally the same that sixteen months later inflicted the first home defeat on England's professionals at Wembley. The most successful player was Dezsö Nowak (HUN)

who won two golds and a bronze from 1960 to 1968. Of the nine other players to win two gold medals only Arthur Berry and Vivian Woodward (both GBR) in 1908–1912 were not Uruguayan. Two of the latter, Antonio and Santos Urdinarán, were the first brothers to win soccer gold medals in 1924, but this feat was surpassed by the three Nordahl brothers, Bertil, Knut and Gunnar, in 1948. One of the most remarkable goals in international football involved the Swedish centre-forward Gunnar Nordahl in the 1948 semi-final against Denmark. Unexpectedly caught offside by a quick reversal of play Nordahl realized that his team were attacking again. With lightning presence of mind he leapt into the back of the Danish goal, taking himself off the field of play, and duly caught the goal headed by his team-mate Henry Carlsson with the goalkeeper on the ground 5 metres away.

The oldest gold medallist was Chelsea player Vivian Woodward (GBR) aged 33yr 32 days in 1912, and the youngest was Pedro Petrone (URU) in 1924 two days short of his 19th birthday.

After many years in the doldrums Olympic soccer had a revival in 1980 when the 56 games of the tournament attracted nearly two million spectators. This was reinforced, albeit surprisingly, in 1984 when nearly 1½ million watched the matches, including 101 799 spectators at the final.

Soccer

	Gold	Silver	Bronze
1900	Great Britain	France	Belgium
1904	Canada	United States	United States
1906	Denmark	Greece	Greece
1908	Great Britain	Denmark	Netherlands
1912	Great Britain	Denmark	Netherlands
1920	Belgium	Spain	Netherlands
1924	Uruguay	Switzerland	Sweden
1928	Uruguay	Argentina	Italy
1936	Italy	Austria	Norway
1948	Sweden	Yugoslavia	Denmark
1952	Hungary	Yugoslavia	Sweden
1956	Soviet Union	Yugoslavia	Bulgaria
1960	Yugoslavia	Denmark	Hungary
1964	Hungary	Czechoslovakia	Germany
1968	Hungary	Bulgaria	Japan
1972	Poland	Hungary	GDR[1]
			Soviet Union[1]
1976	GDR	Poland	Soviet Union
1980	Czechoslovakia	GDR	Soviet Union
1984	France	Brazil	Yugoslavia

[1]Tie declared after extra time played. 1896, 1932 Event not held.

Soccer – Medals

	G	S	B	Total
Hungary	3	1	1	5
Denmark	1	3	1	5
Yugoslavia	1	3	1	5
Soviet Union	1	–	3	4
Great Britain	3	–	–	3
GDR	1	1	1	3
Sweden	1	–	2	3
Netherlands	–	–	3	3
Uruguay	2	–	–	2
Czechoslovakia	1	1	–	2
France	1	1	–	2
Poland	1	1	–	2
Belgium	1	–	1	2
Italy	1	–	1	2
Bulgaria	–	1	1	2
Greece	–	1	1	2
United States	–	1	1	2
Canada	1	–	–	1
Argentina	–	1	–	1
Austria	–	1	–	1
Brazil	–	1	–	1
Spain	–	1	–	1
Switzerland	–	1	–	1
Germany (FRG)	–	–	1	1
Japan	–	–	1	1
Norway	–	–	1	1
	19	19	20[1]	58

[1]Third place tie in 1972.

SWIMMING

The sport has been an integral part of the Games since 1896 when the swimming was held in the Bay of Zea near Piraeus. The first champion was Alfred Hajos (HUN) who won the 100m freestyle in freezing water. The first female champion (women's events were introduced in 1912) was Australia's Fanny Durack, also in the 100m freestyle. The first Olympic competition in a pool was in 1908, in a 100m long tank constructed inside the track at the White City Stadium, London. The first 50m pool was in 1924, outdoors, and the first one indoors was at Wembley, London in 1948. In 1904 Emil Rausch (GER) was the last to win an Olympic title using the side-stroke technique.

The most successful swimmer was Mark Spitz (USA) with nine gold medals plus a silver and a bronze in 1968 and 1972. His seven golds at one Games (1972) is unmatched in any sport. The most individual event golds won is four by Charles Daniels (USA) 1904–1908, Roland Matthes (GDR) 1968–1972, and Spitz in 1972. The most won by a woman are four by Dawn Fraser (AUS) 1956–1964 and Kornelia Ender (GDR) all in 1976 (itself a record for one Games by a woman). Fraser is the only swimmer, male or female, to win the same event (100m freestyle) three times. Three women have won a record eight medals: Fraser and Ender, both with four silvers to add to their four golds; and Shirley Babashoff (USA) who won two gold and six silver medals in 1972 and 1976. Both Spitz and Babashoff set an endurance record of sorts in 1972 and 1976 respectively by taking part in 13 races within eight days.

The oldest gold medallist was Louis Handley (USA) in the 1904 relay team aged 30yr 206 days, and the oldest female champion was Ursula Happe (GER) in the 1956 200m breaststroke aged 30yr 41 days. The oldest medallist was William Henry (GBR), a last minute replacement in the 1906 relay, aged 46yr 301 days. The youngest gold medallist was Lillian 'Pokey' Watson (USA) in the 4 × 100m freestyle in 1964 aged 14yr 96 days. The youngest male champion was Kusuo Kitamura (JPN) in the 15000m in 1932 aged 14yr 309 days, while the youngest known medallist in any sport at the Games was Inge Sörensen (DEN) aged 12yr 24 days winning a bronze in the 200m breaststroke of 1936. Similarly the youngest known competitor in any Summer Games sport was Liana Vicens of Puerto Rico in 1968 aged 11yr 328 days.

The first dead heat in Games swimming came in the 1984 women's 100m freestyle final when Carrie Steinseifer and Nancy Hogshead (both USA) gained a gold medal each. Also in those Games there was a strange situation when the winner of the 400m freestyle 'B' final, Thomas Fahrner (FRG), set an Olympic record faster than the winner of the 'A' final. In 1920 the final was re-swum after the Australian, William Herald, complained that he was impeded by Norman Ross (USA) – this was before lane dividers were used. The original winner, Duke Kahanamoku (USA), won again but in a slower time than before, but his first time of 60.4sec was recognized as a world record. Kahanamoku, the first of the great Hawaiian swimmers, was born into the Hawaiian Royal Family, and was named 'Duke' after the Duke of Edinburgh, Queen Victoria's second son, who was visiting the Palace at the time. He was a pioneer of surfing, made many movies in Hollywood, and was the oldest individual event champion in 1920 when 5 days past his 30th birthday.

Hollywood has attracted a number of Olympians: Romanian-born Johnny Weissmuller (USA) who won five gold medals 1924–1928 and then became the most famous 'Tarzan' of them all; Aileen Riggin (USA), the 1920 diving champion, and Eleanor Holm (USA), the 1932 backstroke champion, both took their good looks into movies; Clarence 'Buster' Crabbe (USA), the 1932 400m freestyle champion, became 'Flash Gordon' and 'Buck Rogers' in children's serials.

Gertrude Ederle (USA) and Greta Andersen (DEN), gold medallists in 1924 and 1948 respectively, both later set Channel swimming records.

Diving

Men's diving was introduced into the Games in 1904, and that for women in 1912. The most successful diver has been Austrian-born Klaus Dibiasi (ITA) with three gold and two silver medals from 1964 to 1976, uniquely winning the same event three times and gaining medals in four Games. Pat McCormick (USA) set a female record of four golds in 1952 and 1956. Dorothy Poynton-Hill (USA) 1928–1936 and Paula Myers-Pope (USA) 1952–1960 have won medals in three separate Games, while Juno Stover-Irwin (USA) competed in four Games placing fifth, third, second and fourth respectively from 1948 to 1960. The oldest gold medallist was Hjalmar Johansson (SWE) aged 34yr 186 days when winning the 1908 plain diving at London, and also the oldest ever medallist four

Arguably the greatest diver of all time, Greg Louganis in action. (All-Sport)

years later in Stockholm with a silver aged 38yr 173 days. The youngest champion, and the youngest individual Olympic champion at any sport, was Marjorie Gestring (USA) who won the 1936 springboard title aged 13yr 268 days. The youngest male diving champion was Albert Zürner (GER) in 1908 aged 18yr 170 days. Dorothy Poynton (USA) was the youngest medallist in 1928 aged 13yr 23 days, while the youngest male medallist was Nils Skoglund (SWE) aged 14yr 10 days in 1928. Greg Louganis (USA) won both diving titles in 1984 (the first male double since 1928) by

the biggest margins ever recorded at the Games.

Four divers, three women and a man, have won medals at swimming as well as diving. The most successful was Aileen Riggin (USA) with gold and silver diving medals in 1920 and 1924, and a bronze in the backstroke at Paris.

Water Polo

The first Olympic contest was won by the Osborne Swimming Club, Manchester, representing Great Britain in 1900. Five players have won three gold medals each: George Wilkinson (GBR) 1900, 1908 and

1912; Paul Radomilovic and Charles Smith (both GBR) 1908–1920; Dezsö Gyarmati and György Kárpáti (HUN) 1952, 1956 and 1964. Of these Radomilovic, Welsh-born of a Greek father and Irish mother, also won a gold in the 4 × 200m team in 1908, and competed in a record six Olympic tournaments 1906–1928. Gyarmati was the most successful player, adding a silver in 1948 and a bronze in 1960, and is one of the few Olympians in any sport to win medals in five Games. He also heads a fine Olympic family, as his wife Eva Szekely won a gold (1952) and a silver (1956) in the 200m breaststroke, and their daughter Andrea won silver and bronze medals in the 1972 backstroke and butterfly events respectively. She then added to the family total of medals by marrying Mihaly Hesz (HUN), a canoeist with a gold (1968 K1) and a silver (1964 K1).

The oldest gold medallist was Charles Smith (GBR) aged 41yr 217 days in 1920, while the youngest was György Kárpáti (HUN) in 1952 aged 17yr 40 days. The first brothers to win gold medals in the same team were Ferenc and Alajos Keserü (HUN) in 1932, and they were matched by Tulio and Franco Pandolfini (ITA) in 1948.

Swimming (Men)

	Gold	Silver	Bronze

100 Metres Freestyle

Year	Gold	Silver	Bronze
1896	Alfred Hajoš (HUN) 1:22.2	Efstathios Choraphas (GRE) 1:23.0	Otto Herschmann (AUT) d.n.a.
1904[1]	Zóltán Halmay (HUN) 1:02.8	Charles Daniels (USA) d.n.a.	Scott Leary (USA) d.n.a.
1906	Charles Daniels (USA) 1:13.4	Zóltán Halmay (HUN) 1:14.2	Cecil Healy (AUS) d.n.a.
1908	Charles Daniels (USA) 1:05.6	Zóltán Halmay (HUN) 1:06.2	Harald Julin (SWE) 1:08.0
1912	Duke Kahanamoku (USA) 1:03.4	Cecil Healy (AUS) 1:04.6	Kenneth Huszagh (USA) 1:05.6
1920	Duke Kahanamoku (USA) 1:01.4	Pua Kealoha (USA) 1:02.2	William Harris (USA) 1:03.0
1924	Johnny Weissmuller (USA) 59.0	Duke Kahanamoku (USA) 1:01.4	Sam Kahanamoku (USA) 1:01.8
1928	Johnny Weissmuller (USA) 58.6	István Bárány (HUN) 59.8	Katsuo Takaishi (JPN) 1:00.0
1932	Yasuji Miyazaki (JPN) 58.2	Tatsugo Kawaishi (JPN) 58.6	Albert Schwartz (USA) 58.8
1936	Ferenc Csik (HUN) 57.6	Masanori Yusa (JPN) 57.9	Shigeo Arai (JPN) 58.0
1948	Walter Ris (USA) 57.3	Alan Ford (USA) 57.8	Géza Kádas (HUN) 58.1
1952	Clarke Scholes (USA) 57.4	Hiroshi Suzuki (JPN) 57.4	Göran Larsson (SWE) 58.2
1956	Jon Henricks (USA) 55.4	John Devitt (AUS) 55.8	Gary Chapman (AUS) 56.7
1960	John Devitt (AUS) 55.2	Lance Larson (USA) 55.2	Manuel dos Santos (BRA) 55.4
1964	Don Schollander (USA) 53.4	Bobbie McGregor (GBR) 53.5	Hans-Joachim Klein (GER) 54.0
1968	Mike Wenden (AUS) 52.2	Ken Walsh (USA) 52.8	Mark Spitz (USA) 53.0
1972	Mark Spitz (USA) 51.22	Jerry Heidenreich (USA) 51.65	Vladimir Bure (URS) 51.77
1976	Jim Montgomery (USA) 49.99	Jack Babashoff (USA) 50.81	Peter Nocke (FRG) 51.31
1980	Jörg Woithe (GDR) 50.40	Per Holmertz (SWE) 50.91	Per Johansson (SWE) 51.29
1984	Ambrose Gaines (USA) 49.80*	Mark Stockwell (AUS) 50.24	Per Johansson (SWE) 50.31

[1]100 yards.   *Olympic record.   1900 Event not held.

200 Metres Freestyle

Year	Gold	Silver	Bronze
1900	Frederick Lane (AUS) 2:25.2	Zóltán Halmay (HUN) 2:31.4	Karl Ruberl (AUT) 2:32.0
1904[1]	Charles Daniels (USA) 2:44.2	Francis Gailey (USA) 2:46.0	Emil Rausch (GER) 2:56.0
1968	Mike Wenden (AUS) 1:55.2	Don Schollander (USA) 1:55.8	John Nelson (USA) 1:58.1
1972	Mark Spitz (USA) 1:52.78	Steven Genter (USA) 1:53.73	Werner Lampe (FRG) 1:53.99
1976	Bruce Furniss (USA) 1:50.29	John Naber (USA) 1:50.50	Jim Montgomery (USA) 1:50.58
1980	Sergey Kopliakov (URS) 1:49.81	Andrej Krylov (URS) 1:50.76	Graeme Brewer (AUS) 1:51.60
1984	Michael Gross (FRG) 1:47.44*	Michael Heath (USA) 1:49.10	Thomas Fahrner (FRG) 1:49.69

[1]220 yards.   *Olympic record   1896, 1906–1964 Event not held.

400 Metres Freestyle

Year	Gold	Silver	Bronze
1896[1]	Paul Neumann (AUT) 8:12.6	Antonios Pepanos (GRE) 30m	Efstathios Choraphas (GRE) d.n.a.
1904[2]	Charles Daniels (USA) 6:16.2	Francis Gailey (USA) 6:22.0	Otto Wahle (AUT) 6:39.0
1906	Otto Scheff (AUT) 6:23.8	Henry Taylor (GBR) 6:24.4	John Jarvis (GBR) 6:27.2
1908	Henry Taylor (GBR) 5:36.8	Frank Beaurepaire (AUS) 5:44.2	Otto Scheff (AUT) 5:46.0
1912	George Hodgson (CAN) 5:24.4	John Hatfield (GBR) 5:25.8	Harold Hardwick (AUS) 5:31.2
1920	Norman Ross (USA) 5:26.8	Ludy Langer (USA) 5:29.2	George Vernot (CAN) 5:29.8
1924	Johnny Weissmuller (USA) 5:04.2	Arne Borg (SWE) 5:05.6	Andrew Charlton (AUS) 5:06.6
1928	Alberto Zorilla (ARG) 5:01.6	Andrew Charlton (AUS) 5:03.6	Arne Borg (SWE) 5:04.6
1932	Buster Crabbe (USA) 4:48.4	Jean Taris (FRA) 4:48.5	Tautomu Oyokota (JPN) 4:52.3
1936	Jack Medica (USA) 4:44.5	Shumpei Uto (JPN) 4:45.6	Shozo Makino (JPN) 4:48.1
1948	William Smith (USA) 4:41.0	James McLane (USA) 4:43.4	John Marshall (AUS) 4:47.7
1952	Jean Boiteux (FRA) 4:30.7	Ford Konno (USA) 4:31.3	Per-Olof Ostrand (SWE) 4:35.2
1956	Murray Rose (AUS) 4:27.3	Tsuyoshi Yamanaka (JPN) 4:30.4	George Breen (AUS) 4:32.5
1960	Murray Rose (AUS) 4:18.3	Tsuyoshi Yamanaka (JPN) 4:21.4	John Konrads (AUS) 4:21.8
1964	Don Schollander (USA) 4:12.2	Frank Wiegand (GER) 4:14.9	Allan Wood (AUS) 4:15.1
1968	Mike Burton (USA) 4:09.0	Ralph Hutton (CAN) 4:11.7	Alain Mosconi (FRA) 4:13.3
1972	Brad Cooper (AUS) 4:00.27	Steven Genter (USA) 4:01.94	Tom McBreen (USA) 4:02.64
1976	Brian Goodell (USA) 3:51.93	Tim Shaw (USA) 3:52.54	Vladimir Raskatov (URS) 3:55.76
1980	Vladimir Salnikov (URS) 3:51.31	Andrej Krylov (URS) 3:53.24	Ivar Stukolkin (URS) 3:53.95
1984	George DiCarlo (USA) 3:51.23*	John Mykkanen (USA) 3:51.49	Justin Lemberg (AUS) 3:51.79

[1]500m.   [2]440 yards.   *Olympic record of 3:50.91 by Thomas Fahrner (FRG) in 'B' Final.   1900 Event not held.

1500 Metres Freestyle

Year	Gold	Silver	Bronze
1896[1]	Alfred Hajós (HUN) 18:22.2	Jean Andreou (GRE) 21:03.4	Efstathios Choraphas (GRE) d.n.a.
1900[2]	John Jarvis (GBR) 13:40.2	Otto Wahle (AUT) 14:53.6	Zóltán Halmay (HUN) 15:16.4
1904[3]	Emil Rausch (GER) 27:18.2	Géza Kiss (HUN) 28:28.2	Francis Gailey (USA) 28:54.0
1906[3]	Henry Taylor (GBR) 28:28.0	John Jarvis (GBR) 30:13.0	Otto Scheff (AUT) 30:59.0
1908	Henry Taylor (GBR) 22:48.4	Sydney Battersby (GBR) 22:51.2	Frank Beaurepaire (AUS) 22:56.2
1912	George Hodgson (CAN) 22:00.0	John Hatfield 22:39.0	Harold Hardwick (AUS) 23:15.4
1920	Norman Ross (USA) 22:23.2	George Vernot (CAN) 22:36.4	Frank Beaurepaire (AUS) 23:04.0
1924	Andrew Charlton (AUS) 20:06.6	Arne Borg (SWE) 20:41.4	Frank Beaurepaire (AUS) 21:48.4

Four Olympic champions (from left): Mickey Galitzen, Georgia Coleman, Buster Crabbe and Helene Madison. (Dave Terry)

	Gold	Silver	Bronze
1928	Arne Borg (SWE) 19:51.8	Andrew Charlton (AUS) 20:02.6	Buster Crabbe (USA) 20:28.8
1932	Kusuo Kitamura (JPN) 19:12.4	Shozo Makino (JPN) 19:14.1	James Christy (USA) 19:39.5
1936	Noboru Terada (JPN) 19:13.7	Jack Medica (USA) 19:34.0	Shumpei Uto (JPN) 19:34.5
1948	James McLane (USA) 19:18.5	John Marshall (AUS) 19:31.3	György Mitró (HUN) 19:43.2
1952	Ford Konno (USA) 18:30.0	Shiro Hashizune (JPN) 18:41.4	Tetsuo Okamoto (JPN) 18:51.3
1956	Murray Rose (AUS) 17:58.9	Tsuyoshi Yamanaka (JPN) 18:00.3	George Breen (USA) 18:08.2
1960	John Konrads (AUS) 17:19.6	Murray Rose (AUS) 17:21.7	George Breen (USA) 17:30.6
1964	Bob Windle (AUS) 17:01.7	John Nelson (USA) 17:03.0	Allan Wood (AUS) 17:07.7
1968	Mike Burton (USA) 16:38.9	John Kinsella (USA) 16:57.3	Greg Brough (AUS) 17:04.7
1972	Mike Burton (USA) 15:52.58	Graham Windeatt (AUS) 15:58.48	Doug Northway (USA) 16:09.25
1976	Brian Goodell (USA) 15:02.40	Bobby Hackett (USA) 15:03.91	Steve Holland (AUS) 15:04.66
1980	Vladimir Salnikov (URS) 14:58.27*	Aleksandr Chaev (URS) 15:14.30	Max Metzker (AUS) 15:14.49
1984	Michael O'Brien (USA) 15:05.20	George DiCarlo (USA) 15:10.59	Stefan Pfeiffer (FRG) 15:12.11

[1]1200m.   [2]1000m.   [3]1 mile.   *Olympic record

100 Metres Backstroke

1904[1]	Walter Brack (GER) 1:16.8	Georg Hoffmann (GER) 1:18.0	Georg Zacharias (GER) 1:19.6
1908	Arno Bieberstein (GER) 1:24.6	Ludvig Dam (DEN) 1:26.6	Herbert Haresnape (GBR) 1:27.0
1912	Harry Hebner (USA) 1:21.2	Otto Fahr (GER) 1:22.4	Paul Kellner (GER) 1:24.0
1920	Warren Kealoha (USA) 1:15.2	Ray Kegeris (USA) 1:16.2	Gérard Blitz (BEL) 1:19.0
1924	Warren Kealoha (USA) 1:13.2	Paul Wyatt (USA) 1:15.4	Károly Bartha (HUN) 1:17.8
1928	George Kojac (USA) 1:08.2	Walter Laufer (USA) 1:10.0	Paul Wyatt (USA) 1:12.0
1932	Masaji Kiyokawa (JPN) 1:08.6	Toshio Irie (JPN) 1:09.8	Kentaro Kawatsu (JPN) 1:10.0
1936	Adolf Kiefer (USA) 1:05.9	Albert Van de Weghe (USA) 1:07.7	Masaji Kiyokawa (JPN) 1:08.4
1948	Allen Stack (USA) 1:06.4	Robert Cowell (USA) 1:06.5	Georges Vallerey (FRA) 1:07.8
1952	Yoshinobu Oyakawa (USA) 1:05.4	Gilbert Bozon (FRA) 1:06.2	Jack Taylor (USA) 1:06.4
1956	David Theile (AUS) 1:02.2	John Monckton (AUS) 1:03.2	Frank McKinney (USA) 1:04.5
1960	David Theile (AUS) 1:01.9	Frank McKinney (USA) 1:02.1	Robert Bennett (USA) 1:02.3
1968	Roland Matthes (GDR) 58.7	Charles Hickcox (USA) 1:10.2	Ronnie Mills (USA) 1:00.5
1972	Roland Matthes (GDR) 56.58	Mike Stamm (USA) 57.70	John Murphy (USA) 58.35
1976	John Naber (USA) 55.49*	Peter Rocca (USA) 56.34	Roland Matthes (GDR) 57.22
1980	Bengt Baron (SWE) 56.53	Viktor Kuznetsov (URS) 56.99	Vladimir Dolgov (URS) 57.63
1984	Richard Carey (USA) 55.79	David Wilson (USA) 56.35	Mike West (CAN) 56.49

[1]100 yards.   *Olympic record.   1896–1900, 1906, 1964 Event not held.

200 Metres Backstroke

1900	Ernst Hoppenberg (GER) 2:47.0	Karl Ruberl (AUT) 2:56.0	Johannes Drost (HOL) 3:01.0
1964	Jed Graef (USA) 2:10.3	Gary Dilley (USA) 2:10.5	Robert Bennett (USA) 2:13.1
1968	Roland Matthes (GDR) 2:09.6	Mitchell Ivey (USA) 2:10.6	Jack Horsley (USA) 2:10.9
1972	Roland Matthes (GDR) 2:02.82	Mike Stamm (USA) 2:04.09	Mitchell Ivey (USA) 2:04.33
1976	John Naber (USA) 1:59.19	Peter Rocca (USA) 2:00.55	Don Harrigan (USA) 2:01.35
1980	Sandor Wladar (HUN) 2:01.93	Zóltán Verraszto (HUN) 2:02.40	Mark Kerry (AUS) 2:03.14
1984	Richard Carey (USA) 2:00.23*	Frederic Delcourt (FRA) 2:01.75	Cameron Henning (CAN) 2:02.37

*Olympic record 1:58.99 in heats.   1896, 1904–1960 Event not held.

100 Metres Breaststroke

1968	Don McKenzie (USA) 1:07.7	Vladimir Kossinsky (URS) 1:08.0	Nikolai Pankin (URS) 1:08.0
1972	Nobutaka Taguchi (JPN) 1:04.94	Tom Bruce (USA) 1:05.43	John Hencken (USA) 1:05.61
1976	John Hencken (USA) 1:03.11	David Wilkie (GBR) 1:03.43	Arvidas Iuozaytis (URS) 1:04.23
1980	Duncan Goodhew (GBR) 1:03.34	Arsen Miskarov (URS) 1:03.82	Peter Evans (AUS) 1:03.96
1984	Steve Lundquist (USA) 1:01.65*	Victor Davis (CAN) 1:01.99	Peter Evans (AUS) 1:02.97

*Olympic record   1896–1964 Event not held.

Gold	Silver	Bronze

200 Metres Breaststroke

Gold	Silver	Bronze
1908 Frederick Holman (GBR) 3:09.2	William Robinson (GBR) 3:12.8	Pontus Hansson (SWE) 3:14.6
1912 Walter Bathe (GER) 3:01.8	Wilhelm Lützow (GER) 3:05.2	Kurt Malisch (GER) 3:08.0
1920 Häken Malmroth (SWE) 3:04.4	Thor Henning (SWE) 3:09.2	Arvo Aaltonen (FIN) 3:12.2
1924 Robert Skelton (USA) 2:56.5	Joseph de Combe (BEL) 2:59.2	William Kirschbaum (USA) 3:01.0
1928 Yoshiyuki Tsuruta (JPN) 2:48.8	Erich Rademacher (GER) 2:50.6	Teofilo Yldefonzo (PHI) 2:56.4
1932 Yoshiyuki Tsuruta (JPN) 2:45.4	Reizo Koike (JPN) 2:46.4	Teofilo Yldefonzo (PHI) 2:47.1
1936 Tetsuo Hamuro (JPN) 2:42.5	Erwin Sietas (GER) 2:42.9	Reizo Koike (JPN) 2:44.2
1948 Joseph Verdeur[1] (USA) 2:39.3	Keith Carter (USA) 2:40.2	Robert Sohl (USA) 2:43.9
1952 John Davies[1] (AUS) 2:34.4	Bowen Stassforth (USA) 2:34.7	Herbert Klein (GER) 2:35.9
1956 Masaru Furukawa[2] (JPN) 2:34.7	Masahiro Yoshimura (JPN) 2:36.7	Charis Yunitschev (URS) 2:36.8
1960 William Mulliken (USA) 2:37.4	Yoshihiko Osaki (JPN) 2:38.0	Wieger Mensonides (HOL) 2:39.7
1964 Ian O'Brien (AUS) 2:27.8	Georgy Prokopenko (URS) 2:28.2	Chester Jastremski (USA) 2:29.6
1968 Felipe Munoz (MEX) 2:28.7	Vladimir Kossinsky (URS) 2:29.2	Brian Job (USA) 2:29.9
1972 John Hencken (USA) 2:21.55	David Wilkie (GBR) 2:23.67	Nobutaka Taguchi (JPN) 2:23.88
1976 David Wilkie (GBR) 2:15.11	John Hencken (USA) 2:17.26	Rick Colella (USA) 2:19.20
1980 Robertas Shulpa (URS) 2:15.85	Alban Vermes (HUN) 2:16.93	Arsen Miskarov (URS) 2:17.28
1984 Victor Davis (CAN) 2:13.34*	Glenn Beringen (AUS) 2:15.79	Etienne Dagon (SUI) 2:17.41

[1]Used then permissible butterfly stroke. [2]Used then permissible underwater technique. *Olympic record. 1896–1906 Event not held.

100 Metres Butterfly

Gold	Silver	Bronze
1968 Doug Russell (USA) 55.9	Mark Spitz (USA) 56.4	Ross Wales (USA) 57.2
1972 Mark Spitz (USA) 54.27	Bruce Robertson (CAN) 55.56	Jerry Heidenreich (USA) 55.74
1976 Matt Vogel (USA) 54.35	Joe Bottom (USA) 54.50	Gary Hall (USA) 54.65
1980 Pär Arvidsson (SWE) 54.92	Roger Pyttel (GDR) 54.94	David Lopez (ESP) 55.13
1984 Michael Gross (FRG) 53.08*	Pedro Morales (USA) 53.23	Glenn Buchanan (AUS) 53.85

*Olympic record. 1896–1964 Event not held.

200 Metres Butterfly

Gold	Silver	Bronze
1956 William Yorzyk (USA) 2:19.3	Takashi Ishimoto (JPN) 2:23.8	György Tumpek (HUN) 2:23.9
1960 Mike Troy (USA) 2:12.8	Neville Hayes (AUS) 2:14.6	David Gillanders (USA) 2:15.3
1964 Kevin Berry (AUS) 2:06.6	Carl Robie (USA) 2:07.5	Fred Schmidt (USA) 2:09.3
1968 Carl Robie (USA) 2:08.7	Martyn Woodroffe (GBR) 2:09.0	John Ferris (USA) 2:09.3
1972 Mark Spitz (USA) 2:00.70	Gary Hall (USA) 2:02.86	Robin Backhaus (USA) 2:03.23
1976 Mike Bruner (USA) 1:59.23	Steven Gregg (USA) 1:59.54	William Forrester (USA) 1:59.96
1980 Sergey Fesenko (URS) 1:59.76	Phil Hubble (GBR) 2:01.20	Roger Pyttel (GDR) 2:01.39
1984 Jon Sieben (AUS) 1:57.04*	Michael Gross (FRG) 1:57.40	Rafael Castro (VEN) 1:57.51

*Olympic record. 1896–1952 Event not held.

200 Metres Individual Medley

Gold	Silver	Bronze
1968 Charles Hickcox (USA) 2:12.0	Greg Buckingham (USA) 2:13.0	John Ferris (USA) 2:13.3
1972 Gunnar Larsson (SWE) 2:07.17	Tim McKee (USA) 2:08.37	Steve Furniss (USA) 2:08.45
1984 Alex Baumann (CAN) 2:01.42*	Pedro Morales (USA) 2:03.05	Neil Cochran (GBR) 2:04.38

*Olympic record. 1896–1964, 1976–1980 Event not held.

400 Metres Individual Medley

Gold	Silver	Bronze
1964 Richard Roth (USA) 4:45.4	Roy Saari (USA) 4:47.1	Gerhard Hetz (GER) 4:51.0
1968 Charles Hickcox (USA) 4:48.4	Gary Hall (USA) 4:48.7	Michael Holthaus (FRG) 4:51.4
1972 Gunnar Larsson (SWE) 4:31.98	Tim McKee (USA) 4:31.98	András Hargitay (HUN) 4:32.70
1976 Rod Strachan (USA) 4:23.68	Tim McKee (USA) 4:24.62	Andrei Smirnov (URS) 4:26.90
1980 Aleksandr Sidorenko (URS) 4:22.89	Sergey Fesenko (URS) 4:23.43	Zóltán Verraszto (HUN) 4:24.24
1984 Alex Baumann (CAN) 4:17.41*	Ricardo Prado (BRA) 4:18.45	Robert Woodhouse (AUS) 4:20.50

*Olympic record. 1896–1960 Event not held.

4 × 100 Metres Freestyle Relay

Gold	Silver	Bronze
1964 United States 3:33.2	Germany 3:37.2	Australia 3:39.1
1968 United States 3:31.7	Soviet Union 3:34.2	Australia 3:34.7
1972 United States 3:26.42	Soviet Union 3:29.72	GDR 3:32.42
1984 United States 3:19.03*	Australia 3:19.68	Sweden 3:22.69

*Olympic record. 1896–1960, 1976–1980 Event not held.

4 × 200 Metres Freestyle Relay

Gold	Silver	Bronze
1906[1] Hungary 16:52.4	Germany 17:16.2	Great Britain n.t.a.
1908 Great Britain 10:55.6	Hungary 10:59.0	United States 11:02.8
1912 Australasia[2] 10:11.6	United States 10:20.2	Great Britain 10:28.2
1920 United States 10:04.4	Australia 10:25.4	Great Britain 10:37.2
1924 United States 9:53.4	Australia 10:02.2	Sweden 10:06.8
1928 United States 9:36.2	Japan 9:41.4	Canada 9:47.8
1932 Japan 8:58.4	United States 9:10.5	Hungary 9:31.4
1936 Japan 8:51.5	United States 9:03.0	Hungary 9:12.3
1948 United States 8:46.0	Hungary 8:48.4	France 9:08.0
1952 United States 8:31.1	Japan 8:33.5	France 8:45.9
1956 Australia 8:23.6	United States 8:31.5	Soviet Union 8:34.7
1960 United States 8:10.2	Japan 8:13.2	Australia 8:13.8
1964 United States 7:52.1	Germany 7:59.3	Japan 8:03.8
1968 United States 7:52.3	Australia 7:53.7	Soviet Union 8:01.6
1972 United States 7:35.78	FRG 7:41.69	Soviet Union 7:45.76
1976 United States 7:23.22	Soviet Union 7:27.97	Great Britain 7:32.11
1980 Soviet Union 7:23.50	GDR 7:28.60	Brazil 7:29.30
1984 United States 7:16.59*	FRG 7:16.73	Great Britain 7:24.78

[1]4 × 250 metres. [2]Composed of three Australians and a New Zealander. *Olympic record. 1896–1904 Event not held.

Gold	Silver	Bronze

4 × 100 Metres Medley Relay

Gold	Silver	Bronze
1960 United States 4:05.4	Australia 4:12.0	Japan 4:12.2
1964 United States 3:58.4	Germany 4:01.6	Australia 4:02.3
1968 United States 3:54.9	GDR 3:57.5	Soviet Union 4:00.7
1972 United States 3:48.16	GDR 3:52.12	Canada 3:52.26
1976 United States 3:42.22	Canada 3:45.94	FRG 3:47.29
1980 Australia 3:45.70	Soviet Union 3:45.92	Great Britain 3:47.71
1984 United States 3:39.30*	Canada 3:43.23	Australia 3:43.25

*Olympic record. 1896–1956 Event not held.

Springboard Diving

Gold	Silver	Bronze
1908 Albert Zurner (GER) 85.5	Kurt Behrens (GER) 85.3	George Gaidzik (USA) 80.8 Gottlob Walz (GER) 80.8
1912 Paul Günther (GER) 79.23	Hans Luber (GER) 76.78	Kurt Behrens (GER) 73.73
1920 Louis Kuehn (USA) 675.4	Clarence Pinkston (USA) 655.3	Louis Balbach (USA) 649.5
1924 Albert White (USA) 696.4	Peter Desjardins (USA) 693.2	Clarence Pinkston (USA) 653
1928 Peter Desjardins (USA) 185.04	Michael Galitzen (USA) 174.06	Farid Simaika (EGY) 172.46
1932 Michael Galitzen (USA) 161.38	Harold Smith (USA) 158.54	Richard Degener (USA) 151.82
1936 Richard Degener (USA) 163.57	Marshall Wayne (USA) 159.56	Al Greene (USA) 146.29
1948 Bruce Harlan (USA) 163.64	Miller Anderson (USA) 157.29	Samuel Lee (USA) 145.52
1952 David Browning (USA) 205.29	Miller Anderson (USA) 199.84	Robert Clotworthy (USA) 184.92
1956 Robert Clotworthy (USA) 159.56	Donald Harper (USA) 156.23	Joaquin Capilla Pérez (MEX) 150.69
1960 Gary Tobian (USA) 170.00	Samuel Hall (USA) 167.08	Juan Botella (MEX) 162.30
1964 Kenneth Sitzberger (USA) 159.90	Francis Gorman (USA) 157.63	Larry Andreasen (USA) 143.77
1968 Bernard Wrightson (USA) 170.15	Klaus Dibiasi (ITA) 159.74	James Henry (USA) 158.09
1972 Vladimir Vasin (URS) 594.09	F Giorgio Cagnotto (ITA) 591.63	Craig Lincoln (USA) 577.29
1976 Philip Boggs (USA) 619.05	F Giorgio Cagnotto (ITA) 570.48	Aleksandr Kosenkov (URS) 567.24
1980 Aleksandr Portnov (URS) 905.025	Carlos Giron (MEX) 892.140	F Giorgio Cagnotto (ITA) 871.500
1984 Greg Louganis (USA) 754.41	Liangde Tan (CHN) 662.31	Ronald Merriott (USA) 661.32

1896–1906 Event not held.

Highboard Diving

Gold	Silver	Bronze
1904[1] George Sheldon (USA) 12.66	Georg Hoffmann (GER) 11.66	Frank Nehoe (USA) 11.33 Alfred Braunschweiger (GER) 11.33
1906 Gottlob Walz (GER) 156.00	Georg Hoffman (GER) 150.20	Otto Satzinger (AUT) 147.40
1908 Hjalmar Johansson (SWE) 83.75	Karl Malström (SWE) 78.73	Arvid Spångberg (SWE) 74.00
1912 Erik Adlerz (SWE) 73.94	Albert Zürner (GER) 72.60	Gustaf Blomgren (SWE) 69.56
1920 Clarence Pinkston (USA) 100.67	Erik Adlerz (SWE) 99.08	Haig Prieste (USA) 93.73
1924 Albert White (USA) 97.46	David Fall (USA) 97.30	Clarence Pinkston (USA) 94.60
1928 Peter Desjardins (USA) 98.74	Farid Simaika (EGY) 99.58	Michael Galitzen (USA) 92.34
1932 Harold Smith (USA) 124.80	Michael Galitzen (USA) 124.28	Frank Kurtz (USA) 121.98
1936 Marshall Wayne (USA) 113.58	Elbert Root (USA) 110.60	Hermann Stork (GER) 110.31
1948 Samuel Lee (USA) 130.05	Bruce Harlan (USA) 122.30	Joaquin Capilla Pérez (MEX) 113.52
1952 Samuel Lee (USA) 156.28	Joaquin Capilla Pérez (MEX) 145.21	Günther Haase (GER) 141.31
1956 Joaquin Capilla Pérez (MEX) 152.44	Gary Tobian (USA) 152.41	Richard Connor (USA) 149.79
1960 Robert Webster (USA) 165.56	Gary Tobian (USA) 165.25	Brian Phelps (GBR) 157.13
1964 Robert Webster (USA) 148.58	Klaus Dibiasi (ITA) 147.54	Thomas Gompf (USA) 146.57
1968 Klaus Dibiasi (ITA) 164.18	Alvaro Gaxiola (MEX) 154.49	Edwin Young (USA) 153.93
1972 Klaus Dibiasi (ITA) 504.12	Richard Rydze (USA) 480.75	F Giorgio Cagnotto (ITA) 475.83
1976 Klaus Dibiasi (ITA) 600.51	Gregory Louganis (USA) 576.99	Vladimir Aleynik (URS) 548.61
1980 Falk Hoffmann (GDR) 835.650	Vladimir Heynik (URS) 819.705	David Ambartsumyan (URS) 817.440
1984 Greg Louganis (USA) 710.91	Bruce Kimball (USA) 643.50	Kongzheng Li (CHN) 638.28

[1]Combined springboard and highboard event. 1896–1900 Event not held.

Swimming (Women)

Gold	Silver	Bronze

100 Metres Freestyle

Gold	Silver	Bronze
1912 Fanny Durack (AUS) 1:22.2	Wilhelmina Wylie (AUS) 1:25.4	Jennie Fletcher (GBR) 1:27.0
1920 Ethelda Bleibtrey (USA) 1:13.6	Irene Guest (USA) 1:17.0	Frances Schroth (USA) 1:17.2
1924 Ethel Lackie (USA) 1:12.4	Mariechen Wehselau (USA) 1:12.8	Gertrude Ederle (USA) 1:14.2
1928 Albina Osipowich (USA) 1:11.0	Eleanor Garatti (USA) 1:11.4	Joyce Cooper (GBR) 1:13.6
1932 Helene Madison (USA) 1:06.8	Willemijntje den Ouden (HOL) 1:07.8	Eleanor Garatti-Saville (USA) 1:08.2
1936 Henrika Mastenbroek (HOL) 1:05.9	Jeanette Campbell (ARG) 1:06.4	Gisela Arendt (USA) 1:06.6
1948 Greta Andersen (DEN) 1:06.3	Ann Curtis (USA) 1:06.5	Marie-Louise Vaessen (HOL) 1:07.6
1952 Katalin Szöke (HUN) 1:06.8	Johanna Termeulen (HOL) 1:07.0	Judit Temes (HUN) 1:07.1
1956 Dawn Fraser (AUS) 1:02.0	Lorraine Crapp (AUS) 1:02.3	Faith Leech (AUS) 1:05.1
1960 Dawn Fraser (AUS) 1:01.2	Chris van Saltza (USA) 1:02.8	Natalie Steward (GBR) 1:03.1
1964 Dawn Fraser (AUS) 59.5	Sharon Stouder (USA) 59.9	Kathleen Ellis (USA) 1:00.8
1968 Jan Henne (USA) 1:00.0	Susan Pedersen (USA) 1:00.3	Linda Gustavson (USA) 1:00.3
1972 Sandra Neilson (USA) 58.59	Shirley Babashoff (USA) 59.02	Shane Gould (AUS) 59.06
1976 Kornelia Ender (GDR) 55.65	Petra Priemer (GDR) 56.49	Enith Brigitha (HOL) 56.65
1980 Barbara Krause (GDR) 54.79*	Caren Metschuck (GDR) 55.16	Ines Diers (GDR) 55.65
1984 Carrie Steinseifer (USA) 55.92 Nancy Hogshead (USA) 55.92	–	Annemarie Verstappen (HOL) 56.08

*Olympic record. 1896–1908 Event not held.

200 Metres Freestyle

Gold	Silver	Bronze
1968 Debbie Meyer (USA) 2:10.5	Jan Henne (USA) 2:11.0	Jane Barkman (USA) 2:11.2
1972 Shane Gould (AUS) 2:03.56	Shirley Babashoff (USA) 2:04.33	Keena Rothhammer (USA) 2:04.92
1976 Kornelia Ender (GDR) 1:59.26	Shirley Babashoff (USA) 2:01.22	Enith Brigitha (HOL) 2:01.40
1980 Barbara Krause (GDR) 1:58.33*	Ines Diers (GDR) 1:59.64	Carmela Schmidt (GDR) 2:01.44
1984 Mary Wayte (USA) 1:59.23	Cynthia Woodhead (USA) 1:59.50	Annemarie Verstappen (HOL) 1:59.69

*Olympic record. 1896–1964 Event not held.

Gold	*Silver*	*Bronze*

400 Metres Freestyle

	Gold	Silver	Bronze
1920[1]	Ethelda Bleibtrey (USA) 4:34.0	Margaret Woodbridge (USA) 4:42.8	Frances Schroth (USA) 4:52.0
1924	Martha Norelius (USA) 6:02.2	Helen Wainwright (USA) 6:03.8	Gertrude Ederle (USA) 6:04.8
1928	Martha Norelius (USA) 5:42.8	Marie Braun (HOL) 5:57.8	Josephine McKim (USA) 6:00.2
1932	Helene Madison (USA) 5:28.5	Lenore Kight (USA) 5:28.6	Jennie Maakal (SAF) 5:47.3
1936	Henrika Mastenbroek (HOL) 5:26.4	Ragnhild Hveger (DEN) 5:27.5	Lenore Kight-Wingard (USA) 5:29.0
1948	Ann Curtis (USA) 5:17.8	Karen Harup (DEN) 5:21.2	Cathy Gibson (GBR) 5:22.5
1952	Valéria Gyenge (HUN) 5:12.1	Eva Nowák (HUN) 5:13.7	Evelyn Kawamoto (USA) 5:14.6
1956	Lorraine Crapp (AUS) 4:54.6	Dawn Fraser (AUS) 5:02.5	Sylvia Ruuska (USA) 5:07.1
1960	Chris von Saltza (USA) 4:50.6	Jane Cederquist (SWE) 4:53.9	Catharina Lagerberg (HOL) 4:56.9
1964	Virginia Duenkel (USA) 4:43.3	Marilyn Ramenofsky (USA) 4:44.6	Terri Stickles (USA) 4:47.2
1968	Debbie Meyer (USA) 4:31.8	Linda Gustavson (USA) 4:35.5	Karen Moras (AUS) 4:37.0
1972	Shane Gould (AUS) 4:19.04	Novella Calligaris (ITA) 4:22.44	Gudrun Wegner (GDR) 4:23.11
1976	Petra Thuemer (GDR) 4:09.89	Shirley Babashoff (USA) 4:10.46	Shannon Smith (CAN) 4:14.60
1980	Ines Diers (GDR) 4:08.76	Petra Schneider (GDR) 4:09.16	Carmela Schmidt (GDR) 4:10.86
1984	Tiffany Cohen (USA) 4:07.10*	Sarah Hardcastle (GBR) 4:10.27	June Croft (GBR) 4:11.49

[1]300 metres. *Olmypic record. 1896–1912 Event not held.

800 Metres Freestyle

	Gold	Silver	Bronze
1968	Debbie Meyer (USA) 9:24.0	Pamela Kruse (USA) 9:35.7	Maria Ramirez (MEX) 9:38.5
1972	Keena Rothhammer (USA) 8:53.68	Shane Gould (AUS) 8:56.39	Novella Calligaris (ITA) 8:57.46
1976	Petra Thuemer (GDR) 8:37.14	Shirley Babashoff (USA) 8:37.59	Wendy Weinberg (USA) 8:42.60
1980	Michelle Ford (AUS) 8:28.90	Ines Diers (GDR) 8:32.55	Heike Dähne (GDR) 8:33.48
1984	Tiffany Cohen (USA) 8:24.95*	Michele Richardson (USA) 8:30.73	Sarah Hardcastle (GBR) 8:32.60

*Olympic record. 1896–1964 Event not held.

100 Metres Backstroke

	Gold	Silver	Bronze
1924	Sybil Bauer (USA) 1:23.2	Phyllis Harding (GBR) 1:27.4	Aileen Riggin (USA) 1:28.2
1928	Marie Braun (HOL) 1:22.0	Ellen King (GBR) 1:22.2	Joyce Cooper (GBR) 1:22.8
1932	Eleanor Holm (USA) 1:19.4	Philomena Mealing (AUS) 1:21.3	Valerie Davies (GBR) 1:22.5
1936	Dina Senff (HOL) 1:18.9	Hendrika Mastenbroek (HOL) 1:19.2	Alice Bridges (USA) 1:19.4
1948	Karen Harup (DEN) 1:14.4	Suzanne Zimmermann (USA) 1:16.0	Judy Davies (AUS) 1:16.7
1952	Joan Harrison (SAF) 1:14.3	Geertje Wielema (HOL) 1:14.5	Jean Stewart (NZL) 1:15.8
1956	Judy Grinham (GBR) 1:12.9	Carin Cone (USA) 1:12.9	Margaret Edwards (GBR) 1:13.1
1960	Lynn Burke (USA) 1:09.3	Natalie Steward (GBR) 1:10.8	Satoko Tanaka (JPN) 1:11.4
1964	Cathy Ferguson (USA) 1:07.7	Cristine Caron (FRA) 1:07.9	Virginia Duenkel (USA) 1:08.0
1968	Kaye Hall (USA) 1:06.2	Elaine Tanner (CAN) 1:06.7	Jane Swaggerty (USA) 1:08.1
1972	Melissa Belote (USA) 1:05.78	Andrea Gyarmati (HUN) 1:06.26	Susie Atwood (USA) 1:06.34
1976	Ulrike Richter (GDR) 1:01.83	Birgit Treiber (GDR) 1:03.41	Nancy Garapick (CAN) 1:03.71
1980	Rica Reinisch (GDR) 1:00.86*	Ina Kleber (GDR) 1:02.07	Petra Riedel (GDR) 1:02.64
1984	Theresa Andrews (USA) 1:02.55	Betsy Mitchell (USA) 1:02.63	Jolanda De Rover (HOL) 1:92.91

*Olympic record. 1896–1920 Event not held.

200 Metres Backstroke

	Gold	Silver	Bronze
1968	Lillian Watson (USA) 2:24.8	Elaine Tanner (CAN) 2:27.4	Kaye Hall (USA) 2:28.9
1972	Melissa Belote (USA) 2:19.19	Susie Atwood (USA) 2:20.38	Donna Marie Gurr (CAN) 2:23.22
1976	Ulrike Richter (GDR) 2:13.43	Birgit Treiber (GDR) 2:14.97	Nancy Garapick (CAN) 2:15.60
1980	Rica Reinisch (GDR) 2:11.77*	Cornelia Polit (GDR) 2:13.75	Birgit Treiber (GDR) 2:14.14
1984	Jolanda De Rover (HOL) 2:12.38	Amy White (USA) 2:13.04	Aneta Patrascoiu (ROM) 2:13.29

*Olympic record. 1896–1964 Event not held.

100 Metres Breaststroke

	Gold	Silver	Bronze
1968	Djurdjica Bjedov (YUG) 1:15.8	Galina Prozumenschchikova (URS) 1:15.9	Sharon Wichman (USA) 1:16.1
1972	Catherine Carr (USA) 1:13.58	Galina Stepanova (URS) 1:14.99	Beverley Whitfield (AUS) 1:15.73
1976	Hannelore Anke (GDR) 1:11.16	Lubov Rusanova (URS) 1:13.04	Marina Kosheveya (URS) 1:13.30
1980	Ute Geweniger (GDR) 1:10.22	Elvira Vasilkova (URS) 1:10.41	Susanne Nielsson (DEN) 1:11.16
1984	Petra Van Staveren (HOL) 1:09.88*	Anne Ottenbrite (CAN) 1:10.69	Catherine Poirot (FRA) 1:10.70

*Olympic record. 1896–1964 Event not held.

200 Metres Breaststroke

	Gold	Silver	Bronze
1924	Lucy Morton (GBR) 3:33.2	Agnes Geraghty (USA) 3:34.0	Gladys Carson (GBR) 3:35.4
1928	Hilde Schrader (GER) 3:12.6	Mietje Baron (HOL) 3:15.2	Lotte Mühe (GER) 3:17.6
1932	Claire Dennis (AUS) 3:06.3	Hideko Maehata (JPN) 3:06.4	Else Jacobson (DEN) 3:07.1
1936	Hideko Maehata (JPN) 3:03.6	Martha Genenger (GER) 3:04.2	Inge Sörensen (DEN) 3:07.8
1948	Petronella van Vliet (HOL) 2:57.2	Nancy Lyons (AUS) 2:57.7	Eva Novák (HUN) 3:00.2
1952	Eva Székely[1] (HUN) 2:51.7	Eva Novák (HUN) 2:54.4	Helen Gordon (GBR) 2:57.6
1956	Ursula Happe[2] (GER) 2:53.1	Eva Ezékely (HUN) 2:54.8	Eva-Maria ten Elsen (GER) 2:55.1
1960	Anita Lonsbrough (GBR) 2:49.5	Wiltrud Urselmann (GER) 2:50.0	Barbara Göbel (GER) 2:53.6
1964	Galina Prozumenshchikova (URS) 2:46.4	Claudia Kolb (USA) 2:47.6	Svetlana Babanina (URS) 2:48.6
1968	Sharon Wichman (USA) 2:44.4	Djurdjica Bjedov (YUG) 2:46.4	Galina Prozumenshchikova (URS) 2:47.0
1972	Beverley Whitfield (AUS) 2:41.71	Dana Schoenfield (USA) 2:42.05	Galina Stepanova (URS) 2:42.36
1976	Marina Kosheveya (URS) 2:33.35	Marina Yurchenia (URS) 2:36.08	Lubov Rusanova (URS) 2:36.22
1980	Lina Kachushite (URS) 2:29.54*	Svetlana Varganova (URS) 2:29.61	Yulia Bogdanova (URS) 2:32.39
1984	Anne Ottenbrite (CAN) 2:30.38	Susan Rapp (USA) 2:31.15	Ingrid Lempereur (BEL) 2:31.40

[1]Used then permitted butterfly stroke. [2]Used then permitted underwater technique. *Olympic record. 1896–1920 Event not held.

100 Metres Butterfly

	Gold	Silver	Bronze
1956	Shelley Mann (USA) 1:11.0	Nancy Ramey (USA) 1:11.9	Mary Sears (USA) 1:14.4
1960	Carolyn Schuler (USA) 1:09.5	Marianne Heemskerk (HOL) 1:10.4	Janice Andrew (AUS) 1:12.2
1964	Sharon Stouder (USA) 1:04.7	Ada Kok (HOL) 1:05.6	Kathleen Ellis (USA) 1:06.0
1968	Lynette McClements (AUS) 1:05.5	Ellie Daniel (USA) 1:05.8	Susan Shields (USA) 1:06.2
1972	Mayumi Aoki (JPN) 1:03.34	Roswitha Beier (GDR) 1:03.61	Andrea Gyarmati (HUN) 1:03.73
1976	Kornelia Ender (GDR) 1:00.13	Andrea Pollack (GDR) 1:00.98	Wendy Boglioli (USA) 1:01.17
1980	Caren Metschuck (GDR) 1:00.42	Andrea Pollack (GDR) 1:00.90	Christiane Knacke (GDR) 1:01.44

The first Olympic swimming dead-heat in history from Carrie Steinseifer and Nancy Hogshead in the 100m freestyle at Los Angeles. (All-Sport)

Gold	*Silver*	*Bronze*
1984 Mary Meagher (USA) 59.26*	Jenna Johnson (USA) 1:00.19	Karin Seick (FRG) 1:00.36

*Olympic record 59.05 in heats.   1896–1952 Event not held.

200 Metres Butterfly

1968 Ada Kok (HOL) 2:24.7	Helga Lindner (GDR) 2:24.8	Ellie Daniel (USA) 2:25.9
1972 Karen Moe (USA) 2:15.57	Lynn Colella (USA) 2:16.34	Ellie Daniel (USA) 2:16.74
1976 Andrea Pollack (GDR) 2:11.41	Ulrike Tauber (GDR) 2:12.50	Rosemarie Gabriel (GDR) 2:12.86
1980 Ines Geissler (GDR) 2:10.44	Sybille Schönrock (GDR) 2:10.45	Michelle Ford (AUS) 2:11.66
1984 Mary Meagher (USA) 2:06.90*	Karen Phillips (AUS) 2:10.56	Ina Beyermann (FRG) 2:11.91

*Olympic record.   1896–1964 Event not held.

200 Metres Individual Medley

1968 Claudia Kolb (USA) 2:24.7	Susan Pedersen (USA) 2:28.8	Jan Henne (USA) 2:31.4
1972 Shane Gould (AUS) 2:23.07	Kornelia Ender (GDR) 2:23.59	Lynn Vidali (USA) 2:24.06
1984 Tracy Caulkins (USA) 2:12.64*	Nancy Hogshead (USA) 2:15.17	Michele Pearson (AUS) 2:15.92

*Olympic record.   1896–1964, 1976–1980 Event not held.

400 Metres Individual Medley

1964 Donna De Varona (USA) 5:18.7	Sharon Finneran (USA) 5:24.1	Martha Randall (USA) 5:24.2
1968 Claudia Kolb (USA) 5:08.5	Lynn Vidali (USA) 5:22.2	Sabine Steinbach (GDR) 5:25.3
1972 Gail Neall (AUS) 5:02.97	Leslie Cliff (CAN) 5:03.57	Novella Calligaris (ITA) 5:03.99
1976 Ulrike Tauber (GDR) 4:42.77	Cheryl Gibson (CAN) 4:48.10	Becky Smith (CAN) 4:50.48
1980 Petra Schneider (GDR) 4:36.29*	Sharron Davies (GBR) 4:46.83	Agnieszka Czopek (POL) 4:48.17
1984 Tracy Caulkins (USA) 4:39.24	Suzanne Landells (AUS) 4:48.30	Petra Zindler (FRG) 4:48.57

*Olympic record.   1896–1960 Event not held.

4 × 100 Metres Freestyle Relay

1912 Great Britain 5:52.8	Germany 6:04.6	Austria 6:17.0
1920 United States 5:11.6	Great Britain 5:40.8	Sweden 5:43.6
1924 United States 4:58.8	Great Britain 5:17.0	Sweden 5:35.6
1928 United States 4:47.6	Great Britain 5:02.8	South Africa 5:13.4
1932 United States 4:38.0	Netherlands 4:47.5	Great Britain 4:52.4
1936 Netherlands 4:36.0	Germany 4:36.8	United States 4:40.2
1948 United States 4:29.2	Denmark 4:29.6	Netherlands 4:31.6
1952 Hungary 4:24.4	Netherlands 4:29.0	United States 4:30.1
1956 Australia 4:17.1	United States 4:19.2	South Africa 4:15.7
1960 United States 4:08.9	Australia 4:11.3	Germany 4:19.7
1964 United States 4:03.8	Australia 4:06.9	Netherlands 4:12.0
1968 United States 4:02.5	GDR 4:05.7	Canada 4:07.2
1972 United States 3:55.19	GDR 3:55.55	FRG 3:57.93
1976 United States 3:44.82	GDR 3:45.50	Canada 3:48.81
1980 GDR 3:42.71*	Sweden 3:48.93	Netherlands 3:49.51
1984 United States 3:43.43	Netherlands 3:44.40	FRG 3:45.56

*Olympic record. 1896–1908 Event not held.

4 × 100 Metres Medley Relay

1960 United States 4:41.1	Australia 4:45.9	Germany 4:47.6
1964 United States 4:33.9	Netherlands 4:37.0	Soviet Union 4:39.2
1968 United States 4:28.3	Australia 4:30.0	FRG 4:36.4
1972 United States 4:20.75	GDR 4:24.91	FRG 4:26.46
1976 GDR 4:07.95	United States 4:14.55	Canada 4:15.22
1980 GDR 4:06.67*	Great Britain 4:12.24	Soviet Union 4:13.61
1984 United States 4:08.34	FRG 4:11.97	Canada 4:12.98

*Olympic record.   1896–1956 Event not held.

Springboard Diving

1920 Aileen Riggin (USA) 539.9	Helen Wainwright USA) 534.8	Thelma Payne (USA) 534.1
1924 Elizabeth Becker (USA) 474.5	Aileen Riggin (USA) 460.4	Caroline Fletcher (USA) 434.4
1928 Helen Meany (USA) 78.62	Dorothy Poynton (USA) 75.62	Georgia Coleman (USA) 73.38
1932 Georgia Coleman (USA) 87.52	Katherine Rawls (USA) 82.56	Jane Fauntz (USA) 82.12
1936 Marjorie Gestring (USA) 89.27	Katherine Rawls (USA) 88.35	Dorothy Poynton-Hill (USA) 82.36
1948 Victoria Draves (USA) 108.74	Zoe Ann Olsen (USA) 108.23	Patricia Elsener (USA) 101.30
1952 Patricia McCormick (USA) 147.30	Madeleine Moreau (FRA) 139.34	Zoe Ann Jensen (USA) 127.57
1956 Patricia McCormick (USA) 142.36	Jeanne Stunyo (USA) 125.89	Irene Macdonald (CAN) 121.40
1960 Ingrid Krämer (GER) 155.81	Paula Myers-Pope (USA) 141.24	Elizabeth Ferris (GBR) 139.09
1964 Ingrid Krämer-Engel (GER) 145.00	Jeanne Collier (USA) 138.36	Mary Willard (USA) 138.18
1968 Sue Gossick (USA) 150.77	Tamara Pogozheva (URS) 145.30	Keala O'Sullivan (USA) 145.23
1972 Micki King (USA) 450.03	Ulrika Knape (SWE) 434.19	Marina Janicke (GDR) 430.92
1976 Jennifer Chandler (USA) 506.19	Christa Kohler (GDR) 469.41	Cynthia McIngvale (USA) 466.83
1980 Irina Kalinina (URS) 725.910	Martina Proeber (GDR) 698.895	Karin Guthke (GDR) 685.245
1984 Sylvie Bernier (CAN) 530.70	Kelly McCormick (USA) 527.46	Christina Seufert (USA) 517.62

1896–1912 Event not held.

Highboard Diving

1912 Greta Johansson (SWE) 39.9	Lisa Regnell (SWE) 36.0	Isabelle White (GBR) 34.0
1920 Stefani Fryland-Clausen (DEN) 34.6	Eileen Armstrong (GBR) 33.3	Eva Ollivier (SWE) 33.3
1924 Caroline Smith (USA) 10.5	Elizabeth Becker (USA) 11.0	Hjördis Töpel (SWE) 15.5
1928 Elizabeth Pinkston (USA) 31.6	Georgia Coleman (USA) 30.6	Lala Sjöqvist (SWE) 29.2
1932 Dorothy Poynton (USA) 40.26	Georgia Coleman (USA) 35.56	Marion Roper (USA) 35.22
1936 Dorothy Poynton-Hill (USA) 33.93	Velma Dunn (USA) 33.63	Käthe Köhler (GER) 33.43
1948 Victoria Draves (USA) 68.87	Patricia Elsener (USA) 66.28	Birte Christoffersen (DEN) 66.04
1952 Patricia McCormick (USA) 79.37	Paula Myers (USA) 71.63	Juno Irwin (USA) 70.49
1956 Patricia McCormick (USA) 84.85	Juno Irwin (USA) 81.64	Paula Myers (USA) 81.58

	Gold	Silver	Bronze
1960	Ingrid Krämer (GER) 91.28	Paula Myers-Pope (USA) 88.94	Ninel Krutova (URS) 86.99
1964	Lesley Bush (USA) 99.80	Ingrid Krämer-Engel (GER) 98.45	Galina Alekseyeva (URS) 97.60
1968	Milena Duchková (TCH) 109.59	Natalia Lobanova (URS) 105.14	Ann Peterson (USA) 101.11
1972	Ulrika Knape (SWE) 390.00	Milena Duchková (TCH) 370.92	Marina Janicke (GDR) 360.54
1976	Elena Vaytsekhovskaya (URS) 406.59	Ulrika Knape (SWE) 402.60	Deborah Wilson (USA) 401.07
1980	Martina Jäschke (GDR) 596.250	Servard Emirzyan (URS) 576.465	Liana Tsotadze (URS) 575.925
1984	Jihong Zhou (CHN) 435.51	Michele Mitchell (USA) 431.19	Wendy Wyland (USA) 422.07

1896–1908 Event not held.

Synchronized Swimming – Duet
1984	United States 195.584	Canada 194.234	Japan 187.992

1896–1980 Event not held.

Synchronized Swimming – Solo
1984	Tracie Ruiz (USA) 198.467	Carolyn Waldo (CAN) 195.300	Miwako Motoyoshi (JPN) 187.050

1896–1980 Event not held

Discontinued Events

50 Yards Freestyle
1904[1]	Zoltán Halmay (HUN) 28.0	Scott Leary (USA) 28.6	Charles Daniels (USA) n.t.a.

[1]Race reswum after judges disagreed on result of first race.

100 Metres Freestyle (Sailors)
1896	Ioannis Malokinis (GRE) 2:20.4	S Chasapis (GRE) n.t.a.	Dimitrios Drivas (GRE) n.t.a.

200 Metres Obstacle Event
1900	Frederick Lane (AUS) 2:38.4	Otto Wahle (AUT) 2:40.0	Peter Kemp (GBR) 2:47.4

400 Metres Breaststroke
1904	Georg Zacharias (GER) 7:23.6	Walter Brack (GER) 20m	Jamison Handy (USA) d.n.a.
1912	Walter Bathe (GER) 6:29.6	Thor Henning (SWE) 6:35.6	Percy Courtman (GBR) 6:36.4
1920	Hakan Malmroth (SWE) 6:31.8	Thor Henning (SWE) 6:45.2	Arvo Aaltonen (FIN) 6:48.0

880 Yards Freestyle
1904	Emil Rausch (GER) 13:11.4	Francis Gailey (USA) 13:23.4	Géza Kiss (HUN) n.t.a.

4000 Metres Freestyle
1900	John Jarvis (GBR) 58:24.0	Zoltán Halmay (HUN) 1:08:55.4	Louis Martin (FRA) 1:13:08.4

Underwater Swimming
1900	Charles de Vendeville (FRA) 188.4	A Six (FRA) 185.4	Peder Lykkeberg (DEN) 147.0

Plunge for Distance
1904	Paul Dickey (USA) 19.05m	Edgar Adams (USA) 17.53m	Leo Goodwin (USA) 17.37m

200 Metres Team Swimming
1900	Germany 32pts	France 51	France 61

4 × 50 Yards Relay
1904	United States (New York AC) 2:04.6	United States (Chicago AC) n.t.a.	United States (Missouri AC) n.t.a.

Plain High Diving
1912	Erik Adlerz (SWE) 40.0	Hjalmar Johansson (SWE) 39.3	John Jansson (SWE) 39.1
1920	Arvid Wallmann (SWE) 183.5	Nils Skoglund (SWE) 183.0	John Jansson (SWE) 175.0
1924	Richmond Eve (AUS) 160.0	John Jansson (SWE) 157.0	Harold Clarke (GBR) 158.0

Water Polo

	Gold	Silver	Bronze
1900[1]	Great Britain	Belgium	France
1904[1]	United States	United States	United States
1908	Great Britain	Belgium	Sweden
1912	Great Britain	Sweden	Belgium
1920	Great Britain	Sweden	Belgium
1924	France	Belgium	United States
1928	Germany	Hungary	France
1932	Hungary	Germany	United States
1936	Hungary	Germany	Belgium
1948	Italy	Hungary	Netherlands
1952	Hungary	Yugoslavia	Italy
1956	Hungary	Yugoslavia	Soviet Union
1960	Italy	Soviet Union	Hungary
1964	Hungary	Yugoslavia	Soviet Union
1968	Yugoslavia	Soviet Union	Hungary
1972	Soviet Union	Hungary	United States
1976	Hungary	Italy	Netherlands
1980	Soviet Union	Yugoslavia	Hungary
1984	Yugoslavia	United States	FRG

[1]Entries were from clubs and not international teams.
1896, 1906 Event not held.

Swimming – Medals
(Excluding diving but including synchronized)

	Men			Women			Total			Total Medals
	G	S	B	G	S	B	G	S	B	
United States	86	64	47	61	40	33	147	104	80	331
Australia	22	18	27	14	12	8	36	30	35	101
GDR	5	4	3	22	20	10	27	24	13	64
Germany (FRG)	11	14	13	2	5	13	13	19	26	58
Great Britain	9	11	11	4	9	12	13	20	23	56
Soviet Union	7	13	13	3	6	8	10	19	21	50
Japan	11	17	11	2	1	2	13	18	13	44
Hungary	7	10	10	4	4	3	11	14	13	38
Netherlands	–	–	2	9	12	10	9	12	12	33
Canada	5	6	5	1	6	9	6	12	14	32
Sweden	7	6	9	–	2	2	7	8	11	26
France	2	5	6	–	1	1	2	6	7	15
Denmark	–	1	1	2	3	3	2	4	4	10
Austria	2	2	5	–	–	1	2	2	6	10
Greece	1	4	3	–	–	–	1	4	3	8
South Africa	–	–	–	1	–	3	1	–	3	4
Brazil	–	1	3	–	–	–	–	1	3	4
Belgium	–	1	1	–	–	1	–	1	2	3
Italy	–	–	–	–	1	2	–	1	2	3
Argentina	1	–	–	–	1	–	1	1	–	2
Yugoslavia	–	–	–	1	1	–	1	1	–	2
Mexico	1	–	–	–	–	1	1	–	1	2
New Zealand	1	–	–	–	–	1	1	–	1	2
Finland	–	–	2	–	–	–	–	–	2	2
Philippines	–	–	2	–	–	–	–	–	2	2
Poland	–	–	–	–	–	1	–	–	1	1
Romania	–	–	–	–	–	1	–	–	1	1
Spain	–	–	1	–	–	–	–	–	1	1
Switzerland	–	–	1	–	–	–	–	–	1	1
Venezuela	–	–	1	–	–	–	–	–	1	1
	178[1]	177	177	126[2]	124	125	304	301	302	907

[1] Extra gold due to double counting of Australia/New Zealand relay team in 1912.
[2] Two golds in 1984 100m freestyle.

Diving – Medals

	Men			Women			Total			Total Medals
	G	S	B	G	S	B	G	S	B	
United States	24	19	19	19	19	17	43	38	36	117
Sweden	4	5	4	2	3	3	6	8	7	21
Germany (FRG)	3	5	5	3	1	1	6	6	6	18
Soviet Union	2	1	3	2	3	3	4	4	6	14
Italy	3	4	2	–	–	–	3	4	2	9
GDR	1	–	–	1	2	3	2	2	3	7
Mexico	1	3	3	–	–	–	1	3	3	7
Great Britain	–	–	2	–	1	2	–	1	4	5
China	–	1	1	1	–	–	1	1	1	3
Czechoslovakia	–	–	–	1	1	–	1	1	–	2
Canada	–	–	–	1	–	1	1	–	1	2
Denmark	–	–	–	1	–	1	1	–	1	2
Egypt	–	1	1	–	–	–	–	1	1	2
Australia	1	–	–	–	–	–	1	–	–	1
France	–	–	–	–	1	–	–	1	–	1
Austria	–	–	1	–	–	–	–	–	1	1
	39	39	41[1]	31	31	31	70	70	72[1]	212

[1] Two bronzes awarded in a 1904 and a 1908 event.

Water Polo – Medals

	G	S	B	Total
Hungary	6	3	3	12
United States	1	2	4	7
Yugoslavia	2	4	–	6
Soviet Union	2	2	2	6
Belgium	–	4	2	6
Great Britain	4	–	–	4
Italy	2	1	1	4
Germany (FRG)	1	2	1	4
France	1	–	2	3
Sweden	–	1	2	3
Netherlands	–	–	2	2
	19	19	19	57

TABLE TENNIS

First recognized as an Olympic sport by the IOC in 1977, table tennis will be included in the 1988 Games. There will be 64 men and 32 women, selected by an agreed international formula, competing in men's and women's singles and doubles events. The sport has never been included in the Olympics before, not even as a demonstration.

TENNIS

The sport was last included in the Games in 1924, although it was a demonstration sport in 1968 and 1984. The first gold medallist was Irish-born John Pius Boland (GBR) in the 1896 singles. He happened to be in Athens, visiting the famous archaeologist Schliemann, and entered the Games at the last minute. The ladies' singles champion in 1900, Charlotte Cooper (GBR), became the first woman to win an Olympic title at any sport. Over the years a number of medal winning pairs were composed of players from two countries, thus Boland combined with a German to win the first mixed doubles title. The most successful player was Max Decugis (FRA) with a total of six medals comprising four golds, one silver and a bronze between 1900 and 1920. Britain's Kitty McKane won a record total for a woman of five (one gold, two silvers and two bronzes) in 1920 and 1924.

The oldest gold medallist was George Hillyard (GBR) in the 1908 men's doubles aged 44yr 160 days. The oldest female was Winifred McNair (GBR) aged 43yr 14 days in the women's doubles of 1920. She was also the oldest British woman to win a gold medal in any sport. The youngest gold medallist in tennis was Helen Wills (USA), winner of the 1924 singles aged 18yr 288 days, while the youngest male was Fritz Traun (GER), Boland's partner in 1896 aged 20yr 13 days. The husband and wife team of Max and Marie Decugis (FRA) won the mixed title in 1906, while brothers Reggie and Laurie Doherty (GBR) added the 1900 Olympic title to the eight Wimbledon doubles championships they won. Many of the greatest names in tennis played in the Games and there were 19 gold medal winners who also were successful at Wimbledon. One of the most remarkable of these was Swiss-born Norris Williams (USA), who survived the sinking of the *Titanic* in 1912 swimming in icy water for over an hour, won the Croix de Guerre and the Legion d'Honneur in the First World War, a Wimbledon title in 1920, an Olympic gold medal in 1924, and died aged 77.

The first female Olympic gold medallist Charlotte Cooper (GBR) also won five Wimbledon titles. (GSL)

Tennis

	Gold	Silver	Bronze

Men's Singles

	Gold	Silver	Bronze
1896	John Boland (GBR)	Demis Kasdaglis (GRE)	–
1900[1]	Hugh Doherty (GBR)	Harold Mahony (GBR)	Reginald Doherty (GBR)
			A B Norris (GBR)
1904	Beals Wright (USA)	Robert LeRoy (USA)	–
1906	Max Decugis (FRA)	Maurice Germot (FRA)	Zdenek Zemla (BOH)
1908	Josiah Ritchie (GBR)	Otto Froitzheim (GER)	Wilberforce Eves (GBR)
1908[2]	Wentworth Gore (GBR)	George Caridia (GBR)	Josiah Ritchie (GBR)
1912	Charles Winslow (SAF)	Harold Kitson (SAF)	Oscar Kreuzer (GER)
1912[2]	André Gobert (FRA)	Charles Dixon (GBR)	Anthony Wilding (NZL)
1920	Louis Raymond (SAF)	Ichiya Kumagae (JPN)	Charles Winslow (GBR)
1924	Vincent Richards (USA)	Henri Cochet (FRA)	Umberto De Morpurgo (ITA)

[1]Two bronze medals in 1900.　[2]Indoor tournaments.

Men's Doubles

	Gold	Silver	Bronze
1896	GBR/Germany	Greece	–[1]
1900[2]	Great Britain	USA/France	France
			Great Britain
1904	United States	United States	–[1]
1906	France	Greece	Bohemia
1908	Great Britain	Great Britain	Great Britain
1908[3]	Great Britain	Great Britain	Sweden
1912	South Africa	Austria	France
1912[3]	France	Sweden	Great Britain
1920	Great Britain	Japan	France
1924	United States	France	France

[1]No bronze medal.　[2]Two bronze medals in 1900.　[3]Indoor tournaments.

Mixed Doubles

	Gold	Silver	Bronze
1900[1]	Great Britain	France/GBR	Bohemia/GBR
			United States/GBR
1906	France	Greece	Greece
1912	Germany	Sweden	France
1912[2]	Great Britain	Great Britain	Sweden
1920	France	Great Britain	Czechoslovakia
1924	United States	United States	Netherlands

[1]Two bronze medals in 1900.　[2]Indoor tournament.

Women's Singles

	Gold	Silver	Bronze
1900[1]	Charlotte Cooper (GBR)	Hélène Prévost (FRA)	Marion Jones (USA)
			Hedwiga Rosenbaumova (BOH)
1906	Esmeé Simiriotou (GRE)	Sophia Marinou (GRE)	Euphrosine Paspati (GRE)
1908	Dorothea Chambers (GBR)	Dorothy Boothby (GBR)	Joan Winch (GBR)
1908[2]	Gwen Eastlake-Smith (GBR)	Angela Greene (GBR)	Märtha Adlerstråhle (SWE)
1912	Marguerite Broquedis (FRA)	Dora Köring (GER)	Molla Bjurstedt (NOR)
1912[2]	Ethel Hannam (GBR)	Thora Castenschiold (DEN)	Mabel Parton (GBR)
1920	Suzanne Lenglen (FRA)	Dorothy Holman (GBR)	Kitty McKane (GBR)
1924	Helen Wills (USA)	Julie Vlasto (FRA)	Kitty McKane (GBR)

[1]Two bronze medals.　[2]Indoor tournaments.

Women's Doubles

	Gold	Silver	Bronze
1920	Great Britain	Great Britain	France
1924	United States	Great Britain	Great Britain

Tennis – Medals

	G	S	B	Total
Great Britain	16	13	15	44
France	8	7	6	21
United States	7	4	2	13
Greece	1	5	2	8
Germany (FRG)	2	2	1	5
Bohemia (Czechoslovakia)	–	–	5	5
Sweden	–	2	3	5
South Africa	3	1	–	4
Japan	–	2	–	2
Austria	–	1	–	1
Denmark	–	1	–	1
Italy	–	–	1	1
Netherlands	–	–	1	1
New Zealand	–	–	1	1
Norway	–	–	1	1
	37	38	38	113[1]

[1]Two-country pairs counted as two separate medals.

TRACK AND FIELD ATHLETICS

The track and field events have been the centre-piece of every Olympic Games since 1896. From 1920 until the International Amateur Athletics Federation inaugurated their first world title meeting in 1983, the Olympic events were also official world championships. The first champion in modern Olympic history was James Connolly (USA) who won the triple jump (then called the hop, step and jump) on 6 April 1896. He also won medals in the high and long jumps, and was later a novelist and war correspondent. The first winner of an Olympic event was Francis Lane (USA) who had won the first heat of the 100m earlier the same day. Women's events were introduced in 1928 and the first female gold medallist was Halina Konopacka (POL) in the discus. Again the first winner of an Olympic women's event was Anni Holdmann (GER) who took the first heat of the 100m the day before.

A record ten gold medals was won by Ray Ewry (USA) in the standing jumps from 1900 to 1908. A feat unsurpassed in any sport, and achieved despite the fact that Ewry had contracted polio as a child. The Finnish distance runner Paavo

Nine gold and three silver medals were won by the legendary Paavo Nurmi (FIN), and he could have won more in 1932. (All-Sport)

Nurmi won a total of twelve medals from 1920 to 1928, comprising nine golds and three silvers. He won them in an unmatched seven different events, and his five golds in 1924 is a record for one Games. Incidentally Ewry had won three of his titles on the same day in 1900. However, the most individual titles at one Games is four by Alvin Kraenzlein (USA) in 1900. This total was equalled by Jesse Owens (USA) in 1936 and Carl Lewis (USA) in 1984, but they only gained three individual events – 100m, 200m and long jump – with the fourth gold medal in the relay. Nurmi's team-mate Ville Ritola won a record six medals in 1924, consisting of four golds and two silvers, incurring eight races in eight days. In 1912 the forerunner of all the 'Flying Finns', Hannes Kolehmainen, had won six races within nine days.

Four gold medals have been won by three women: Fanny Blankers-Koen (HOL) in 1948, which is also a female record for one Games, as is the three individual titles included; Betty Cuthbert (AUS) in 1956 and 1964; and Bärbel Wöckel (neé Eckert) (GDR) in 1976 and 1980. Shirley Strickland (later de la Hunty) (AUS) won a record seven medals from 1948 to 1956, comprising three golds, one silver and three bronzes. This total was equalled by Irena Szewinska (née Kirszenstein) (POL) with three golds, two silvers and two bronzes from 1964 to 1976. Szewinska is the only woman to win medals at three successive Games, and also in five different events. Incidentally study of photo-finish evidence indicates that Strickland also came third in the 200m of 1948, but no move has been made to change the result officially.

A unique track and field achievement, equalling that of yachting's Paul Elvström, was the four successive gold medals in the discus by Al Oerter (USA) 1956–1968. Almost as worthy were the three golds and one silver won by Viktor Saneyev (URS) in the triple jump 1968–1980. Mildred Didrikson (USA) – who later achieved golf fame as Babe Zaharias – achieved a unique triple in 1932 when she won medals in a run (80m hurdles – gold), a jump (high jump – silver) and a throw (javelin – gold).

Another unusual spread of medals was by Micheline Ostermeyer (FRA) in 1948 with golds in the shot and discus and a bronze in the high jump. Perhaps even more unusual was the fact that she was a concert pianist. The best male equivalent was Robert Garrett (USA) with golds in the shot and discus, and silvers in the high and long jumps, in 1896. Stanley Rowley won bronze medals in the 60m, 100m and 200m in 1900 representing Australasia (he was Australian), and then was drafted into the British team for the 5000m team race and won a gold medal although he did not finish the race.

The oldest gold medallist was Patrick 'Babe' McDonald (USA) winning the 56lb weight throw in 1920 aged 42yr 23 days. The youngest gold medallist was Barbara Jones (USA) in the 1952 sprint relay aged 15yr 123 days, while the youngest individual event champion was Ulrike Meyfarth (FRG) who won the high jump in 1972 aged exactly one year older. The youngest male champion was Robert Mathias (USA) who won the 1948 decathlon aged 17yr 263 days, and later (1966) became a US Congressman. The oldest female champion was Lia Manoliu (ROM) in the 1968 discus aged 36yr 176 days. She is also co-holder of another female record, that of attending six Games (1952–1968). At least eight men have attended five Games. The oldest medallist was Tebbs Lloyd Johnson (GBR) in the 50km walk of 1952 aged 48yr 115 days, and the oldest female medallist was Dana Zatopkova (TCH) in the 1960 javelin aged 37yr 248 days. Jones (see above) was also the youngest medallist, while the youngest male medallist was Pal Simon (HUN) in the 1908 medley relay aged 17yr 206 days.

The first brothers to win medals were Patrick and Con Leahy, Irishmen representing Great Britain, in 1900 and 1906 respectively. The first to gain medals at the same Games were Platt and Ben Adams (USA) who came first and second in the 1912 standing high jump. The most successful siblings were the Press sisters (URS), Tamara with three golds and a silver, and Irina, with two golds, in 1960 and 1964. The only twins to win medals were Patrick and Pascal

In 1908 George Larner (GBR) won the 3500m walk, the only time it was ever held. (GSL)

Barré (FRA) in the bronze medal sprint relay of 1980.

Father and son gold medallists are represented by two families. Werner Järvinen (FIN) won the 1906 Greek style discus, his son Matti won the javelin in 1932, and another son, Akilles, gained silver medals in the 1928 and 1932 decathlons. In 1948 Imre Nemeth (HUN) won the hammer, and 28 years later his son Miklos won the javelin with a world record throw. The most successful mother/daughter combination were Elizabeta Bagriantseva (URS) with a silver in the 1952 discus, and Irina Nazarova with a gold in the 4 × 400m relay of 1980. One of the more poignant Olympic stories relates to Marie Dollinger who was one of the girls involved in dropping the baton in the 1936 sprint relay when the German girls 'couldn't lose'. One imagines the thoughts of her daughter Brunhilde Hendrix in the 1960 relay final – happily she won a silver medal.

The only married couple to win gold medals were Emil and Dana Zatopek (TCH). Even more remarkable is the fact that Dana won her javelin title on the same afternoon as one of Emil's in 1952 – both of them were also born on the same day.

Frank Wykoff (USA) is the only sprinter to win gold medals in three Games, in relay teams from 1928 to 1936.

The first Olympic athlete to be disqualified for contravening the drug regulations was Danuta Rosani (POL) in the 1976 discus. The scrutiny or 'sex testing' of women was introduced into the Games in 1968, many years too late in the opinion of many. They had in mind the case of Dora Ratjen (GER) who placed fourth in the 1936 high jump and was later found to be a man posing as a woman. Less clear cut was the case of Stella Walasiewicz (later Walsh), Polish-born but later an American citizen, who won gold and silver medals in the 100m of 1932 and 1936 respectively, and was reported, after her violent death in 1980, to have 'primary male characteristics'.

The shortest time that an athlete has held an Olympic record was 0.4sec by Olga Rukavishnikova (URS) in the 1980 pentathlon. That is the difference between her second place time of 2min 04.8sec in the final 800m event of the five-event contest, and the time of the third-placed Nadyezda Tkachenko (URS) whose overall points score exceeded her team-mate's by 146.

Tug of War

This sport was part of the athletics programme 1900–1920. Three men won a record two golds and one silver from 1908 to 1920: John Shepherd, Frederick Humphreys and Edwin Mills, all from Great Britain. The oldest gold medallist was Humphreys aged 42yr 204 days in 1920, while the youngest was Karl Staaf (SWE) aged 19yr 101 days in 1900. There were some strange team compositions in the early days: the winning 1900 team was composed of three Swedes and three Danes; the 1904 competition was between American clubs; the 1908 tournament was between British Police Clubs with London City Police beating their colleagues from Liverpool.

Track and Field (Men)

(Prior to 1972 automatic timings to one-hundredths of a second are shown additionally, where known.)

Gold	Silver	Bronze
100 Metres		
1896 Thomas Burke (USA) 12.0	Fritz Hofmann (GER) 12.2	Alajos Szokolyi (HUN) 12.6
1900 Frank Jarvis (USA) 11.0	Walter Tewksbury (USA) 11.1	Stanley Rowley (AUS) 11.2
1904 Archie Hahn (USA) 11.0	Nathaniel Cartmell (USA) 11.2	William Hogenson (USA) 11.2
1906 Archie Hann (USA) 11.2	Fay Moulton (USA) 11.3	Nigel Barker (AUS) 11.3
1908 Reginald Walker (SAF) 10.8	James Rector (USA) 10.9	Robert Kerr (CAN) 11.0
1912 Ralph Craig (USA) 10.8	Alvah Meyer (USA) 10.9	Donald Lippincott (USA) 10.9
1920 Charles Paddock (USA) 10.8	Morris Kirksey (USA) 10.8	Harry Edward (GBR) 11.0
1924 Harold Abrahams (GBR) 10.6	Jackson Scholz (USA) 10.7	Arthur Porritt (NZL) 10.8
1928 Percy Williams (CAN) 10.8	Jack London (GBR) 10.9	George Lammers (GER) 10.9
1932 Eddie Tolan (USA) 10.3 (10.38)	Ralph Metcalfe (USA) 10.3 (10.38)	Arthur Jonath (GER) 10.4 (10.50)
1936 Jesse Owens (USA) 10.3	Ralph Metcalfe (USA) 10.4	Martinus Osendarp (HOL) 10.5
1948 Harrison Dillard (USA) 10.3	Norwood Ewell (USA) 10.4	Lloyd LaBeach (PAN) 10.4
1952 Lindy Remigino (USA) 10.4 (10.79)	Herb McKenley (JAM) 10.4 (10.79)	Emmanuel McD Bailey (GBR) 10.4 (10.83)
1956 Bobby-Joe Morrow (USA) 10.5 (10.62)	Thane Baker (USA) 10.5 (10.77)	Hector Hogan (AUS) 10.6 (10.77)
1960 Armin Hary (GER) 10.2 (10.32)	David Sime (USA) 10.2 (10.35)	Peter Radford (GBR) 10.3 (10.42)
1964 Bob Hayes (USA) 10.0 (10.06)	Enrique Figuerola (CUB) 10.2 (10.20)	Harry Jerome (CAN) 10.2 (10.27)
1968 James Hines (USA) 9.9 (9.95)*	Lennox Miller (JAM) 10.0 (10.04)	Charles Greene (USA) 10.0 (10.07)
1972 Valeriy Borzov (URS) 10.14	Robert Taylor (USA) 10.24	Lennox Miller (JAM) 10.33
1976 Hasely Crawford (TRI) 10.06	Don Quarrie (JAM) 10.08	Valeriy Borzov (URS) 10.14
1980 Allan Wells (GBR) 10.25	Silvio Leonard (CUB) 10.25	Petar Petrov (BUL) 10.39
1984 Carl Lewis (USA) 9.99	Sam Graddy (USA) 10.19	Ben Johnson (CAN) 10.22

*Olympic record.

Gold	Silver	Bronze
200 Metres		
1900 Walter Tewksbury (USA) 22.2	Norman Pritchard (IND) 22.8	Stanley Rowley (AUS) 22.9
1904[1] Archie Hahn (USA) 21.6	Nathaniel Cartmell (USA) 21.9	William Hogenson (USA) d.n.a.
1908 Robert Kerr (CAN) 22.6	Robert Cloughen (USA) 22.6	Nathaniel Cartmell (USA) 22.7
1912 Ralph Craig (USA) 21.7	Donald Lippincott (USA) 21.8	Willie Applegarth (GBR) 22.0
1920 Allen Woodring (USA) 22.0	Charles Paddock (USA) 22.1	Harry Edward (GBR) 22.2
1924 Jackson Scholz (USA) 21.6	Charles Paddock (USA) 21.7	Eric Liddell (GBR) 21.9
1928 Percy Williams (CAN) 21.8	Walter Rangeley (GBR) 21.9	Helmut Kornig[2] (GER) 21.9
1932 Eddie Tolan (USA) 21.2 (21.12)	George Simpson (USA) 21.4	Ralph Metcalfe[3] (USA) 21.5
1936 Jesse Owens (USA) 20.7	Mack Robinson (USA) 21.1	Martinus Osendarp (HOL) 21.3
1948 Mel Patton (USA) 21.1	Norwood Ewell (USA) 21.1	Lloyd LaBeach (PAN) 21.2
1952 Andrew Stanfield (USA) 20.7 (20.81)	Thane Baker (USA) 20.8 (20.97)	James Gathers (USA) 20.8 (21.08)
1956 Bobby-Joe Morrow (USA) 20.6 (20.75)	Andrew Stanfield (USA) 20.7 (20.97)	Thane Baker (USA) 20.9 (21.05)
1960 Livio Berutti (ITA) 20.5 (20.62)	Lester Carney (USA) 20.6 (20.69)	Abdoulaye Seye (FRA) 20.7 (20.83)
1964 Henry Carr (USA) 20.3 (20.36)	Paul Drayton (USA) 20.5 (20.58)	Edwin Roberts (TRI) 20.6 (20.63)

	Gold	Silver	Bronze
1968	Tommie Smith (USA) 19.8 (19.83)	Peter Norman (AUS) 20.0 (20.06)	John Carlos (USA) 20.0 (20.10)
1972	Valeriy Borzov (URS) 20.00	Larry Black (USA) 20.19	Pietro Mennea (ITA) 20.30
1976	Don Quarrie (JAM) 20.23	Millard Hampton (USA) 20.29	Dwayne Evans (USA) 20.43
1980	Pietro Mennea (ITA) 20.19	Allan Wells (GBR) 20.21	Don Quarrie (JAM) 20.29
1984	Carl Lewis (USA) 19.80*	Kirk Baptiste (USA) 19.96	Thomas Jefferson (USA) 20.26

[1]Race over straight course. Hahn's three opponents were all given 2yd handicaps for false starting.   [2]Awarded bronze medal when Scholz (USA) refused to re-run after tie.   [3]Metcalfe's lane was later found to be 1½m too long.   *Olympic record.   1896, 1906 Event not held.

400 Metres

1896	Thomas Burke (USA) 54.2	Herbert Jamison (USA) 55.2	Fritz Hofmann (GER) 55.6
1900	Maxwell Long (USA) 49.4	William Holland (USA) 49.6	Ernst Schultz (DEN) 15m
1904	Harry Hillman (USA) 49.2	Frank Waller (USA) 49.9	Herman Groman (USA) 50.0
1906	Paul Pilgrim (USA) 53.2	Wyndham Halswelle (GBR) 53.8	Nigel Barker (AUS) 54.1
1908[1]	Wyndham Halswelle (GBR) 50.0	–	–
1912	Charles Reidpath (USA) 48.2	Hanns Braun (GER) 48.3	Edward Lindberg (USA) 48.4
1920	Bevil Rudd (SAF) 49.6	Guy Butler (GBR) 49.9	Nils Engdahl (SWE) 50.0
1924	Eric Liddell (GBR) 47.6	Horatio Fitch (USA) 48.4	Guy Butler (GBR) 48.6
1928	Ray Barbuti (USA) 47.8	James Ball (CAN) 48.0	Joachim Büchner (GER) 48.2
1932	William Carr (USA) 46.2 (46.28)	Ben Eastman (USA) 46.4 (46.50)	Alexander Wilson (CAN) 47.4
1936	Archie Williams (USA) 46.5 (46.66)	Godfrey Brown (GBR) 46.7 (46.68)	James LuValle (USA) 46.8 (46.84)
1948	Arthur Wint (JAM) 46.2	Herb McKenley (JAM) 46.4	Mal Whitfield (USA) 46.6
1952	George Rhoden (JAM) 45.9 (46.09)	Herb McKenley (JAM) 45.9 (46.20)	Ollie Matson (USA) 46.8 (46.94)
1956	Charles Jenkins (USA) 46.7 (46.85)	Karl-Friedrich Haas (GER) 46.8 (47.12)	Voitto Hellsten (URS) 47.0 (47.15) Ardalion Ignatyev (URS) 47.0 (47.15)
1960	Otis Davis (USA) 44.9 (45.07)	Carl Kaufmann (GER) 44.9 (45.08)	Mal Spence (SAF) 45.5 (45.60)
1964	Mike Larrabee (USA) 45.1 (45.15)	Wendell Mottley (TRI) 45.2 (45.24)	Andrzej Badenski (POL) 45.6 (45.63)
1968	Lee Evans (USA) 43.8 (43.86)*	Lawrence James (USA) 43.9 (43.97)	Ron Freeman (USA) 44.4 (44.41)
1972	Vince Matthews (USA) 44.66	Wayne Collett (USA) 44.80	Julius Sang (KEN) 44.92
1976	Alberto Juantorena (CUB) 44.26	Fred Newhouse (USA) 44.40	Herman Frazier (USA) 44.95
1980	Viktor Markin (URS) 44.60	Rick Mitchell (AUS) 44.84	Frank Schaffer (GDR) 44.87
1984	Alonzo Babers (USA) 44.27	Gabriel Tiacoh (CIV) 44.54	Antonio McKay (USA) 44.71

[1]Re-run ordered after John Carpenter (USA) disqualified in first final. Only Halswelle showed up and 'walked over' for the title.   *Olympic record.

800 Metres

1896	Edwin Flack (AUS) 2:11.0	Nándor Dáni (HUN) 2:11.8	Dimitrios Golemis (GRE) 2:28.0
1900	Alfred Tysoe (GBR) 2:01.2	John Cregan (USA) 2:03.0	David Hall (USA) d.n.a.
1904	James Lightbody (USA) 1:56.0	Howard Valentine (USA) 1:56.3	Emil Breitkreutz (USA) 1:56.4
1906	Paul Pilgrim (USA) 2:01.5	James Lightbody (USA) 2:01.6	Wyndham Halswelle (GBR) 2:03.0
1908	Mel Sheppard (USA) 1:52.8	Emilio Lunghi (ITA) 1:54.2	Hanns Braun (GER) 1:55.2
1912	James Meredith (USA) 1:51.9	Mel Sheppard (USA) 1:52.0	Ira Davenport (USA) 1:52.0
1920	Albert Hill (GBR) 1:53.4	Earl Eby (USA) 1:53.6	Bevil Rudd (SAF) 1:54.0
1924	Douglas Lowe (GBR) 1:52.4	Paul Martin (SUI) 1:52.6	Schuyler Enck (USA) 1:53.0
1928	Douglas Lowe (GBR) 1:51.8	Erik Bylehn (SWE) 1:52.8	Hermann Engelhardt (GER) 1:53.2
1932	Thomas Hampson (GBR) 1:49.7	Alexander Wilson (CAN) 1:49.9	Phil Edwards (CAN) 1:51.5
1936	John Woodruff (USA) 1:52.9	Mario Lanzi (ITA) 1:53.3	Phil Edwards (CAN) 1:53.6
1948	Mal Whitfield (USA) 1:49.2	Arthur Wint (JAM) 1:49.5	Marcel Hansenne (FRA) 1:49.8
1952	Mal Whitfield (USA) 1:49.2	Arthur Wint (JAM) 1:49.4	Heinz Ulzheimer (GER) 1:49.7
1956	Tom Courtney (USA) 1:47.7	Derek Johnson (GBR) 1:47.8	Audun Boysen (NOR) 1:48.1
1960	Peter Snell (NZL) 1:46.3	Roger Moens (BEL) 1:46.5	George Kerr[1] (BWI) 1:47.1
1964	Peter Snell (NZL) 1:45.1	Bill Crothers (CAN) 1:45.6	Wilson Kiprugut (KEN) 1:45.9
1968	Ralph Doubell (AUS) 1:44.3	Wilson Kiprugut (KEN) 1:44.5	Tom Farrell (USA) 1:45.4
1972	Dave Wottle (USA) 1:45.9	Yevgeniy Arzhanov (URS) 1:45.9	Mike Boit (KEN) 1:46.0
1976	Alberto Juantorena (CUB) 1:43.5	Ivo Van Damme (BEL) 1:43.9	Richard Wohlhuter (USA) 1:44.1
1980	Steve Ovett (GBR) 1:45.4	Sebastian Coe (GBR) 1:45.9	Nikolai Kirov (URS) 1:46.0
1984	Joaquim Cruz (BRA) 1:43.00*	Sebastian Coe (GBR) 1:43.64	Earl Jones (USA) 1:43.83

[1]Kerr was a Jamaican in the combined British West Indies team.   *Olympic record.

1500 Metres

1896	Edwin Flack (AUS) 4:33.2	Arthur Blake (USA) 4:34.0	Albin Lermusiaux (FRA) 4:36.0
1900	Charles Bennett (GBR) 4:06.2	Henri Deloge (FRA) 4:06.6	John Bray (USA) 4:07.2
1904	James Lightbody (USA) 4:05.4	William Verner (USA) 4:06.8	Lacey Hearn (USA) d.n.a.
1906	James Lightbody (USA) 4:12.0	John McGough (GBR) 4:12.6	Kristian Hellström (SWE) 4:13.4
1908	Mel Sheppard (USA) 4:03.4	Harold Wilson (GBR) 4:03.6	Norman Hallows (GBR) 4:04.0
1912[1]	Arnold Jackson (GBR) 3:56.8	Abel Kiviat (USA) 3:56.9	Norman Taber (USA) 3:56.9
1920	Albert Hill (GBR) 4:01.8	Philip Baker[1] (GBR) 4:02.4	Lawrence Shields (USA) 4:03.1
1924	Paavo Nurmi (FIN) 3:53.6	Willy Schärer (SUI) 3:55.0	Henry Stallard (GBR) 3:55.6
1928	Harri Larva (FIN) 3:53.2	Jules Ladoumègue (FRA) 3:53.8	Eino Purje (FIN) 3:56.4
1932	Luigi Beccali (ITA) 3:51.2	John Cornes (GBR) 3:52.6	Phil Edwards (CAN) 3:52.8
1936	Jack Lovelock (NZL) 3:47.8	Glenn Cunningham (USA) 3:48.4	Luigi Beccali (ITA) 3:49.2
1948	Henry Eriksson (SWE) 3:49.8	Lennart Strand (SWE) 3:50.4	Willem Slijkhuis (HOL) 3:50.4
1952	Josef Barthel (LUX) 3:45.1	Bob McMillen (USA) 3:45.2	Werner Lueg (GER) 3:45.4
1956	Ron Delany (IRL) 3:41.2	Klaus Richtzenhain (GER) 3:42.0	John Landy (AUS) 3:42.0
1960	Herb Elliott (AUS) 3:35.6	Michel Jazy (FRA) 3:38.4	István Rózsavölgyi (HUN) 3:39.2
1964	Peter Snell (NZL) 3:38.1	Josef Odlozil (TCH) 3:39.6	John Davies (NZL) 3:39.6
1968	Kipchoge Keino (KEN) 3:34.9	Jim Ryun (USA) 3:37.8	Bodo Tümmler (FRG) 3:39.0
1972	Pekka Vasala (FIN) 3:36.3	Kipchoge Keino (KEN) 3:36.8	Rod Dixon (NZL) 3:37.5
1976	John Walker (NZL) 3:39.2	Ivo Van Damme (BEL) 3:39.3	Paul-Heinz Wellmann (FRG) 3:39.3
1980	Sebastian Coe (GBR) 3:38.4	Jürgen Straub (GDR) 3:38.8	Steve Ovett (GBR) 3:39.0
1984	Sebastian Coe (GBR) 3:32.53*	Steve Cram (GBR) 3:33.40	Jose Abascal (ESP) 3:34.30

[1]Jackson later changed name to Strode-Jackson and Baker changed to Noel-Baker.   *Olympic record.

5000 Metres

1912	Hannes Kolehmainen (FIN) 14:36.6	Jean Bouin (FRA) 14:36.7	George Hutson (GBR) 15:07.6
1920	Joseph Guillemot (FRA) 14:55.6	Paavo Nurmi (FIN) 15:00.0	Erik Backman (SWE) 15:13.0
1924[1]	Paavo Nurmi (FIN) 14:31.2	Ville Ritola (FIN) 14:31.4	Edvin Wide (SWE) 15:01.8
1928	Ville Ritola (FIN) 14:38.0	Paavo Nurmi (FIN) 14:40.0	Edvin Wide (SWE) 14:41.2

Gold	Silver	Bronze
1932 Lauri Lehtinen (FIN) 14:30.0	Ralph Hill (USA) 14:30.0	Lauri Virtanen (FIN) 14:44.0
1936 Gunnar Höckert (FIN) 14:22.2	Lauri Lehtinen (FIN) 14:25.8	Henry Jonsson[2] (SWE) 14:29.0
1948 Gaston Rieff (BEL) 14:17.6	Emil Zatopek (TCH) 14:17.8	Willem Slijkhuis (HOL) 14:26.8
1952 Emil Zatopek (TCH) 14:06.6	Alain Mimoun (FRA) 14:07.4	Herbert Schade (GER) 14:08.6
1956 Vladimir Kuts (URS) 13:39.6	Gordon Pirie (GBR) 13:50.6	Derek Ibbotson (GBR) 13:54.4
1960 Murray Halberg (NZL) 13:43.4	Hans Grodotzki (GER) 13:44.6	Kazimierz Zimny (POL) 13:44.8
1964 Bob Schul (USA) 13:48.8	Harald Norpoth (GER) 13:49.6	Bill Dellinger (USA) 13:49.8
1968 Mohamed Gammoudi (TUN) 14:05.0	Kipchoge Keino (KEN) 14:05.2	Naftali Temu (KEN) 14:06.4
1972 Lasse Viren (FIN) 13:26.4	Mohamed Gammoudi (TUN) 13:27.4	Ian Stewart (GBR) 13:27.6
1976 Lasse Viren (FIN) 13:24.8	Dick Quax (NZL) 13:25.2	Klaus-Peter Hildenbrand (FRG) 13:25.4
1980 Miruts Yifter (ETH) 13:21.0	Suleiman Nyambui (TAN) 13:21.6	Kaarlo Maaninka (FIN) 13:22.0
1984 Said Aouita (MAR) 13:05.59*	Markus Ryffel (SUI) 13:07.54	Antonio Leitao (POR) 13:09.20

[1]Nurmi won 5000m only 1½ hours after winning the 1500m.   [2]Jonsson later changed name to Kälarne.   *Olympic record.   1896–1908 Event not held.

10 000 Metres

1906[1] Henry Hawtrey (GBR) 26:11.8	John Svanberg (SWE) 26:19.4	Edward Dahl (SWE) 26:26.2
1908[1] Emil Voigt (GBR) 25:11.2	Edward Owen (GBR) 25:24.0	John Svanberg (SWE) 25:37.2
1912 Hannes Kolehmainen (FIN) 31:20.8	Louis Tewanima (USA) 32:06.6	Albin Stenroos (FIN) 32:21.8
1920 Paavo Nurmi (FIN) 31:45.8	Joseph Guillemot (FRA) 31:47.2	James Wilson (GBR) 31:50.8
1924 Ville Ritola (FIN) 30:23.2	Edvin Wide (SWE) 30:55.2	Eero Berg (FIN) 31:43.0
1928 Paavo Nurmi (FIN) 30:18.8	Ville Ritola (FIN) 30:19.4	Edvin Wide (SWE) 31:00.8
1932 Janusz Kusocinski (POL) 30:11.4	Volmari Iso-Hollo (FIN) 30:12.6	Lauri Virtanen (FIN) 30:35.0
1936 Ilmari Salminen (FIN) 30:15.4	Arvo Askola (FIN) 30:15.6	Volmari Iso-Hollo (FIN) 30:20.2
1948 Emil Zatopek (TCH) 29:59.6	Alain Mimoun (FRA) 30:47.4	Bertil Albertsson (SWE) 30:53.6
1952 Emil Zatopek (TCH) 29:17.0	Alain Mimoun (FRA) 29:32.8	Aleksandr Anufriyev (URS) 29:48.2
1956 Vladimir Kuts (URS) 28:45.6	József Kovács (HUN) 28:52.4	Allan Lawrence (AUS) 28:53.6
1960 Pyotr Bolotnikov (URS) 28:32.2	Hans Grodotzki (GER) 28:37.0	David Power (AUS) 28:38.2
1964 Billy Mills (USA) 28:24.4	Mohamed Gammoudi (TUN) 28:24.8	Ron Clarke (AUS) 28:25.8
1968 Naftali Temu (KEN) 29:27.4	Mamo Wolde (ETH) 29:28.0	Mohamed Gammoudi (TUN) 29:34.2
1972 Lasse Viren (FIN) 27:38.4*	Emiel Puttemans (BEL) 27:39.6	Miruts Yifter (ETH) 27:41.0
1976 Lasse Viren (FIN) 27:44.4	Carlos Lopes (POR) 27:45.2	Brendan Foster (GBR) 27:54.9
1980 Miruts Yifter (ETH) 27:42.7	Kaarlo Maaninka (FIN) 27:44.3	Mohammed Kedir (ETH) 27:44.7
1984 Alberto Cova (ITA) 27:47.54	Mike McLeod (GBR) 28:06.22[2]	Mike Musyoki (KEN) 28:06.46

[1]5 miles (8046m).   [2]Martti Vainio (FIN) finished second but failed a drugs test.   *Olympic record (27:38.35)   1896–1904 Event not held.

Marathon

The length of the marathon was standardized at the 1908 distance of 26 miles 385 yards (42 195 metres) from 1924. Previously the distances had been: 1896 & 1904 – 40 000m, 1900 – 40 260m, 1906 – 41 860m, 1912 – 40 200m, 1920 – 42 750m.

1896 Spyridon Louis (GRE) 2h 58:50	Charilaos Vasilakos (GRE) 3h 06:03	Gyula Kellner (HUN) 3h 09:35
1900 Michel Theato (FRA) 2h 59:45	Emile Champion (FRA) 3h 04:17	Ernst Fast (SWE) 3h 37:14
1904 Thomas Hicks (USA) 3h 28:35	Albert Coray[1] (FRA) 3h 34:52	Arthur Newton (USA) 3h 47:33
1906 William Sherring (CAN) 2h 51:23.6	John Svanberg (SWE) 2h 58:20.8	William Frank (USA) 3h 00:46.8
1908[2] John Hayes (USA) 2h 55:18.4	Charles Hefferon (SAF) 2h 56:06.0	Joseph Forshaw (USA) 2h 57:10.4
1912 Kenneth McArthur (SAF) 2h 36:54.8	Christian Gitsham (SAF) 2h 37:52.0	Gaston Strobino (USA) 2h 38:42.4
1920 Hannes Kolehmainen (FIN) 2h 32:35.8	Jüri Lossman (EST) 2h 32:48.6	Valerio Arri (ITA) 2h 36:32.8
1924 Albin Stenroos (FIN) 2h 41:22.6	Romeo Bertini (ITA) 2h 47:19.6	Clarence DeMar (USA) 2h 48:14.0
1928 Mohamed El Ouafi (FRA) 2h 32:57	Miguel Plaza (CHI) 2h 33:23	Martti Marttelin (FIN) 2h 35:02
1932 Juan Carlos Zabala (ARG) 2h 31:36	Sam Ferris (GBR) 2h 31:55	Armas Toivonen (FIN) 2h 32:12
1936 Kitei Son (JPN) 2h 29:19.2	Ernest Harper (GBR) 2h 31:23.2	Shoryu Nan (JPN) 2h 31:42.0
1948 Delfo Cabrera (ARG) 2h 34:51.6	Tom Richards (GBR) 2h 35:07.6	Etienne Gailly (BEL) 2h 35:33.6
1952 Emil Zatopek (TCH) 2h 23:03.2	Reinaldo Gorno (ARG) 2h 25:35.0	Gustaf Jansson (SWE) 2h 26:07.0
1956 Alain Mimoun (FRA) 2h 25:00	Franjo Mihalic (YUG) 2h 26:32	Veikko Karvonen (FIN) 2h 27:47
1960 Abebe Bikila (ETH) 2h 15:16.2	Rhadi Ben Abdesselem (MAR) 2h 15:41.6	Barry Magee (NZL) 2h 17:18.2
1964 Abebe Bikila (ETH) 2h 12:11.2	Basil Heatley (GBR) 2h 16:19.2	Kokichi Tsuburaya (JPN) 2h 16:22.8
1968 Mamo Wolde (ETH) 2h 20:26.4	Kenji Kimihara (JPN) 2h 23:31.0	Michael Ryan (NZL) 2h 23:45.0
1972 Frank Shorter (USA) 2h 12:19.8	Karel Lismont (BEL) 2h 14:31.8	Mamo Wolde (ETH) 2h 15:08.4
1976 Waldemar Cierpinski (GDR) 2h 09:55.0	Frank Shorter (USA) 2h 10:45.8	Karel Lismont (BEL) 2h 11:12.6
1980 Waldemar Cierpinski (GDR) 2h 11:03	Gerard Nijboer (HOL) 2h 11:20	Satymkul Dzhumanazarov (URS) 2h 11:35
1984 Carlos Lopes (POR) 2h 09:21*	John Treacy (IRL) 2h 09.56	Charles Spedding (GBR) 2h 09:58

[1]Usually shown as an American incorrectly.   [2]Dorando Pietri (ITA) finished first but was disqualified due to assistance by officials on last lap of the track.   *Olympic record.

3000 Metres Steeplechase

1900[1] George Orton (CAN) 7:34.4	Sidney Robinson (GBR) 7:38.0	Jacques Chastanié (FRA) d.n.a.
1900[2] John Rimmer (GBR) 12:58.4	Charles Bennett (GBR) 12:58.6	Sidney Robinson (GBR) 12:58.8
1904[3] James Lightbody (USA) 7:39.6	John Daly (GBR) 7:40.6	Arthur Newton (USA) 25m
1908[4] Arthur Russell (GBR) 10:47.8	Archie Robertson (GBR) 10:48.4	John Eisele (USA) 20m
1920 Percy Hodge (GBR) 10:00.4	Patrick Flynn (USA) 100m	Ernesto Ambrosini (ITA) 30m
1924 Ville Ritola (FIN) 9:33.6	Elias Katz (FIN) 9:44.0	Paul Bontemps (FRA) 9:45.2
1928 Toivo Loukola (FIN) 9:21.8	Paavo Nurmi (FIN) 9:31.2	Ove Andersen (FIN) 9:35.6
1932[5] Volmari Iso-Hollo (FIN) 10:33.4	Tom Evenson (GBR) 10:46.0	Joseph McCluskey (USA) 10:46.2
1936 Volmari Iso-Hollo (FIN) 9:03.8	Kaarlo Tuominen (FIN) 9:06.8	Alfred Dompert (GER) 9:07.2
1948 Tore Sjöstrand (SWE) 9:04.6	Erik Elmsäter (SWE) 9:08.2	Göte Hagström (SWE) 9:11.8
1952 Horace Ashenfelter (USA) 8:45.4	Vladimir Kazantsev (URS) 8:51.6	John Disley (GBR) 8:51.8
1956 Chris Brasher (GBR) 8:41.2	Sándor Rozsnyói (HUN) 8:43.6	Ernst Larsen (NOR) 8:44.0
1960 Zdzislaw Krzyszkowiak (POL) 8:34.2	Nikolai Sokolov (URS) 8:36.4	Semyon Rzhischin (URS) 8:42.2
1964 Gaston Roelants (BEL) 8:30.8	Maurice Herriott (GBR) 8:32.4	Ivan Belyayev (URS) 8:33.8
1968 Amos Biwott (KEN) 8:51.0	Benjamin Kogo (KEN) 8:51.6	George Young (USA) 8:51.8
1972 Kipchoge Keino (KEN) 8:23.6	Benjamin Jipcho (KEN) 8:24.6	Tapio Kantanen (FIN) 8:24.8
1976 Anders Garderud (SWE) 8:08.0*	Bronislaw Malinowski (POL) 8:09.1	Frank Baumgartl (GDR) 8:10.4
1980 Bronislaw Malinowski (POL) 8:09.7	Filbert Bayi (TAN) 8:12.5	Eshetu Tura (ETH) 8:13.6
1984 Julius Korir (KEN) 8:11.80	Joseph Mahmoud (FRA) 8:13.31	Brian Diemer (USA) 8:14.06

[1]2500m.   [2]4000m.   [3]2590m.   [4]3200m.   [5]3460m in final due to lap scoring error. Iso-Hollo clocked 9:14.6 in a heat.   *Olympic record (8:08.02).   1896, 1906, 1912 Event not held.

Gold	*Silver*	*Bronze*

110 Metres Hurdles

	Gold	Silver	Bronze
1896[1]	Thomas Curtis (USA) 17.6	Grantley Goulding (GBR) 18.0	–
1900	Alvin Kraenzlein (USA) 15.4	John McLean (USA) 15.5	Fred Moloney (USA) 15.6
1904	Frederick Schule (USA) 16.0	Thaddeus Shideler (USA) 16.3	Lesley Ashburner (USA) 16.4
1906	Robert Leavitt (USA) 16.2	Alfred Healey (GBR) 16.2	Vincent Duncker (SAF) 16.3
1908	Forrest Smithson (USA) 15.0	John Garrels (USA) 15.7	Arthur Shaw (USA) 15.8
1912	Frederick Kelly (USA) 15.1	James Wendell (USA) 15.2	Martin Hawkins (USA) 15.3
1920	Earl Thomson (CAN) 14.8	Harold Barron (USA) 15.1	Frederick Murray (USA) 15.2
1924	Daniel Kinsey (USA) 15.0	Sydney Atkinson (SAF) 15.0	Sten Pettersson (SWE) 15.4
1928	Sydney Atkinson (SAF) 14.8	Stephen Anderson (USA) 14.8	John Collier (USA) 15.0
1932	George Saling (USA) 14.6 (14.56)	Percy Beard (USA) 14.7	Don Finlay (GBR) 14.8
1936	Forrest Towns (USA) 14.2	Don Finlay (GBR) 14.4	Fred Pollard (USA) 14.4
1948	William Porter (USA) 13.9	Clyde Scott (USA) 14.1	Craig Dixon (USA) 14.1
1952	Harrison Dillard (USA) 13.7 (13.91)	Jack Davis (USA) 13.7 (14.00)	Art Barnard (USA) 14.1 (14.40)
1956	Lee Calhoun (USA) 13.5 (13.70)	Jack Davis (USA) 13.5 (13.73)	Joel Shankle (USA) 14.1 (14.25)
1960	Lee Calhoun (USA) 13.8 (13.98)	Willie May (USA) 13.8 (13.99)	Hayes Jones (USA) 14.0 (14.17)
1964	Hayes Jones (USA) 13.6 (13.67)	Blaine Lindgren (USA) 13.7 (13.74)	Anatoliy Mikhailov (URS) 13.7 (13.78)
1968	Willie Davenport (USA) 13.3 (13.33)	Ervin Hall (USA) 13.4 (13.42)	Eddy Ottoz (ITA) 13.4 (13.46)
1972	Rod Milburn (USA) 13.24	Guy Drut (FRA) 13.34	Tom Hill (USA) 13.48
1976	Guy Drut (FRA) 13.30	Alejandro Casanas (CUB) 13.33	Willie Davenport (USA) 13.38
1980	Thomas Munkelt (GDR) 13.39	Alejandro Casanas (CUB) 13.40	Aleksandr Puchkov (URS) 13.44
1984	Roger Kingdom (USA) 13.20*	Greg Foster (USA) 13.23	Arto Bryggare (FIN) 13.40

[1]Only two finalists. *Olympic record.

400 Metres Hurdles

	Gold	Silver	Bronze
1900	Walter Tewksbury (USA) 57.6	Henri Tauzin (FRA) 58.3	George Orton (CAN) d.n.a.
1904[1]	Harry Hillman (USA) 53.0	Frank Waller (USA) 53.2	George Poage (USA) 30m
1908	Charles Bacon (USA) 55.0	Harry Hillman (USA) 55.3	Leonard Tremeer (GBR) 57.0
1920	Frank Loomis (USA) 54.0	John Norton (USA) 54.3	August Desch (USA) 54.5
1924	Morgan Taylor (USA) 52.6[2]	Erik Vilen (FIN) 53.8	Ivan Riley (USA) 54.2
1928	Lord Burghley (GBR) 53.4	Frank Cuhel (USA) 53.6	Morgan Taylor (USA) 53.6
1932	Bob Tisdall (IRL) 51.7[2] (51.67)	Glenn Hardin (USA) 51.9 (51.85)	Morgan Taylor (USA) 52.0 (51.96)
1936	Glenn Hardin (USA) 52.4	John Loaring (CAN) 52.7	Miguel White (PHI) 52.8
1948	Roy Cochran (USA) 51.1	Duncan White (SRI) 51.8	Rune Larsson (SWE) 52.2
1952	Charlie Moore (USA) 50.8 (51.06)	Yuriy Lituyev (URS) 51.3 (51.51)	John Holland (NZL) 52.2 (52.26)
1956	Glenn Davis (USA) 50.1 (50.29)	Eddie Southern (USA) 50.8 (50.94)	Josh Culbreath (USA) 51.6 (51.74)
1960	Glenn Davis (USA) 49.3 (49.51)	Cliff Cushman (USA) 49.6 (49.77)	Dick Howard (USA) 49.7 (49.90)
1964	Rex Cawley (USA) 49.6 (49.69)	John Cooper (GBR) 50.1 (50.19)	Salvadore Morale (ITA) 50.1
1968	David Hemery (GBR) 48.1 (48.12)	Gerhard Hennige (FRG) 49.0 (49.02)	John Sherwood (GBR) 49.0 (49.03)
1972	John Akii-Bua (UGA) 47.82	Ralph Mann (USA) 48.51	David Hemery (GBR) 48.52
1976	Edwin Moses (USA) 47.64*	Mike Shine (USA) 48.69	Yevgeniy Gavrilenko (URS) 49.45
1980	Volker Beck (GDR) 48.70	Vasiliy Arkhipenko (URS) 48.86	Gary Oakes (GBR) 49.11
1984	Edwin Moses (USA) 47.75	Danny Harris (USA) 48.13	Harald Schmid (FRG) 48.19

[1]Hurdles only *2ft 6in* 76.2cm high instead of usual *3ft* 91.4cm. [2]Record not allowed because hurdle knocked down. *Olympic record. 1896, 1906, 1912 Event not held.

4 × 100 Metres Relay

	Gold	Silver	Bronze
1912[1]	Great Britain 42.4	Sweden 42.6	–
1920	United States 42.2	France 42.6	Sweden 42.9
1924	United States 41.0	Great Britain 41.2	Netherlands 41.8
1928	United States 41.0	Germany 41.2	Great Britain 41.8
1932	United States 40.0	Germany 40.9	Italy 41.2
1936	United States 39.8	Italy 41.1	Germany 41.2
1948[2]	United States 40.6	Great Britain 41.3	Italy 41.5
1952	United States 40.1 (40.26)	Soviet Union 40.3 (40.58)	Hungary 40.5 (40.83)
1956	United States 39.5 (39.60)	Soviet Union 39.8 (39.92)	Germany 40.3 (40.34)
1960	Germany 39.5 (39.66)	Soviet Union 40.1 (40.24)	Great Britain 40.2 (40.32)
1964	United States 39.0 (39.06)	Poland 39.3 (39.36)	France 39.3 (39.36)
1968	United States 38.2 (38.24)	Cuba 38.3 (38.40)	France 38.4 (38.43)
1972	United States 38.19	Soviet Union 38.50	FRG 38.79
1976	United States 38.33	GDR 38.66	Soviet Union 38.78
1980	Soviet Union 38.26	Poland 38.33	France 38.53
1984	United States 37.83*	Jamaica 38.62	Canada 38.70

[1]German team finished second but was disqualified. [2]United States disqualified but later reinstated. *Olympic record. 1896–1908 Event not held.

4 × 400 Metres Relay

	Gold	Silver	Bronze
1908[1]	United States 3:29.4	Germany 3:32.4	Hungary 3:32.5
1912	United States 3:16.6	France 3:20.7	Great Britain 3:23.2
1920	Great Britain 3:22.2	South Africa 3:24.2	France 3:24.8
1924	United States 3:16.0	Sweden 3:17.0	Great Britain 3:17.4
1928	United States 3:14.2	Germany 3:14.8	Canada 3:15.4
1932	United States 3:08.2	Great Britain 3:11.2	Canada 3:12.8
1936	Great Britain 3:09.0	United States 3:11.0	Germany 3:11.8
1948	United States 3:10.4	France 3:14.8	Sweden 3:16.3
1952	Jamaica 3:03.9 (3:04.04)	United States 3:04.0 (3:04.21)	Germany 3:06.6 (3:06.78)
1956	United States 3:04.8 (3:04.81)	Australia 3:06.2 (3:06.19)	Great Britain 3:07.2 (3:07.19)
1960	United States 3:02.2 (3:02.37)	Germany 3:02.7 (3:02.84)	British West Indies[2] 3:04.0 (3:04.13)
1964	United States 3:00.7 (3:00.71)	Great Britain 3:01.6 (3:01.69)	Trinidad 3:01.7
1968	United States 2:56.1 (2:56.16)*	Kenya 2:59.6 (2:59.64)	FRG 3:00.5 (3:00.57)
1972	Kenya 2:59.83	Great Britain 3:00.46	France 3:00.65
1976	United States 2:58.65	Poland 3:01.43	FRG 3:01.98
1980	Soviet Union 3:01.08	GDR 3:01.26	Italy 3:04.3
1984	United States 2:57.91	Great Britain 2:59.13	Nigeria 2:59.32

[1]Medley relay – 200m, 200m, 400m, 800m. [2]Three from Jamaica, one from Trinidad. *Olympic record. 1896–1906 Event not held.

Gold	Silver	Bronze

20 000 Metres Road Walk

	Gold	Silver	Bronze
1956	Leonid Spirin (URS) 1h 31:27.4	Antonas Mikenas (URS) 1h 32:03.0	Bruno Junk (URS) 1h 32:12.0
1960	Vladimir Golubnichiy (URS) 1h 34:07.2	Noel Freeman (AUS) 1h 34:16.4	Stan Vickers (GBR) 1h 34:56.4
1964	Ken Matthews (GBR) 1h 29:34.0	Dieter Lindner (GER) 1h 31:13.2	Vladimir Golubnichiy (URS) 1h 31:59.4
1968	Vladimir Golubnichiy (URS) 1h 33:58.4	José Pedraza (MEX) 1h 34:00.0	Nikolai Smaga (URS) 1h 34:03.4
1972	Peter Frenkel (GDR) 1h 26:42.4	Vladimir Golubnichiy (URS) 1h 26:55.2	Hans Reimann (GDR) 1h 27:16.6
1976	Daniel Bautista (MEX) 1h 24:40.6	Hans Reimann (GDR) 1h 25:13.8	Peter Frenkel (GDR) 1h 25:29.4
1980	Maurizio Damilano (ITA) 1h 23:35.5	Pyotr Pochenchuk (URS) 1h 24:45.4	Roland Wieser (GDR) 1h 25:58.2
1984	Ernesto Canto (MEX) 1h 23:13*	Raul Gonzalez (MEX) 1h 23:20	Maurizio Damilano (ITA) 1h 23:26

*Olympic record.   1896–1952 Event not held.

50 000 Metres Road Walk

	Gold	Silver	Bronze
1932	Thomas Green (GBR) 4h 50:10	Janis Dalinsh (LAT) 4h 47:20	Ugo Frigerio (ITA) 4h 59:06
1936	Harold Whitlock (GBR) 4h 30:41.1	Arthur Schwab (SUI) 4h 32:09.2	Adalberts Bubenko (LAT) 4h 32:42.2
1948	John Ljunggren (SWE) 4h 41:52	Gaston Godel (SUI) 4h 48:17	Tebbs Lloyd Johnson (GBR) 4h 48:31
1952	Giuseppe Dordoni (ITA) 4h 28:07.8	Josef Dolezal (TCH) 4h 30:17.8	Antal Róka (HUN) 4h 31:27.2
1956	Norman Read (NZL) 4h 30:42.8	Yevgeniy Maskinkov (URS) 4h 32:57.0	John Ljunggren (SWE) 4h 35:02.0
1960	Don Thompson (GBR) 4h 25:30.0	John Ljunggren (SWE) 4h 25:47.0	Abdon Pamich (ITA) 4h 27:55.4
1964	Abdon Pamich (ITA) 4h 11:12.4	Paul Nihill (GBR) 4h 11:31.2	Ingvar Pettersson (SWE) 4h 14:17.4
1968	Christoph Höhne (GDR) 4h 20:13.6	Antal Kiss (HUN) 4h 30:17.0	Larry Young (USA) 4h 31:55.4
1972	Bernd Kannenberg (FRG) 3h 56:11.6	Venjamin Soldatenko (URS) 3h 58:24.0	Larry Young (USA) 4h 00:46.0
1980	Hartwig Gauder (GDR) 3h 49:24	Jorge Llopart (ESP) 3h 51:25	Yevgeniy Ivchenko (URS) 3h 56:32
1984	Raul Gonzalez (MEX) 3h 47:26*	Bo Gustafsson (SWE) 3h 53.19	Sandro Bellucci (ITA) 3h 53:45

*Olympic record.   1896–1928, 1976 Event not held.

High Jump

	Gold	Silver	Bronze
1896	Ellery Clark (USA) 1.81m	James Connolly (USA) 1.65m Robert Garrett (USA) 1.65m	–

Olympic champions and world record holders in the 4 × 100m relay are Jesse Owens, Ralph Metcalfe, Foy Draper and Frank Wykoff. (Dave Terry)

	Gold	*Silver*	*Bronze*
1900	Irving Baxter (USA) 1.90m	Patrick Leahy (GBR) 1.78m	Lajos Gönczy (HUN) 1.75m
1904	Samuel Jones (USA) 1.80m	Garrett Serviss (USA) 1.77m	Paul Weinstein (GER) 1.77m
1906	Con Leahy (GBR) 1.77m	Lajos Gönczy (HUN) 1.75m	Herbert Kerrigan (USA) 1.72m
			Themistoklis Diakidis (GRE) 1.72m
1908	Harry Porter (USA) 1.905m	Con Leahy (GBR) 1.88m	–
		István Somodi (HUN) 1.88m	
		Georges André (FRA) 1.88m	
1912	Alma Richards (USA) 1.93m	Hans Liesche (GER) 1.91m	George Horine (USA) 1.89m
1920	Richmond Landon (USA) 1.94m	Harold Muller (USA) 1.90m	Bo Ekelund (SWE) 1.90m
1924	Harold Osborn (USA) 1.98m	Leroy Brown (USA) 1.95m	Pierre Lewden (FRA) 1.92m
1928	Robert King (USA) 1.94m	Ben Hedges (USA) 1.91m	Claude Ménard (FRA) 1.91m
1932	Duncan McNaughton (CAN) 1.97m	Robert Van Osdel (USA) 1.97m	Simeon Toribio (PHI) 1.97m
1936	Cornelius Johnson (USA) 2.03m	David Albritton (USA) 2.00m	Delos Thurber (USA) 2.00m
1948	John Winter (AUS) 1.98m	Björn Paulsen (NOR) 1.95m	George Stanich (USA) 1.95m
1952	Walt Davis (USA) 2.04m	Ken Wiesner (USA) 2.01m	Jose Telles da Conceicao (BRA) 1.98m
1956	Charlie Dumas (USA) 2.12m	Chilla Porter (AUS) 2.10m	Igor Kashkarov (URS) 2.08m
1960	Robert Shavlakadze (URS) 2.16m	Valeriy Brumel (URS) 2.16m	John Thomas (USA) 2.14m
1964	Valeriy Brumel (URS) 2.18m	John Thomas (USA) 2.18m	John Rambo (USA) 2.16m
1968	Dick Fosbury (USA) 2.24m	Ed Caruthers (USA) 2.22m	Valentin Gavrilov (URS) 2.20m
1972	Yuriy Tarmak (URS) 2.23m	Stefan Junge (GDR) 2.21m	Dwight Stones (USA) 2.21m
1976	Jacek Wszola (POL) 2.25m	Greg Joy (CAN) 2.23m	Dwight Stones (USA) 2.21m
1980	Gerd Wessig (GDR) 2.36m*	Jacek Wszola (POL) 2.31m	Jörg Freimuth (GDR) 2.31m
1984	Dietmar Mögenburg (FRG) 2.35m	Patrik Sjöberg (SWE) 2.33m	Zhu Jianhua (CHN) 2.31m

*Olympic record.

Pole Vault

	Gold	*Silver*	*Bronze*
1896	William Hoyt (USA) 3.30m	Albert Tyler (USA) 3.25m	Evangelos Damaskos (GRE) 2.85m
1900	Irving Baxter (USA) 3.30m	Meredith Colkett (USA) 3.25m	Carl-Albert Andersen (NOR) 3.20m
1904	Charles Dvorak (USA) 3.50m	LeRoy Samse (USA) 3.43m	Louis Wilkins (USA) 3.43m
1906	Fernand Gonder (FRA) 3.40m	Bruno Söderström (SWE) 3.40m	Ernest Glover (USA) 3.35m
1908	Edward Cooke (USA) 3.70m	–	Edward Archibald (CAN) 3.58m
	Alfred Gilbert (USA) 3.70m		Charles Jacobs (USA) 3.58m
			Bruno Söderström (SWE) 3.58m
1912	Harry Babcock (USA) 3.95m	Frank Nelson (USA) 3.85m	–
		Marcus Wright (USA) 3.85m	
1920	Frank Foss (USA) 4.09m	Henry Petersen (DEN) 3.70m	Edwin Meyers (USA) 3.60m
1924	Lee Barnes (USA) 3.95m	Glenn Graham (USA) 3.95m	James Brooker (USA) 3.90m
1928	Sabin Carr (USA) 4.20m	William Droegemuller (USA) 4.10m	Charles McGinnis (USA) 3.95m
1932	William Miller (USA) 4.31m	Shuhei Nishida (JPN) 4.26m	George Jefferson (USA) 4.19m
1936	Earle Meadows (USA) 4.35m	Shuhei Nishida (JPN) 4.25m	Sueo Oe (JPN) 4.25m
1948	Guinn Smith (USA) 4.30m	Erkki Kataja (FIN) 4.20m	Bob Richards (USA) 4.20m
1952	Bob Richards (USA) 4.55m	Don Laz (USA) 4.50m	Ragnar Lundberg (SWE) 4.40m
1956	Bob Richards (USA) 4.56m	Bob Gutowski (USA) 4.53m	Georgios Roubanis (GRE) 4.50m
1960	Don Bragg (USA) 4.70m	Ron Morris (USA) 4.60m	Eeles Landström (FIN) 4.55m
1964	Fred Hansen (USA) 5.10m	Wolfgang Reinhardt (GER) 5.05m	Klaus Lehnertz (GER) 5.00m
1968	Bob Seagren (USA) 5.40m	Claus Schiprowski (FRG) 5.40m	Wolfgang Nordwig (GDR) 5.40m
1972	Wolfgang Nordwig (GDR) 5.50m	Bob Seagren (USA) 5.40m	Jan Johnson (USA) 5.35m
1976	Tadeusz Slusarski (POL) 5.50m	Antti Kalliomaki (FIN) 5.50m	David Roberts (USA) 5.50m
1980	Wladislaw Kozakiewicz (POL) 5.78m*	Tadeusz Slusarski (POL) 5.65m	–
		Konstantin Volkov (URS) 5.65m	
1984	Pierre Quinon (FRA) 5.75m	Mike Tully (USA) 5.65m	Earl Bell (USA) 5.60m
			Thierry Vigneron (FRA) 5.60m

*Olympic record.

Long Jump

	Gold	*Silver*	*Bronze*
1896	Ellery Clark (USA) 6.35m	Robert Garrett (USA) 6.18m	James Connolly (USA) 6.11m
1900	Alvin Kraenzlein (USA) 7.18m	Myer Prinstein (USA) 7.17m	Patrick Leahy (GBR) 6.95m
1904	Myer Prinstein (USA) 7.34m	Daniel Frank (USA) 6.89m	Robert Stangland (USA) 6.88m
1906	Myer Prinstein (USA) 7.20m	Peter O'Connor (GBR) 7.02m	Hugo Friend (USA) 6.96m
1908	Francis Irons (USA) 7.48m	Daniel Kelly (USA) 7.09m	Calvin Bricker (CAN) 7.08m
1912	Albert Gutterson (USA) 7.60m	Calvin Bricker (CAN) 7.21m	Georg Aberg (SWE) 7.18m
1920	William Pettersson (SWE) 7.15m	Carl Johnson (USA) 7.09m	Erik Abrahamsson (SWE) 7.08m
1924	William DeHart Hubbard (USA) 7.44m	Ed Gourdin (USA) 7.27m	Sverre Hansen (NOR) 7.26m
1928	Edward Hamm (USA) 7.73m	Silvio Cator (HAI) 7.58m	Alfred Bates (USA) 7.40m
1932	Ed Gordon (USA) 7.63m	Lambert Redd (USA) 7.60m	Chuhei Nambu (JPN) 7.44m
1936	Jesse Owens (USA) 8.06m	Luz Long (GER) 7.87m	Naoto Tajima (JPN) 7.74m
1948	Willie Steele (USA) 7.82m	Thomas Bruce (AUS) 7.55m	Herbert Douglas (USA) 7.54m
1952	Jerome Biffle (USA) 7.57m	Meredith Gourdine (USA) 7.53m	Odön Földessy (HUN) 7.30m
1956•	Greg Bell (USA) 7.83m	John Bennett (USA) 7.68m	Jorma Valkama (FIN) 7.48m
1960	Ralph Boston (USA) 8.12m	Irvin Roberson (USA) 8.11m	Igor Ter-Ovanesyan (URS) 8.04m
1964	Lynn Davies (GBR) 8.07m	Ralph Boston (USA) 8.03m	Igor Ter-Ovanesyan (URS) 7.99m
1968	Bob Beamon (USA) 8.90m*	Klaus Beer (GDR) 8.19m	Ralph Boston (USA) 8.16m
1972	Randy Williams (USA) 8.24m	Hans Baumgartner (FRG) 8.18m	Arnie Robinson (USA) 8.03m
1976	Arnie Robinson (USA) 8.35m	Randy Williams (USA) 8.11m	Frank Wartenberg (GDR) 8.02m
1980	Lutz Dombrowski (GDR) 8.54m	Frank Paschek (GDR) 8.21m	Valeriy Podluzhny (URS) 8.18m
1984	Carl Lewis (USA) 8.54m	Gary Honey (AUS) 8.24m	Giovanni Evangelisti (ITA) 8.24m

*Olympic record.

Triple Jump
(Formerly known as the Hop, step and jump)

	Gold	*Silver*	*Bronze*
1896[1]	James Connolly (USA) 13.71m	Alexander Tuffere (FRA) 12.70m	Ioannis Persakis (GRE) 12.52m
1900	Myer Prinstein (USA) 14.47m	James Connolly (USA) 13.97m	Lewis Sheldon (USA) 13.64m
1904	Myer Prinstein (USA) 14.35m	Frederick Englehardt (USA) 13.90m	Robert Stangland (USA) 13.36m
1906	Peter O'Connor (GBR) 14.07m	Con Leahy (GBR) 13.98m	Thomas Cronan (USA) 13.70m
1908	Tim Ahearne (GBR) 14.91m	Garfield McDonald (CAN) 14.76m	Edvard Larsen (NOR) 14.39m
1912	Gustaf Lindblom (SWE) 14.76m	Georg Aberg (SWE) 14.51m	Erik Almlöf (SWE) 14.17m
1920	Vilho Tuulos (FIN) 14.50m	Folke Jansson (SWE) 14.48m	Erik Almlöf (SWE) 14.27m

	Gold	Silver	Bronze
1924	Anthony Winter (AUS) 15.52m	Luis Brunetto (ARG) 15.42m	Vilho Tuulos (FIN) 15.37m
1928	Mikio Oda (JPN) 15.21m	Levi Casey (USA) 15.17m	Vilho Tuulos (FIN) 15.11m
1932	Chuhei Nambu (JPN) 15.72m	Erik Svensson (SWE) 15.32m	Kenkichi Oshima (JPN) 15.12m
1936	Naoto Tajima (JPN) 16.00m	Masao Harada (JPN) 15.66m	John Metcalfe (AUS) 15.50m
1948	Arne Ahman (SWE) 15.40m	George Avery (AUS) 15.36m	Ruhi Sarialp (TUR) 15.02m
1952	Adhemar Ferreira da Silva (BRA) 16.22m	Leonid Shcherbakov (URS) 15.98m	Arnoldo Devonish (VEN) 15.52m
1956	Adhemar Ferreira da Silva (BRA) 16.35m	Vilhjalmur Einarsson (ISL) 16.26m	Vitold Kreyer (URS) 16.02m
1960	Jozef Schmidt (POL) 16.81m	Vladimir Goryayev (URS) 16.63m	Vitold Kreyer (URS) 16.43m
1964	Jozef Schmidt (POL) 16.85m	Oleg Fedoseyev (URS) 16.58m	Viktor Kravchenko (URS) 16.57m
1968	Viktor Saneyev (URS) 17.39m*	Nelson Prudencio (BRA) 17.27m	Giuseppe Gentile (ITA) 17.22m
1972	Viktor Saneyev (URS) 17.35m	Jörg Drehmel (GDR) 17.31m	Nelson Prudencio (BRA) 17.05m
1976	Viktor Saneyev (URS) 17.29m	James Butts (USA) 17.18m	Joao de Oliveira (BRA) 16.90m
1980	Jaak Uudmäe (URS) 17.35m	Viktor Saneyev (URS) 17.24m	Joao de Oliveira (BRA) 17.22m
1984	Al Joyner (USA) 17.26m	Mike Conley (USA) 17.18m	Keith Connor (GBR) 16.87m

[1]Winner took two hops with his right foot, contrary to present rules.   *Olympic record.

Shot Put

	Gold	Silver	Bronze
1896[1]	Robert Garrett (USA) 11.22m	Miltiades Gouskos (GRE) 11.15m	Georgios Papasideris (GRE) 10.36m
1900[1]	Richard Sheldon (USA) 14.10m	Josiah McCracken (USA) 12.85m	Robert Garrett (USA) 12.37m
1904[1]	Ralph Rose (USA) 14.80m	Wesley Coe (USA) 14.40m	Leon Feuerbach (USA) 13.37m
1906	Martin Sheridan (USA) 12.32m	Maihály Dávid (HUN) 11.83m	Erik Lemming (SWE) 11.26m
1908	Ralph Rose (USA) 14.21m	Dennis Horgan (GBR) 13.61m	John Garrels (USA) 13.18m
1912	Patrick McDonald (USA) 15.34m	Ralph Rose (USA) 15.25m	Lawrence Whitney (USA) 14.15m
1920	Ville Pörhölä (FIN) 14.81m	Elmer Niklander (FIN) 14.155m	Harry Liversedge (USA) 14.15m
1924	Clarence Houser (USA) 14.99m	Glenn Hartranft (USA) 14.98m	Ralph Hills (USA) 14.64m
1928	John Kuck (USA) 15.87m	Herman Brix (USA) 15.75m	Emil Hirschfeld (GER) 15.72m
1932	Leo Sexton (USA) 16.00m	Harlow Rothert (USA) 15.67m	Frantisek Douda (TCH) 15.60m
1936	Hans Woellke (GER) 16.20m	Sulo Bärlund (FIN) 16.12m	Gerhard Stöck (GER) 15.66m
1948	Wilbur Thompson (USA) 17.12m	Jim Delaney (USA) 16.68m	Jim Fuchs (USA) 16.42m
1952	Parry O'Brien (USA) 17.41m	Darrow Hooper (USA) 17.39m	Jim Fuchs (USA) 17.06m
1956	Parry O'Brien (USA) 18.57m	Bill Nieder (USA) 18.18m	Jiri Skobla (TCH) 17.65m
1960	Bill Nieder (USA) 19.68m	Parry O'Brien (USA) 19.11m	Dallas Long (USA) 19.01m
1964	Dallas Long (USA) 20.33m	Randy Matson (USA) 20.20m	Vilmos Varju (HUN) 19.39m
1968	Randy Matson (USA) 20.54m	George Woods (USA) 20.12m	Eduard Grishchin (URS) 20.09m
1972	Wladyslaw Komar (POL) 21.18m	George Woods (USA) 21.17m	Hartmut Briesenick (GDR) 21.14m
1976	Udo Beyer (GDR) 21.05m	Yevgeniy Mironov (URS) 21.03m	Aleksandr Baryshnikov (URS) 21.00m
1980	Vladimir Kiselyev (URS) 21.35m*	Aleksandr Baryshnikov (URS) 21.08m	Udo Beyer (GDR) 21.06m
1984	Alessandro Andrei (ITA) 21.26m	Michael Carter (USA) 21.09m	Dave Laut (USA) 20.97m

[1]From a 7ft 2.13m square.   *Olympic record.

Discus

	Gold	Silver	Bronze
1896[1]	Robert Garrett (USA) 29.15m	Panagotis Paraskevopoulos (GRE) 28.95m	Sotirios Versis (GRE) 28.78m
1900	Rudolf Bauer (HUN) 36.04m	Frantisek Janda-Suk (BOH) 35.25m	Richard Sheldon (USA) 34.60m
1904[2]	Martin Sheridan (USA) 39.28m	Ralph Rose (USA) 39.28m	Nicolaos Georgantas (GRE) 37.68m
1906	Martin Sheridan (USA) 41.46m	Nicolaos Georgantas (GRE) 38.06m	Werner Järvinen (FIN) 36.82m
1908	Martin Sheridan (USA) 40.89m	Merritt Giffin (USA) 40.70m	Marquis Horr (USA) 39.44m
1912	Armas Taipale (FIN) 45.21m	Richard Byrd (USA) 42.32m	James Duncan (USA) 42.28m
1920	Elmer Niklander (FIN) 44.68m	Armas Taipale (FIN) 44.19m	Augustus Pope (USA) 42.13m
1924	Clarence Houser (USA) 46.15m	Vilho Niittymaa (FIN) 44.95m	Thomas Lieb (USA) 44.83m
1928	Clarence Houser (USA) 47.32m	Antero Kivi (FIN) 47.23m	James Corson (USA) 47.10m
1932	John Anderson (USA) 49.49m	Henri Laborde (USA) 48.47m	Paul Winter (FRA) 47.85m
1936	Ken Carpenter (USA) 50.48m	Gordon Dunn (USA) 49.36m	Giorgio Oberweger (ITA) 49.23m
1948	Adolfo Consolini (ITA) 52.78m	Giuseppe Tosi (ITA) 51.78m	Fortune Gordien (USA) 50.77m
1952	Sim Iness (USA) 55.03m	Adolfo Consolini (ITA) 53.78m	James Dillion (USA) 53.28m
1956	Al Oerter (USA) 56.36m	Fortune Gordien (USA) 54.81m	Des Koch (USA) 54.40m
1960	Al Oerter (USA) 59.18m	Rink Babka (USA) 58.02m	Dick Cochran (USA) 57.16m
1964	Al Oerter (USA) 61.00m	Ludvik Danek (TCH) 60.52m	Dave Weill (USA) 59.49m
1968	Al Oerter (USA) 64.78m	Lothar Milde (GDR) 63.08m	Ludvik Danek (TCH) 62.92m
1972	Ludvik Danek (TCH) 64.40m	Jay Silvester (USA) 63.50m	Ricky Bruch (SWE) 63.40m
1976	Mac Wilkins (USA) 67.50m*	Wolfgang Schmidt (GDR) 66.22m	John Powell (USA) 65.70m
1980	Viktor Rashchupkin (URS) 66.64m	Imrich Bugár (TCH) 66.38m	Luis Delis (CUB) 66.32m
1984	Rolf Danneberg (FRG) 66.60m	Mac Wilkins (USA) 66.30m	John Powell (USA) 65.46m

[1]From 2.50m square.   [2]First place decided by a throw-off.   *Olympic record 68.28m in qualifying round.

Hammer

	Gold	Silver	Bronze
1900[1]	John Flanagan (USA) 49.73m	Truxton Hare (USA) 49.13m	Josiah McCracken (USA) 42.46m
1904	John Flanagan (USA) 51.23m	John De Witt (USA) 50.26m	Ralph Rose (USA) 45.73m
1908	John Flanagan (USA) 51.92m	Matt McGrath (USA) 51.18m	Con Walsh (CAN) 48.50m
1912	Matt McGrath (USA) 54.74m	Duncan Gillis (CAN) 48.39m	Clarence Childs (USA) 48.17m
1920	Patrick Ryan (USA) 52.87m	Carl Lind (SWE) 48.43m	Basil Bennett (USA) 48.25m
1924	Fred Tootell (USA) 53.29m	Matt McGrath (USA) 50.84m	Malcolm Nokes (GBR) 48.87m
1928	Patrick O'Callaghan (IRL) 51.39m	Ossian Skiöld (SWE) 51.29m	Edmund Black (USA) 49.03m
1932	Patrick O'Callaghan (IRL) 53.92m	Ville Pörhölä (FIN) 52.27m	Peter Zaremba (USA) 50.33m
1936	Karl Hein (GER) 56.49m	Erwin Blask (GER) 55.04m	Fred Warngard (SWE) 54.83
1948	Imre Németh (HUN) 56.07m	Ivan Gubijan (YUG) 54.27m	Bob Bennett (USA) 53.73m
1952	József Csermák (HUN) 60.34m	Karl Storch (GER) 58.86m	Imre Németh (HUN) 57.74m
1956	Harold Connolly (USA) 63.19m	Mikhail Krivonosov (URS) 63.03m	Anatoliy Samotsvetov (URS) 62.56m
1960	Vasiliy Rudenkov (URS) 67.10m	Gyula Zsivótzky (HUN) 65.79m	Tadeusz Rut (POL) 65.64m
1964	Romuald Klim (URS) 69.74m	Gyula Zsivótzky (HUN) 69.09m	Uwe Beyer (GER) 68.09m
1968	Gyula Zsivótzky (HUN) 73.36m	Romuald Klim (URS) 73.28m	Lázár Lovász (HUN) 69.78m
1972	Anatoliy Bondarchuk (URS) 75.50m	Jochen Sachse (GDR) 74.96m	Vasiliy Khmelevski (URS) 74.04m
1976	Yuriy Sedykh (URS) 77.52m	Aleksey Spiridinov (URS) 76.08m	Anatoliy Bondarchuk (URS) 75.48m
1980	Yuriy Sedykh (URS) 81.80m*	Sergey Litvinov (URS) 80.64m	Yuriy Tamm (URS) 78.96m
1984	Juha Tiainen (FIN) 78.08m	Karl-Hans Riehm (FRG) 77.98m	Klaus Ploghaus (FRG) 76.68m

[1]From a 9ft 2.74m circle.   *Olympic record.   1896, 1906 Event not held.

	Gold	Silver	Bronze

Javelin

	Gold	Silver	Bronze
1906	Erik Lemming (SWE) 53.90m	Knut Lindberg (SWE) 45.17m	Bruno Söderström (SWE) 44.92m
1908	Erik Lemming (SWE) 54.82m	Arne Halse (NOR) 50.57m	Otto Nilsson (SWE) 47.09m
1912	Erik Lemming (SWE) 60.64m	Juho Saaristo (FIN) 58.66m	Mór Kóczán (HUN) 55.50m
1920	Jonni Myyrä (FIN) 65.78m	Urho Peltonen (FIN) 63.50m	Pekka Johansson (FIN) 63.09m
1924	Jonni Myyrä (FIN) 62.96m	Gunnar Lindström (SWE) 60.92m	Eugene Oberst (USA) 58.35m
1928	Erik Lundkvist (SWE) 66.60m	Béla Szepes (HUN) 65.26m	Olav Sunde (NOR) 63.97m
1932	Matti Järvinen (FIN) 72.71m	Matti Sippala (FIN) 69.79m	Eino Penttila (FIN) 68.69m
1936	Gerhard Stöck (GER) 71.84m	Yrjö Nikkanen (FIN) 70.77m	Kalervo Toivonen (FIN) 70.72m
1948	Tapio Rautavaara (FIN) 69.77m	Steve Seymour (USA) 67.56m	József Várszegi (HUN) 67.03m
1952	Cyrus Young (USA) 73.78m	Bill Miller (USA) 72.46m	Toivo Hyytiainen (FIN) 71.89m
1956	Egil Danielsen (NOR) 85.71m	Janusz Sidlo (POL) 79.98	Viktor Tsibulenko (URS) 79.50m
1960	Viktor Tsibulenko (URS) 84.64m	Walter Krüger (GER) 79.36m	Gergely Kulcsár (HUN) 78.57m
1964	Pauli Nevala (FIN) 82.66m	Gergely Kulcsár (HUN) 82.32m	Janis Lusis (URS) 80.57m
1968	Janis Lusis (URS) 90.10m	Jorma Kinnunen (FIN) 88.58m	Gergely Kulcsár (HUN) 87.06m
1972	Klaus Wolfermann (FRG) 90.48m	Janis Lusis (URS) 90.46m	Bill Schmidt (USA) 84.42m
1976	Miklos Németh (HUN) 94.58m*	Hannu Siitonen (FIN) 87.92m	Gheorghe Megelea (ROM) 87.16m
1980	Dainis Kula (URS) 91.20m	Aleksandr Makarov (URS) 89.64m	Wolfgang Hanisch (GDR) 86.72m
1984	Arto Härkonen (FIN) 86.76m	David Ottley (GBR) 85.74m	Kenth Eldebrink (SWE) 83.72m

*Olympic record.   1896–1904 Event not held.

Decathlon[1,2]

	Gold	Silver	Bronze
1904[3]	Thomas Kiely (GBR) 6036pts	Adam Gunn (USA) 5907	Truxton Hare (USA) 5813
1912[4]	Hugo Wieslander (SWE) 6162pts	Charles Lomberg (SWE) 5943	Gösta Holmer (SWE) 5956
1920	Helge Lövland (NOR) 5970pts	Brutus Hamilton (USA) 5912	Bertil Ohlsson (SWE) 5825
1924	Harold Osborn (USA) 6668pts	Emerson Norton (USA) 6360	Aleksandr Klumberg (EST) 6260
1928	Paavo Yrjölä (FIN) 6774pts	Akilles Järvinen (FIN) 6815	Ken Doherty (USA) 6593
1932	Jim Bausch (USA) 6986pts	Akilles Järvinen (FIN) 7038	Wolrad Eberle (GER) 6830
1936	Glenn Morris (USA) 7421pts	Robert Clark (USA) 7226	Jack Parker (USA) 6918
1948	Bob Mathias (USA) 6826pts	Ignace Heinrich (FRA) 6740	Floyd Simmons (USA) 6711
1952	Bob Mathias (USA) 7731pts	Milt Campbell (USA) 7132	Floyd Simmons (USA) 7069
1956	Milt Campbell (USA) 7708pts	Rafer Johnson (USA) 7568	Vasiliy Kuznetsov (URS) 7461
1960	Rafer Johnson (USA) 8001pts	Chuan-Kwang Yang (TAI) 7930	Vasiliy Kuznetsov (URS) 7624
1964	Willi Holdorf (GER) 7887pts	Rein Aun (URS) 7842	Hans-Joachim Walde (GER) 7809
1968	Bill Toomey (USA) 8193pts	Hans-Joachim Walde (FRG) 8111	Kurt Bendlin (FRG) 8064
1972	Nikolai Avilov (URS) 8454pts	Leonid Litvinenko (URS) 8035	Ryszard Katus (POL) 7984
1976	Bruce Jenner (USA) 8617pts	Guido Kratschmer (FRG) 8411	Nikolai Avilov (URS) 8369
1980	Daley Thompson (GBR) 8495pts	Yuriy Kutsenko (URS) 8331	Sergey Zhelanov (URS) 8135
1984	Daley Thompson (GBR) 8798pts*	Jürgen Hingsen (FRG) 8673	Siegfried Wentz (FRG) 8412

[1]The decathlon consists of 100m, long jump, shot put, high jump, 400m, 110m hurdles, discus, pole vault, javelin and 1500m. The competition occupies two days, but in 1912 it occupied three days.   [2]The scores given above have all been calculated on the 1962 tables. The 1912 scores were based on the then Olympic records; the 1920–1932 scores on the Olympic records after the 1912 Games; the 1936 and 1948 scores on the 1934 tables; and the 1952–1960 scores on the 1952 tables. Note that in 1912, 1928 and 1932 the original medal order would have been different had the 1962 tables then been in use.   [3]Consisted of 100yd, 1 mile, 120yd hurdles, 880yd walk, high jump, long jump, pole vault, shot put, hammer and 56-lb weight.   [4]Jim Thorpe (USA) finished first with 6845pts but was later disqualified for a breach of the then amateur rules. He was reinstated posthumously by the IOC in 1982, but only as joint first.
*Olympic record – under 1986 tables 8847pts.   1896–1900, 1906–1908 Event not held.

Track and Field (Women)

	Gold	Silver	Bronze

100 Metres

	Gold	Silver	Bronze
1928	Elizabeth Robinson (USA) 12.2	Fanny Rosenfeld (CAN) 12.3	Ethel Smith (CAN) 12.3
1932	Stanislawa Walasiewicz (POL) 11.9	Hilda Strike (CAN) 11.9	Wilhelmina von Bremen (USA) 12.0
1936	Helen Stephens (USA) 11.5	Stanislawa Walasiewicz (POL) 11.7	Kathe Krauss (GER) 11.9
1948	Fanny Blankers-Koen (HOL) 11.9	Dorothy Manley (GBR) 12.2	Shirley Strickland (AUS) 12.2
1952	Marjorie Jackson (AUS) 11.5 (11.67)	Daphne Hasenjager (SAF) 11.8 (12.05)	Shirley Strickland (AUS) 11.9 (12.12)
1956	Betty Cuthbert (AUS) 11.5 (11.82)	Christa Stubnick (GER) 11.7 (11.92)	Marlene Matthews (AUS) 11.7 (11.94)
1960	Wilma Rudolph (USA) 11.0 (11.18)	Dorothy Hyman (GBR) 11.3 (11.43)	Giuseppina Leone (ITA) 11.3 (11.48)
1964	Wyomia Tyus (USA) 11.4 (11.49)	Edith Maguire (USA) 11.6 (11.62)	Ewa Klobukowska (POL) 11.6 (11.64)
1968	Wyomia Tyus (USA) 11.0 (11.08)	Barbara Ferrell (USA) 11.1 (11.15)	Irena Szewinska (POL) 11.1 (11.19)
1972	Renate Stecher (GDR) 11.07	Raelene Boyle (AUS) 11.23	Silvia Chivas (CUB) 11.24
1976	Annegret Richter (FRG) 11.08	Renate Stecher (GDR) 11.13	Inge Helten (FRG) 11.17
1980	Ludmila Kondratyeva (URS) 11.06	Marlies Göhr (GDR) 11.07	Ingrid Auerswald (GDR) 11.14
1984	Evelyn Ashford (USA) 10.97*	Alice Brown (USA) 11.13	Merlene Ottey-Page (JAM) 11.16

*Olympic record.

200 Metres

	Gold	Silver	Bronze
1948	Fanny Blankers-Koen (HOL) 24.4	Audrey Williamson (GBR) 25.1	Audrey Patterson[1] (USA) 25.2
1952	Marjorie Jackson (AUS) 23.7 (23.89)	Bertha Brouwer (GBR) 24.2 (24.25)	Nadyezda Khnykina (URS) 24.2 (24.37)
1956	Betty Cuthbert (AUS) 23.4 (23.55)	Christa Stubnick (GER) 23.7 (23.89)	Marlene Matthews (AUS) 23.8 (24.10)
1960	Wilma Rudolph (USA) 24.0 (24.13)	Jutta Heine (GER) 24.4 (24.58)	Dorothy Hyman (GBR) 24.7 (24.82)
1964	Edith Maguire (USA) 23.0 (23.05)	Irena Kirszenstein (POL) 23.1 (23.13)	Marilyn Black (AUS) 23.1 (23.18)
1968	Irena Szewinska (POL) 22.5 (22.58)	Raelene Boyle (AUS) 22.7 (22.74)	Jennifer Lamy (AUS) 22.8 (22.88)
1972	Renate Stecher (GDR) 22.40	Raelene Boyle (AUS) 22.45	Irena Szewinska (POL) 22.74
1976	Bärbel Eckert (GDR) 22.37	Annegret Richter (FRG) 22.39	Renate Stecher (GDR) 22.47
1980	Bärbel Wöckel (GDR) 22.03	Natalya Bochina (URS) 22.19	Merlene Ottey (JAM) 22.20
1984	Valerie Brisco-Hooks (USA) 21.81*	Florence Griffith (USA) 22.04	Merlene Ottey-Page (JAM) 22.09

[1]A recently discovered photo-finish picture indicates that Shirley Strickland (AUS) was third.   *Olympic record.   1928–1936 Event not held.

400 Metres

	Gold	Silver	Bronze
1964	Betty Cuthbert (AUS) 52.0 (52.01)	Ann Packer (GBR) 52.2 (52.20)	Judith Amoore (AUS) 53.4
1968	Colette Besson (FRA) 52.0 (52.03)	Lillian Board (GBR) 52.1 (52.12)	Natalya Pechenkina (URS) 52.2 (52.25)
1972	Monika Zehrt (GDR) 51.08	Rita Wilden (FRG) 51.21	Kathy Hammond (USA) 51.64

Al Oerter (USA) winning the first of his unique sequence of Olympic titles. (All-Sport)

Gold	*Silver*	*Bronze*
1976 Irena Szewinska (POL) 49.29	Christina Brehmer (GDR) 50.51	Ellen Streidt (GDR) 50.55
1980 Marita Koch (GDR) 48.88	Jarmila Kratochvilova (TCH) 49.46	Christina Lathan (GDR) 49.66
1984 Valerie Brisco-Hooks (USA) 48.83*	Chandra Cheeseborough (USA) 49.05	Kathy Cook (GBR) 49.43

*Olympic record. 1928–1960 Event not held.

800 Metres

1928 Lina Radke (GER) 2:16.8	Kinuye Hitomi (JPN) 2:17.6	Inga Gentzel (SWE) 2:17.8
1960 Ludmila Shevtsova (URS) 2:04.3	Brenda Jones (AUS) 2:04.4	Ursula Donath (GER) 2:05.6
1964 Ann Packer (GBR) 2:01.1	Maryvonne Dupureur (FRA) 2:01.9	Marise Chamberlain (NZL) 2:02.8
1968 Madeline Manning (USA) 2:00.9	Iloha Silai (ROM) 2:02.5	Maria Gommers (HOL) 2:02.6
1972 Hildegard Falck (FRG) 1:58.6	Niole Sabaite (URS) 1:58.7	Gunhild Hoffmeister (GDR) 1:59.2
1976 Tatyana Kazankina (URS) 1:54.9	Nikolina Shtereva (BUL) 1:55.4	Elfi Zinn (GDR) 1:55.6
1980 Nadyezda Olizarenko (URS) 1:53.5*	Olga Mineyeva (URS) 1:54.9	Tatyana Providokhina (URS) 1:55.5
1984 Doina Melinte (ROM) 1:57.60	Kim Gallagher (USA) 1:58.63	Fita Lovin (ROM) 1:58.83

*Olympic record (1:53.43). 1932–1956 Event not held.

1500 Metres

1972 Ludmila Brágina (URS) 4:01.4	Gunhild Hoffmeister (GDR) 4:02.8	Paola Cacchi-Pigni (ITA) 4:02.9
1976 Tatyana Kazankina (URS) 4:05.5	Gunhild Hoffmeister (GDR) 4:06.0	Ulrike Klapezynski (GDR) 4:06.1
1980 Tatyana Kazankina (URS) 3:56.6*	Christiane Wartenberg (GDR) 3:57.8	Nadyezda Olizarenko (URS) 3:59.6
1984 Gabriella Dorio (ITA) 4:03.25	Doina Melinte (ROM) 4:03.76	Maricica Puica (ROM) 4:04.15

*Olympic record (3:56.56). 1928–1968 Event not held.

3000 Metres

1984 Maricica Puica (ROM) 8:35.96*	Wendy Sly (GBR) 8:39.47	Lynn Williams (CAN) 8:42.14

*Olympic record. 1928–1980 Event not held.

Marathon

1984 Joan Benoit (USA) 2h 24:52*	Grete Waitz (NOR) 2h 26:18	Rosa Mota (POR) 2h 26:57

*Olympic record. 1928–1980 Event not held.

100 Metres Hurdles

(Over 80m hurdles 1932–1968)

1932 Mildred Didrikson (USA) 11.7	Evelyne Hall (USA) 11.7	Marjorie Clark (SAF) 11.8
1936 Trebisonda Valla (ITA) 11.7 (11.73)	Anny Steuer (GER) 11.7 (11.81)	Elizabeth Taylor (CAN) 11.7 (11.81)
1948 Fanny Blankers-Koen (HOL) 11.2	Maureen Gardner (GBR) 11.2	Shirley Strickland (AUS) 11.4
1952 Shirley de la Hunty (AUS) 10.9 (11.01)	Maria Golubnichaya (URS) 11.1 (11.24)	Maria Sander (GER) 11.1 (11.38)
1956 Shirley de la Hunty (AUS) 10.7 (10.96)	Gisela Köhler (GER) 10.9 (11.12)	Norma Thrower (AUS) 11.0 (11.25)
1960 Irina Press (URS) 10.8 (10.93)	Carol Quinton (GBR) 10.9 (10.99)	Gisela Birkemeyer (GER) 11.0 (11.13)
1964 Karin Balzer (GER) 10.5 (10.54)	Tereza Ciepla (POL) 10.5 (10.55)	Pam Kilborn (AUS) 10.5 (10.56)
1968 Maureen Caird (AUS) 10.3 (10.39)	Pam Kilborn (AUS) 10.4 (10.46)	Chi Cheng (TAI) 10.4 (10.51)
1972 Annelie Ehrhardt (GDR) 12.59	Valeria Bufanu (ROM) 12.84	Karin Balzer (GDR) 12.90
1976 Johanna Schaller (GDR) 12.77	Tatyana Anisimova (URS) 12.78	Natalya Lebedeva (URS) 12.80
1980 Vera Komisova (URS) 12.56*	Johanna Klier (GDR) 12.63	Lucyna Langer (POL) 12.65
1984 Benita Fitzgerald-Brown (USA) 12.84	Shirley Strong (GBR) 12.88	Kim Turner (USA) 13.06
		Michele Chardonnet (FRA) 13.06

*Olympic record. 1928 Event not held.

400 Metres Hurdles

1984 Nawal El Moutawakel (MAR) 54.61*	Judi Brown (USA) 55.20	Cristina Cojocaru (ROM) 55.41

*Olympic record. 1928–1980 Event not held.

4 × 100 Metres Relay

1928 Canada 48.4	United States 48.8	Germany 49.2
1932 United States 47.0	Canada 47.0	Great Britain 47.6
1936 United States 46.9	Great Britain 47.6	Canada 47.8
1948 Netherlands 47.5	Australia 47.6	Canada 47.8
1952 United States 45.9 (46.14)	Germany 45.9 (46.18)	Great Britain 46.2 (46.41)
1956 Australia 44.5 (44.65)	Great Britain 44.7 (44.70)	United States 44.9 (45.04)
1960 United States 44.5 (44.72)	Germany 44.8 (45.00)	Poland 45.0 (45.19)
1964 Poland 43.6 (43.69)	United States 43.9 (43.92)	Great Britain 44.0 (44.09)
1968 United States 42.8 (42.88)	Cuba 43.3 (43.36)	Soviet Union 43.4 (43.41)
1972 FRG 42.81	GDR 42.95	Cuba 43.36
1976 GDR 42.55	FRG 42.59	Soviet Union 43.09
1980 GDR 41.60*	Soviet Union 42.10	Great Britain 42.43
1984 United States 41.65	Canada 42.77	Great Britain 43.11

*Olympic record

4 × 400 Metres Relay

1972 GDR 3:22.95	United States 3:25.15	FRG 3:26.51
1976 GDR 3:19.23	United States 3:22.81	Soviet Union 3:24.24
1980 Soviet Union 3:20.12	GDR 3:20.35	Great Britain 3:27.5
1984 United States 3:18.29*	Canada 3:21.21	FRG 3:22.98

*Olympic record. 1928–1968 Event not held.

High Jump

1928 Ethel Catherwood (CAN) 1.59m	Carolina Gisolf (HOL) 1.56m	Mildred Wiley (USA) 1.56m
1932 Jean Shiley (USA) 1.65m[1]	Mildred Didrikson (USA) 1.657m[1]	Eva Dawes (CAN) 1.60m
1936 Ibolya Csák (HUN) 1.60m	Dorothy Odam (GBR) 1.60m	Elfriede Kaun (GER) 1.60m
1948 Alice Coachman (USA) 1.68m	Dorothy Tyler (GBR) 1.68m	Micheline Ostermeyer (FRA) 1.61m
1952 Esther Brand (SAF) 1.67m	Sheila Lerwill (GBR) 1.65m	Aleksandra Chudina (URS) 1.63m

	Gold	Silver	Bronze
1956	Mildred McDaniel (USA) 1.76m	Thelma Hopkins (GBR) 1.67m	–
		Maria Pisaryeva (URS) 1.67m	
1960	Iolanda Balas (ROM) 1.85m	Jaroslawa Jozwiakowska (POL) 1.71m	–
		Dorothy Shirley (GBR) 1.71m	
1964	Iolanda Balas (ROM) 1.90m	Michelle Brown (AUS) 1.80m	Taisia Chenchik (URS) 1.78m
1968	Miloslava Rezkova (TCH) 1.82m	Antonina Okorokova (URS) 1.80m	Valentina Kozyr (URS) 1.80m
1972	Ulrike Meyfarth (FRG) 1.92m	Yordanka Blagoyeva (BUL) 1.88m	Ilona Gusenbauer (AUT) 1.88m
1976	Rosemarie Ackermann (GDR) 1.93m	Sara Simeoni (ITA) 1.91m	Yordanka Blagoyeva (BUL) 1.91m
1980	Sara Simeoni (ITA) 1.97m	Urszula Kielan (POL) 1.94m	Jutta Kirst (GDR) 1.94m
1984	Ulrike Meyfarth (FRG) 2.02m*	Sara Simeoni (ITA) 2.00m	Joni Huntley (USA) 1.97m

[1]Some sources suggest 1.66m.   *Olympic record.

Long Jump

1948	Olga Gyarmati (HUN) 5.69m	Noemi Simonetto de Portela (ARG) 5.60m	Ann-Britt Leyman (SWE) 5.57m
1952	Yvette Williams (NZL) 6.24m	Aleksandra Chudina (URS) 6.14m	Shirley Cawley (GBR) 5.92m
1956	Elzbieta Krzesinska (POL) 6.35m	Willye White (USA) 6.09m	Nadyezda Dvalishvili (URS) 6.07m
1960	Vera Krepkina (URS) 6.37m	Elzbieta Krzesinska (POL) 6.27m	Hildrun Claus (GER) 6.21m
1964	Mary Rand (GBR) 6.76m	Irena Kirszenstein (POL) 6.60m	Tatyana Schelkanova (URS) 6.42m
1968	Viorica Viscopoleanu (ROM) 6.82m	Sheila Sherwood (GBR) 6.68m	Tatyana Talysheva (URS) 6.66m
1972	Heidemarie Rosendahl (FRG) 6.78m	Diana Yorgova (BUL) 6.77m	Eva Suranova (TCH) 6.67m
1976	Angela Voigt (GDR) 6.72m	Kathy McMillan (USA) 6.66m	Lidia Alfeyeva (URS) 6.60m
1980	Tatyana Kolpakova (URS) 7.06m*	Brigitte Wujak (GDR) 7.04m	Tatyana Skatchko (URS) 7.01m
1984	Anisoara Stanciu (ROM) 6.96m	Vali Ionescu (ROM) 6.81m	Susan Hearnshaw (GBR) 6.80m

*Olympic record. 1928–1936 Event not held.

Shot Put

1948	Micheline Ostermeyer (FRA) 13.75m	Amelia Piccinini (ITA) 13.09m	Ina Schäffer (AUT) 13.08m
1952	Galina Zybina (URS) 15.28m	Marianne Werner (GER) 14.57m	Klavdia Tochenova (URS) 14.50m
1956	Tamara Tyshkevich (URS) 16.59m	Galina Zybina (URS) 16.53m	Marianne Werner (GER) 15.61m
1960	Tamara Press (URS) 17.32m	Johanna Lüttge (GER) 16.61m	Earlene Brown (USA) 16.42m
1964	Tamara Press (URS) 18.14m	Renate Garisch (GDR) 17.61m	Galina Zybina (URS) 16.42m
1968	Margitta Gummel (GDR) 19.61m	Marita Lange (GDR) 18.78m	Nadyezda Chizhova (URS) 18.19m
1972	Nadyezda Chizhova (URS) 21.03m	Margitta Gummel (GDR) 20.22m	Ivanka Khristova (BUL) 19.35m
1976	Ivanka Khristova (BUL) 21.16m	Nadyezda Chizhova (URS) 20.96m	Helena Fibingerova (TCH) 20.67m
1980	Ilona Slupianek (GDR) 22.41m*	Svetlana Krachevskaya (URS) 21.42m	Margitta Pufe (GDR) 21.20m
1984	Claudia Losch (FRG) 20.48m	Mihaela Loghin (ROM) 20.47m	Gael Martin (AUS) 19.19m

*Olympic record. 1928–1936 Event not held.

Discus

1928	Helena Konopacka (POL) 39.62m	Lillian Copeland (USA) 37.08m	Ruth Svedberg (SWE) 35.92m
1932	Lillian Copeland (USA) 40.58m	Ruth Osburn (USA) 40.11m	Jadwiga Wajsówna (POL) 38.73m
1936	Gisela Mauermayer (GER) 47.63m	Jadwiga Wajsówna (POL) 46.22m	Paula Mollenhauer (GER) 39.80m
1948	Micheline Ostermeyer (FRA) 41.92m	Edera Gentile (ITA) 41.17m	Jacqueline Mazeas (FRA) 40.47m
1952	Nina Romashkova (URS) 51.42	Elizaveta Bagriantseva (URS) 47.08m	Nina Dumbadze (URS) 46.29m
1956	Olga Fikotova (TCH) 53.69m	Irina Beglyakova (URS) 52.54m	Nina Ponomaryeva (URS) 52.02m
1960	Nina Ponomaryeva (URS) 55.10m	Tamara Press (URS) 52.59m	Lia Manoliu (ROM) 52.36m
1964	Tamara Press (URS) 57.27m	Ingrid Lotz (GER) 57.21m	Lia Manoliu (ROM) 56.97m
1968	Lia Manoliu (ROM) 58.28m	Liesel Westermann (FRG) 57.76m	Jolán Kleiber (HUN) 54.90m
1972	Faina Melnik (URS) 66.62	Argentina Menis (ROM) 65.06m	Vasilka Stoyeva (BUL) 64.34m
1976	Evelin Schlaak (GDR) 69.00m	Maria Vergova (BUL) 67.30m	Gabriele Hinzmann (GDR) 66.84m
1980	Evelin Jahl (GDR) 69.96m*	Maria Petkova (BUL) 67.90m	Tatyana Lesovaya (URS) 67.40m
1984	Ria Stalman (HOL) 65.36m	Leslie Deniz (USA) 64.86m	Florenta Craciunescu (ROM) 63.64m

*Olympic record.

Javelin

1932	Mildred Didrikson (USA) 43.68m	Ellen Braumüller (GER) 43.49m	Tilly Fleischer (GER) 43.40m
1936	Tilly Fleischer (GER) 45.18m	Luise Krüger (GER) 43.29m	Marja Kwasniewska (POL) 41.80m
1948	Herma Bauma (AUT) 45.57m	Kaisa Parviainen (FIN) 43.79m	Lily Carlstedt (DEN) 42.08m
1952	Dana Zatopková (TCH) 50.47m	Aleksandra Chudina (URS) 50.01m	Yelena Gorchakova (URS) 49.76m
1956	Ines Jaunzeme (URS) 53.86m	Marlene Ahrens (CHI) 50.38m	Nadyezda Konyayeva (URS) 50.28m
1960	Elvira Ozolina (URS) 55.98m	Dana Zatopková (TCH) 53.78m	Birute Kalediene (URS) 53.45m
1964	Mihaela Penes (ROM) 60.64m	Märta Rudas (HUN) 58.27m	Yelena Gorchakova (URS) 57.06m
1968	Angela Németh (HUN) 60.36m	Mihaela Penes (ROM) 59.92m	Eva Janko (AUT) 58.04m
1972	Ruth Fuchs (GDR) 63.88m	Jacqueline Todten (GDR) 62.54m	Kathy Schmidt (USA) 59.94m
1976	Ruth Fuchs (GDR) 65.94m	Marion Becker (FRG) 64.70m	Kathy Schmidt (USA) 63.96m
1980	Maria Colon (CUB) 68.40m	Saida Gunba (URS) 67.76m	Ute Hommola (GDR) 66.56m
1984	Tessa Sanderson (GBR) 69.56m*	Tiina Lillak (FIN) 69.00m	Fatima Whitbread (GBR) 67.14m

*Olympic record. 1928 Event not held.

Pentathlon[1]

1964	Irina Press (URS) 5246pts	Mary Rand (GBR) 5035	Galina Bystrova (URS) 4956
1968	Ingrid Becker (FRG) 5098pts	Liese Prokop (AUT) 4966	Annamaria Tóth (HUN) 4959
1972[2]	Mary Peters (GBR) 4801pts	Heidemarie Rosendahl (FRG) 4791	Burglinde Pollak (GDR) 4768
1976[3]	Siegrun Siegl (GDR) 4745pts	Christine Laser (GDR) 4745	Burglinde Pollak (GDR) 4740
1980	Nadyezda Tkachenko (URS) 5083pts	Olga Rukavishnikova (URS) 4937	Olga Kuragina (URS) 4875

[1]The pentathlon consisted of 100m hurdles, shot put, high jump, long jump and 200m from 1964 to 1976. In 1980 the 200m was replaced by 800m.   [2]New scoring tables were introduced in May 1971.   [3]Siegl finished ahead of Laser in three events.   1928–1960 Event not held.

Heptathlon[4]

(Replaced Pentathlon in 1984)

1984	Glynis Nunn (AUS) 6390pts*	Jackie Joyner (USA) 6385	Sabine Everts (FRG) 6363

[4]The Heptathlon consists of 100m hurdles, high jump, shot, 200m on the first day; long jump, javelin and 800m on the second day.   *Olympic record – under 1986 tables 6387pts.

Gold	*Silver*	*Bronze*

Women who have won medals under both their maiden and married names:

Becker – Mickler (FRG)
Brehmer – Lathan (GDR)
Eckert – Wöckel (GDR)
Foulds – Paul (GBR)
Khnykina – Dvalishvili (URS)
Kirszenstein – Szewinska (POL)
Köhler – Birkemeyer (GDR)
Manning – Jackson (USA)

Odam – Tyler (GBR)
Richter – Górecka (POL)
Romashkova – Ponomaryeva (URS)
Schaller – Klier (GDR)
Schlaak – Jahl (GDR)
Vergova – Petkova (BUL)
Wieczorek – Ciepla (POL)
Zharkova – Maslakova (URS)

Discontinued Events

60 Metres
1900 Alvin Kraenzlein (USA) 7.0	Walter Tewksbury (USA) 7.1	Stanley Rowley (AUS) 7.2
1904 Archie Hahn (USA) 7.0	William Hogenson (USA) 7.2	Fay Moulton (USA) 7.2

3000 Metres Team Race
1912 United States 9pts	Sweden 13	Great Britain 23
1920 United States 10pts	Great Britain 20	Sweden 24
1924 Finland 8pts	Great Britain 14	United States 25

3 Miles Team Race
1908 Great Britain 6pts	United States 19	France 32

5000 Metres Team Race
1900 Great Britain 26pts	France 29	–

Individual Cross-Country
1912[1] Hannes Kolehmainen (FIN) 45:11.6	Hjalmar Andersson (SWE) 45:44.8	John Eke (SWE) 46:37.6
1920[2] Paavo Nurmi (FIN) 27:15.0	Erick Backman (SWE) 27:17.6	Heikki Liimatainen (FIN) 27:37.4
1924[3] Paavo Nurmi (FIN) 32:54.8	Ville Ritola (FIN) 34:19.4	Earl Johnson (USA) 35:21.0

[1]12 000 metres. [2]8000 metres. [3]10 000 metres.

Team Cross-Country
1904 United States (New York AC)	United States (Chicago AA)	–
1912 Sweden 10pts	Finland 11	Great Britain 49
1920 Finland 10pts	Great Britain 21	Sweden 23
1924 Finland 11pts	United States 14	France 20

200 Metres Hurdles
1900 Alvin Kraenzlein (USA) 25.4	Norman Pritchard (IND) 26.6	Walter Tewksbury (USA) n.t.a.
1904 Harry Hillman (USA) 24.6	Frank Castleman (USA) 24.9	George Poage (USA) n.t.a.

1500 Metres Walk
1906 George Bonhag (USA) 7:12.6	Donald Linden (CAN) 7:19.8	Konstantin Spetsiotis (GRE) 7:22.0

3000 Metres Walk
1906 György Sztantics (HUN) 15:13.2	Hermann Müller (GER) 15:20.0	Georgios Saridakis (GRE) 15:33.0
1920 Ugo Frigerio (ITA) 13:14.2	George Parker (AUS) n.t.a.	Richard Remer (USA) n.t.a.

3500 Metres Walk
1908 George Larner (GBR) 14:55.0	Ernest Webb (GBR) 15:07.4	Harry Kerr (NZL) 15:43.4

10 000 Metres Walk
1912 George Goulding (CAN) 46:28.4	Ernest Webb (GBR) 46:50.4	Fernando Altimani (ITA) 47:37.6
1920 Ugo Frigerio (ITA) 48:06.2	Joseph Pearman (USA) n.t.a.	Charles Gunn (GBR) n.t.a.
1924 Ugo Frigerio (ITA) 47:49.0	Gordon Goodwin (GBR) 200m	Cecil McMaster (SAF) 300m
1948 John Mikaelsson (SWE) 45:13.2	Ingemar Johansson (SWE) 45:43.8	Fritz Schwab (SUI) 46:00.2
1952 John Mikaelsson (SWE) 45:02.8	Fritz Schwab (SUI) 45:41.0	Bruno Junk (URS) 45:41.2

1928–1936 Event not held.

10 Miles Walk
1908 George Larner (GBR) 1:15:57.4	Ernest Webb (GBR) 1:17:31.0	Edward Spencer (GBR) 1:21:20.2

Pentathlon
1906[1] Hjalmar Mellander (SWE) 24pts	Istvan Mudin (HUN) 25	Erik Lemming (SWE) 29
1912[2,3] Ferdinand Bie (NOR) 16pts	James Donahue (USA) 24	Frank Lukeman (CAN) 24
1920[2] Eero Lehtonen (FIN) 14pts	Everett Bradley (USA) 24	Hugo Lahtinen (FIN) 26
1924[2] Eero Lehtonen (FIN) 14pts	Elemér Somfay (HUN) 16	Robert LeGendre (USA) 18

[1]Consisted of standing long jump, discus (Greek style), javelin, one-lap race (192m), Greco-Roman wrestling. [2]Consisted of long jump, javelin, 200m, discus, 1500m. [3]Jim Thorpe (USA) finished first with 7 points but was subsequently disqualified. He was reinstated posthumously in 1982, but as joint first.

Standing High Jump
1900 Ray Ewry (USA) 1.655m	Irving Baxter (USA) 1.525	Lewis Sheldon (USA) 1.50
1904 Ray Ewry (USA) 1.50m	James Stadler (USA) 1.45	Lawson Robertson (USA) 1.45
1906 Ray Ewry (USA) 1.565m	Martin Sheridan (USA) 1.40	–
	Léon Dupont (BEL) 1.40	
	Lawson Robertson (USA) 1.40	
1908 Ray Ewry (USA) 1.575m	Konstantin Tsiklitiras (GRE) 1.55	–
	John Biller (USA) 1.55	
1912 Platt Adams (USA) 1.63m	Benjamin Adams (USA) 1.60	Konstantin Tsiklitiras (GRE) 1.55m

Gold	Silver	Bronze

Standing Long Jump

	Gold	Silver	Bronze
1900	Ray Ewry (USA) 3.21m	Irving Baxter (USA) 3.135	Emile Torcheboeuf (FRA) 3.03
1904	Ray Ewry (USA) 3.476m	Charles King (USA) 3.28	John Biller (USA) 3.26
1906	Ray Ewry (USA) 3.30m	Martin Sheridan (USA) 3.095	Lawson Robertson (USA) 3.05
1908	Ray Ewry (USA) 3.335m	Konstantin Tsiklitiras (GRE) 3.23	Martin Sheridan (USA) 3.225
1912	Konstantin Tsiklitiras (GRE) 3.37m	Platt Adams (USA) 3.36	Benjamin Adams (USA) 3.28

Standing Triple Jump

	Gold	Silver	Bronze
1900	Ray Ewry (USA) 10.58m	Irving Baxter (USA) 9.95	Robert Garrett (USA) 9.50
1904	Ray Ewry (USA) 10.55m	Charles King (USA) 10.16	James Stadler (USA) 9.53

Stone (6.40kg) Put

	Gold	Silver	Bronze
1906	Nicolaos Georgantas (GRE) 19.925m	Martin Sheridan (USA) 19.035	Michel Dorizas (GRE) 18.585

Shot (Both Hands)[1]

	Gold	Silver	Bronze
1912	Ralph Rose (USA) 27.70m	Patrick McDonald (USA) 27.53	Elmer Niklander (FIN) 27.14

[1]Aggregate of throws with right and left hands.

Discus (Both Hands)[1]

	Gold	Silver	Bronze
1912	Armas Taipale (FIN) 82.86m	Elmer Niklander (FIN) 77.96	Emil Magnusson (SWE) 77.37

[1]Aggregate of throws with right and left hands.

Discus (Greek Style)

	Gold	Silver	Bronze
1906	Werner Järvinen (FIN) 35.17m	Nicolaos Georgantas (GRE) 32.80	Istvan Mudin (HUN) 31.91
1908	Martin Sheridan (USA) 38.00m	Marquis Horr (USA) 37.325	Werner Järvinen (FIN) 36.48

Javelin (Both Hands)[1]

	Gold	Silver	Bronze
1912	Julius Saaristo (FIN) 109.42m	Väinö Siikaniemi (FIN) 101.13	Urho Peltonen (FIN) 100.24

[1]Aggregate of throws with right and left hands.

Javelin (Free Style)

	Gold	Silver	Bronze
1908	Erik Lemming (SWE) 54.445m	Michel Dorizas (GRE) 51.36	Arne Halse (NOR) 49.73

56-Pound (25.4kg) Weight Throw

	Gold	Silver	Bronze
1904	Etienne Desmarteau (CAN) 10.465m	John Flanagan (USA) 10.16	James Mitchel (USA) 10.135
1920	Patrick McDonald (USA) 11.265m	Patrick Ryan (USA) 10.965	Carl Lind (SWE) 10.25

Renate Stecher (GDR) and Irena Szewinska (Pol), between them won a total of six gold, four silver and three bronze medals.

Tug of War

	Gold	**Silver**	**Bronze**
1900	Sweden/Denmark	United States	France
1904	United States	United States	United States
1906	Germany	Greece	Sweden
1908	Great Britain	Great Britain	Great Britain
1912	Sweden	Great Britain	–
1920	Great Britain	Netherlands	Belgium

Track and Field Medals – (including Tug-of-War)

| | Men | | | Women | | | Total | | | Total Medals |
	G	S	B	G	S	B	G	S	B	
United States	235	175	148	26	19	10	261	194	158	613
Soviet Union	29	31	36	25	18	28	54	49	64	167
Great Britain	42	52	38	4	18	11	46	70	49	165
Germany (FRG)	11	28	32	12	19	14	23	47	46	116[1]
Finland	46	32	28	–	2	–	46	34	28	108
Sweden	19	24	41	–	–	3	19	24	44	87
GDR	11	11	11	21	14	14	32	25	25	82
Australia	6	9	11	10	7	11	16	16	22	54
France	7	20	19	3	1	2	10	21	21	52
Canada	9	9	15	2	5	6	11	14	21	46
Italy	12	6	17	3	4	2	15	10	19	44
Poland	9	7	4	6	8	7	15	15	11	41
Hungary	6	13	16	3	1	2	9	14	18	41
Greece	3	9	11	–	–	–	3	9	11	23
Romania	–	–	1	8	7	6	8	7	7	22
Czechoslovakia	5	6	3	3	2	2	8	8	5	21
Jamaica	4	8	4	–	–	3	4	8	7	19
New Zealand	7	1	7	1	–	1	8	1	8	17
Kenya	6	6	5	–	–	–	6	6	5	17
South Africa	4	4	4	1	1	1	5	5	5	15
Netherlands	–	2	5	5	2	1	5	4	6	15
Japan	4	4	6	–	1	–	4	5	6	15
Norway	3	2	7	–	1	–	3	3	7	13
Cuba	2	5	1	1	1	2	3	6	3	12
Belgium	2	6	3	–	–	–	2	6	3	11
Ethiopia	5	1	4	–	–	–	5	1	4	10
Bulgaria	–	–	1	1	5	3	1	5	4	10
Brazil	3	1	4	–	–	–	3	1	4	8
Switzerland	–	6	1	–	–	–	–	6	1	7
Ireland	4	1	–	–	–	–	4	1	–	5
Mexico	3	2	–	–	–	–	3	2	–	5
Argentina	2	2	–	–	1	–	2	3	–	5
Austria	–	–	–	1	1	3	1	1	3	5
Trinidad	1	1	3	–	–	–	1	1	3	5
Tunisia	1	2	1	–	–	–	1	2	1	4
Denmark	1	1	1	–	–	1	1	1	2	4
Portugal	1	1	1	–	–	1	1	1	2	4
Morocco	1	1	–	1	–	–	2	1	–	3
Chile	–	1	–	–	1	–	–	2	–	2
India	–	2	–	–	–	–	–	2	–	2
Tanzania	–	2	–	–	–	–	–	2	–	2
Yugoslavia	–	2	–	–	–	–	–	2	–	2
Estonia	–	1	1	–	–	–	–	1	1	2
Latvia	–	1	1	–	–	–	–	1	1	2
Spain	–	1	1	–	–	–	–	1	1	2
Taiwan (Taipei)	–	1	–	–	–	1	–	1	1	2
Panama	–	–	2	–	–	–	–	–	2	2
Philippines	–	–	2	–	–	–	–	–	2	2
Luxembourg	1	–	–	–	–	–	1	–	–	1
Uganda	1	–	–	–	–	–	1	–	–	1
Haiti	–	1	–	–	–	–	–	1	–	1
Iceland	–	1	–	–	–	–	–	1	–	1
Ivory Coast	–	1	–	–	–	–	–	1	–	1
Sri Lanka (Ceylon)	–	1	–	–	–	–	–	1	–	1
China	–	–	1	–	–	–	–	–	1	1
Nigeria	–	–	1	–	–	–	–	–	1	1
Turkey	–	–	1	–	–	–	–	–	1	1
Venezuela	–	–	1	–	–	–	–	–	1	1
	506	504	498	137	139	135	643	643	633	1919

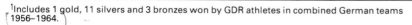

[1]Includes 1 gold, 11 silvers and 3 bronzes won by GDR athletes in combined German teams 1956–1964.

VOLLEYBALL

Introduced into the Games in 1964 for men and women, volleyball has been dominated by Soviet teams. Their men's teams played 39 matches losing only four from 1964 to 1980, and their women played 28 matches, losing only two in the same period.

The most successful player was Inna Ryskal (URS) with two gold and two silver medals 1964–1976. The best by a male player was two golds and a silver by Yuriy Poyarkov (URS) 1964–1972. The oldest gold medallist was Ludmila Buldakova (URS) aged 34yr 105 days in 1972, and the oldest male was Edward Skorek (POL) aged 33yr 47 days in 1976. The youngest gold medallist was Ludmila Borozna (URS) in 1972 aged 18yr 249 days, and the youngest male was Oleg Antropov (URS) aged 20yr 357 days in 1968. The oldest medallist was Bohumil Golián (TCH) winning a bronze in 1968 aged 37yr 215 days.

Volleyball (Men)

	Gold	Silver	Bronze
1964	Soviet Union	Czechoslovakia	Japan
1968	Soviet Union	Japan	Czechoslovakia
1972	Japan	GDR	Soviet Union
1976	Poland	Soviet Union	Cuba
1980	Soviet Union	Bulgaria	Romania
1984	United States	Brazil	Italy

1896–1960 Event not held.

Volleyball (Women)

1964	Japan	Soviet Union	Poland
1968	Soviet Union	Japan	Poland
1972	Soviet Union	Japan	North Korea
1976	Japan	Soviet Union	South Korea
1980	Soviet Union	GDR	Bulgaria
1984	China	United States	Japan

1896–1960 Event not held.

Volleyball – Medals

	Men			Women			
	G	S	B	G	S	B	Total
Soviet Union	3	1	1	3	2	–	10
Japan	1	1	1	2	2	1	8
Poland	1	–	–	–	–	2	3
United States	1	–	–	–	1	–	2
GDR	–	1	–	–	1	–	2
Bulgaria	–	1	–	–	–	1	2
Czechoslovakia	–	1	1	–	–	–	2
China	–	–	–	1	–	–	1
Brazil	–	1	–	–	–	–	1
Cuba	–	–	1	–	–	–	1
Italy	–	–	1	–	–	–	1
Korea	–	–	–	–	–	1	1
North Korea (PRK)	–	–	–	–	–	1	1
Romania	–	–	1	–	–	–	1
	6	6	6	6	6	6	36

WEIGHTLIFTING

Two events were held in 1896, consisting of one-arm and two-arm lifts. The first Olympic weightlifting champion was Viggo Jensen (DEN) who won the two-arm competition from Launceston Eliot (GBR); both had lifted the same weight but the Briton had moved one of his feet. An amusing incident occurred when an attendant was having great trouble moving one of the weights. Prince George of Greece, a member of the organizing committee and an immensely big and strong man, bent down and easily lifted it aside.

In 1920 the contests were decided on the aggregate of a one-hand snatch, a one-hand jerk, and a two-hands jerk. In 1924 an additional two lifts were included, two-hands press and snatch. From 1928 to 1972 the result depended on the aggregate of three two-handed lifts: the press, snatch, and clean and jerk.

In 1976 the press was eliminated, owing to difficulty in judging it correctly, and the total now is for the snatch and the clean and jerk. At the suggestion of the IOC the forerunner of the International Weightlifting Federation was formed in 1920 to control the sport.

Of the ten men to win two gold medals only Tommy Kono (USA) and Norair Nurikyan (BUL) have won them in different categories. Kono won the 67.5kg (1952) and the 82.5kg (1956), while more unusually Nurikyan moved down from the 60kg (1972) to the 56kg (1976). Norbert Schemansky (USA) has won the most medals with one gold, one silver and two bronze medals from 1948 to 1964. The oldest gold medallist was Rudolf Plukfelder (URS) in the 8.25kg class of 1964 aged 36yr 40 days, while Schemansky was the oldest medallist in 1964 aged 40yr 141 days. The youngest gold medallist was Zeng Guoqiang (CHN) who won the 52kg class in 1984 aged 19yr 133 days, and the youngest ever medallist

was Andrei Socaci (ROM) who won a 1984 silver in the 67.5kg category aged 17yr 330 days. The oldest known competitor was 56-year-old Teunist Jonck (SAF) in 1952, and the youngest known was 13-year-old M Djemal (TUR) in 1924.

The only brothers to win medals in the same event at the same Games were Yoshinobu and Yoshiyuki Miyake (JPN) who won gold and bronze medals respectively in the 60kg in 1968. Yoshinobu also won another gold and a silver, but Peter and James George (USA) hold the family record for medals with one gold, three silvers and a bronze from 1948 to 1960. The silver medallist in the 82.5kg class in 1948, Harold Sakata (USA), later gained fame portraying 'Oddjob' in the James Bond film Goldfinger.

Disqualification due to use of drugs has affected this sport more than most with the first cases, gold medallist Zbigniev Kaczmarek (POL) and silver medallist Blagoi Blagoyev (BUL), being disqualified in 1976.

John Davis won two Olympic heavyweight titles to add to his eight world titles. (All-Sport)

Weightlifting

	Gold	*Silver*	*Bronze*

Flyweight
(Up to 52kg)

	Gold	Silver	Bronze
1972	Zygmunt Smalcerz (POL) 337.5kg	Lajos Szuecs (HUN) 330kg	Sandor Holczreiter (HUN) 327.5kg
1976	Aleksandr Voronin (URS) 242.5kg	Gyorgy Koszegi (HUN) 237.5kg	Mohammad Nassiri (IRN) 235kg
1980	Kanybek Osmonoliev (URS) 245kg*	Bong Chol Ho (PRK) 245kg	Gyong Si Han (PRK) 245kg
1984	Zeng Guoqiang (CHN) 235kg	Zhou Peishun (CHN) 235kg	Kazushito Manabe (JPN) 232.5kg

*Olympic record.   1896–1968 Event not held.

Bantamweight
(Up to 56kg)

	Gold	Silver	Bronze
1948	Joseph de Pietro (USA) 307.5kg	Julian Creus (GBR) 297.5kg	Richard Tom (USA) 295kg
1952	Ivan Udodov (URS) 315kg	Mahmoud Namdjou (IRN) 307.5kg	Ali Mirzai (IRN) 300kg
1956	Charles Vinci (USA) 342.5kg	Vladimir Stogov (URS) 337.5kg	Mahmoud Namdjou (IRN) 332.5kg
1960	Charles Vinci (USA) 345kg	Yoshinobu Miyake (JPN) 337.5kg	Esmail Khan (IRN) 330kg
1964	Aleksey Vakhonin (URS) 357.5kg	Imre Földi (HUN) 355kg	Shiro Ichinoseki (JPN) 347.5kg
1968	Mohammad Nassiri (IRN) 367.5kg	Imre Földi (HUN) 367.5kg	Henryk Trebicki (POL) 357.5kg
1972	Imre Földi (HUN) 377.5kg	Mohammad Nassiri (IRN) 370kg	Gennadiy Chetin (URS) 367.5kg
1976	Norair Nurikyan (BUL) 262.5kg	Grzegorz Cziura (POL) 252.5kg	Kenkichi Ando (JPN) 250kg
1980	Daniel Nunez (CUB) 275kg*	Yurik Sarkisian (URS) 270kg	Tadeusz Dembonczyk (POL) 265kg
1984	Wu Shude (CHN) 267.5kg	Lai Runming (CHN) 265kg	Masahiro Kotaka (JPN) 252.5kg

*Olympic record.   1896–1936 Event not held.

Featherweight
(Up to 60kg)

	Gold	Silver	Bronze
1920	Frans de Haes (BEL) 220kg	Alfred Schmidt (EST) 212.5kg	Eugène Ryther (SUI) 210kg
1924[1]	Pierino Gabetti (ITA) 402.5kg	Andreas Stadler (AUT) 385kg	Arthur Reinmann (SUI) 382.5kg
1928	Franz Andrysek (AUT) 287.5kg	Pierino Gabetti (ITA) 282.5kg	Hans Wölpert (GER) 282.5kg
1932	Raymond Suvigny (FRA) 287.5kg	Hans Wölpert (GER) 282.5kg	Anthony Terlazzo (USA) 280kg
1936	Anthony Terlazzo (USA) 312.5kg	Saleh Mohammed Soliman (EGY) 305kg	Ibrahim Shams (EGY) 300kg
1948	Mahmoud Fayad (EGY) 332.5kg	Rodney Wilkes (TRI) 317.5kg	Jaffar Salmassi (IRN) 312.5kg
1952	Rafael Chimishkyan (URS) 337.5kg	Nikolai Saksonov (URS) 332.5kg	Rodney Wilkes (TRI) 322.5kg
1956	Isaac Berger (USA) 352.5kg	Yevgeniy Minayev (URS) 342.5kg	Marian Zielinski (POL) 335kg
1960	Yevgeniy Minayev (URS) 372.5kg	Isaac Berger (USA) 362.5kg	Sebastiano Mannironi (ITA) 352.5kg
1964	Yoshinobu Miyake (JPN) 397.5kg	Isaac Berger (USA) 382.5kg	Mieczyslaw Nowak (POL) 377.5kg
1968	Yoshinobu Miyake (JPN) 392.5kg	Dito Shanidze (URS) 387.5kg	Yoshiyuki Miyake (JPN) 385kg
1972	Norair Nurikyan (BUL) 402.5kg	Dito Shanidze (URS) 400kg	Janos Benedek (HUN) 390kg
1976	Nikolai Kolesnikov (URS) 285kg	Georgi Todorov (BUL) 280kg	Kuzumasa Hirai (JPN) 275kg
1980	Viktor Mazin (URS) 290kg*	Stefan Dimitrov (BUL) 287.5kg	Marek Seweryn (POL) 282.5kg
1984	Chen Weiqiang (CHN) 282.5kg	Gelu Radu (ROM) 280kg	Wen-Yee Tsai (TPE) 272.5kg

[1]Aggregate of five lifts.   *Olympic record.   1896–1912 Event not held.

Lightweight
(Up to 67.5kg)

	Gold	Silver	Bronze
1920	Alfred Neuland (EST) 257.5kg	Louis Williquet (BEL) 240kg	Florimond Rooms (BEL) 230kg
1924[1]	Edmond Decottignies (FRA) 440kg	Anton Zwerina (AUT) 427.5kg	Bohumil Durdis (TCH) 425kg
1928[2]	Kurt Helbig (GER) 322.5kg Hans Haas (AUT) 322.5kg	–	Fernand Arnout (FRA) 302.5kg
1932	René Duverger (FRA) 325kg	Hans Haas (AUT) 307.5kg	Gastone Pierini (ITA) 302.5kg
1936[2]	Anwar Mohammed Mesbah (EGY) 342.5kg Robert Fein (AUT) 342.5kg	–	Karl Jansen (GER) 327.5kg
1948	Ibrahim Shams (EGY) 360kg	Attia Hamouda (EGY) 360kg	James Halliday (GBR) 340kg
1952	Tommy Kono (USA) 362.5kg	Yevgeniy Lopatin (URS) 350kg	Verne Barberis (AUS) 350kg
1956	Igor Rybak (URS) 380kg	Ravil Khabutdinov (URS) 372.5kg	Chang-Hee Kim (KOR) 370kg
1960	Viktor Bushuyev (URS) 397.5kg	Howe-Liang Tan (SIN) 380kg	Abdul Wahid Aziz (IRQ) 380kg
1964	Waldemar Baszanowski (POL) 432.5kg	Vladimir Kaplunov (URS) 432.5kg	Marian Zielinski (POL) 420kg
1968	Waldemar Baszanowski (POL) 437.5kg	Parviz Jalayer (IRN) 422.5kg	Marian Zielinski (POL) 420kg
1972	Mukharbi Kirzhinov (URS) 460kg	Mladen Koutchev (BUL) 450kg	Zbigniev Kaczmarek (POL) 437.5kg
1976[3]	Pyotr Korol (URS) 305kg	Daniel Senet (FRA) 300kg	Kazimierz Czarnecki (POL) 295kg
1980	Yanko Rusev (BUL) 342.5kg*	Joachim Kunz (GDR) 335kg	Mintcho Pachov (BUL) 325kg
1984	Yao Jingyuan (CHN) 320kg	Andrei Socaci (ROM) 312.5kg	Jouni Gronman (FIN) 312.5kg

[1]Aggregate of five lifts.   [2]Tie-breaker rule relating to bodyweight not yet introduced.   [3]Zbigniev Kaczmarek (POL) finished in first place with 307.5kg but was subsequently disqualified.   *Olympic record.   1896–1912 Event not held.

Middleweight
(Up to 75kg)

	Gold	Silver	Bronze
1920	Henri Gance (FRA) 245kg	Pietro Bianchi[1] (ITA) 237.5kg	Albert Pettersson (SWE) 237.5kg
1924[2]	Carlo Galimberti (ITA) 492.5kg	Alfred Neuland (EST) 455kg	Jaan Kikas (EST) 450kg
1928	Roger Francois (FRA) 335kg	Carlo Galimberti (ITA) 332.5kg	August Scheffer (HOL) 327.5kg
1932	Rudolf Ismayr (GER) 345kg	Carlo Galimberti (ITA) 340kg	Karl Hipfinger (AUT) 337.5kg
1936	Khadr El Thouni (EGY) 387.5kg	Rudolf Ismayr (GER) 352.5kg	Adolf Wagner (GER) 352.5kg
1948	Frank Spellman (USA) 390kg	Peter George (USA) 382.5kg	Sung-Jip Kim (KOR) 380kg
1952	Peter George (USA) 400kg	Gerard Gratton (CAN) 390kg	Sung-Jip Kim (KOR) 382.5kg
1956	Fyodor Bogdanovski (URS) 420kg	Peter George (USA) 412.5kg	Ermanno Pignatti (ITA) 382.5kg
1960	Aleksandr Kurinov (URS) 437.5kg	Tommy Kono (USA) 427.5kg	Gyözö Veres (HUN) 405kg
1964	Hans Zdrazila (TCH) 445kg	Viktor Kurentsov (URS) 440kg	Masashi Ouchi (JPN) 437.5kg
1968	Viktor Kurentsov (URS) 475kg	Masashi Ouchi (JPN) 455kg	Károly Bakos (HUN) 440kg
1972	Yordan Bikov (BUL) 485kg	Mohamed Trabulsi (LIB) 472.5kg	Anselmo Silvino (ITA) 470kg
1976	Yordan Mitkov (BUL) 335kg	Vartan Militosyan (URS) 330kg	Peter Wenzel (GDR) 327.5kg
1980	Asen Zlatev (BUL) 360kg*	Aleksandr Pervy (URS) 357.5kg	Nedeltcho Kolev (BUL) 345kg

	Gold	Silver	Bronze
1984	Karl-Heinz Radschinsky (FRG) 340kg	Jacques Demers (CAN) 335kg	Dragomir Cioroslan (ROM) 332.5kg

[1]Bianchi and Pettersson drew lots for the silver medal. [2]Aggregate of five lifts. *Olympic record. 1896–1912 Event not held.

Light-Heavyweight
(Up to 82.5kg)

	Gold	Silver	Bronze
1920	Ernest Cadine (FRA) 290kg	Fritz Hünenberger (SUI) 275kg	Erik Pettersson (SWE) 272.5kg
1924[1]	Charles Rigoulot (FRA) 502.5kg	Fritz Hünenberger (SUI) 490kg	Leopold Friedrich (AUT) 490kg
1928	Said Nosseir (EGY) 355kg	Louis Hostin (FRA) 352.5kg	Johannes Verheijen (HOL) 337.5kg
1932	Louis Hostin (FRA) 372.5kg	Svend Olsen (DEN) 360kg	Henry Duey (USA) 330kg
1936	Louis Hostin (FRA) 372.5kg	Eugen Deutsch (GER) 365kg	Ibrahim Wasif (EGY) 360kg
1948	Stanley Stanczyk (USA) 417.5kg	Harold Sakata (USA) 380kg	Gösta Magnusson (SWE) 375kg
1952	Trofim Lomakin (URS) 417.5kg	Stanley Stanczyk (USA) 415kg	Arkadiy Vorobyev (URS) 407.5kg
1956	Tommy Kono (USA) 447.5kg	Vassiliy Stepanov (URS) 427.5kg	James George (USA) 417.5kg
1960	Ireneusz Palinski (POL) 442.5kg	James George (USA) 430kg	Jan Bochenek (POL) 420kg
1964	Rudolf Plukfelder (URS) 475kg	Géza Toth (HUN) 467.5kg	Gyözö Veres (HUN) 467.5kg
1968	Boris Selitsky (URS) 485kg	Vladimir Belyayev (URS) 485kg	Norbert Ozimek (POL) 472.5kg
1972	Leif Jenssen (NOR) 507.5kg	Norbert Ozimek (POL) 497.5kg	György Horvath (HUN) 495kg
1976[2]	Valeriy Shary (URS) 365kg	Trendachil Stoichev (BUL) 360kg	Peter Baczako (HUN) 345kg
1980	Yurik Vardanyan (URS) 400kg*	Blagoi Blagoyev (BUL) 372.5kg	Dusan Poliacik (TCH) 367.5kg
1984	Petre Becheru (ROM) 355kg	Robert Kabbas (AUS) 342.5kg	Ryoji Isaoka (JPN) 340kg

[1]Aggregate of five lifts. [2]Blagoi Blagoyev (BUL) finished in second place with 362.5kg but was subsequently disqualified. *Olympic record. 1896–1912 Event not held.

Middle-Heavyweight
(Up to 90kg)

	Gold	Silver	Bronze
1952	Norbert Schemansky (USA) 445kg	Grigoriy Nowak (URS) 410kg	Lennox Kilgour (TRI) 402.5kg
1956	Arkadiy Vorobyev (URS) 462.5kg	David Sheppard (USA) 442.5kg	Jean Debuf (FRA) 425kg
1960	Arkadiy Vorobyev (URS) 472.5kg	Trofim Lomakin (URS) 457.5kg	Louis Martin (GBR) 445kg
1964	Vladimir Golovanov (URS) 487.5kg	Louis Martin (GBR) 475kg	Ireneusz Palinski (POL) 467.5kg
1968	Kaarlo Kangasniemi (FIN) 517.5kg	Jan Talts (URS) 507.5kg	Marek Golab (POL) 495kg
1972	Andon Nikolov (BUL) 525kg	Atanas Chopov (BUL) 517.5kg	Hans Bettembourg (SWE) 512.5kg
1976	David Rigert (URS) 382.5kg	Lee James (USA) 362.5kg	Atanas Chopov (BUL) 360kg
1980	Peter Baczako (HUN) 377.5kg	Rumen Alexandrov (BUL) 375kg	Frank Mantek (GDR) 375kg
1984	Nicu Vlad (ROM) 392.5kg*	Dumitru Petre (ROM) 360kg	David Mercer (GBR) 352.5kg

*Olympic record. 1896–1948 Event not held.

Up to 100kg

	Gold	Silver	Bronze
1980	Ota Zaremba (TCH) 395kg*	Igor Nikitin (URS) 392.5kg	Alberto Blanco (CUB) 385kg
1984	Rolf Milser (FRG) 385kg	Vasile Gropa (ROM) 382.5kg	Pekka Niemi (FIN) 367.5kg

*Olympic record. 1896–1976 Event not held.

Heavyweight
(From 1920 to 1948 class was over 82.5kg. From 1952 to 1968 class was over 90kg. Since 1972 weight limit has been up to 110kg)

	Gold	Silver	Bronze
1896[1]	Launceston Eliot (GBR) 71kg	Viggo Jensen (DEN) 57.2kg	Alexandros Nikolopoulos (GRE) 57.2kg
1896[2]	Viggo Jensen (DEN) 111.5kg	Launceston Eliot (GBR) 111.5kg	Sotirios Versis (GRE) 100kg
1904[3]	Oscar Osthoff (USA) 48pts	Frederick Winters (USA) 45pts	Frank Kungler (USA) 10pts
1904[2]	Perikles Kakousis (GRE) 111.58kg	Oscar Osthoff (USA) 84.36kg	Frank Kungler (USA) 79.83kg
1906[1]	Josef Steinbach (AUT) 76.55kg	Tullio Camilotti (ITA) 73.75kg	Heinrich Schneidereit (GER) 70.75kg
1906[2]	Dimitrios Tofalos (GRE) 142.5kg	Josef Steinbach (AUT) 136.5kg	Alexandre Maspoli (FRA) 129.5kg
			Heinrich Rondl (GER) 129.5kg
			Heinrich Schneidereit (GER) 129.5kg
1920	Filippo Bottino (ITA) 270kg	Joseph Alzin (LUX) 255kg	Louis Bernot (FRA) 250kg
1924[4]	Giuseppe Tonani (ITA) 517.5kg	Franz Aigner (AUT) 515kg	Harald Tammer (EST) 497.5kg
1928	Josef Strassberger (GER) 372.5kg	Arnold Luhaäär (EST) 360kg	Jaroslav Skobla (TCH) 357.5kg
1932	Jaroslav Skobla (TCH) 380kg	Václav Psenicka (TCH) 377.5kg	Josef Strassberger (GER) 377.5kg
1936	Josef Manger (AUT) 410kg	Václav Psenicka (TCH) 402.5kg	Arnold Luhaäär (EST) 400kg
1948	John Davis (USA) 452.2kg	Norbert Schemansky (USA) 425kg	Abraham Charité (HOL) 412.5kg
1952	John Davis (USA) 460kg	James Bradford (USA) 437.5kg	Humberto Selvetti (ARG) 432.5kg
1956	Paul Anderson (USA) 500kg	Humberto Selvetti (ARG) 500kg	Alberto Pigaiani (ITA) 452.5kg
1960	Yuriy Vlasov (URS) 537.5kg	James Bradford (USA) 512.5kg	Norbert Schemansky (USA) 500kg
1964	Leonid Zhabotinsky (URS) 572.5kg	Yuriy Vlasov (URS) 570kg	Norbert Schemansky (USA) 537.5kg
1968	Leonid Zhabotinsky (URS) 572.5kg	Serge Reding (BEL) 555kg	Joseph Dube (USA) 555kg
1972	Jan Talts (URS) 580kg	Alexandre Kraitchev (BUL) 562.5kg	Stefan Grützner (GDR) 555kg
1976[5]	Yuriy Zaitsev (URS) 385kg	Krastio Semerdiev (BUL) 385kg	Tadeusz Rutkowski (POL) 377.5kg
1980	Leonid Taranenko (URS) 422.5kg*	Valentin Christov (BUL) 405kg	György Szalai (HUN) 390kg
1984	Norberto Oberburger (ITA) 390kg	Stefan Tasnadi (ROM) 380kg	Guy Carlton (USA) 377.5kg

[1]One-hand lift. [2]Two-hand lift. [3]Dumbell lift. [4]Aggregate of five lifts. [5]Valentin Christov (BUL) finished in first place with 400kg but was subsequently disqualified. *Olympic record. 1900, 1908–1912 Event not held.

Super-Heavyweight
(Over 110kg)

	Gold	Silver	Bronze
1972	Vasiliy Alexeyev (URS) 640kg	Rudolf Mang (GDR) 610kg	Gerd Bonk (GDR) 572.5kg
1976	Vasiliy Alexeyev (URS) 440kg*	Gerd Bonk (GDR) 405kg	Helmut Losch (GDR) 387.5kg
1980	Sultan Rakhmanov (URS) 440kg*	Jürgen Heuser (GDR) 410kg	Tadeusz Rutkowski (POL) 407.5kg
1984	Dinko Lukin (AUS) 412.5kg	Mario Martinez (USA) 410kg	Manfred Nerlinger (FRG) 397.5kg

*Olympic record. 1896–1968 Event not held.

*Verner Weckman and Yrjö Saarela (both FIN)
wrestle for the light-heavyweight
Greco-Roman title in 1908. (GLS)*

Weightlifting – Medals

	G	S	B	Total
Soviet Union	33	19	2	54
United States	15	16	10	41
Poland	4	2	15	21
Bulgaria	7	10	3	20
Germany (FRG)	5	3	8	16
France	9	2	4	15
Italy	5	5	5	15
Hungary	2	5	8	15
Austria	5	5	2	12
Japan	2	2	8	12
Egypt	5	2	2	9
Iran	1	3	5	9
GDR	–	4	5	9
Czechoslovakia	3	2	3	8
Romania	2	5	1	8
Estonia	1	3	3	7
Great Britain	1	3	3	7
China	4	2	–	6
Greece	2	–	2	4
Belgium	1	2	1	4
Switzerland	–	2	2	4
Sweden	–	–	4	4
Denmark	1	2	–	3
Australia	1	1	1	3
Finland	1	–	2	3
Trinidad	–	1	2	3
Korea	–	–	3	3
Netherlands	–	–	3	3
Cuba	1	–	1	2
Canada	–	2	–	2
Argentina	–	1	1	2
North Korea (PRK)	–	1	1	2
Norway	1	–	–	1
Lebanon	–	1	–	1
Luxembourg	–	1	–	1
Singapore	–	1	–	1
Iraq	–	–	1	1
Taiwan (Taipei)	–	–	1	1
	112	108	112	332

WRESTLING

Wrestling was the most popular sport in the ancient Games with victors recorded from 708 BC. The most famous was Milon of Kroton, a five-time winner. Greco-Roman wrestling was included in the 1896 Games and freestyle in 1904. There was no bodyweight limit at Athens and it was won, surprisingly, by gymnastics triple gold medallist Carl Schuhmann (GER), who was only 1.63m *5ft 4in* tall, and who defeated Games weightlifting champion Launceston Eliot (GBR) in the preliminaries.

Until a time limit was set in 1924 bouts often lasted for remarkable lengths of time. The most extreme was that between Martin Klein, an Estonian representing Russia, and Alfred 'Alpo' Asikáinen (FIN) in the 1912 Greco-Roman middleweight class which lasted for 11 hours 40 minutes. Klein won. In the light-heavy final that year Anders Ahlgren (SWE) and Ivar Böhling (FIN) were declared equal second after 9 hours without a decision,

and no gold medal was awarded.

Three men have won three gold medals: Carl Westergren (SWE); Ivar Johansson (SWE) and Aleksandr Medved (URS). Johansson and Kristjan Palusalu (FIN) are the only men to win titles in both styles at the same Games. Wilfried Dietrich (GER/FRG) won most medals with one gold, two silvers and two bronzes at both styles from 1956 to 1968. Dietrich and George Mackenzie (GBR) competed at a record five Games, 1956–1972 and 1908–1928 respectively, while Mackenzie also competed over a record span of 20 years. The most successful brothers have been Kustaa and Hermanni Pihlajamäki (FIN) with three golds, one silver and a bronze between 1924 and 1936. The only twins to win gold medals were Anatoliy and Sergey Beloglazov (URS) in 1980. Uniquely two pairs of brothers, Ed and Lou Banach and Dave and Mark Schultz, all from the United States, won titles in 1984. The only father and son to become champions were Kaarlo (1928 freestyle) and Rauno (1956 Greco-Roman) Mäkinen (FIN).

The oldest gold medallist was Anatoliy Roschin (URS) in 1972 aged 40yr 184 days, while the youngest was Saban Trstena (YUG) in 1984 aged 19yr 222 days. The heaviest competitor ever in any Olympic event was the 1972 free-style super-heavyweight bronze medallist Chris Taylor (USA) who weighed between 182kg *401lb* and 190kg *419lb*.

When Osamu Watanabe (JPN) won the 1964 freestyle feather-weight title it was his 186th successive victory in the sport.

Wrestling

The contemporary descriptions of some bodyweight classes have varied during the history of the Games. Current descriptions are used in the lists below.

Gold	*Silver*	*Bronze*

Free-Style – Light Flyweight
(Weight up to 48kg)

	Gold	Silver	Bronze
1904	Robert Curry (USA)	John Heim (USA)	Gustav Thiefenthaler (USA)
1972	Roman Dmitriev (URS)	Ognian Nikolov (BUL)	Ebrahim Javadpour (IRN)
1976	Khassan Issaev (BUL)	Roman Dmitriev (URS)	Akira Kudo (JPN)
1980	Claudio Pollio (ITA)	Se Hong Jang (PRK)	Sergey Kornilayev (URS)
1984	Robert Weaver (USA)	Takashi Irie (JPN)	Gab-Do Son (KOR)

1896–1900, 1906–1968 Event not held.

Free-Style – Flyweight
Note: 1904 weight up to *115lb* 52.16kg. From 1948 weight up to 52kg.

	Gold	Silver	Bronze
1904	George Mehnert (USA)	Gustave Bauer (USA)	William Nelson (USA)
1948	Lennart Viitala (FIN)	Halit Balamir (TUR)	Thure Johansson (SWE)
1952	Hasan Gemici (TUR)	Yushu Kitano (JPN)	Mahmoud Mollaghassemi (IRN)
1956	Mirian Tsalkalamanidze (URS)	Mohamad-Ali Khojastehpour (IRN)	Hüseyin Akbas (TUR)
1960	Ahmet Bilek (TUR)	Masayuki Matsubara (JPN)	Mohamad Saifpour Saidabadi (IRN)
1964	Yoshikatsu Yoshida (JPN)	Chang-sun Chang (KOR)	Said Aliaakbar Haydari (IRN)
1968	Shigeo Nakata (JPN)	Richard Sanders (USA)	Surenjav Sukhbaatar (MGL)
1972	Kiyomi Kato (JPN)	Arsen Alakhverdiev (URS)	Hyong Kim Gwong (PRK)
1976	Yuji Takada (JPN)	Aleksandr Ivanov (URS)	Hae-Sup Jeon (KOR)
1980	Anatoliy Beloglazov (URS)	Wladyslaw Stecyk (POL)	Nermedin Selimov (BUL)
1984	Saban Trstena (YUG)	Jong-Kyu Kim (KOR)	Yuji Takada (JPN)

1896–1900, 1906–1936 Event not held.

Free-Style – Bantamweight
Note: The weight limit for this event has been: 1904, *125lb* 56.70kg; 1908, *119lb* 54kg; 1924–1936, 56kg and from 1948, 57kg.

	Gold	Silver	Bronze
1904	Isidor Niflot (USA)	August Wester (USA)	Z B Strebler (USA)
1908	George Mehnert (USA)	William Press (GBR)	Aubert Côté (CAN)
1924	Kustaa Pihlajamäki (FIN)	Kaarlo Mäkinen (FIN)	Bryant Hines (USA)
1928	Kaarlo Mäkinen (FIN)	Edmond Spapen (BEL)	James Trifunov (CAN)
1932	Robert Pearce (USA)	Ödön Zombori (HUN)	Aatos Jaskari (FIN)
1936	Ödön Zombori (HUN)	Ross Flood (USA)	Johannes Herbert (GER)
1948	Nasuk Akar (TUR)	Gerald Leeman (USA)	Charles Kouyos (FRA)
1952	Shohachi Ishii (JPN)	Rashid Mamedbekov (URS)	Kha-Shaba Jadav (IND)
1956	Mustafa Dagistanli (TUR)	Mohamad Yaghoubi (IRN)	Mikhail Chakhov (URS)
1960	Terrence McCann (USA)	Nejdet Zalev (BUL)	Tadeusz Trojanowski (POL)
1964	Yojiro Uetake (JPN)	Hüseyin Akbas (TUR)	Aidyn Ibragimov (URS)
1968	Yojiro Uetake (JPN)	Donald Behm (USA)	Abutaleb Gorgori (IRN)
1972	Hideaki Yanagide (JPN)	Richard Sanders (USA)	László Klinga (HUN)
1976	Vladimir Yumin (URS)	Hans-Dieter Brüchert (GDR)	Masao Arai (JPN)
1980	Sergey Beloglazov (URS)	Ho Pyong Li (PRK)	Dugarsuren Ouinbold (MGL)
1984	Hideyaki Tomiyama (JPN)	Barry Davis (USA)	Eui-Kon Kim (KOR)

1896–1900, 1906, 1912–1920 Event not held.

Free-Style – Featherweight
Note: The weight limit for this event has been: 1904, *135lb* 61.24kg; 1908, *133lb* 60.30kg; 1920, 60kg; 1924–1936, 61kg; 1948–1960, and 1972, 62kg; 1964–1968, 63kg; 1984, 62kg.

	Gold	Silver	Bronze
1904	Benjamin Bradshaw (USA)	Theodore McLear (USA)	Charles Clapper (USA)
1908	George Dole (USA)	James Slim (GBR)	William McKie (GBR)
1920	Charles Ackerly (USA)	Samuel Gerson (USA)	P W Bernard (GBR)
1924	Robin Reed (USA)	Chester Newton (USA)	Katsutoshi Naito (JPN)
1928	Allie Morrison (USA)	Kustaa Pihlajamäki (FIN)	Hans Minder (SUI)
1932	Hermanni Pihlajamäki (FIN)	Edgar Nemir (USA)	Einar Karlsson (SWE)
1936	Kustaa Pihlajamäki (FIN)	Francis Millard (USA)	Gösta Jönsson (SWE)
1948	Gazanfer Bilge (TUR)	Ivar Sjölin (SWE)	Adolf Müller (SUI)
1952	Bayram Sit (TUR)	Nasser Guivehtchi (IRN)	Josiah Henson (USA)
1956	Shozo Sasahara (JPN)	Joseph Mewis (BEL)	Erkki Penttilä (FIN)
1960	Mustafa Dagistanli (TUR)	Stantcho Ivanov (BUL)	Vladimir Rubashvili (URS)
1964	Osamu Watanabe (JPN)	Stantcho Ivanov (BUL)	Nodar Khokhashvili (URS)
1968	Masaaki Kaneko (JPN)	Enyu Todorov (BUL)	Shamseddin Seyed-Abbassi (IRN)
1972	Zagalav Abdulbekov (URS)	Vehbi Akdag (TUR)	Ivan Krastev (BUL)
1976	Jung-Mo Yang (KOR)	Zeveg Oidov (MGL)	Gene Davis (USA)
1980	Magomedgasan Abushev (URS)	Mikho Doukov (BUL)	Georges Hadjiioannidis (GRE)
1984	Randy Lewis (USA)	Kosei Akaishi (JPN)	Jung-Keun Lee (KOR)

1896–1900, 1906, 1912 Event not held.

Gold	Silver	Bronze

Free-Style – Lightweight

Note: The weight limit for this event has been: 1904, *145lb* 65.77kg, 1908, *146¾lb* 66.60kg; 1920 67.5kg; 1924 to 1936, 66kg; 1948 to 1960, 67kg; 1964 and 1968, 70kg and from 1972, 68kg.

	Gold	Silver	Bronze
1904	Otto Roehm (USA)	Rudolf Tesing (USA)	Albert Zirkel (USA)
1908	George de Relwyskow (GBR)	William Wood (GBR)	Albert Gingell (GBR)
1920	Kalle Anttila (FIN)	Gottfrid Svensson (SWE)	Peter Wright (GBR)
1924	Russell Vis (USA)	Volmart Wickström (FIN)	Arvo Haavisto (FIN)
1928	Osvald Käpp (EST)	Charles Pacôme (FRA)	Eino Leino (FIN)
1932	Charles Pacôme (FRA)	Károly Kárpáti (HUN)	Gustaf Klarén (SWE)
1936	Károly Kárpáti (HUN)	Wolfgang Ehrl (GER)	Hermanni Pihlajamäki (FIN)
1948	Celál Atik (TUR)	Gösta Frandfors (SWE)	Hermann Baumann (SUI)
1952	Olle Anderberg (SWE)	Thomas Evans (USA)	Djahanbakte Tovfighe (IRN)
1956	Emamali Habibi (IRN)	Shigeru Kasahara (JPN)	Alimberg Bestayev (URS)
1960	Shelby Wilson (USA)	Viktor Sinyavskiy (URS)	Enyu Dimov (BUL)
1964	Enyu Valtschev[1] (BUL)	Klaus-Jürgen Rost (GER)	Iwao Horiuchi (JPN)
1968	Abdollah Movahed Ardabili (IRN)	Enyu Valtschev[1] (BUL)	Sereeter Danzandarjaa (MGL)
1972	Dan Gable (USA)	Kikuo Wada (JPN)	Ruslan Ashuraliev (URS)
1976	Pavel Pinigin (URS)	Lloyd Keaser (USA)	Yasaburo Sagawara (JPN)
1980	Saipulla Absaidov (URS)	Ivan Yankov (BUL)	Saban Sejdi (YUG)
1984	In-Tak You (KOR)	Andrew Rein (USA)	Jukka Rauhala (FIN)

[1]Valtschev competed as Dimov in 1960.   1896–1900, 1906, 1912 Event not held.

Free-Style – Welterweight

Note: The weight limit for this event has been: 1904, *158lb* 71.67kg; 1924 to 1936, 72kg; 1948 to 1960, 73kg; from 1972, 74kg.

	Gold	Silver	Bronze
1904	Charles Erickson (USA)	William Beckmann (USA)	Jerry Winholtz (USA)
1924	Hermann Gehri (SUI)	Eino Leino (FIN)	Otto Müller (SUI)
1928	Arvo Haavisto (FIN)	Lloyd Appleton (USA)	Maurice Letchford (CAN)
1932	Jack van Bebber (USA)	Daniel MacDonald (CAN)	Eino Leino (FIN)
1936	Frank Lewis (USA)	Ture Andersson (SWE)	Joseph Schleimer (CAN)
1948	Yasar Dogu (TUR)	Richard Garrard (AUS)	Leland Merrill (USA)
1952	William Smith (USA)	Per Berlin (SWE)	Abdullah Modjtabavi (IRN)
1956	Mitsuo Ikeda (JPN)	Ibrahim Zengin (TUR)	Vakhtang Balavadze (URS)
1960	Douglas Blubaugh (USA)	Ismail Ogan (TUR)	Mohammed Bashir (PAK)
1964	Ismail Ogan (TUR)	Guliko Sagaradze (URS)	Mohamad-Ali Sanatkaran (IRN)
1968	Mahmut Atalay (TUR)	Daniel Robin (FRA)	Dagvasuren Purev (MGL)
1972	Wayne Wells (USA)	Jan Karlsson (SWE)	Adolf Seger (FRG)
1976	Jiichiro Date (JPN)	Mansour Barzegar (IRN)	Stanley Dziedzic (USA)
1980	Valentin Raitchev (BUL)	Jamtsying Davaajav (MGL)	Dan Karabin (TCH)
1984	David Schultz (USA)	Martin Knosp (FRG)	Saban Sejdi (YUG)

1896–1900, 1906–1920 Event not held.

Freestyle – Middleweight

Note: The weight limit for this event has been: 1908, *161lb* 73kg; 1920, *165¼lb* 75kg; 1924 to 1960, 79kg; 1964 and 1968, 87kg; from 1972, 82kg.

	Gold	Silver	Bronze
1908	Stanley Bacon (GBR)	George de Relwyskow (GBR)	Frederick Beck (GBR)
1920	Eino Leino (FIN)	Väinö Penttala (FIN)	Charles Johnson (USA)
1924	Fritz Hagmann (SUI)	Pierre Ollivier (BEL)	Vilho Pekkala (FIN)
1928	Ernst Kyburz (SUI)	Donald Stockton (CAN)	Samuel Rabin (GBR)
1932	Ivar Johansson (SWE)	Kyösti Luukko (FIN)	József Tunyogi (HUN)
1936	Emile Poilvé (FRA)	Richard Voliva (USA)	Ahmet Kireiçci (TUR)
1948	Glen Brand (USA)	Adil Candemir (TUR)	Erik Lindén (SWE)
1952	David Tsimakuridze (URS)	Gholamheza Takhti (IRN)	György Gurics (HUN)
1956	Nikola Stantschev (BUL)	Daniel Hodge (USA)	Georgiy Skhirtladze (URS)
1960	Hasan Güngör (TUR)	Georgiy Skhirtladze (URS)	Hans Antonsson (SWE)
1964	Prodan Gardschev (BUL)	Hasan Güngör (TUR)	Daniel Brand (USA)
1968	Boris Gurevitch (URS)	Munkbat Jigjid (MGL)	Prodan Gardschev (BUL)
1972	Levan Tediashvili (URS)	John Peterson (USA)	Vasile Jorga (ROM)
1976	John Peterson (USA)	Viktor Novoshilev (URS)	Adolf Seger (FRG)
1980	Ismail Abilov (BUL)	Magomedhan Aratsilov (URS)	Istvan Kovacs (HUN)
1984	Mark Schultz (USA)	Hideyuki Nagashima (JPN)	Chris Rinke (CAN)

1896–1906, 1912 Event not held.

Free-Style – Light-Heavyweight

Note: The weight limit for this event has been: 1920, 82.5kg; 1924 to 1960, 87kg; 1964 and 1968, 97kg; from 1972, 90kg.

	Gold	Silver	Bronze
1920	Anders Larsson (SWE)	Charles Courant (SUI)	Walter Maurer (USA)
1924	John Spellman (USA)	Rudolf Svensson (SWE)	Charles Courant (SUI)
1928	Thure Sjöstedt (SWE)	Anton Bögli (SUI)	Henri Lefèbre (FRA)
1932	Peter Mehringer (USA)	Thure Sjöstedt (SWE)	Eddie Scarf (AUS)
1936	Knut Fridell (SWE)	August Neo (EST)	Erich Siebert (GER)
1948	Henry Wittenberg (USA)	Fritz Stöckli (SUI)	Bengt Fahlkvist (SWE)
1952	Wiking Palm (SWE)	Henry Wittenberg (USA)	Adil Atan (TUR)
1956	Gholam Reza Tahkti (IRN)	Boris Kulayev (URS)	Peter Blair (USA)
1960	Ismet Atli (TUR)	Cholam Reza Tahkti (IRN)	Anatoliy Albul (URS)
1964	Aleksandr Medved (URS)	Ahmet Ayik (TUR)	Said Mustafafov (BUL)
1968	Ahmet Ayik (TUR)	Shota Lomidze (URS)	József Csatári (HUN)
1972	Ben Peterson (USA)	Gennadiy Strakhov (URS)	Karoly Bajko (HUN)
1976	Levan Tediashvili (URS)	Ben Peterson (USA)	Stelica Morcov (ROM)
1980	Sanasar Oganesyan (URS)	Uwe Neupert (GDR)	Aleksandr Cichon (POL)
1984	Ed Banach (USA)	Akira Ohta (JPN)	Noel Loban (GBR)

1896–1912 Event not held.

Gold	Silver	Bronze

Free-Style – Heavyweight

Note: The weight limit for this event has been: 1904, over *158lb* 71.6kg; 1908, over 73kg; 1920, over 82.5kg; 1924 to 1960, over 87kg; 1964 and 1968, over 97kg; from 1972, up to 100kg.

Gold	Silver	Bronze
1904 Bernhuff Hansen (USA)	Frank Kungler (USA)	Fred Warmbold (USA)
1908 George O'Kelly (GBR)	Jacob Gundersen (NOR)	Edmond Barrett (GBR)
1920 Robert Roth (SUI)	Nathan Pendleton (USA)	Ernst Nilsson (SWE)[1]
		Frederick Meyer (USA)
1924 Harry Steele (USA)	Henry Wernli (SUI)	Andrew McDonald (GBR)
1928 Johan Richthoff (SWE)	Aukusti Sihovla (FIN)	Edmond Dame (FRA)
1932 Johan Richthoff (SWE)	John Riley (USA)	Nikolaus Hirschl (AUT)
1936 Kristjan Palusalu (EST)	Josef Klapuch (TCH)	Hjalmar Nyström (FIN)
1948 Gyula Bóbis (HUN)	Bertil Antonsson (SWE)	Joseph Armstrong (AUS)
1952 Arsen Mekokishvili (URS)	Bertil Antonsson (SWE)	Kenneth Richmond (GBR)
1956 Hamit Kaplan (TUR)	Hussein Mekhmedov (BUL)	Taisto Kangasniemi (FIN)
1960 Wilfried Dietrich (GER)	Hamit Kaplan (TUR)	Savkus Dzarassov (URS)
1964 Aleksandr Ivanitsky (URS)	Liutvi Djiber (BUL)	Hamit Kaplan (TUR)
1968 Aleksandr Medved (URS)	Osman Duraliev (BUL)	Wilfried Dietrich (FRG)
1972 Ivan Yarygin (URS)	Khorloo Baianmunkh (MGL)	József Csatári (HUN)
1976 Ivan Yarygin (URS)	Russell Hellickson (USA)	Dimo Kostov (BUL)
1980 Ilya Mate (YUG)	Slavtcho Tchervenkov (BUL)	Julius Strnisko (TCH)
1984 Lou Banach (USA)	Joseph Atiyeh (SYR)	Vasile Pascasu (ROM)

[1]Tie for third place.   1896–1900, 1906, 1912 Event not held.

Free-Style – Super-Heavyweight

(Weight over 100kg)

Gold	Silver	Bronze
1972 Aleksandr Medved (URS)	Osman Duraliev (BUL)	Chris Taylor (USA)
1976 Soslan Andiev (URS)	Jozsef Balla (HUN)	Ladislau Simon (ROM)
1980 Soslan Andiev (URS)	Jozsef Balla (HUN)	Adam Sandurski (POL)
1984 Bruce Baumgartner (USA)	Bob Molle (CAN	Ayhan Taskin (TUR)

1896–1968 Event not held.

Greco-Roman – Light-Flyweight

(Weight up to 48kg)

Gold	Silver	Bronze
1972 Gheorghe Berceanu (ROM)	Rahim Ahabadi (IRN)	Stefan Anghelov (BUL)
1976 Aleksey Shumakov (URS)	Gheorghe Berceanu (ROM)	Stefan Anghelov (BUL)
1980 Zaksylik Ushkempirov (URS)	Constantin Alexandru (ROM)	Ferenc Seres (HUN)
1984 Vincenzo Maenza (ITA)	Markus Scherer (FRG)	Ikuzo Saito (JPN)

1896–1968 Event not held.

Greco-Roman – Flyweight

(Weight up to 52kg)

Gold	Silver	Bronze
1948 Pietro Lombardi (ITA)	Kenan Olcay (TUR)	Reino Kangasmäki (FIN)
1952 Boris Gurevich (URS)	Ignazio Fabra (ITA)	Leo Honkala (FIN)
1956 Nikolai Solovyov (URS)	Ignazio Fabra (ITA)	Durum Ali Egribas (TUR)
1960 Dumitru Pirvulescu (ROM)	Osman Sayed (UAR)	Mohamad Paziraye (IRN)
1964 Tsutomu Hanahara (JPN)	Angel Kerezov (BUL)	Dumitru Pirvulescu (ROM)
1968 Petar Kirov (BUL)	Vladimir Bakulin (URS)	Miroslav Zeman (TCH)
1972 Petar Kirov (BUL)	Koichiro Hirayama (JPN)	Giuseppe Bognanni (ITA)
1976 Vitaliy Konstantinov (URS)	Nicu Ginga (ROM)	Koichiro Hirayama (JPN)
1980 Vakhtang Blagidze (URS)	Lajos Racz (HUN)	Mladen Mladenov (BUL)
1984 Atsuji Miyahara (JPN)	Daniel Aceves (MEX)	Dae-Du Bang (KOR)

1896–1936 Event not held.

Greco-Roman – Bantamweight

Note: The weight limit for this event has been: 1924 to 1928, 58kg; 1932 to 1936, 56kg; since 1948, 57kg.

Gold	Silver	Bronze
1924 Eduard Pütsep (EST)	Anselm Ahlfors (FIN)	Väinö Ikonen (FIN)
1928 Kurt Leucht (GER)	Jindrich Maudr (TCH)	Giovanni Gozzi (ITA)
1932 Jakob Brendel (GER)	Marcello Nizzola (ITA)	Louis François (FRA)
1936 Márton Lörincz (HUN)	Egon Svensson (SWE)	Jakob Brendel (GER)
1948 Kurt Pettersén (SWE)	Aly Mahmoud Hassan (EGY)	Habil Kaya (TUR)
1952 Imre Hódos (HUN)	Zakaria Chihab (LIB)	Artem Teryan (URS)
1956 Konstantin Vyrupayev (URS)	Evdin Vesterby (SWE)	Francisco Horvat (ROM)
1960 Oleg Karavayev (URS)	Ion Cernea (ROM)	Petrov Dinko (BUL)
1964 Masamitsu Ichiguchi (JPN)	Vladlen Trostiansky (URS)	Ion Cernea (ROM)
1968 János Varga (HUN)	Ion Baciu (ROM)	Ivan Kochergin (URS)
1972 Rustem Kazakov (URS)	Hans-Jürgen Veil (FRG)	Risto Björlin (FIN)
1976 Pertti Ukkola (FIN)	Ivan Frgic (YUG)	Farhat Mustafin (URS)
1980 Shamil Serikov (URS)	Jozef Lipien (POL)	Benni Ljungbeck (SWE)
1984 Pasquale Passarelli (FRG)	Masaki Eto (JPN)	Haralambos Holidis (GRE)

1896–1920 Event not held.

Greco-Roman – Featherweight

Note: The weight limit for this event has been: 1912 to 1920, 60kg; 1924 to 1928, 1948 to 1960 and since 1972, 62kg; 1932 to 1936, 61kg; 1964 to 1968, 63kg.

Gold	Silver	Bronze
1912 Kaarlo Koskelo (FIN)	Georg Gerstacker (GER)	Otto Lasanen (FIN)
1920 Oskari Friman (FIN)	Hekki Kähkönen (FIN)	Fridtjof Svensson (SWE)
1924 Kalle Antila (FIN)	Aleksanteri Toivola (FIN)	Erik Malmberg (SWE)
1928 Voldemar Väli (EST)	Erik Malmberg (SWE)	Giacomo Quaglia (ITA)
1932 Giovanni Gozzi (ITA)	Wolfgang Ehrl (GER)	Lauri Koskela (FIN)
1936 Yasar Erkan (TUR)	Aarne Reini (FIN)	Einar Karlsson (SWE)
1948 Mehmet Oktav (TUR)	Olle Anderberg (SWE)	Ferenc Tóth (HUN)

	Gold	Silver	Bronze
1952	Yakov Punkin (URS)	Imre Polyák (HUN)	Abdel Rashed (EGY)
1956	Rauno Mäkinen (FIN)	Imre Polyák (HUN)	Roman Dzneladze (URS)
1960	Mu4zahir Sille (TUR)	Imre Polyák (HUN)	Konstantin Vyrupayev (URS)
1964	Imre Polyák (HUN)	Roman Rurua (URS)	Branko Martinovič (YUG)
1968	Roman Rurua (URS)	Hideo Fujimoto (JPN)	Simeon Popescu (ROM)
1972	Gheorghi Markov (BUL)	Heinz-Helmut Wehling (GDR)	Kazimierz Lipien (POL)
1976	Kazimierz Lipien (POL)	Nelson Davidian (URS)	Laszlo Reczi (HUN)
1980	Stilianos Migiakis (GRE)	Istvan Toth (HUN)	Boris Kramorenko (URS)
1984	Weon-Kee Kim (KOR)	Kentolle Johansson (SWE)	Hugo Dietsche (SUI)

1896–1908 Event not held.

Greco-Roman – Lightweight

Note: The weight limit for this event has been: 1906, 75kg; 1908, 66.6kg; 1912 to 1928, 67.5kg; 1932 to 1936, 66kg; 1948 to 1960, 67kg; 1964 to 1968, 70kg; since 1972, 68kg.

1906	Rudolf Watzl (AUT)	Karl Karlsen (DEN)	Ferenc Holuban (HUN)
1908	Enrico Porro (ITA)	Nikolay Orlov (URS)	Avid Lindén-Linko (FIN)
1912	Eemil Wäre (FIN)	Gustaf Malmström (SWE)	Edvin Matiasson (SWE)
1920	Eemil Wäre (FIN)	Taavi Tamminen (FIN)	Fritjof Andersen (NOR)
1924	Oskari Friman (FIN)	Lajos Keresztes (HUN)	Kalle Westerlund (FIN)
1928	Lajos Keresztes (HUN)	Eduard Sperling (GER)	Eduard Westerlund (FIN)
1932	Erik Malmberg (SWE)	Abraham Kurland (DEN)	Eduard Sperling (GER)
1936	Lauri Koskela (FIN)	Josef Herda (TCH)	Voldemar Väli (EST)
1948	Gustaf Freij (SWE)	Aage Eriksen (NOR)	Károly Ferencz (HUN)
1952	Shazam Safin (URS)	Gustaf Freij (SWE)	Mikuláš Athanasov (TCH)
1956	Kyösti Lehtonen (FIN)	Riza Dogan (TUR)	Gyul Tóth (HUN)
1960	Avtandil Koridze (URS)	Branislav Martinovic (YUG)	Gustaf Freij (SWE)
1964	Kazim Ayvaz (TUR)	Valeriu Bularca (ROM)	David Gvantseladze (URS)
1968	Munji Mumemura (JPN)	Stevan Horvat (YUG)	Petros Galaktopoulos (GRE)
1972	Shamil Khisamutdinov (URS)	Stoyan Apostolov (BUL)	Gian Matteo Ranzi (ITA)
1976	Suren Nalbandyan (URS)	Stefan Rusu (ROM)	Heinz-Helmut Wehling (GDR)
1980	Stefan Rusu (ROM)	Andrzej Supron (POL)	Lars-Erik Skiold (SWE)
1984	Vlado Lisjak (YUG)	Tapio Sipila (FIN)	James Martinez (USA)

1896–1904 Event not held.

Greco-Roman – Welterweight

Note: the weight limit for this event has been: 1932 to 1936, 72kg; 1948 to 1960, 73kg; 1964 to 1968, 78kg; since 1972, 74kg.

1932	Ivar Johansson (SWE)	Väinö Kajander (FIN)	Ercole Gallegatti (ITA)
1936	Rudolf Svedberg (SWE)	Fritz Schäfer (GER)	Eino Virtanen (FIN)
1948	Gösta Andersson (SWE)	Miklós Szilvási (HUN)	Henrik Hansen (DEN)
1952	Miklós Szilvási (HUN)	Gösta Andersson (SWE)	Khalil Taha (LIB)
1956	Mithat Bayrak (TUR)	Vladimir Maneyev (URS)	Per Berlin (SWE)
1960	Mithat Bayrak (TUR)	Günther Maritschnigg (GER)	René Schiermeyer (FRA)
1964	Anatoliy Kolesov (URS)	Cyril Todorov (BUL)	Bertil Nyström (SWE)
1968	Rudolf Vesper (GDR)	Daniel Robin (FRA)	Károly Bajkó (HUN)
1972	Vitezslav Macha (TCH)	Petros Galaktopoulos (GRE)	Jan Karlsson (SWE)
1976	Anatoliy Bykov (URS)	Vitezslav Macha (TCH)	Karlheinz Helbing (FRG)
1980	Ferenc Kocsis (HUN)	Anatoliy Bykov (URS)	Mikko Huhtala (FIN)
1984	Jonko Salomaki (FIN)	Roger Tallroth (SWE)	Stefan Rusu (ROM)

1896–1928 Event not held.

Greco-Roman – Middleweight

Note: The weight limit for this event has been: 1906, 85kg; 1908, 73kg; 1912 to 1928, 75kg; 1932 to 1960, 79kg; 1964 to 1968, 87kg; since 1972, 82kg.

1906	Verner Weckman (FIN)	Rudolf Lindmayer (AUT)	Robert Bebrens (DEN)
1908	Frithiof Märtensson (SWE)	Mauritz Andersson (SWE)	Anders Andersen (DEN)
1912	Claes Johansson (SWE)	Martin Klein (URS)	Alfred Asikainen (FIN)
1920	Carl Westergren (SWE)	Artur Lindfors (FIN)	Matti Perttila (FIN)
1924	Eduard Westerlund (FIN)	Artur Lindfors (FIN)	Roman Steinberg (EST)
1928	Väinö Kokkinen (FIN)	László Papp (HUN)	Albert Kusnetz (EST)
1932	Väinö Kokkinen (FIN)	Jean Földeák (GER)	Axel Cadier (SWE)
1936	Ivar Johansson (SWE)	Ludwig Schweikert (GER)	József Palotás (HUN)
1948	Axel Grönberg (SWE)	Muhlis Tayfur (TUR)	Ercole Gallegatti (ITA)
1952	Axel Grönberg (SWE)	Kalervo Rauhala (FIN)	Nikolai Belov (URS)
1956	Givi Kartoziya (URS)	Dimiter Dobrev (BUL)	Rune Jansson (SWE)
1960	Dimiter Dobrev (BUL)	Lothar Metz (GER)	Ion Taranu (ROM)
1964	Branislav Simič (YUG)	Jiri Kormanik (TCH)	Lothar Metz (GER)
1968	Lothar Metz (GDR)	Valentin Olenik (URS)	Branislav Simič (YUG)
1972	Csaba Hegedus (HUN)	Anatoliy Nazarenko (URS)	Milan Nenadic (YUG)
1976	Momir Petkovic (YUG)	Vladimir Cheboksarov (URS)	Ivan Kolev (BUL)
1980	Gennadiy Korban (URS)	Jan Polgowicz (POL)	Pavel Pavlov (BUL)
1984	Ion Draica (ROM)	Dimitrios Thanapoulos (GRE)	Soren Claeson (SWE)

1896–1904 Event not held.

Greco-Roman – Light-Heavyweight

Note: The weight limit in this event has been: 1908, 93kg; 1912 to 1928, 82.5kg; 1932 to 1960, 87kg; 1964 to 1968, 97kg; since 1972, 90kg.

1908	Verner Weckman (FIN)	Yrjö Saarela (FIN)	Carl Jensen (DEN)
1912	–[1]	Anders Ahlgren (SWE) Ivor Böhling (FIN)	Béla Varga (HUN)
1920	Claes Johansson (SWE)	Edil Rosenqvist (FIN)	Johannes Eriksen (DEN)
1924	Carl Westergren (SWE)	Rudolf Svensson (SWE)	Onni Pellinen (FIN)
1928	Ibrahim Moustafa (EGY)	Adolf Rieger (GER)	Onni Pellinen (FIN)
1932	Rudolf Svensson (SWE)	Onni Pellinen (FIN)	Mario Gruppioni (ITA)
1936	Axel Cadier (SWE)	Edwins Bietags (LAT)	August Néo (EST)
1948	Karl-Erik Nilsson (SWE)	Kaelpo Gröndahl (FIN)	Ibrahim Orabi (EGY)

	Gold	Silver	Bronze
1952	Kaelpo Gröndahl (FIN)	Shalva Shikhladze (URS)	Karl-Erik Nilsson (SWE)
1956	Valentin Nikolayev (URS)	Petko Sirakov (BUL)	Karl-Erik Nilsson (SWE)
1960	Tevfik Kis (TUR)	Krali Bimbalov (BUL)	Givi Kartoziya (URS)
1964	Boyan Radev (BUL)	Per Svensson (SWE)	Heinz Kiehl (GER)
1968	Boyan Radev (BUL)	Nikolai Yakovlev (URS)	Nicolae Martinescu (ROM)
1972	Valeriy Rezantsev (URS)	Josip Corak (YUG)	Czeslaw Kwiecinski (POL)
1976	Valeriy Rezantsev (URS)	Stoyan Ivanov (BUL)	Czeslaw Kwiecinski (POL)
1980	Norbert Nottny (HUN)	Igor Kanygin (URS)	Petre Disu (ROM)
1984	Steven Fraser (USA)	Ilie Matei (ROM)	Frank Andersson (SWE)

[1]Ahlgren and Böhling declared equal second after 9 hours of wrestling.   1896–1906 Event not held.

Greco-Roman – Heavyweight

Note: The weight limit for this event has been: 1896, open; 1906, over 85kg; 1908, over 93kg; 1912 to 1928, over 82.5kg; 1932 to 1960, over 81kg; 1964 to 1968, over 91kg; since 1972, up to 100kg.

1896	Carl Schuhmann (GER)	Georgios Tsitas (GRE)	Stephanos Christopoulos (GRE)
1906	Sören Jensen (DEN)	Henri Baur (AUT)	Marcel Dubois (BEL)
1908	Richard Weisz (HUN)	Aleksandr Petrov (URS)	Sören Jensen (DEN)
1912	Yrjö Saarela (FIN)	Johan Olin (FIN)	Sören Jensen (DEN)
1920	Adolf Lindfors (FIN)	Poul Hansen (DEN)	Martti Nieminen (FIN)
1924	Henri Deglane (FRA)	Edil Rosenqvist (FIN)	Raymund Badó (HUN)
1928	Rudolf Svensson (SWE)	Hjalmar Nyström (FIN)	Georg Gehring (GER)
1932	Carl Westergren (SWE)	Josef Urban (TCH)	Nikolaus Hirschl (AUT)
1936	Kristjan Palusalu (EST)	John Nyman (SWE)	Kurt Hornfischer (GER)
1948	Ahmet Kireçci (TUR)	Tor Nilsson (SWE)	Guido Fantoni (ITA)
1952	Johannes Kotkas (URS)	Josef Ružička (TCH)	Tauno Kovanen (FIN)
1956	Anatoliy Parfenov (URS)	Wilfried Dietrich (GER)	Adelmo Bulgarelli (ITA)
1960	Ivan Bogdan (URS)	Wilfried Dietrich (GER)	Bohumil Kubat (TCH)
1964	István Kozma (HUN)	Anatoliy Roschin (URS)	Wilfried Dietrich (GER)
1968	István Kozma (HUN)	Anatoliy Roschin (URS)	Petr Kment (TCH)
1972	Nicolae Martinescu (ROM)	Nikolai Yakovenko (URS)	Ferenc Kiss (HUN)
1976	Nikolai Bolboshin (URS)	Kamen Goranov (BUL)	Andrzej Skrzylewski (POL)
1980	Gheorghi Raikov (BUL)	Roman Bierla (POL)	Vasile Andrei (ROM)
1984	Vasile Andrei (ROM)	Greg Gibson (USA)	Jozef Tertelje (YUG)

1900–1904 Event not held.

Greco-Roman – Super-Heavyweight

(Weight over 100kg)

1972	Anatoliy Roschin (URS)	Alexandre Tomov (BUL)	Victor Dolipschi (ROM)
1976	Aleksandr Kolchinsky (URS)	Alexandre Tomov (BUL)	Roman Codreanu (ROM)
1980	Aleksandr Kolchinsky (URS)	Alexandre Tomov (BUL)	Hassan Bchara (LIB)
1984	Jeffrey Blatnick (USA)	Refik Memisevic (YUG)	Victor Dolipschi (ROM)

1896–1968 Event not held.

Wrestling – Medals

	Freestyle			Greco-Roman			
	G	S	B	G	S	B	Total
Soviet Union	23	12	12	30	18	9	104
United States	36	29	18	1	1	1	87
Finland	8	7	10	19	18	17	79
Sweden	8	10	8	19	15	16	76
Bulgaria	6	13	6	7	11	6	49
Hungary	3	4	7	12	8	11	45
Turkey	15	9	5	8	3	2	42
Japan	14	8	6	4	3	2	37
Germany (FRG)	1	3	5	4	13	8	34
Romania	–	–	4	6	8	12	30
Iran	3	6	9	–	1	1	20
Italy	1	–	–	4	3	9	17
Great Britain	3	4	10	–	–	–	17
Yugoslavia	2	–	2	3	5	4	16
Switzerland	4	4	5	–	–	1	14
Czechoslovakia	–	1	2	1	6	4	14
Poland	–	1	3	1	4	4	13
France	2	2	3	1	1	2	11
Denmark	–	–	–	1	3	7	11
Estonia	2	1	–	3	–	4	10
Korea	2	2	4	1	–	1	10
Greece	–	–	1	1	3	3	8
Mongolia	–	4	4	–	–	–	8
Canada	–	3	5	–	–	–	8
GDR	–	2	–	2	1	1	6
Austria	–	–	1	1	2	1	5
Egypt (UAR)	–	–	–	1	2	2	5
Belgium	–	3	–	–	–	1	4
Norway	–	1	–	–	1	1	3
North Korea (PRK)	–	2	1	–	–	–	3
Australia	–	1	2	–	–	–	3
Lebanon	–	–	–	–	1	2	3
Latvia	–	–	–	–	1	–	1
Mexico	–	–	–	–	1	–	1
Syria	–	1	–	–	–	–	1
India	–	–	1	–	–	–	1
Pakistan	–	–	1	–	–	–	1
	133	133	135	131	133	132	797

YACHTING

The first Olympic regatta should have been held in the Bay of Salamis, but it was cancelled due to bad weather. Since 1900 the classes were changed regularly until very recently when some measure of standardization was imposed. The current classes are as follows: Finn, 470, Tornado, Star, Flying Dutchman, Soling, Board Sailing; and in 1988 a women's 470 will be introduced. In each class there are seven races over a prescribed course in which the fastest time wins. Yachts count their six best results.

The only event which has been a permanent fixture is the Olympic monotype, ie one-man dinghy, albeit represented by different classes of boat prior to 1952 (now the Finn).

The most successful yachtsman is Paul Elvström (DEN) who won four successive Olympic monotype titles 1948–1960 – the first man to achieve such a run in any sport. He competed again in the 1968 Star (fourth) and 1972 Soling (seventh), and then again in 1984, his seventh Games, when he came fourth in the Tornado class partnering his daughter Trine. Frances Clytie Rivett-Carnac (GBR) was the first female gold medallist in the 7m class of 1908 with her husband, and she was the first woman to win in an event not restricted to women or mixed pairs in any sport. The oldest gold medallist was Everard Endt (USA) in the 1952 6m class aged 59yr 112 days, while the oldest in a single-handed event was Leon Huybrechts (BEL) aged 47yr 215 days in 1924. The youngest was Franciscus Hin (HOL), in the 1920 12-foot dinghy event with his brother Johannes, aged 14yr 163 days. The oldest medallist was Louis Noverraz (SUI) in the 5.5m category in 1968 aged 66yr 154 days.

Outstanding family achievements have occurred in Olympic yachting. In 1912 four Norwegian brothers, Henrik, Jan, Ole and Kristian Östervold won gold medals in the 12m (1907 rating) class. The full crew of the winning 5.5m in 1968 were brothers Ulf, Jörgen and Peter Sundelin (SWE), and the winning 6m in 1912 was crewed by Amédée, Gaston and Jacques Thubé (FRA). The only twins to win gold were Sumner and Edgar White (USA) in the 5.5m of 1952. The first father and son to win together were Emile and Florimond Cornellie (BEL) in the 6m (1907 rating) in 1920. However, the greatest Olympic yachting family must be the Norwegians Lunde: Eugen won a gold in the 1924 6m class, his son Peder and daughter-in-law Vibeke along with Vibeke's brother won a silver in the 5.5m in 1952, and grandson Peder Jr won a gold in the 1960 Flying Dutchman contest.

Rodney Pattison and Iain Macdonald-Smith (GBR) scored the lowest number of penalty points (three) ever achieved in Olympic yachting when they won the 1968 Flying Dutchman class with five wins, a second place and a disqualification in their seven starts. Their boat *Superdocious* is now in the National Maritime Museum, Greenwich.

In 1948 Magnus Konow (NOR) equalled the longest span of Olympic competition when he took part in the 6m event 40 years after his debut in the 8m class of 1908. He won two golds and a silver in 1912, 1920 and 1936, the only other Games he attended. Durward Knowles competed in a record seven Games (equalled by Elvström in 1984) from 1948 when he competed for Great Britain. He represented the Bahamas in the next six celebrations.

In the 1984 Games all thirteen members of the United States team won either gold or silver medals, a unique team achievement. An attempt has been made to bring some method of comparison to the Olympic results, made particularly difficult due to the wide variety of classes and types of boat used over the years. Where boats have been superseded by those of similar type, they have been listed in the same table. Purists may be unhappy but the general reader will find it easier to follow.

Yachting

Gold	Silver	Bronze
Olympic Monotype		
1920[1] Netherlands	Netherlands	–
Franciscus Hin	Arnoud van der Biesen	
Joahannes Hin	Petrus Beikers	
1920[2] Great Britain	–	–
F A Richards		
T Hedberg		
1924[3] Léon Huybrechts (BEL)	Henrik Robert (NOR)	Hans Dittmar (FIN)
1928[4] Sven Thorell (SWE)	Henrik Robert (NOR)	Bertil Broman (FIN)
1932[5] Jacques Lebrun (FRA)	Adriaan Maas (HOL)	Santiago Cansino (ESP)
1936[6] Daniel Kagchelland (HOL)	Werner Krogmann (GER)	Peter Scott (GBR)
1948[7] Paul Elvström (DEN)	Ralph Evans (USA)	Jacobus de Jong (HOL)
1952[8] Paul Elvström (DEN)	Charles Currey (GBR)	Rickard Sarby (SWE)
1956 Paul Elvström (DEN)	André Nelis (BEL)	John Marvin (USA)
1960 Paul Elvström (DEN)	Aleksandr Chuchelov (URS)	André Nelis (BEL)
1964 Willi Kuhweide (GER)	Peter Barrett (USA)	Henning Wind (DEN)
1968 Valentin Mankin (URS)	Hubert Raudaschl (AUT)	Fabio Albarelli (ITA)
1972 Serge Maury (FRA)	Ilias Hatzipavlis (GRE)	Viktor Potapov (URS)
1976 Jochen Schümann (GDR)	Andrei Balashov (URS)	John Bertrand (AUS)
1980 Esko Rechardt (FIN)	Wolfgang Mayrhofer (AUT)	Andrei Balashov (URS)
1984 Russell Coutts (NZL)	John Bertrand (USA)	Terry Neilson (CAN)

[1]12-foot dinghy (note two-handed), no bronze medal. [2]18-foot dinghy (note two-handed), no silver and bronze medals. [3]Meulan class, 12-foot dinghy. [4]International 12-foot class. [5]Snowbird class. [6]International Olympia class. [7]Firefly class. [8]Since 1952 Finn class. 1896–1912 Event not held.

Windglider Class

1984 Steve Van Den Berg (HOL)	Randall Steele (USA)	Bruce Kendall (NZL)

1896–1980 Event not held.

	Gold	Silver	Bronze

International Soling

	Gold	Silver	Bronze
1972	United States	Sweden	Canada
1976	Denmark	United States	GDR
1980	Denmark	Soviet Union	Greece
1984	United States	Brazil	Canada

1896–1968 Event not held.

International 470

	Gold	Silver	Bronze
1976	FRG	Spain	Australia
1980	Brazil	GDR	Finland
1984	Spain	United States	France

1896–1972 Event not held.

International Tornado

	Gold	Silver	Bronze
1976	Great Britain	United States	FRG
1980	Brazil	Denmark	Sweden
1984	New Zealand	United States	Australia

1896–1972 Event not held.

International Star

	Gold	Silver	Bronze
1932	United States	Great Britain	Sweden
1936	Germany	Sweden	Netherlands
1948	United States	Cuba	Netherlands
1952	Italy	United States	Portugal
1956	United States	Italy	Bahamas
1960	Soviet Union	Portugal	United States
1964	Bahamas	United States	Sweden
1968	United States	Norway	Italy
1972	Australia	Sweden	FRG
1980	Soviet Union	Austria	Italy
1984	United States	FRG	Italy

1896–1928, 1976 Event not held.

Flying Dutchman

	Gold	Silver	Bronze
1956[1]	New Zealand	Australia	Great Britain
1960	Norway	Denmark	Germany
1964	New Zealand	Great Britain	United States
1968	Great Britain	FRG	Brazil
1972	Great Britain	France	FRG
1976	FRG	Great Britain	Brazil
1980	Spain	Ireland	Hungary
1984	United States	Canada	Great Britain

[1]Sharpie class.   1896–1952 Event not held.

Discontinued Events

Swallow

	Gold	Silver	Bronze
1948	Great Britain	Portugal	United States

International Tempest

	Gold	Silver	Bronze
1972	Soviet Union	Great Britain	United States
1976	Sweden	Soviet Union	United States

Dragon

	Gold	Silver	Bronze
1948	Norway	Sweden	Denmark
1952	Norway	Sweden	Germany
1956	Sweden	Denmark	Great Britain
1960	Greece	Argentina	Italy
1964	Denmark	Germany	United States
1968	United States	Denmark	GDR
1972	Australia	GDR	United States

30 Square Metres

	Gold	Silver	Bronze
1920	Sweden	—[1]	—[1]

[1]No silver or bronze medals.

40 Square Metres

	Gold	Silver	Bronze
1920	Sweden	Sweden	—[1]

[1]No bronze medal.

5.5 Metres

	Gold	Silver	Bronze
1952	United States	Norway	Sweden
1956	Sweden	Great Britain	Australia
1960	United States	Denmark	Switzerland
1964	Australia	Sweden	United States
1968	Sweden	Switzerland	Great Britain

6 Metres

	Gold	Silver	Bronze
1908	Great Britain	Belgium	France
1912	France	Denmark	Sweden
1920	Norway	Belgium	—[1]
1924	Norway	Denmark	Netherlands
1928	Norway	Denmark	Estonia
1932	Sweden	United States	Canada
1936	Great Britain	Norway	Sweden
1948	United States	Argentina	Sweden
1952	United States	Norway	Finland

[1]No bronze medal.

6 Metres (1907 Rating)

	Gold	Silver	Bronze
1920	Belgium	Norway	Norway

6.5 Metres

	Gold	Silver	Bronze
1920	Netherlands	France	—[1]

[1]No bronze medal.

7 Metres

	Gold	Silver	Bronze
1908	Great Britain	—[1]	—[1]
1920	Great Britain	—[1]	—[1]

[1]No silver or bronze medals.   1912 Event not held.

8 Metres

	Gold	Silver	Bronze
1908	Great Britain	Sweden	Great Britain
1912	Norway	Sweden	Finland
1920	Norway	Norway	Belgium
1924	Norway	Great Britain	France
1928	France	Netherlands	Sweden
1932	United States	Canada	—[1]
1936	Italy	Norway	Germany

[1]No bronze medal.

8 Metres (1907 Rating)

	Gold	Silver	Bronze
1920	Norway	Norway	—[1]

[1]No bronze medal.

10 Metres

	Gold	Silver	Bronze
1912	Sweden	Finland	Russia

10 Metres (1907 Rating)

	Gold	Silver	Bronze
1920	Norway	—[1]	—[1]

[1]No silver or bronze medals.

12 Metres

	Gold	Silver	Bronze
1908	Great Britain	Great Britain	—[1]
1912	Norway	Sweden	Finland

[1]No bronze medal.

12 Metres (1907 Rating)

	Gold	Silver	Bronze
1920	Norway	—[1]	—[1]

[1]No silver or bronze medals.

12 Metres (1919 Rating)

	Gold	Silver	Bronze
1920	Norway	—[1]	—[1]

[1]No silver or bronze medals.

½ Ton Class

	Gold	Silver	Bronze
1900	France	France	France

½–1 Ton Class

	Gold	Silver	Bronze
1900	Great Britain	France	France

1–2 Ton Class

	Gold	Silver	Bronze
1900	Germany	Switzerland	France

2–3 Ton Class

	Gold	Silver	Bronze
1900	Great Britain	France	France

3–10 Ton Class

	Gold	Silver	Bronze
1900	France	Netherlands	Great Britain[1] France

[1]Tie for third place.

10–20 Ton Class

	Gold	Silver	Bronze
1900	France	France	Great Britain

Open Class

	Gold	Silver	Bronze
1900	Great Britain	Germany	France

Crown Prince Olav (later King Olav V of Norway) winning the 6m class of 1928 in Norna. (GSL)

Yachting – Medals

	G	S	B	Total
United States	14	11	9	34
Great Britain	14	8	8	30
Sweden	9	10	9	28
Norway	14	10	1	25
France	7	6	9	22
Denmark	7	8	2	17
Germany (FRG)	5	5	6	16
Netherlands	4	4	4	12
Soviet Union	4	4	3	11
Australia	3	1	4	8
Italy	2	1	5	8
Finland	1	1	6	8
Belgium	2	3	2	7
Canada	–	2	4	6
New Zealand	4	–	1	5
Brazil	2	1	2	5
GDR	1	2	2	5
Spain	2	1	1	4
Greece	1	1	1	3
Austria[2]	–	3	–	3
Portugal	–	2	1	3
Switzerland[2]	–	2	1	3
Bahamas	1	–	1	2
Argentina	–	2	–	2
Cuba	–	1	–	1
Ireland	–	1	–	1
Estonia	–	–	1	1
Hungary[2]	–	–	1	1
	97	90[1]	84[1]	271

[1]Some events in the early Games had no silver and/or bronze medallists.
[2]It is worth noting that Austria, Hungary and Switzerland do not have direct access to the sea.

DISCONTINUED SPORTS

In the early celebrations of the Games there were a number of sports included, often of a purely local interest to the host country. The last of these was polo which had its final outing in 1936. Below are listed all the medallists in these sports.

Cricket
On the only occasion that cricket was played at the Games, in 1900, Great Britain, represented by the Devon Wanderers CC, beat a French team, consisting of mainly expatriate Britons, in a 12-a-side match scoring 117 and 145 for five declared, against the French score of 73 and 26.

Croquet
It was only contested in 1900 when all the competitors were French. Only gold medals were awarded in the singles (simple à la boule), won by Aumoitte, and the doubles, won by Aumoitte and John. In the singles (simple à deux boules) the three medals went respectively to Waydelick, Vignerot and Sautereau.

Golf
George Lyon (CAN) was 46yr 59 days when he won the 1904 title, while the most medals were won by Chandler Egan (USA) with a team gold and an individual silver in 1904.

Golf

	Gold	Silver	Bronze
Men's singles			
1900	Charles Sands (USA)	Walter Rutherford (GBR)	David Robertson (GBR)
1904	George Lyon (CAN)	Chandler Egan (USA)	Burt McKinnie (USA)
Men's Team			
1904	United States	United States	–
Women's singles			
1904	Margaret Abbott (USA)	Polly Whittier (USA)	Daria Pratt (USA)

Polo

	Gold	Silver	Bronze
1900	Great Britain	Great Britain	France
1908	Great Britain	Great Britain	Great Britain
1920	Great Britain	Spain	United States
1924	Argentina	United States	Great Britain
1936	Argentina	Great Britain	Mexico

Rugby Union

	Gold	Silver	Bronze
1900	France	Germany	Great Britain
1908	Australia	Great Britain	–
1920	United States	France	–
1924	United States	France	Romania

Jeu de Paume
Held only once, in 1908, it was a demonstration sport in 1928. The medals in 1908 were won by Jay Gould (USA), Eustace Miles (GBR) and Neville Lytton (GBR).

Lacrosse
Held in 1904 and 1908, both were won by Canada, with the silvers going to the United States and Great Britain respectively. Only two teams competed each time. The highest score was when Canada beat Great Britain 14-10 in 1908.Demonstrations were held in 1928, 1932 and 1948.

Motorboating
Only held in 1908, when only one boat finished in each of the three classes. The Open class was won by France, the 60-foot and 8-metre classes went to Great Britain.

Polo
Only Sir John Wodehouse (GBR), the 3rd Earl of Kimberley, won a silver (1908) to add to a gold (1920). The oldest gold medallist was Manuel Andrada (ARG) in 1936 aged 46yr 211 days, and the youngest was his team-mate Roberto Cavanagh aged 21yr 269 days. The biggest winning margin was 16-2 by Argentina v Spain and Great Britain v France, both in 1924, and by Mexico v Hungary in 1936.

Roque
Only held in 1904 with all competitors from the United States. The medals were won by Charles Jacobus, Smith Streeter and Charles Brown respectively.

Rackets
Only held in 1908, the singles went to Evan Noel (GBR), from Henry Leaf (GBR) and John Jacob Astor (GBR), with Great Britain gaining all three medals in the team event.

Rugby Union
Only six countries competed in the four tournaments held – Australia, France, Germany, Great Britain, Romania and the United States. The 1908 title was won by Australia while the Wallabies were on their first tour of Britain. The team they beat in the final was Cornwall, the English County Champions. Five American players won two gold medals in 1920 and 1924: Charles Doe, John O'Neil, Colby Slater, John Patrick and Rudolph Scholz. Additionally, Daniel Carroll won his second gold with the 1920 US team, having been on the 1908 Australian squad when only 16yr 149 days. This makes him the youngest player ever to represent his country at the sport, although 'purists' have never considered the Olympic matches to be 'full' internationals. The highest score was when France beat Romania 61-3 in 1924. In 1920 sprint relay gold medallist Morris Kirksey, also runner-up in the 100m, won another gold in the winning US rugby team. It always comes as a shock to enthusiasts to realize that the United States is the reigning Olympic champions at Rugby. Incidentally, after their Paris victory they played in Britain and were beaten by the Harlequins and Blackheath club teams. The game was probably in the Olympics originally because Baron de Coubertin was a keen follower and actually refereed France's first international match, against New Zealand, in 1906.

DEMONSTRATION SPORTS

Since 1904 there have been a variety of demonstration sports held as part of the Games but not as official events eligible for medals. Some of them have later become official sports and they have been mentioned elsewhere. Other than those there have been the following:

American Football
In 1932 two teams representing the East and West of America played an exhibition which the West won 7-6.

Australian Rules Football
Two amateur Australian teams played an exhibition in 1956 which resulted in a 250-135 score.

Badminton
In 1972 twenty-five competitors from eleven countries provided a competition of the highest quality, highlighted by the men's singles victory of Rudy Hartono (INA).

Bandy
A tournament was included in the 1952 Winter Games. Final placings were decided on goal average with Sweden winning from Norway and Finland.

Baseball
There have been five occasions when American baseball has been exhibited, plus a demonstration of Finnish baseball in 1952. In 1912 the USA, containing many track and field medallists, beat Sweden 13-3. In 1936 a 'World Amateurs' team beat an American 'Olympic' team before 100 000 spectators in the Berlin Olympic stadium. In 1956 an American Services team beat an Australian team 11-5 in front of an estimated 114 000 people, a record crowd for a single baseball game anywhere. At Tokyo in 1964 a USA team beat two Japanese teams, and in 1984 Japan won an eight-nation tournament.

Budo
Exhibitions of Japanese archery, wrestling and fencing were given in 1964.

Curling
A three-country contest was held in 1924, won by Great Britain from Sweden and France. In 1932 there were four Canadian Provincial and four American club teams. The Canadians took the first four places with the title won by Manitoba. In 1936 eight teams from Austria (3),

Germany (3) and Czechoslovakia (2) competed in a specialized version of the game, German curling, with the Austrian number one team, from the Tyrol, winning. The Austrians demonstrated the game again in 1964 at Innsbruck, and it will be a demonstration sport again in 1988.

Dog Sled Racing
A race for twelve sled teams, seven dogs to a sled, was held in 1932. There were actually two races of approximately 25 miles *40km* each, with the aggregate times added together. Emile St Goddard (CAN) won easily finishing first both times in a combined 4hr 23min 12.5sec, nearly 8 minutes ahead of Lennard Seppala (USA).

Gliding
Fourteen countries took part in an exhibition in 1936, but the main demonstrations were by German gliders.

Military Patrol
Held at four Winter Games, it is considered to be the forerunner of the official biathlon contests introduced in 1960. Switzerland won in 1924 and 1948, Norway won in 1928, and Italy took the 1936 title.

Pelota Basque
Demonstrated in 1924 by teams from Spain and France, and again in 1968 when the same countries were joined by Mexico, Argentina and Uruguay.

Water Skiing
Held at Kiel in 1972 with 36 competitors from 20 countries, with many of the best skiers in the world. Events were won by Roby Zucchi (ITA), Ricky McCormick (USA), Willy Stähle (HOL), Liz Allan-Shetter (USA) and Sylvie Maurial (FRA).

Winter Pentathlon
Held in 1948 and comprising a 10km cross-country skiing race, a pistol shoot, fencing, downhill skiing and horse riding over a distance of about 3500m. Gustaf Lindh (SWE) came first, with his team-mate Willie Grut second. Grut later won the modern pentathlon in the Summer Games by a record margin. In sixth place was Derek Allhusen (GBR) who 20

Christel Cranz (GER) won the Alpine Combined event the only time it was contested in 1936. (GSL)

years later in his 55th year won an equestrian gold medal at Mexico City.

ALPINE SKIING

Separate Alpine skiing events were first introduced into the Games in 1948, but this style held in 1936 as an Alpine combination event consisting of an aggregate of points scored in a downhill and slalom race. Toni Sailer (AUT) in 1956 and Jean-Claude Killy (FRA) in 1968 both won a record three gold medals. Five girls have won two golds each but only German-born Hanni Wenzel (LIE) also won a silver and a bronze to make her the only Alpine skier, male or female, to win four medals. Uniquely, for Alpine skiers, Trude Jochum-Beiser (AUT) and Marielle Goitschel (FRA) gained gold medals in two Games.

The oldest gold medallist was Zeno Colo (ITA) who won the 1952 downhill aged 31yr 231 days, while the youngest was Michela Figini (SUI) aged 17yr 314 days when winning the 1984 downhill. The youngest male winner was Sailer (see above) aged 20yr 73 days in the 1956 giant slalom, and the oldest female champion was Ossi Reichert (GER) in the 1956 giant slalom aged 30yr 33 days. Heinrich Messner (AUT) was the oldest medallist with the downhill bronze in 1972 aged 32yr 159 days, and the youngest medallist was Gertrud 'Traudl' Hecher (AUT) aged 16yr 145 days with the bronze in the 1960 downhill race. The youngest male medallist was Alfred Matt (AUT) with the 1968 slalom bronze aged 19yr 281 days, and the oldest female medallist was Dorothea Hochleitner (AUT) aged 30yr 201 days when she

won the 1956 giant slalom bronze medal.

The highest average speed attained in an Olympic downhill race was 104.532km/h *64.953 mph* by Bill Johnson (USA) in 1984.

The greatest margin of victory in downhill was 4.7sec by Madeleine Berthod (FRA) in 1956, while the best in the male race was 4.1sec by Henri Oreiller (FRA) in 1948. The smallest margin was 0.05sec in the 1984 women's race while that for men was 0.08sec in 1968. The greatest margin in slalom was 11.3sec by Cristel Cranz (GER) in the 1936 combination event, when that in the men's equivalent was 5.9sec by Franz Pfnür (GER). Since

then Toni Sailer (AUT) won by 4.0sec in 1956 and Anne Heggtveit (CAN) the 1960 women's race by 3.3sec. The smallest margin was 0.02sec in the 1972 women's event, with a 0.09sec margin in the 1968 men's race.

In the giant slalom the biggest margin was 6.2sec by Sailer in 1956, while that for women was 2.64sec by Nancy Greene (CAN) in 1968. The smallest margin was 0.1sec (before electronic timing) by Yvonne Rüegg (SUI) in 1960, and 0.12sec by Kathy Kreiner (CAN) in 1976. The smallest for men was 0.20sec by Heini Hemmi (SUI) in 1976.

Alpine Skiing (Men)

	Gold	*Silver*	*Bronze*

Slalom
1948	Edi Reinalter (SUI) 2:10.3	James Couttet (FRA) 2:10.8	Henri Oreiller (FRA) 2:12.8
1952	Othmar Schneider (AUT) 2:00.0	Stein Eriksen (NOR) 2:01.2	Guttorm Berge (NOR) 2:01.7
1956	Anton Sailer (AUT) 3:14.7	Chiharu Igaya (JPN) 3:18.7	Stig Sollander (SWE) 3:20.2
1960	Ernst Hinterseer (AUT) 2:08.9	Matthias Leitner (AUT) 2:10.3	Charles Bozon (FRA) 2:10.4
1964	Josef Stiegler (AUT) 2:21.13	William Kidd (USA) 2:21.27	James Huega (USA) 2:21.52
1968	Jean-Claude Killy (FRA) 1:39.73	Herbert Huber (AUT) 1:39.82	Alfred Matt (AUT) 1:40.09
1972	Francisco Fernandez Ochoa (ESP) 1:49.27	Gustavo Thoeni (ITA) 1:50.28	Rolando Thoeni (ITA) 1:50.30
1976	Piero Gros (ITA) 2:03.29	Gustavo Thoeni (ITA) 2:03.73	Willy Frommelt (LIE) 2:04.28
1980	Ingemar Stenmark (SWE) 1:44.26	Phil Mahre (USA) 1:44.76	Jacques Lüthy (SUI) 1:45.06
1984	Phil Mahre (USA) 1:39.21	Steve Mahre (USA) 1:39.62	Didier Bouvet (FRA) 1:40.20

1908–1936 Event not held.

Giant Slalom
1952	Stein Eriksen (NOR) 2:25.0	Christian Pravda (AUT) 2:26.9	Toni Spiss (AUT) 2:28.8
1956	Anton Sailer (AUT) 3:00.1	Andreas Molterer (AUT) 3:06.3	Walter Schuster (AUT) 3:07.2
1960	Roger Staub (SUI) 1:48.3	Josef Stiegler (AUT) 1:48.7	Ernst Hinterseer (AUT) 1:49.1
1964	Francois Bonlieu (FRA) 1:46.71	Karl Schranz (AUT) 1:47.09	Josef Stiegler (AUT) 1:48.05
1968	Jean-Claude Killy (FRA) 3:29.28	Willy Favre (SUI) 3:31.50	Heinrich Messner (AUT) 3:31.83
1972	Gustavo Thoeni (ITA) 3:09.62	Edmund Bruggmann (SUI) 3:10.75	Werner Mattle (SUI) 3:10.99
1976	Heini Hemmi (SUI) 3:26.97	Ernst Good (SUI) 3:27.17	Ingemar Stenmark (SWE) 3:27.41
1980	Ingemar Stenmark (SWE) 2:40.74	Andreas Wenzel (LIE) 2:41.49	Hans Enn (AUT) 2:42.51
1984	Max Julen (SUI) 2:41.18	Juriy Franko (YUG) 2:41.41	Andreas Wenzel (LIE) 2:41.75

1908–1948 Event not held.

Downhill
1948	Henri Oreiller (FRA) 2:55.0	Franz Gabl (AUT) 2:59.1	Karl Molitor (SUI) 3:00.3 Rolf Olinger (SUI) 3:00.3
1952	Zeno Colo (ITA) 2:30.8	Othmar Schneider (AUT) 2:32.0	Christian Pravda (AUT) 2:32.4
1956	Anton Sailer (AUT) 2:52.2	Raymond Fellay (SUI) 2:55.7	Andreas Molterer (AUT) 2:56.2
1960	Jean Vuarnet (FRA) 2:06.0	Hans-Peter Lanig (GER) 2:06.5	Guy Perillat (FRA) 2:06.9
1964	Egon Zimmermann (AUT) 2:18.16	Leo Lacroix (FRA) 2:18.90	Wolfgang Bartels (GER) 2:19.48
1968	Jean-Claude Killy (FRA) 1:59.85	Guy Périllat (FRA) 1:59.93	Jean-Daniel Dätwyler (SUI) 2:00.32
1972	Bernhard Russi (SUI) 1:51.43	Roland Collombin (SUI) 1:52.07	Heinrich Messner (AUT) 1:52.40
1976	Franz Klammer (AUT) 1:45.73	Bernhard Russi (SUI) 1:46.06	Herbert Plank (ITA) 1:46.59
1980	Leonhard Stock (AUT) 1:45.50	Peter Wirnsberger (AUT) 1:46.12	Steve Podborski (CAN) 1:46.62
1984	Bill Johnson (USA) 1:45.59	Peter Mueller (SUI) 1:45.86	Anton Steiner (AUT) 1:45.95

1908–1936 Event not held.

Alpine Combination (Downhill and Slalom)
1936	Franz Pfnür (GER) 99.25pts	Gustav Lantschner (GER) 96.26pts	Emile Allais (FRA) 94.69pts
1948	Henri Oreiller (FRA) 3.27pts	Karl Molitor (SUI) 6.44pts	James Couttet (FRA) 6.95pts

1952–1984 Event not held.

Alpine Skiing (Women)

	Gold	*Silver*	*Bronze*

Slalom
1948	Gretchen Fraser (USA) 1:57.2	Antoinette Meyer (SUI) 1:57.7	Erika Mahringer (AUT) 1:58.0
1952	Andrea Mead-Lawrence (USA) 2:10.6	Ossi Reichert (GER) 2:11.4	Annemarie Buchner (GER) 2:13.3
1956	Renée Colliard (SUI) 1:52.3	Regina Schöpf (AUT) 1:55.4	Jevginija Sidorova (URS) 1:56.7
1960	Anne Heggtveit (CAN) 1:49.6	Betsy Snite (USA) 1:52.9	Barbi Henneberger (GER) 1:56.6

Gold	*Silver*	*Bronze*
1964 Christine Goitschel (FRA) 1:29.86	Marielle Goitschel (FRA) 1:30.77	Jean Saubert (USA) 1:31.36
1968 Marielle Goitschel (FRA) 1:25.86	Nancy Greene (CAN) 1:26.15	Annie Famose (FRA) 1:27.89
1972 Barbara Cochran (USA) 1:31.24	Danielle Debernard (FRA) 1:31.26	Florence Steurer (FRA) 1:32.69
1976 Rosi Mittermaier (FRG) 1:30.54	Claudia Giordani (ITA) 1:30.87	Hanni Wenzel (LIE) 1:32.20
1980 Hanni Wenzel (LIE) 1:25.09	Christa Kinshofer (FRG) 1:26.50	Erika Hess (SUI) 1:27.89
1984 Paoletta Magoni (ITA) 1:36.47	Perrine Pelen (FRA) 1:37.38	Ursula Konsett (LIE) 1:37.50

1908–1936 Event not held.

Giant Slalom

1952 Andrea Mead-Lawrence (USA) 2:06.8	Dagmar Rom (AUT) 2:09.0	Annemarie Buchner (GER) 2:10.0
1956 Ossi Reichert (GER) 1:56.5	Josefine Frandl (AUT) 1:57.8	Dorothea Hochleitner (AUT) 1:58.2
1960 Yvonne Rüegg (SUI) 1:39.9	Penelope Pitou (USA) 1:40.0	Giuliana Chenal-Minuzzo (ITA) 1:40.2
1964 Marielle Goitschel (FRA) 1:52.24	Christine Goitschel (FRA) 1:53.11	Jean Saubert (USA) 1:53.11
1968 Nancy Greene (CAN) 1:51.97	Annie Famose (FRA) 1:54.61	Fernande Bochatay (SUI) 1:54.74
1972 Marie-Therèse Nadig (SUI) 1:29.90	Annemarie Pröll (AUT) 1:30.75	Wiltrud Drexel (AUT) 1:32.35
1976 Kathy Kreiner (CAN) 1:29.13	Rosi Mittermaier (FRG) 1:29.25	Danielle Debernard (FRA) 1:29.95
1980 Hanni Wenzel (LIE) 2:41.66	Irene Epple (FRG) 2:42.12	Perrine Pelen (FRA) 2:42.41
1984 Debbie Armstrong (USA) 2:20.98	Christin Cooper (USA) 2:21.38	Perrine Pelen (FRA) 2:21.40

1908–1948 Event not held.

Downhill

1948 Hedy Schlunegger (SUI) 2:28.3	Trude Beiser (AUT) 2:29.1	Resi Hammerer (AUT) 2:30.2
1952 Trude Jochum-Beiser (AUT) 1:47.1	Annemarie Buchner (GER) 1:48.0	Giuliana Minuzzo (ITA) 1:49.0
1956 Madeleine Berthod (SUI) 1:40.7	Frieda Dänzer (SUI) 1:45.4	Lucile Wheeler (CAN) 1:45.9
1960 Heidi Biebl (GER) 1:37.6	Penelope Pitou (USA) 1:38.6	Traudl Hecher (AUT) 1:38.9
1964 Christl Haas (AUT) 1:55.39	Edith Zimmerman (AUT) 1:56.42	Traudl Hecher (AUT) 1:56.66
1968 Olga Pall (AUT) 1:40.87	Isabelle Mir (FRA) 1:41.33	Christl Haas (AUT) 1:41.41
1972 Marie-Therèse Nadig (SUI) 1:36.68	Annemarie Pröll (AUT) 1:37.00	Susan Corrock (USA) 1:37.68
1976 Rosi Mittermaier (FRG) 1:46.16	Brigitte Totschnig (AUT) 1:46.68	Cindy Nelson (USA) 1:47.50
1980 Annemarie Moser-Pröll (AUT) 1:37.52	Hanni Wenzel (LIE) 1:38.22	Marie-Therèse Nadig (SUI) 1:38.36
1984 Michela Figini (SUI) 1:13.36	Maria Walliser (SUI) 1:13.41	Olga Chartova (TCH) 1:13.53

1908–1936 Event not held.

Alpine Combination (Downhill and Slalom)

1936 Christel Cranz (GER) 97.06pts	Käthe Grasegger (GER) 95.26pts	Laila Schou Nilsen (NOR) 93.48pts
1948 Trude Beiser (AUT) 6.58pts	Gretchen Fraser (USA) 6.95pts	Erika Mahringer (AUT) 7.04pts

1952–1984 Event not held.

Alpine Skiing – Medals

	Men			Women			
	G	S	B	G	S	B	Total
Austria	9	9	11	5	8	8	50
Switzerland	5	8	5	7	3	3	31
France	7	3	6	3	6	5	30
United States	2	3	1	5	5	4	20
Germany (FRG)	1	2	1	5	6	3	18
Italy	3	2	2	1	1	2	11
Liechtenstein	–	1	2	2	1	2	8
Canada	–	–	1	3	1	1	6
Sweden	2	–	2	–	–	–	4
Norway	1	1	1	–	–	1	4
Spain	1	–	–	–	–	–	1
Japan	–	1	–	–	–	–	1
Yugoslavia	–	1	–	–	–	–	1
Czechoslovakia	–	–	–	–	–	1	1
Soviet Union	–	–	–	–	–	1	1
	31	31	32	31	31	31	187

BOBSLEDDING

A bob competition for 4-man sleds was first held in 1924. The rules allowed 4- or 5-men teams in 1924 and 1928. The 2-man event was introduced in 1932. Both competitions have been held ever since except for 1960 when the Squaw Valley Organizing Committee refused to build a run.

In 1952 a situation arose which led to changes in the rules governing the overall weight of teams and bobs. The Germans combined their heaviest men from their two vehicles into one 4-man sled averaging over 118kg per man, and won easily. Resulting complaints led to rules stipulating that the maximum weight of the bobs, with crews, must not exceed 375kg (2-man) and 630kg (4-man), but that extra weights may be added within those limits.

The most gold medals won by an individual is three by Bernhard Germeshausen (GDR) and Meinhard Nehmer (GDR) both in the 1976 and 1980 4-man events and the 1976 2-man competition. The most medals won is six (two golds, two silvers, two bronzes) by Eugenio Monti (ITA) from 1956 to 1968.

The oldest gold medallist was Giacomo Conti (ITA) in the 2-man in 1956 aged 47yr 218 days, which also makes him the oldest gold medallist in Winter Games history. The youngest champion was William Fiske (USA) who piloted the winning 5-man bob in 1928 aged 16yr 260 days, which makes him the youngest male Winter Games gold medallist ever. He also had the distinction of being the first American to join the RAF in the Second World War – he was killed in the Battle of Britain. Conti was also the oldest medallist, while the youngest was Thomas Doe Jr (USA) aged 15yr 127 days in Fiske's bob, making him the youngest Winter Games male medallist ever. The tallest gold medallist was Edy Hubacher (SUI) in the 1972 4-man bob at 2.01m *6ft 7in*. He had competed in the 1968 Summer Games shot event.

The first brothers to win gold medals were Alfred and Heinrich Schläppi (SUI) in the 4-man bob of 1924, while the inaugural 2-man event of 1932 was won by Hubert and Curtis Stevens (USA).

The closest finish in Olympic bobsledding occurred in the 2-man of 1968 when Italy I and FRG I had identical aggregate times after the four runs. The title went to Italy, driven by the 40-year-old Monti, as they had the fastest single run.

Bobsledding

	Gold	Silver	Bronze		Gold	Silver	Bronze
2-Man Bob				**4-Man Bob**			
1932	United States I 8:14.14	Switzerland II 8:16.28	United States II 8:29.15	1924	Switzerland I 5:45.54	Great Britain II 4:48.83	Belgium I 6:02.29
1936	United States I 5:29.29	Switzerland II 5:30.64	United States II 5:33.96	1928[1]	United States II 3:20.5	United States I 3:21.0	Germany II 3:21.9
1948	Switzerland II 5:29.2	Switzerland I 5:30.4	United States II 5:35.3	1932	United States I 7:53.68	United States I 7:55.70	Germany I 8:00.04
1952	Germany I 5:24.54	United States I 5:26.89	Switzerland I 5:27.71	1936	Switzerland II 5:19.85	Switzerland I 5:22.73	Great Britain I 5:23.41
1956	Italy I 5:30.14	Italy II 5:31.45	Switzerland I 5:37.46	1948	United States II 5:20.1	Belgium 5:21.3	United States I 5:21.5
1964	Great Britain I 4:21.90	Italy II 4:22.02	Italy I 4:22.63	1952	Germany 5:07.84	United States I 5:10.48	Switzerland I 5:11.70
1968	Italy I 4:41.54	FRG I 4:41.54	Romania I 4:44.46	1956	Switzerland I 5:10.44	Italy II 5:12.10	United States I 5:12.39
1972	FRG II 4:47.07	FRG I 4:58.84	Switzerland I 4:59.33	1964	Canada I 4:14.46	Austria I 4:15.48	Italy II 4:15.60
1976	GDR II 3:44.42	FRG I 3:44.99	Switzerland I 3:45.70	1968[2]	Italy I 2:17.39	Austria I 2:17.48	Switzerland I 2:18.04
1980	Switzerland II 4:09.36	GDR II 4:10.93	GDR I 4:11.08	1972	Switzerland I 4:43.07	Italy I 4:43.83	FRG I 4:43.92
1984	GDR II 3:28.56	GDR I 3:26.04	Soviet Union II 3:26.16	1976	GDR I 3:40.43	Switzerland II 3:40.89	FRG I 3:41.37
				1980	GDR I 3:59.92	Switzerland I 4:00.87	GDR II 4:00.97
				1984	GDR I 3:20.22	GDR II 3:20.78	Switzerland I 3:21.39

1908–1928, 1960 Event not held.

The winning US 4-man bob in 1932 with the only summer and winter Games gold medallist, Eddie Eagan, in second position. (Dave Terry)

[1]Five-man team in 1928; aggregate of two runs. [2]Aggregate of two runs. 1908–1920, 1960 Event not held.

Bobsledding – Medals

	G	S	B	Total
Switzerland	6	6	7	19
United States	5	4	5	14
GDR	5	3	2	10
Germany (FRG)	3	3	4	10
Italy	3	4	2	9
Great Britain	1	1	1	3
Austria	–	2	–	2
Belgium	–	1	1	2
Canada	1	–	–	1
Romania	–	–	1	1
Soviet Union	–	–	1	1
	24	24	24	72

FIGURE SKATING

The first Olympic title at a Winter Games event was won by Ulrich Salchow (SWE) in 1908 at the Prince's Rink, London. Salchow gave his name to one of the most popular jumps. In those 1908 Games there was also a special figures event which was won by a Russian (Czarist variety), Nikolai Panin, who had been too ill to compete in the main event. The first women's title went to Madge Syers (GBR), who six years previously had entered the World championships, ostensibly for men only, and had placed second to Salchow.

The most gold medals won by a figure skater is three by Gillis Grafström (SWE) 1920–1928, Sonja Henie (NOR) 1928–1936, and Irina Rodnina (URS) in the pairs 1972–1980. Of these only Grafström also won a silver, in 1932, and thus is the only skater to win medals in four Games. No skater has doubled completely successfully in singles and pairs at the Games. The best have been Ernst Baier (GER) with a pairs gold and a singles silver in 1936, and Madge Syers (GBR) with a singles gold and pairs bronze in 1908. The oldest gold medallist was Walter Jakobsson (FIN) who won the pairs with his German-born wife Ludowika aged 38yr 80 days. Ludowika was the oldest ever female winner aged 35yr 276 days. The youngest was Maxi Herber (GER) aged 15yr 128 days in the 1936 pairs with Baier, whom she later married. The youngest male champion was Richard Button (USA) aged 18yr 202 days winning the 1948 singles. Sonja Henie (NOR) was remarkably 50 days short of her 16th birthday when she

Anna Hübler and Heinrich Burger (Germany), winners of the first Olympic Pairs Skating in 1908.

won her first title in 1928, after some last minute coaching by Britain's Alex Adams. She had been eighth and last in 1924 when still under 12 years of age. However, the youngest ever Winter Games competitor was her rival of 1936, who had been 11yr 73 days at the 1932 Games. The youngest medallist was Scott Allen (USA) 2 days short of his 15th birthday taking the 1964 singles bronze, while the youngest female medallist was Marina Tcherkasova (URS) just three days past her 15th birthday in the 1980 silver-winning pair. The oldest medallist was Martin Stixrud (NOR) with the 1920 singles bronze aged 44yr 78 days.

Sonja Henie won three Olympic, six European and ten World titles before turning professional and making an estimated $47 million in ice shows and films. She is usually credited with introducing jumps into the women's event, but in 1920 Theresa Weld (USA), the bronze medallist, included a salchow in her programme which brought a reprimand from the judges and a threat that she would be penalized if she continued with such 'unfeminine behaviour'.

A change of marking in the sport was brought about by Trixie Schuba (AUT) winning the 1972 title primarily on the basis of her excellent set figures (she was only placed seventh in free skating). At that time the marks had been divided 50-50 between the two sections, but they were changed to give greater emphasis to free skating.

On the subject of marks, Jayne Torvill and Christopher Dean (GBR) were awarded a maximum nine sixes for their artistic impression in the 1984 ice dancing

event, as well as another three sixes for technical merit – unsurpassed marking at the Games.

In 1972, although Irina Rodnina and Aleksey Ulanov (URS) won the pairs it was the latter's dalliance with Ludmila Smirnova, silver medallist with Andrei Suraikin, which caught the interest. The result was a break-up of the top

Soviet pair. Rodnina then teamed with Aleksandr Zaitsev, while Ulanov and Smirnova got married. In the World championships the Rodnina/Zaitsev partnership beat the other pair and, getting married themselves in 1975, they went on to win two Olympic titles, the second less than a year after the birth of a son.

Figure Skating

	Gold	Silver	Bronze

Figure Skating (Men)

	Gold	Silver	Bronze
1908[1]	Nikolai Panin (URS) 219pts	Arthur Cumming (GBR) 164	George Hall-Say (GBR) 104
1908	Ulrich Salchow (SWE) 1886.5pts	Richard Johansson (SWE) 1826.0	Per Thorén (SWE) 1787.0
1920	Gillis Gräfström (SWE) 2838.5pts	Andreas Krogh (NOR) 2634	Martin Stixrud (NOR) 2561.5
1924	Gillis Gräfström (SWE) 2575.25pts	Willy Böckl (AUT) 2518.75	Georges Gautschi (SUI) 2233.5
1928	Gillis Gräfström (SWE) 2698.25pts	Willy Böckl (AUT) 2682.50	Robert v. Zeebroeck (BEL) 2578.75
1932	Karl Schäfer (AUT) 2602.0pts	Gillis Gräfström (SWE) 2514.5	Montgomery Wilson (CAN) 2448.3
1936	Karl Schäfer (AUT) 2959.0pts	Ernst Baier (GER) 2805.3	Felix Kaspar (AUT) 2801.0
1948	Richard Button (USA) 1720.6pts	Hans Gerschwiler (SUI) 1630.1	Edi Rada (AUT) 1603.2
1952	Richard Button (USA) 1730.3pts	Helmut Seibt (AUT) 1621.3	James Grogan (USA) 1627.4
1956	Hayes Alan Jenkins (USA) 1497.95pts	Ronald Robertson (USA) 1492.15	David Jenkins (USA) 1465.41
1960	David Jenkins (USA) 1440.2pts	Karol Divin (TCH) 1414.3	Donald Jackson (CAN) 1401.0
1964	Manfred Schnelldorfer (GER) 1916.9pts	Alain Calmat (FRA) 1876.5	Scott Allen (USA) 1873.6
1968	Wolfgang Schwarz (AUT) 1894.1pts	Tim Woods (USA) 1891.6	Patrick Péra (FRA) 1864.5
1972	Ondrej Nepela (TCH) 2739.1pts	Sergey Tchetveroukhin (URS) 2672.4	Patrick Péra (FRA) 2653.1
1976	John Curry (GBR) 192.74pts	Vladimir Kovalev (URS) 187.64	Toller Cranston (CAN) 187.38
1980	Robin Cousins (GBR) 189.48pts	Jan Hoffmann (GDR) 189.72	Charles Tickner (USA) 187.06
1984	Scott Hamiliton (USA) 3.4pl	Brian Oser (CAN) 5.6	Jozef Sabovtchik (TCH) 7.4

[1]Special Figures competition. 1912 Event not held.

Figure Skating (Women)

	Gold	Silver	Bronze
1908	Madge Syers (GBR) 1262.5pts	Elsa Rendschmidt (GER) 1055.0	Dorothy Greenhough-Smith (GBR) 960.5
1920	Magda Julin-Mauroy (SWE) 913.5pts	Svea Norén (SWE) 887.75	Theresa Weld (USA) 898.0
1924	Herma Planck-Szabo (AUT) 2094.25pts	Beatrix Loughran (USA) 1959.0	Ethel Muckelt (GBR) 1750.50
1928	Sonja Henie (NOR) 2452.25pts	Fritzi Burger (AUT) 2248.50	Beatrix Loughran (USA) 2254.50
1932	Sonja Henie (NOR) 2302.5pts	Fritzi Burger (AUT) 2167.1	Maribel Vinson (USA) 2158.5
1936	Sonja Henie (NOR) 2971.4pts	Cecilia Colledge (GBR) 2926.8	Vivi-Anne Hultén (SWE) 2763.2
1948	Barbara Scott (USA) 1467.7pts	Eva Pawlik (AUT) 1418.3	Jeanette Altwegg (GBR) 1405.5
1952	Jeanette Altwegg (GBR) 1455.8pts	Tenley Albright (USA) 1432.2	Jacqueline du Bief (FRA) 1422.0
1956	Tenley Albright (USA) 1866.39pts	Carol Heiss (USA) 1848.24	Ingrid Wendl (AUT) 1753.91
1960	Carol Heiss (USA) 1490.1pts	Sjoukje Dijkstra (HOL) 1424.8	Barbara Roles (USA) 1414.8
1964	Sjoukje Dijkstra (HOL) 2018.5pts	Regine Heitzer (AUT) 1945.5	Petra Burka (CAN) 1940.0
1968	Peggy Fleming (USA) 1970.5pts	Gabrielle Seyfert (GDR) 1882.3	Hana Maskova (TCH) 1828.8
1972	Beatrix Schuba (AUT) 2751.5pts	Karen Magnussen (CAN) 2673.2	Janet Lynn (USA) 2663.1
1976	Dorothy Hamill (USA) 193.80pts	Dianne De Leeuw (HOL) 190.24	Christine Errath (GDR) 188.16
1980	Anett Pötzsch (GDR) 189.00pts	Linda Fratianne (USA) 188.30	Dagmar Lurz (FRG) 183.04
1984	Katarina Witt (GDR) 3.2pl	Rosalyn Sumners (USA) 4.6	Kira Ivanova (URS) 9.2

1912 Event not held.

	Gold	Silver	Bronze

Pairs

	Gold	Silver	Bronze
1908	Germany 56.0pts	Great Britain 51.5	Great Britain 48.0
1920	Finland 80.75pts	Norway 72.75	Great Britain 66.25
1924	Austria 74.50pts	Finland 71.75	France 69.25
1928	France 100.50pts	Austria 99.25	Austria 93.25
1932	France 76.7pts	United States 77.5	Hungary 76.4
1936	Germany 103.3pts	Austria 102.7	Hungary 97.6
1948	Belgium 123.5pts	Hungary 122.2	Canada 121.0
1952	Germany 102.6pts	United States 100.6	Hungary 97.4
1956	Austria 101.8pts	Canada 101.9	Hungary 99.3
1960	Canada 80.4pts	Germany 76.8	United States 76.2
1964[1]	Soviet Union 104.4pts	Canada 98.5	United States 98.2
1968	Soviet Union 315.2pts	Soviet Union 312.3	FRG 304.4
1972	Soviet Union 420.4pts	Soviet Union 419.4	GDR 411.8
1976	Soviet Union 140.54pts	GDR 136.35	GDR 134.57
1980	Soviet Union 147.26pts	Soviet Union 143.80	GDR 140.52
1984	Soviet Union 1.4pl	United States 2.8	Soviet Union 3.8

[1]Marika Kilius and Hansjürgen Bäumler (GER) finished second but were subsequently disqualified. 1912 Event not held.

Ice Dance

	Gold	Silver	Bronze
1976	Soviet Union 209.92pts	Soviet Union 204.88	United States 202.64
1980	Soviet Union 205.48pts	Hungary 204.52	Soviet Union 201.86
1984	Great Britain 2.0pl	Soviet Union 4.0	Soviet Union 7.0

1908–1972 Event not held.

Figure Skating – Medals

	G	S	B	Total
United States	9	10	12	31
Soviet Union	9	7	4	20
Austria	7	9	4	20
Great Britain	5	3	6	14
Canada	2	4	5	11
Sweden	5	3	2	10
Germany (FRG)	4	3	2	9
GDR	2	3	4	9
France	2	1	4	7
Norway	3	2	1	6
Hungary	–	2	4	6
Czechoslovakia	1	1	2	4
Netherlands	1	2	–	3
Finland	1	1	–	2
Belgium	1	–	1	2
Switzerland	–	1	1	2
	52	52	52	156

ICE HOCKEY

The game was introduced in 1920 as part of the Summer Games. The tournament was won by Canada, the first of a run of six victories only interrupted by Great Britain in 1936. The Canadians were always represented by a club side, not a national one, so that the first Olympic champions were actually the Winnipeg Falcons. Since 1948 the tournament has been decided on a championship format and not, as previously, on a knock-out basis – thus there is no Olympic final as such. The game has been the centre of much bitter argument about amateur/professional status, and in 1972 Canada withdrew in protest against alleged 'professionalism' of the Eastern European teams in particular. Happily they returned in 1980. In 1948 there was a strange situation when two teams turned up to represent the United States, one from the Amateur Hockey Association (AHA) and the other picked by the US Olympic Committee. The AHA, while not affiliated to the USOC, was a member of the International Hockey Federation (IHF), the governing body of most of the other teams present in St Moritz. The IHF threatened to withdraw all the other teams if the AHA did not play, while the USOC threatened to withdraw the whole American Olympic team if the AHA did play. Initially the IOC barred both teams, but then agreed to allow the AHA team to compete. They eventually finished fourth, but a year later were disqualified for non-affiliation to the Olympic movement. Strangely the USOC hockey team members marched in the opening ceremony.

Five Soviet players have won a record three gold medals, but only goalminder Vladislaw Tretyak, 1972–1984, also won a silver. Richard 'Bibi' Torriani (SUI) won a bronze in 1928 and another in 1948, for a record 20 year span. The oldest gold medallist was George Abel (CAN) in 1952 on the day after his 36th birthday. The youngest was Mike Ramsey (USA) in 1980 aged 19yr 83 days, while the youngest medallist was Richard Torriani (SUI) at 16yr 141 days in 1928. The

oldest medallist was Erich Romer (GER) in 1932 aged 37yr 256 days. The first brothers to win gold were Herbert, Hugh and Roger Plaxton along with Frank and Joseph Sullivan in the 1928 Canadian team. The only twins were Boris and Yevgeniy Maiorov (URS) in 1964. The highest score and aggregate in Olympic ice hockey was the 33-0 victory by Canada over Switzerland in 1924. In that tournament the Canadians totalled 110 goals in five matches with only three against.

When the Czechs won the 1948 silver medal a member of the team was 1954 Wimbledon tennis champion Jaroslav Drobny.

Ice Hockey

	Gold	Silver	Bronze
1920	Canada	United States	Czechoslovakia
1924	Canada	United States	Great Britain
1928	Canada	Sweden	Switzerland
1932	Canada	United States	Germany
1936	Great Britain	Canada	United States
1948	Canada	Czechoslovakia	Switzerland
1952	Canada	United States	Sweden
1956	Soviet Union	United States	Canada
1960	United States	Canada	Soviet Union
1964	Soviet Union	Sweden	Czechoslovakia
1968	Soviet Union	Czechoslovakia	Canada
1972	Soviet Union	United States	Czechoslovakia
1976	Soviet Union	Czechoslovakia	FRG[1]
1980	United States	Soviet Union	Sweden
1984	Soviet Union	Czechoslovakia	Sweden

[1]Three-way tie for bronze with the United States and Finland decided on goal average.

Ice Hockey – Medals

	G	S	B	Total
Canada	6	2	2	10
United States	2	6	1	9
Soviet Union	6	1	1	8
Czechoslovakia	–	4	3	7
Sweden	–	2	3	5
Great Britain	1	–	1	2
Germany (FRG)	–	–	2	2
Switzerland	–	–	2	2
	15	15	15	45

NORDIC SKIING

Cross-Country Skiing
This was the first form of skiing in the Olympics. The most successful competitor was Sixten Jernberg (SWE) with four gold, three silver and two bronze medals, for a record total of nine medals from 1956 to 1964. The best by a woman was four gold, two silver and two bronze medals, a record total of eight, by Galina Kulakova (URS) from 1968 to 1980. Only Jernberg has won individual titles in three successive

Games. Marja-Liisa Hämäläinen (FIN) won a record three individual gold medals at one Games in 1984.

The oldest gold medallist was Veikko Hakulinen (FIN) aged 35yr 52 days in the 1960 relay, and the youngest was Gunde Swan (SWE) who won the 15km race in 1984 aged 22yr 32 days. The oldest male medallist was Olaf Ökern (NOR) in the 1948 relay aged 36yr 235 days, and the youngest male medallist was Ivar Formo (NOR) in the 1972 relay aged 20yr 234 days. The oldest female gold medallist was Galina Kulakova (URS) in the 1976 relay aged 33yr 289 days, and the youngest was Carola Anding (GDR) aged 19yr 54 days in the 1980 relay.

Kulakova was also the oldest medallist, male or female, aged 37yr 298 days in the 1980 relay, and the youngest female medallist was Marjo Matikainen (FIN) in the 1984 relay aged 19yr 12 days.

Nordic Combination
The event was the 'blue riband' of Nordic skiing in the early Games. The all-round title, comprising a cross-country race and a jump, was won three successive times by Ulrich Wehling (GDR) 1972–1980. The oldest medallist was Simon Slattvik (NOR) who won the title in 1952 aged 34yr 209 days, and the youngest was Wehling in 1972 aged 19yr 212 days.

Biathlon
The combination of skiing and shooting was introduced in 1960. Aleksandr Tikhonov (URS) set a Winter Games record by winning a gold medal in the relay on four successive occasions 1968–1980. The oldest gold medallist was Magnar Solberg (NOR) uniquely

defending his title in 1972 aged 35yr 5 days. The youngest gold medallist was Yuriy Kachkarov (URS) in the 1984 relay aged 20yr 75 days, while Frank Peter Roetsch (GDR) won a silver in the 20km event in 1984 aged only 19yr 298 days.

Ski Jumping

Introduced in 1924 the most successful jumper has been Birger Ruud (NOR) with two golds and a silver medal from 1932 to 1948, and the only man to win twice. He also came fourth in the Alpine Combination event of 1936, winning the downhill segment. His brother Sigmund won a silver in 1928, while a third brother, Asbjorn, was seventh in 1948. The longest jump achieved in Olympic competition was 117m by gold medallist Juoko Törmänen (FIN) and by unplaced Hansjoers Sumi (SUI) in 1980 on the 90m hill.

The oldest gold medallist was Yukio Kasaya (JPN) aged 28yr 173 days in 1972, while the youngest was Wojciech Fortuna (POL) also in 1972 aged 19yr 189 days. The oldest medallist was Birger Ruud in 1948 aged 36yr 168 days, and the youngest Toni Innauer (AUT) in 1976 aged 17yr 320 days. Sepp Bradl (AUT) – the first man ever to jump over 100m – competed over a period of 20 years, 1936–1956, but never won a medal.

Nordic Skiing (Men)

Gold	Silver	Bronze

15 000 Metres

1924[1] Thorleif Haug (NOR) 1h 14:31.0	Johan Gröttumsbraaten (NOR) 1h 15:51.0	Tipani Niku (FIN) 1h 26:26.0
1928[2] Johan Gröttumsbraaten (NOR) 1h 37:01.0	Ole Hegge (NOR) 1h 39:01.0	Reidar Ödegaard (NOR) 1h 40:11.0
1932[3] Sven Utterström (SWE) 1h 23:07.0	Axel Wikström (SWE) 1h 25:07.0	Veli Saarinen (FIN) 1h 25:24.0
1936[1] Erik-August Larsson (SWE) 1h 14:38.0	Oddbjörn Hagen (NOR) 1h 15:33.0	Pekka Niemi (FIN) 1h 16:59.0
1948[1] Martin Lundström (SWE) 1h 13:50.0	Nils Östensson (SWE) 1h 14:22.0	Gunnar Eriksson (SWE) 1h 16:06.6
1952[1] Hallgeir Brenden (NOR) 1h 1:34.0	Tapio Mäkelä (FIN) 1h 2:09.0	Paavo Lonkila (FIN) 1h 2:20.0
1956 Hallgeir Brenden (NOR) 49:39.0	Sixten Jernberg (SWE) 50:14.0	Pavel Koltschin (URS) 50:17.0
1960 Haakon Brusveen (NOR) 51:55.5	Sixten Jernberg (SWE) 51:58.6	Veikko Hakulinen (FIN) 52:03.0
1964 Eero Mäntyranta (FIN) 50:54.1	Harald Grönningen (NOR) 51:34.8	Sixten Jernberg (SWE) 51:42.2
1968 Harald Grönningen (NOR) 47:54.2	Eero Mäntyranta (FIN) 47:56.1	Gunnar Larsson (SWE) 48:33.7
1972 Sven-Ake Lundback (SWE) 45:28.24	Fedor Simaschov (URS) 46:00.84	Ivar Formo (NOR) 46:02.86
1976 Nikolai Bajukov (URS) 43:58.47	Yevgenly Beliayev (URS) 44:01.10	Arto Koivisto (FIN) 44:19.25
1980 Thomas Wassberg (SWE) 41:57.63	Juha Mieto (FIN) 41:57.64	Ove Aunli (NOR) 42:28.62
1984 Gunde Swan (SWE) 41:25.6	Aki Karvonen (FIN) 41:34.9	Harri Kirvesniemi (FIN) 41:45.6

[1]The distance was 18km. [2]The distance was 19.7km. [3]The distance was 18.2km. 1908–1920 Event not held.

30 000 Metres

1956 Veikko Hakulinen (FIN) 1h 44:06.0	Sixten Jernberg (SWE) 1h 44:30.0	Pavel Koltschin (URS) 1h 45:45.0
1960 Sixten Jernberg (SWE) 1h 51:03.9	Rolf Rämgård (SWE) 1h 51:16.9	Nikolai Anikin (URS) 1h 52:28.2
1964 Eero Mäntyranta (FIN) 1h 30:50.7	Harald Grönningen (NOR) 1h 32:02.3	Igor Voronchikin (URS) 1h 32:15.8
1968 Franco Nones (ITA) 1h 35:39.2	Odd Martinsen (NOR) 1h 36:28.9	Eero Mäntyranta (FIN) 1h 36:55.3
1972 Vyacheslav Vedenine (URS) 1h 36:31.2	Paal Tyldum (NOR) 1h 37:25.3	Johs Harviken (NOR) 1h 37:32.4
1976 Sergey Savelyev (URS) 1h 30:29.38	William Koch (USA) 1h 30:57.84	Ivan Garanin (URS) 1h 31:09.29
1980 Nikolai Simyatov (URS) 1h 27:02.80	Vasiliy Rochev (URS) 1h 27:34.22	Ivan Lebanov (URS) 1h 28:03.87
1984 Nikolai Simyatov (URS) 1h 28:56.3	Alexandre Zavialov (URS) 1h 29:23.3	Gunde Swan (SWE) 1h 29:35.7

1908–1952 Event not held.

50 000 Metres

1924 Thorleif Haug (NOR) 3h 44:32.0	Thoralf Strömstad (NOR) 3h 46:23.0	Johan Gröttumsbraaten (NOR) 3h 47:46.0
1928 Per Erik Hedlund (SWE) 4h 52:03.0	Gustaf Jonsson (SWE) 5h 05:30.0	Volger Andersson (SWE) 5h 05:46.0
1932 Veli Saarinen (FIN) 4h 28:00.0	Väinö Likkanen (FIN) 4h 28:20.0	Arne Rustadstuen (NOR) 4h 31:53.0
1936 Elis Wiklund (SWE) 3h 30:11.0	Axel Wikström (SWE) 3h 33:20.0	Nils-Joel Englund (SWE) 3h 34:10.0
1948 Nils Karlsson (SWE) 3h 47:48.0	Harald Eriksson (SWE) 3h 52:20.0	Benjamin Vanninen (FIN) 3h 57:28.0
1952 Veikko Hakulinen (FIN) 3h 33:33.0	Eero Kolehmainen (FIN) 3h 38:11.0	Magnar Estenstad (NOR) 3h 38:28.0
1956 Sixten Jernberg (SWE) 2h 50:27.0	Veikko Hakulinen (FIN) 2h 51:45.0	Fedor Terentyev (URS) 2h 53:32.0
1960 Kalevi Hämäläinen (FIN) 2h 59:06.3	Veikko Hakulinen (FIN) 2h 59:26.7	Rolf Rämgård (SWE) 3h 02:46.7
1964 Sixten Jernberg (SWE) 2h 43:52.6	Assar Rönnlund (SWE) 2h 44:58.2	Arto Tiainen (FIN) 2h 45:30.4
1968 Olle Ellefsaeter (NOR) 2h 28:45.8	Vyacheslav Vedenine (URS) 2h 29:02.5	Josef Haas (SUI) 2h 29:14.8
1972 Paal Tyldrum (NOR) 2h 43:14.75	Magne Myrmo (NOR) 2h 43:29.45	Vyacheslav Vedenine (URS) 2h 44:00.19
1976 Ivar Formo (NOR) 2h 37:30.50	Gert-Dietmar Klause (GDR) 2h 38:13.21	Benny Södergren (SWE) 2h 39:39.21
1980 Nikolai Simyatov (URS) 2h 27:24.60	Juha Mieto (FIN) 2h 30:20.52	Aleksandr Savyalov (URS) 2h 30:51.52
1984 Thomas Wassberg (SWE) 2h 15:55.8	Gunde Swan (SWE) 2h 16:00.7	Aki Karvonen (FIN) 2h 17:04.7

1908–1920 Event not held.

4 × 10 000 Metres Relay

1936 Finland 2h 41:33.0	Norway 2h 41:39.0	Sweden 2h 43:03.0
1948 Sweden 2h 32:08.0	Finland 2h 41:06.0	Norway 2h 44:33.0
1952 Finland 2h 20:16.0	Norway 2h 23:13.0	Sweden 2h 24:13.0
1956 Soviet Union 2h 15:30.0	Finland 2h 16:31.0	Sweden 2h 17:42.0
1960 Finland 2h 18:45.6	Norway 2h 18:46.4	Soviet Union 2h 21:21.6
1964 Sweden 2h 18:34.6	Finland 2h 18:42.4	Soviet Union 2h 18:46.9
1968 Norway 2h 08:33.5	Sweden 2h 10:13.2	Finland 2h 10:56.7
1972 Soviet Union 2h 04:47.94	Norway 2h 04:57.6	Switzerland 2h 07:00.06
1976 Finland 2h 07:59.72	Norway 2h 09:58.36	Soviet Union 2h 10:51.46
1980 Soviet Union 1h 57:03.6	Norway 1h 58:45.77	Finland 2h 00:00.18
1984 Sweden 1h 55:06.3	Soviet Union 1h 55:16.5	Finland 1h 56:31.4

1908–1932 Event not held.

Oddbjörn Hagen (NOR) won the Nordic Combined event in 1936. (GSL)

Nordic Skiing (Women)

	Gold	Silver	Bronze

5000 Metres

	Gold	Silver	Bronze
1964	Klaudia Boyarskikh (URS) 17:50.5	Mirja Lehtonen (FIN) 17:52.9	Alevtina Koltschina (URS) 18:08.4
1968	Toini Gustafsson (SWE) 16:45.2	Galina Kulakova (URS) 16:48.4	Alevtina Koltschina (URS) 16:51.6
1972	Galina Kulakova (URS) 17:00.50	Marjatta Kajosmaa (FIN) 17:05.50	Helena Sikolova (TCH) 17:07.32
1976	Helena Takalo (FIN) 15:48.69	Raisa Smetanina (URS) 15:49.73	Nina Baldycheva[1] (URS) 16:12.82
1980	Raisa Smetanina (URS) 15:06.92	Hilkka Riihivuori (FIN) 15:11.96	Kvetoslava Jeriova (TCH) 15:23.44
1984	Marja-Liisa Hämäläinen (FIN) 17:04.0	Berit Aunli (NOR) 17:14.1	Kvetoslava Jeriova (TCH) 17:18.3

[1]Galina Kulakova (URS) finished third but was disqualified.   1908–1960 Event not held.

10 000 Metres

	Gold	Silver	Bronze
1952	Lydia Wideman (FIN) 41:40.0	Mirja Hietamies (FIN) 42:39.0	Siiri Rantanen (FIN) 42:50.0
1956	Lubov Kozyryeva (URS) 38:11.0	Radya Yeroschina (URS) 38:16.0	Sonja Edström (SWE) 38:23.0
1960	Maria Gusakova (URS) 39:46.6	Lubov Baranova-Kozyryeva (URS) 40:04.2	Radya Yeroschina (URS) 40:06.0
1964	Klaudia Boyarskikh (URS) 40:24.3	Yevdokia Mekshilo (URS) 40:26.6	Maria Gusakova (URS) 40:46.6
1968	Toini Gustafsson (SWE) 36:46.5	Berit Mördre (NOR) 37:54.6	Inger Aufles (NOR) 37:59.9
1972	Galina Kulakova (URS) 34:17.8	Alevtina Olunina (URS) 34:54.1	Marjatta Kajosmaa (FIN) 34:56.5
1976	Raisa Smetanina (URS) 30:13.41	Helena Takalo (FIN) 30:14.28	Galina Kulakova (URS) 30:38.61
1980	Barbara Petzold (GDR) 30:31.54	Hilkka Riihivuori (FIN) 30:35.05	Helena Takalo (FIN) 30:45.25
1984	Marja-Liisa Hämäläinen (FIN) 31:44.2	Raisa Smetanina (URS) 32:02.9	Brit Pettersen (NOR) 32:12.7

1908–1948 Event not held.

20 000 Metres

	Gold	Silver	Bronze
1984	Marja-Liisa Hämäläinen (FIN) 1h 01:45.0	Raisa Smetanina (URS) 1h 02:26.7	Anne Jahren (NOR) 1h 03:13.6

1908–1980 Event not held.

4[1] × 5000 Metres Relay

	Gold	Silver	Bronze
1956	Finland 1h 09:01.0	Soviet Union 1h 09:28.0	Sweden 1h 09:48.0
1960	Sweden 1h 04:21.4	Soviet Union 1h 05:02.6	Finland 1h 06:27.5
1964	Soviet Union 59:20.2	Sweden 1h 01:27.0	Finland 1h 02:45.1
1968	Norway 57:30.0	Sweden 57:51.0	Soviet Union 58:13.6
1972	Soviet Union 48:46.15	Finland 49:19.37	Norway 49:51.49
1976	Soviet Union 1h 07:49.75	Finland 1h 08:36.57	GDR 1h 09:57.95
1980	GDR 1h 02:11.10	Soviet Union 1h 03:18.30	Norway 1h 04:13.50
1984	Norway 1h 06:49.7	Czechoslovakia 1h 07:34.7	Finland 1h 07:36.7

[1]Over three stages prior to 1976.   1908–1952 Event not held.

Biathlon

	Gold	Silver	Bronze

10 000 Metres

	Gold	Silver	Bronze
1980	Frank Ullrich (GDR) 32:10.69	Vladimir Alikin (URS) 32:53.10	Anatoliy Alyabiev (URS) 33:09.16
1984	Eirik Kvalfoss (NOR) 30:53.8	Peter Angerer (FRG) 31:02.4	Matthias Jacob (GDR) 31:10.5

1908–1976 Event not held.

20 000 Metres

	Gold	Silver	Bronze
1960	Klas Lestander (SWE) 1h 33:21.6	Antti Tyrväinen (FIN) 1h 33:57.7	Aleksandr Privalov (URS) 1h 34:54.2
1964	Vladimir Melyanin (URS) 1h 20:26.8	Aleksandr Privalov (URS) 1h 23:42.5	Olav Jordet (NOR) 1h 24:38.8
1968	Magnar Solberg (NOR) 1h 13:45.9	Aleksandr Tikhonov (URS) 1h 14:40.4	Vladimir Gundartsev (URS) 1h 18:27.4
1972	Magnar Solberg (NOR) 1h 15:55.5	Hans-Jürg Knauthe (GDR) 1h 16:07.6	Lars Arvidsson (SWE) 1h 16:27.03
1976	Nikolai Kruglov (URS) 1h 14:12.26	Heikki Ikola (FIN) 1h 15:54.10	Aleksandr Elizarov (URS) 1h 16:05.57
1980	Anatoliy Alyabiev (URS) 1h 08:16.31	Frank Ullrich (GDR) 1h 08:27.79	Eberhard Rösch (GDR) 1h 11:11.73
1984	Peter Angerer (FRG) 1h 11:52.7	Frank-Peter Roetsch (GDR) 1h 13:21.4	Eirik Kvalfoss (NOR) 1h 14:02.4

1908–1956 Event not held.

Biathlon Relay (4 × 7500 Metres)

	Gold	Silver	Bronze
1968	Soviet Union 2h 13:02.4	Norway 2h 14:50.2	Sweden 2h 17:26.3
1972	Soviet Union 1h 51:44.92	Finland 1h 54:37.22	GDR 1h 54:57.67
1976	Soviet Union 1h 57:55.64	Finland 2h 01:45.58	GDR 2h 04:08.61
1980	Soviet Union 1h 34:03.27	GDR 1h 34:56.99	FRG 1h 37:30.26
1984	Soviet Union 1h 38:51.7	Norway 1h 39:03.9	FRG 1h 39:05.1

1908–1964 Event not held.

Nordic Combined (15 000 Metres[1] and Jumping)

	Gold	Silver	Bronze
1924[2]	Thorleif Haug (NOR)	Thoralf Strömstad (NOR)	Johan Gröttumsbraaten (NOR)
1928[2]	Johan Gröttumsbraaten (NOR)	Hans Vinjarengen (NOR)	John Snersrud (NOR)
1932	Johan Gröttumsbraaten (NOR) 446.0pts	Ole Stenen (NOR) 436.05	Hans Vinjarengen (NOR) 434.60
1936	Oddbjörn Hagen (NOR) 430.30pts	Olaf Hoffsbakken (NOR) 419.80	Sverre Brodahl (NOR) 408.10
1948	Heikki Hasu (FIN) 448.80pts	Martti Huhtala (FIN) 433.65	Sven Israelsson (SWE) 433.40
1952	Simon Slåttvik (NOR) 451.621pts	Heikki Hasu (FIN) 447.50	Sverre Stenersen (NOR) 436.335
1956	Sverre Stenersen (NOR) 455.0pts	Bengt Eriksson (SWE) 437.4	Franciszek Gron-Gasienica (POL) 436.8
1960	Georg Thoma (GER) 457.952pts	Tormod Knutsen (NOR) 453.000	Nikolai Gusakow (URS) 452.000
1964	Tormod Knutsen (NOR) 469.28pts	Nikolai Kiselyev (URS) 453.04	Georg Thoma (GER) 452.88
1968	Frantz Keller (FRG) 449.04pts	Alois Kälin (SUI) 447.94	Andreas Kunz (GDR) 444.10
1972	Ulrich Wehling (GDR) 413.34pts	Rauno Miettinen (FIN) 405.55	Karl-Heinz Luck (GDR) 398.80
1976	Ulrich Wehling (GDR) 423.39pts	Urban Hettich (FRG) 418.90	Konrad Winkler (GDR) 417.47

	Gold	Silver	Bronze
1980	Ulrich Wehling (GDR) 432.20pts	Jouko Karjalainen (FIN) 429.50	Konrad Winkler (GDR) 425.32
1984	Tom Sandberg (NOR) 422.595pts	Jouko Karjalainen (FIN) 416.900	Jukka Ylipulli (FIN) 410.825

[1]From 1924–1952 distance was 18km. [2]In 1924 and 1928, the scoring was decided upon a different basis from that used from 1932 onwards.   1908–1920 Event not held.

Ski Jumping

	Gold	Silver	Bronze

70 Metre Hill

	Gold	Silver	Bronze
1924[1]	Jacob Tullin Thams (NOR) 18 960pts	Narve Bonna (NOR) 18 689	Anders Haugen 17 916
1928	Alf Andersen (NOR) 19 208pts	Sigmund Ruud (NOR) 18 542	Rudolf Burkert (TCH) 17 937
1932	Birger Ruud (NOR) 228.1pts	Hans Beck (NOR) 227.0	Kaare Wahlberg (NOR) 219.5
1936	Birger Ruud (NOR) 232.0pts	Sven Eriksson (SWE) 230.5	Reidar Andersen (NOR) 228.9
1948	Petter Hugsted (NOR) 228.1pts	Birger Ruud (NOR) 226.6	Thorleif Schjeldrup (NOR) 225.1
1952	Arnfinn Bergmann (NOR) 226.0pts	Torbjörn Falkanger (NOR) 221.5	Karl Holmström (SWE) 219.5
1956	Antti Hyvärinen (FIN) 227.0pts	Aulis Kallakorpi (FIN) 225.0	Harry Glass (GER) 224.5
1960	Helmut Recknagel (GER) 227.2pts	Niilo Halonen (FIN) 222.6	Otto Leodolter (AUT) 219.4
1964	Veikko Kankkonen (FIN) 229.9pts	Toralf Engan (NOR) 226.3	Torgeir Brandtzaeg (NOR) 222.9
1968	Jiri Raska (TCH) 216.5pts	Reinhold Bachler (AUT) 214.2	Baldur Preiml (AUT) 212.6
1972	Yukio Kasaya (JPN) 244.2pts	Akitsugu Konno (JPN) 234.8	Seiji Aochi (JPN) 229.5
1976	Hans-Georg Aschenbach (GDR) 252.0pts	Jochen Danneberg (GDR) 246.2	Karl Schnabl (AUT) 242.0
1980	Toni Innauer (AUT) 266.3pts	Manfred Deckert (GDR) 249.2 Hirokazu Yagi (JPN) 249.2	–
1984	Jens Weissflog (GDR) 215.2pts	Matti Nykaenen (FIN) 214.0	Jari Puikkonen (FIN) 212.8

[1]Originally Thorleif Haug (NOR) placed third due to incorrect calculations at time. Error discovered and corrected in 1974.   1908–1920 Event not held.

90 Metre Hill

	Gold	Silver	Bronze
1964	Toralf Engan (NOR) 230.7pts	Véikko Kankkonen (FIN) 228.9	Torgeir Brandtzaeg (NOR) 227.2
1968	Vladimir Belousov (URS) 231.3pts	Jiri Raska (TCH) 229.4	Lars Grini (NOR) 214.3
1972	Wojciech Fortuna (POL) 219.9pts	Walter Steiner (SUI) 219.8	Rainer Schmidt (GDR) 219.3
1976	Karl Schnabl (AUT) 234.8pts	Toni Innauer (AUT) 232.9	Henry Glass (GDR) 221.7
1980	Jouko Törmänen (FIN) 271.0pts	Hubert Neuper (AUT) 262.4	Jari Puikkonen (FIN) 248.5
1984	Matti Nykaenen (FIN) 232.2pts	Jens Weissflog (GDR) 213.7	Pavel Ploc (TCH) 202.9

1908–1960 Event not held.

Nordic Skiing – Medals
(Including Nordic Combination, Biathlon and Ski Jumping)

	Men			Women			
	G	S	B	G	S	B	Total
Norway	29	28	21	2	2	5	87
Finland	15	25	17	6	8	6	77
Soviet Union	18	10	17	11	11	7	74
Sweden	17	14	15	3	2	2	53
GDR	6	8	10	2	–	1	27
Germany (FRG)	4	2	4	–	–	–	10
Austria	2	3	3	–	–	–	8
Czechoslovakia	1	1	2	–	1	3	8
Japan	1	2	1	–	–	–	4
Switzerland	–	2	2	–	–	–	4
Poland	1	–	1	–	–	–	2
United States	–	1	1	–	–	–	2
Italy	1	–	–	–	–	–	1
	95	96	94	24	24	24	357

SPEED SKATING

The sport was introduced into the Olympics in 1924, with the first official events for women in 1960. There have been two major controversies over the years. In 1928 the 10km event was cancelled by the Norwegian referee due to bad weather. That caused much ill-feeling in the American camp because at the time Irving Jaffee (USA) was the surprise leader and as all the best skaters had competed the medal positions seemed assured. Despite vigorous protests by all nationalities no medals were awarded. The other occasion was in 1932 when the American 'mass start' system was used, for the only time in Olympic competition. This undoubtedly gave the Americans and Canadians a tremendous advantage as the Europeans were completely unfamiliar with the tactics involved – only two medals were won by European skaters.

Lydia Skoblikova (URS) won a record six gold medals in 1960 and 1964, which is also a record for any sport in the Winter Games for either a male or female competitor. The most by a man is five by Clas Thunberg (FIN) in 1924 and 1928, and by Eric Heiden (USA) with all five in 1980. There have only been five events for men since 1976. The most medals won is seven by Thunberg, who added a silver and a bronze to his golds, and by Ivar Ballangrud (NOR) who won four golds, two silvers and a bronze from 1928 to 1936. Skoblikova won her four golds on four successive days.

The oldest gold medallist was Thunberg aged 35yr 315 days in the

1928 1500m. The youngest winner was Anne Henning (USA) in the 500m in 1952 aged 16yr 157 days. The youngest male champion was Igor Malkov (URS) winning the 10km in 1984 aged 19yr 9 days, while the oldest woman was Chistina Baas-Kaiser (HOL) who won the 3000m title in 1972 aged 33yr 268 days.

Frank Stack (CAN) competed over a 20 year period from 1932 to 1952 winning a bronze in 1932, and Cornelius 'Kees' Broekman (HOL) competed at four Games from 1948 to 1960, winning two silvers, and starting in thirteen events in all.

Of the many speed skaters who have found a happy affinity with cycle racing, the most successful has been Sheila Young (USA) who won the 500m title in 1976 and the world amateur sprint cycle championship later that year.

Speed Skating (Men)

	Gold	Silver	Bronze
500 Metres			
1924	Charles Jewtraw (USA) 44.0	Oskar Olsen (NOR) 44.2	Roald Larsen (NOR) 44.8
			Clas Thunberg (FIN) 44.8
1928	Clas Thunberg (FIN) 43.4	–	John Farrell (USA) 43.6
	Bernt Evensen (NOR) 43.4		Roald Larsen (NOR) 43.6
			Jaako Friman (FIN) 43.6
1932	John Shea (USA) 43.4	Bernt Evensen (NOR) 5m	Alexander Hurd (CAN) 8m
1936	Ivar Ballangrud (NOR) 43.4	Georg Krog (NOR) 43.5	Leo Freisinger (USA) 44.0
1948	Finn Helgesen (NOR) 43.1	Kenneth Bartholomew (USA) 43.2	–
		Thomas Byberg (NOR) 43.2	
		Robert Fitzgerald (USA) 43.2	
1952	Kenneth Henry (USA) 43.2	Donald McDermott (USA) 43.9	Arne Johansen (NOR) 44.0
			Gordon Audley (CAN) 44.0
1956	Yevgeniy Grischin (URS) 40.2	Rafael Gratsch (URS) 40.8	Alv Gjestvang (NOR) 41.0
1960	Yevgeniy Grischin (URS) 40.2	William Disney (USA) 40.3	Rafael Gratsch (URS) 40.4
1964	Richard McDermott (USA) 40.1	Yevgeniy Grischin (URS) 40.6	–
		Vladimir Orlov (URS) 40.6	
		Alv Gjestvang (NOR) 40.6	
1968	Erhard Keller (FRG) 40.3	Richard McDermott (USA) 40.5	–
		Magne Thomassen (NOR) 40.5	
1972	Erhard Keller (FRG) 39.44	Hasse Borjes (SWE) 39.69	Valeriy Muratov (URS) 39.80
1976	Yevgeniy Kulikov (URS) 39.17	Valeriy Muratov (URS) 39.25	Daniel Immerfall (USA) 39.54
1980	Eric Heiden (USA) 38.03*	Yevgeniy Kulikov (URS) 38.37	Lieuwe de Boer (HOL) 38.48
1984	Sergey Fokitchev (URS) 38.19	Yoshihiro Kitazawa (JPN) 38.30	Gaetan Boucher (CAN) 38.39

*Olympic record. 1908–1920 Event not held.

1000 Metres			
1976	Peter Mueller (USA) 1:19.32	Jorn Didriksen (NOR) 1:20.45	Valeriy Muratov (URS) 1:20.57
1980	Eric Heiden (USA) 1:15.18*	Gaetan Boucher (CAN) 1:16.68	Frode Rönning (NOR) 1:16.91
			Vladimir Lobanov (URS) 1:16.91
1984	Gaetan Boucher (CAN) 1:15.80	Sergey Khlebnikov (URS) 1:16.63	Kai Arne Engelstad (NOR) 1:16.75

*Olympic record. 1908–1972 Event not held.

1500 Metres			
1924	Clas Thunberg (FIN) 2:20.8	Roald Larsen (NOR) 2:22.0	Sigurd Moen (NOR) 2:25.6
1928	Clas Thunberg (FIN) 2:21.1	Bernt Evensen (NOR) 2:21.9	Ivar Ballangrud (NOR) 2:22.6
1932	John Shea (USA) 2:57.5	Alexander Hurd (CAN) 5m	William Logan (CAN) 6m
1936	Charles Mathiesen (NOR) 2:19.2	Ivar Ballangrud (NOR) 2:20.2	Birger Wasenius (FIN) 2:20.9
1948	Sverre Farstad (NOR) 2:17.6	Ake Seyffarth (SWE) 2:18.1	Odd Lundberg (NOR) 2:18.9
1952	Hjalmar Andersen (NOR) 2:20.4	Willem van der Voort (HOL) 2:20.6	Roald Aas (NOR) 2:21.6
1956	Yevgeniy Grischin (URS) 2:08.6	–	Toivo Salonen (FIN) 2:09.4
	Yuriy Michailov (URS) 2:08.6		
1960	Roald Aas (NOR) 2:10.4	–	Boris Stenin (URS) 2:11.5
	Yevgeniy Grischin (URS) 2:10.4		
1964	Ants Antson (URS) 2:10.3	Cornelis Verkerk (HOL) 2:10.6	Villy Haugen (NOR) 2:11.25
1968	Cornelis Verkerk (HOL) 2:03.4	Ard Schenk (HOL) 2:05.0	–
		Ivar Eriksen (NOR) 2:05.0	
1972	Ard Schenk (HOL) 2:02.96	Roar Gronvold (NOR) 2:04.26	Goran Clässon (SWE) 2:05.89
1976	Jan Egil Storholt (NOR) 1:59.38	Yuriy Kondakov (URS) 1:59.97	Hans Van Helden (HOL) 2:00.87
1980	Eric Heiden (USA) 1:55.44*	Kai Stenshjemmet (NOR) 1:56.81	Jerje Andersen (NOR) 1:56.92
1984	Gaetan Boucher (CAN) 1:58.36	Sergey Khlebnikov (URS) 1:58.83	Oleg Bogiev (URS) 1:58.89

*Olympic record. 1908–1920 Event not held.

5000 Metres			
1924	Clas Thunberg (FIN) 8:39.0	Julius Skutnabb (FIN) 8:48.4	Roald Larsen (NOR) 8:50.2
1928	Ivar Ballangrud (NOR) 8:50.5	Julius Skutnabb (FIN) 8:59.1	Bernt Evensen (NOR) 9:01.1
1932	Irving Jaffee (USA) 9:40.8	Edward Murphy (USA) 2m	William Logan (CAN) 4m
1936	Ivar Ballangrud (NOR) 8:19.6	Birger Wasenius (FIN) 8:23.3	Antero Ojala (FIN) 8:30.1
1948	Reidar Liaklev (NOR) 8:29.4	Odd Lundberg (NOR) 8:32.7	Göthe Hedlund (SWE) 8:34.8
1952	Hjalmar Andersen (NOR) 8:10.6	Kees Broekman (HOL) 8:21.6	Sverre Haugli (NOR) 8:22.4
1956	Boris Schilkov (URS) 7:48.7	Sigvard Ericsson (SWE) 7:56.7	Oleg Gontscharenko (URS) 7:57.5
1960	Yiktor Kositschkin (URS) 7:51.3	Knut Johannesen (NOR) 8:00.8	Jan Pesman (HOL) 8:05.1
1964	Knut Johannesen (NOR) 7:38.4	Per Moe (NOR) 7:38.6	Anton Maier (NOR) 7:42.0
1968	Anton Maier (NOR) 7:22.4	Cornelis Verkerk (HOL) 7:23.2	Petrus Nottet (HOL) 7:25.5
1972	Ard Schenk (HOL) 7:23.6	Roar Gronvold (NOR) 7:28.18	Sten Stensen (NOR) 7:33.39
1976	Sten Stensen (NOR) 7:24.48	Piet Kleine (HOL) 7:26.47	Hans Van Helden (HOL) 7:26.54
1980	Eric Heiden (USA) 7:02.29*	Kai Stenshjemmet (NOR) 7:03.28	Tom Oxholm (NOR) 7:05.59
1984	Tomas Gustafson (SWE) 7:12.28	Igor Malkov (URS) 7:12.30	Rene Schoefisch (GDR) 7:17.49

*Olympic record. 1908–1920 Event not held.

A most unusual sight – Irving Jaffee (USA) winning the 'mass start' 5000m in 1932. (Dave Terry)

10 000 Metres

1924	Julius Skutnabb (FIN) 18:04.8	Clas Thunberg (FIN) 18:97.8	Roald Larsen (NOR) 18:12.2
1932	Irving Jaffee (USA) 19:13.6	Ivar Ballangrud (NOR) 5m	Frank Stack (CAN) 6m
1936	Ivar Ballangrud (NOR) 17:24.3	Birger Wasenius (FIN) 17:28.2	Max Stiepl (AUT) 17:30.0
1948	Ake Seyffarth (SWE) 17:26.3	Lauri Parkkinen (FIN) 17:36.0	Pentti Lammio (FIN) 17:42.7
1952	Hjalmar Andersen (NOR) 16:45.8	Kees Broekman (HOL) 17:10.6	Carl-Erik Asplund (SWE) 17:16.6
1956	Sigvard Ericsson (SWE) 16:35.9	Knut Johannesen (NOR) 16:36.9	Oleg Gontscharenko (URS) 16:42.3
1960	Knut Johannesen (NOR) 15:46.6	Viktor Kositschkin (URS) 15:49.2	Kjell Bäckman (SWE) 16:14.2
1964	Jonny Nilsson (SWE) 15:50.1	Anton Maier (NOR) 16:06.0	Knut Johannesen (NOR) 16:06.3
1968	Johnny Höglin (SWE) 15:23.6	Anton Maier (NOR) 15:23.9	Örjan Sandler (SWE) 15:31.8
1972	Ard Schenk (HOL) 15:01.35	Cornelis Verkerk (HOL) 15:04.70	Sten Stensen (NOR) 15:07.08
1976	Piet Kleine (HOL) 14:50.59	Sten Stensen (NOR) 14:53.30	Hans Van Helden (HOL) 15:02.02
1980	Eric Heiden (USA) 14:28.13*	Piet Kleine (HOL) 14:36.03	Tom Oxholm (NOR) 14:36.60
1984	Igor Malkov (URS) 14:39.90	Tomas Gustafson (SWE) 14:39.95	Rene Schoefisch (GDR) 14:46.91

*Olympic record.   1908–1920 Event not held. 1928 Event abandoned.

Discontinued Event

All-Round Championship

(Aggregate of placings in 500m, 1500m, 5km and 10km)

1924	Clas Thunberg (FIN) 5.5pts	Roald Larsen (NOR) 9.5pts	Julius Skutnabb (FIN) 11pts

Speed Skating (Women)

	Gold	*Silver*	*Bronze*

500 Metres

1960	Helga Haase (GER) 45.9	Natalya Dontschenko (URS) 46.0	Jeanne Ashworth (USA) 46.1
1964	Lydia Skoblikova (URS) 45.0	Irina Yegorova (URS) 45.4	Tatyana Sidorova (URS) 45.5
1968	Ludmila Titova (URS) 46.1	Mary Meyers (USA) 46.3 Dianne Holum (USA) 46.3 Jennifer Fish (USA) 46.3	–
1972	Anne Henning (USA) 43.33	Vera Krasnova (URS) 44.01	Ludmila Titova (URS) 44.45
1976	Sheila Young (USA) 42.76	Catherine Priestner (CAN) 43.12	Tatyana Averina (URS) 43.17
1980	Karin Enke (GDR) 41.78	Leah Poulos-Mueller (USA) 42.26	Natalya Petruseva (URS) 42.42
1984	Christa Rothenburger (GDR) 41.02*	Karin Enke (GDR) 41.28	Natalya Chive (URS) 41.50

*Olympic record.

1000 Metres

1960	Klara Guseva (URS) 1:34.1	Helga Haase (GER) 1:34.3	Tamara Rylova (URS) 1:34.8
1964	Lydia Skoblikova (URS) 1:33.2	Irina Yegorova (URS) 1:34.3	Kaija Mustonen (FIN) 1:34.8
1968	Carolina Geijssen (HOL) 1:32.6	Ludmila Titova (URS) 1:32.9	Dianne Holum (USA) 1:33.4
1972	Monika Pflug (FRG) 1:31.40	Atje Keulen-Deelstra (HOL) 1:31.61	Anne Henning (USA) 1:31.62
1976	Tatyana Averina (URS) 1:28.43	Leah Poulos (USA) 1:28.57	Sheila Young (USA) 1:29.14
1980	Natalya Petruseva (URS) 1:24.10	Leah Poulos-Mueller (USA) 1:25.41	Sylvia Albrecht (GDR) 1:26.46
1984	Karin Enke (GDR) 1:21.61*	Andrea Schoene (GDR) 1:22.83	Natalya Petruseva (URS) 1:23.21

*Olympic record.

1500 Metres

1960	Lydia Skoblikova (URS) 2:25.2	Elvira Seroczynska (POL) 2:25.7	Helena Pilejevk (POL) 2:27.1
1964	Lydia Skoblikova (URS) 2:22.6	Kaija Mustonen (FIN) 2:25.5	Berta Kolokoltseva (URS) 2:27.1

	Gold	Silver	Bronze
1968	Kaija Mustonen (FIN) 2:22.4	Carolina Geijssen (HOL) 2:22.7	Christina Kaiser (HOL) 2:24.5
1972	Dianne Holum (USA) 2:20.85	Christina Baas-Kaiser (HOL) 2:21.05	Atje Keulen-Deelstra (HOL) 2:22.05
1976	Galina Stepanskaya (URS) 2:16.58	Sheila Young (USA) 2:17.06	Tatyana Averina (URS) 2:17.96
1980	Annie Borckink (HOL) 2:10.95	Ria Visser (HOL) 2:12.35	Sabine Becker (GDR) 2:12.38
1984	Karin Enke (GDR) 2:03.42*	Andrea Schoene (GDR) 2:05.29	Natalya Petruseva (URS) 2:05.78

*Olympic record.

3000 Metres

	Gold	Silver	Bronze
1960	Lydia Skoblikova (URS) 5:14.3	Valentina Stenina (URS) 5:16.9	Eevi Huttunen (FIN) 5:21.0
1964	Lydia Skoblikova (URS) 5:14.9	Valentina Stenina (URS) 5:18.5 Pil-Hwa Han (PRK) 5:18.5	–
1968	Johanna Schut (HOL) 4:56.2	Kaija Mustonen (FIN) 5:01.0	Christina Kaiser (HOL) 5:01.3
1972	Christina Baas-Kaiser (HOL) 4:52.14	Dianne Holum (USA) 4:58.67	Atje Keulen-Deelstra (HOL) 4:59.91
1976	Tatyana Averina (URS) 4:45.19	Andrea Mitscherlich (GDR) 4:45.23	Lisbeth Korsmo (NOR) 4:45.24
1980	Björg Eva Jensen (NOR) 4:32.13	Sabine Becker (GDR) 4:32.79	Beth Heiden (USA) 4:33.77
1984	Andrea Schoene (GDR) 4:24.79*	Karin Enke (GDR) 4:26.33	Gabi Schoenbrunn (GDR) 4:33.13

*Olympic record.

Speed Skating – Medals

	Men			Women			
	G	S	B	G	S	B	Total
Norway	18	24	22	1	–	1	66
Soviet Union	11	10	8	12	7	10	58
United States	13	6	3	3	8	5	38
Netherlands	5	9	6	4	4	4	32
Finland	6	6	7	1	2	2	24
GDR	–	–	2	5	6	3	16
Sweden	5	4	5	–	–	–	14
Canada	2	2	6	–	1	–	11
Germany (FRG)	2	–	–	2	1	–	5
Poland	–	–	–	–	1	1	2
Japan	–	1	–	–	–	–	1
North Korea (PRK)	–	–	–	–	1	–	1
Austria	–	–	1	–	–	–	1
	62	62	60	28	31	26	269

TOBOGGANING–LUGEING

In 1928 and 1948 there were one-man skeleton sled races held on the famous Cresta Run at St Moritz. In those events the contestants laid face down. Luge racing, in which contestants sit up or lie back, was introduced in 1964.

The most successful luger was Thomas Köhler (GDR) with two gold medals and a silver in 1964 and 1968. Hans Rinn (GDR) won the 2-man event twice (with Norbert Hahn) and a bronze in the singles.

The most successful woman was Margit Schumann (GDR) with a gold in 1976 added to her 1972 bronze. The oldest gold medallist was Paul Hildgartner (ITA) aged 31yr 249 days in the 1984 singles, while the youngest was Manfred Stengl (AUT) in the 2-man in 1964 aged 17yr 310 days. The youngest female winner was Ortrun Enderlein (GER) aged 20yr 65 days in 1964, and the oldest was Vera Sosulya (URS) in 1980 aged 24yr 35 days.

Probably the heaviest winner of a luge title was Hans Stangassinger (FRG) in the 2-man of 1984 at a weight of 111kg *244lb*.

The Heaton brothers (USA) deserve mention for their exploits on the skeleton sleds as well as on bobs. Jennison won the 1928 skeleton event and a silver in the 5-man bob that year. Brother John was second in the 1928 skeleton, won a bronze in the 1932 2-man bob and then returned in 1948, in his 40th year, to win another skeleton silver.

In 1968 a scandal shook the Games when the first, second and fourth placed women from the GDR were all disqualified for illegally heating the runners of their sleds. The leading girl, Ortrun Enderlein, would have been the only female luger to retain her title.

Lugeing

	Gold	Silver	Bronze

Singles (Men)

	Gold	Silver	Bronze
1964	Thomas Köhler (GER) 3:26.77	Klaus Bonsack (GER) 3:27.04	Hans Plenk (GER) 3:30.15
1968	Manfred Schmid (AUT) 2:52.48	Thomas Köhler (GDR) 2:52.66	Klaus Bonsack (GDR) 2:55.33
1972	Wolfgang Scheidel (GDR) 3:27.58	Harald Ehrig (GDR) 3:28.39	Wolfram Fiedler (GDR) 3:28.73
1976	Detlef Günther (GDR) 3:27.688	Josef Fendt (FRG) 3:28.196	Hans Rinn (GDR) 3:28.574
1980	Bernhard Glass (GDR) 2:54.796	Paul Hildgartner (ITA) 2:55.372	Anton Winkler (FRG) 2:56.545
1984	Paul Hildgartner (ITA) 3:04.258	Sergey Danilin (URS) 3:04.962	Valeriy Dudin (URS) 3:05.012

1908–1960 Event not held.

2-Man

	Gold	Silver	Bronze
1964	Austria 1:41.62	Austria 1:41.91	Italy 1:42.87
1968	GDR 1:35.85	Austria 1:36.34	FRG 1:37.29
1972	Italy 1:28.35 GDR 1:28.35	–	GDR 1:29.16
1976	GDR 1:25.604	FRG 1:25.889	Austria 1:25.919
1980	GDR 1:19.331	Italy 1:19.606	Austria 1:19.795
1984	FRG 1:23.620	Soviet Union 1:23.660	GDR 1:23.887

1908–1960 Event not held.

Gold	Silver	Bronze

Singles (Women)

	Gold	Silver	Bronze
1964	Ortrun Enderlein (GER) 3:24.67	Ilse Geisler (GER) 3:27.42	Helene Thurrier (AUT) 3:29.06
1968	Erica Lechner (ITA) 2:28.66	Christa Schmuck (FRG) 2:29.37	Angelika Dünhaupt (FRG) 2:29.56
1972	Anna-Maria Müller (GDR) 2:59.18	Ute Rührold (GDR) 2:59.49	Margit Schumann (GDR) 2:59.54
1976	Margit Schumann (GDR) 2:50.621	Ute Rührold (GDR) 2:50.846	Elisabeth Demleitner (FRG) 2:51.056
1980	Vera Sosulya (URS) 2:36.537	Melitta Sollmann (GDR) 2:37.657	Ingrida Amantova (URS) 2:37.817
1984	Steffi Martin (GDR) 2:46.570	Bettine Schmidt (GDR) 2:46.873	Ute Weiss (GDR) 2:47.248

1908–1960 Event not held.

Discontinued Event

Tobogganing – Skeleton Sled

	Gold	Silver	Bronze
1928[1]	Jennison Heaton (USA) 3:01.8	John Heaton (USA) 3:02.8	Earl of Northesk (GBR) 3:05.1
1948[2]	Nino Bibbia (ITA) 5:23.2	John Heaton (USA) 5:24.6	John Crammond (GBR) 5:25.1

[1]Aggregate of three runs.   [2]Aggregate of six runs.

Lugeing (and Skeleton Sled) – Medals

	G	S	B	Total
GDR	10	6	7	23
Germany (FRG)	3	5	5	13
Italy	4	2	1	7
Austria	2	2	3	7
Soviet Union	1	2	2	5
United States	1	2	–	3
Great Britain	–	–	2	2
	21	19	20	60

DOUBLES ACROSS SPORT

There has been a number of multi-talented sports people who have won Olympic medals in different sports. The only one to win gold medals in both Summer and Winter Games was Eddie Eagan (USA) who won the 1920 light-heavyweight boxing title, and was a member of the 1932 winning 4-man bob.

In the Summer Games the earliest double gold winner at two sports was Carl Schumann (GER), with three gymnastic events and the wrestling in 1896.

Morris Kirksey (USA) won gold medals in the 4 × 100m relay and as a member of the American Rugby team in 1920. Examples of women excelling in two Olympic sports are rare, with the most outstanding probably being Roswitha Krause (GDR) who won a 1968 silver in the 4 × 100m freestyle relay, and then won silver and bronze medals in the 1976 and 1980 handball tournaments.

One of the more unusual doubles was that of Fernand de Montigny (BEL) in 1920, who won a gold, two silver and two bronze medals in fencing and another bronze on the hockey field.

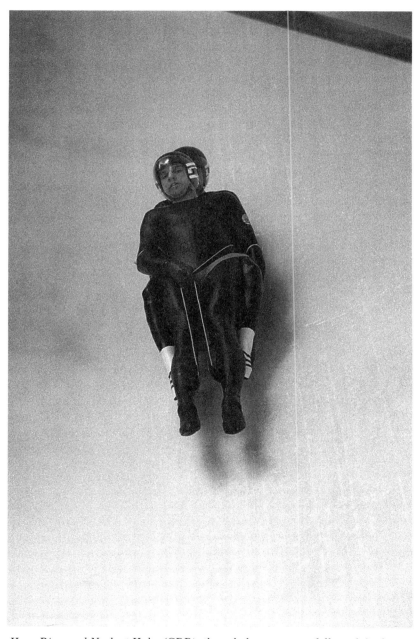

Hans Rinn and Norbert Hahn (GDR), the only lugers successfully to defend an Olympic title. (All-Sport)

Track and Field Conversion Tables

1.55 metres =	5ft 1in	7.50	24ft 7¼in	13.50	44ft 3½in	54.00	177ft 2in
1.60	5ft 3in	7.75	25ft 5¼in	14.00	45ft 11¼in	56.00	183ft 9in
1.65	5ft 5in	8.00	26ft 3in	14.50	47ft 7in	58.00	190ft 3in
1.70	5ft 7in	8.25	27ft 0¾in	15.00	49ft 2½in	60.00	196ft 10in
1.75	5ft 8¾in	8.50	27ft 10¾in	15.50	50ft 10¼in	62.00	203ft 5in
1.80	5ft 10¾in	8.75	28ft 8½in	16.00	52ft 6in	64.00	210ft 0in
1.85	6ft 0¾in	9.00	29ft 6½in	16.50	54ft 1¾in	66.00	216ft 6in
1.90	6ft 2¾in			17.00	55ft 9¼in		
1.95	6ft 4¾in	3.00 metres =	9ft 10in	17.50	57ft 5in	68.00	223ft 1in
2.00	6ft 6¾in	3.20	10ft 6in	18.00	59ft 0¾in	70.00	229ft 8in
2.05	6ft 8¾in	3.40	11ft 1¾in	18.50	60ft 8½in	72.00	236ft 3in
2.10	6ft 10¾in	3.60	11ft 9¾in	19.00	62ft 4in	74.00	242ft 9in
2.15	7ft 0½in	3.80	12ft 5½in	19.50	63ft 11¾in	76.00	249ft 4in
2.20	7ft 2½in	4.00	13ft 1½in	20.00	65ft 7½in	78.00	255ft 11in
2.25	7ft 4½in	4.20	13ft 9¼in	20.50	67ft 3¼in	80.00	262ft 5in
2.30	7ft 6½in	4.40	14ft 5¼in	21.00	68ft 10¾in	82.00	269ft 0in
2.35	7ft 8½in	4.60	15ft 1in	21.50	70ft 6½in	84.00	275ft 7in
2.40	7ft 10½in	4.80	15ft 9in	22.00	72ft 2¼in	86.00	282ft 2in
		5.00	16ft 4¾in	22.50	73ft 10in	88.00	288ft 8in
5.50 metres =	18ft 0½in	5.20	17ft 0¾in			90.00	295ft 3in
5.75	18ft 10½in	5.40	17ft 8½in	40.00 metres =	131ft 3in	92.00	301ft 10in
6.00	19ft 8¼in	5.60	18ft 4½in	42.00	137ft 9in	94.00	308ft 5in
6.25	20ft 6¼in	5.80	19ft 0¼in	44.00	144ft 4in	96.00	314ft 11in
6.50	21ft 4in	6.00	19ft 8¼in	46.00	150ft 11in	98.00	321ft 6in
6.75	22ft 1¾in			48.00	157ft 6in	100.00	328ft 1in
7.00	22ft 11¾in	12.50 metres =	41ft 0¼in	50.00	164ft 0in		
7.25	23ft 9½in	13.00	42ft 8in	52.00	170ft 7in		

Weightlifting Conversion Table

kg	lb
100.................	220¼
125.................	275½
150.................	330½
175.................	385¾
200.................	440¾
225.................	496
250.................	551
275.................	606¼
300.................	661¼
325.................	716½
350.................	771½
375.................	826½
400.................	881¾
425.................	936¾
450.................	992
475.................	1047
500.................	1102¼
525.................	1157¼
550.................	1212¼
575.................	1267½
600.................	1322¾

Index